BEYOND THE IMAGINED

+ BUILDING

EACHING

05

CON

AUTHOR <

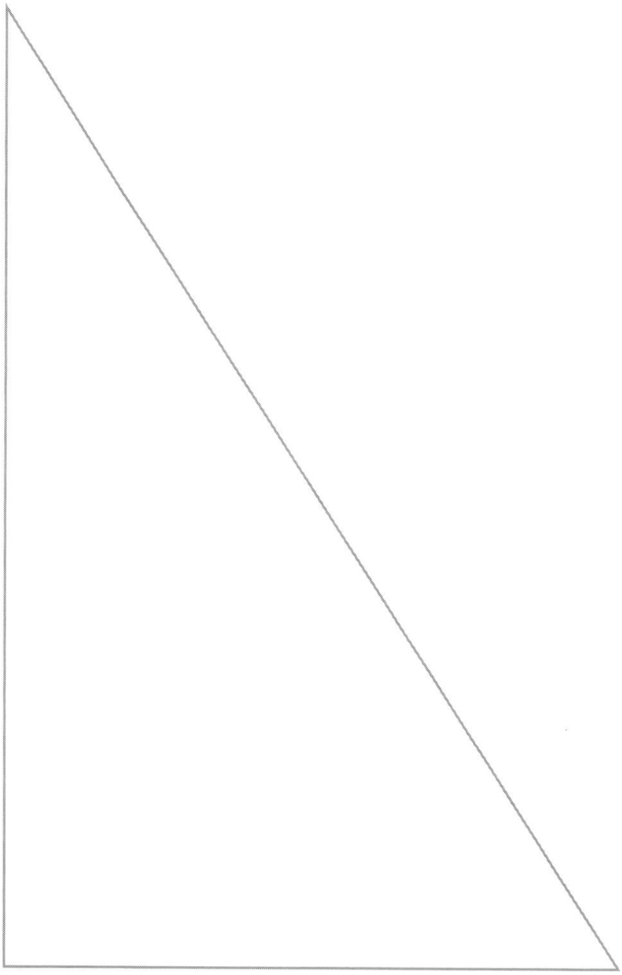

306090 05:

TEACHING + BUILDING

Emily Abruzzo
Jonathan D. Solomon
Editors

Brigid Boyle
Lynne DeSilva Johnson
Eva Hagberg
Cara Soh
Assistant Editors

Andrew Yang
Special Projects Editor

Alexander Briseno
Jonathan D. Solomon
Series Editors & Publishers

Cover by John Wagner
www.workstudios.net

Branding by ORG
www.o-r-g.com

306090 is an independent architectural journal published and distributed semi-annually. 306090 seeks to publish diverse, inquisitive projects by students and young professionals that have not been published elsewhere.

Opinions expressed in 306090 are the author's alone and do not necessarily reflect those of the editors.

Distributed By:
Princeton Architectural Press
37 East Seventh Street
New York, NY 10003
1-800-722.-657
www.papress.com

Contact publisher for Library of Congress Cataloging-in-Publication Data

www.306090.org info@306090.org

306090, Inc. is a non-profit institution registered in the state of New Jersey. Your donations are tax deductible. For information on how to contribute or to submit work please contact us at: info@306090.org or visit our Website. For ordering information contact the Princeton Architectural Press at orders@papress.com

06 05 04 03 6 5 4 3 2 First Edition
ISBN 1-56898-432-4

BEYOND THE IMAGI

CUTTING CLASS

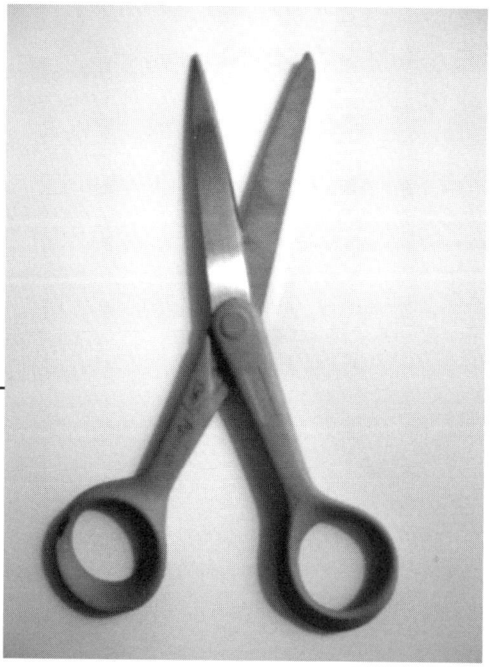

Design-build. Ugh.

Contemporary attention to design-build is too often presented as the product of pure virtuoso—as in the stirring efforts of the Auburn Rural Studio, for example—or it is relegated to the realm of preconstruction. This second category, often viewed as architecture's pre-med, is as beleaguered by its naysayers as it is hyped by its proponents.

To discount design-build projects for their inherent relationship to the practices of industry (and subsequent distance from the practice of academy), however, would be unfortunate. We believe that the projects in this volume—well-executed design-build projects at a variety of scales—offer unique and valuable opportunities for learning, if in a less traditional sense.

More important, however, may be what begins to become evident when the projects are looked at as a whole. The possible directions in which the traditional design-build model can be taken—as exemplified here in the projects by Tonino Vicari and Studio 804—are often stunning in their efforts and outcomes. At the same time, what we see in this issue at large is the emergence of a new way of thinking what design-build could be.

NED

Seemingly central to this shift is the notion of *cutting*. No longer confined to the realm of pre-fab construction pieces for economical reasons, architects are now freed from the 2x4 by tools such as laser cutters and milling machines. Along with this shift comes a change in design approach that often starts at a project's very inception.

306090 05 can be read as an introductory anthology of new construction techniques and the environments in which they develop, where the traditionally separate processes of design, fabrication and assembly no longer exist independently. The results happily indicate that the process of building may no longer be so foreign from the kind of playful invention that characterizes the design studio.

The *How to Build Your Own* instructions that have been included with some articles are meant not literally to act as Do-It-Yourself guides, but to emphasize the *realness* of the projects—the notion that they exist in a realm beyond the imagined, a place that architectural education does not often wander. In addition to projects with a physical presence, we have attempted to offer a selection of projects that, while speculative, address and examine real-life systems that affect building processes worldwide.

As students and as educators, young people in architecture are continually faced with conflicting discourses of the built and the imagined. We are interested in architecture that occupies the fine line between teaching and building; built projects by young design professors; students who are simultaneously involved in design studios and construction projects; students who teach; teachers who learn.

Design, build. Now!

Playfulness. This is issue five.

A STRUCTU
AND CULTURAL E

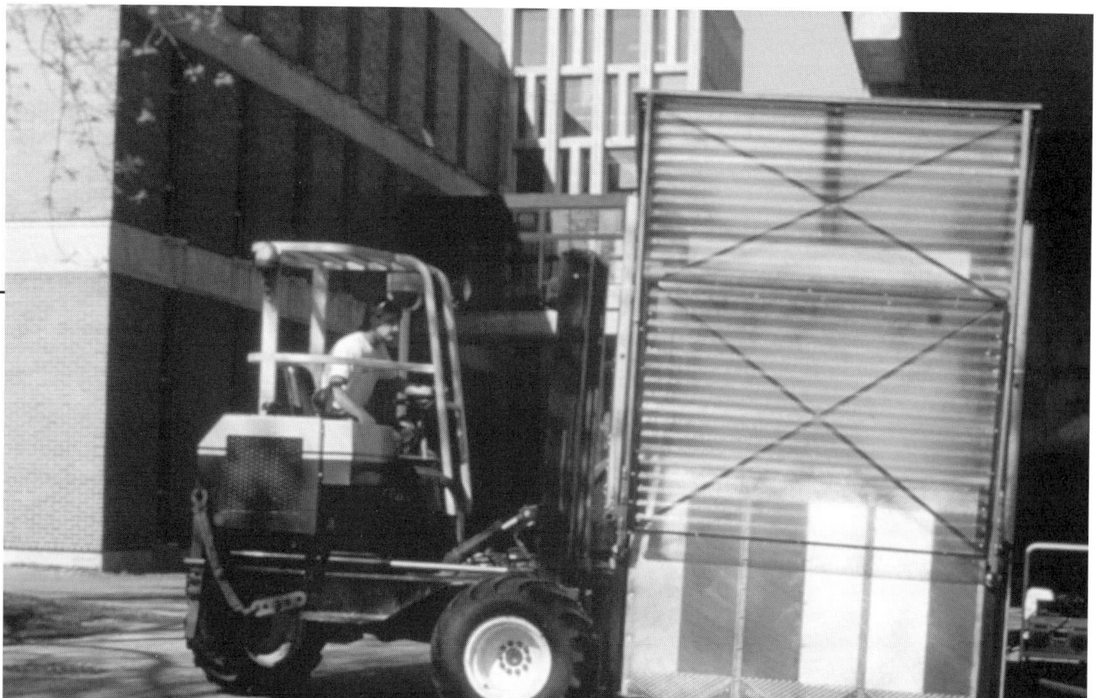

Design-build at Carleton University

RE FOR SOCIAL XCHANGE

by Yvan-pier Cazabon

Building on a growing portfolio of research and design-build projects, Carleton University's School of Architecture established the Carleton Center for Applied Architectural Research (CCAAR). This formal research unit was conceived and developed as a vehicle that would allow students of architecture to explore theoretical as well as practical issues within the full spectrum of architectural investigation using specific and academically relevant projects conceived by clients from both the immediate and distant community.

The following article will introduce the two most recent projects by the CCAAR—one in Ottawa, Ontario, Canada, the other in distant Zambia, Southern Africa.

Yvan-pier Cazabon holds a diploma in Architectural Technology from Algonquin College, a professional degree in architecture from Carleton University and a post-professional MArch degree from McGill University. He is an Assistant Professor at Carleton University's School of Architecture where he teaches undergraduate and graduate design studios (including design-build studios), Architectural Technology and a Theater Production and Set Design Workshop. He is currently the Chair of the CCAAR. Professor Cazabon is also involved in a number of local theater productions providing set designs and improvisational theater space design. He shares a small residential design practice with his partner / spouse Janet Bousquet in Ottawa, Canada.

The Architect's Pub

The first project, a design-build endeavor, sponsored by the Royal Architectural Institute of Canada (RAIC) and the Ottawa Builder's Association, served to tighten the relationship between the architectural profession and its academic counterpart. The positive spirit of this exchange, stemming from the RAIC's Millennium Celebration, served as program and inspiration for the project.

The school of Architecture was commissioned to design and build *The Architect's Pub*, a refreshment area and centerpiece for a trade show and seminar held at Ottawa's Landsdowne Park in the heart of the national Capital and within the grand 19th century Aberdeen Pavilion. Local architects would serve food and drink to members of the National Architectural Institute as well as the local representatives of associations of architects, builders and suppliers gathered for this special event.

During the design phase the instructors, research investigators, volunteer consultants and students of architecture developed various prototypes in drawing and model form. From this process a final strategy of creating a theatrical setting using three architectural characters to define a center within the large gathering space was adopted. These three characters were then further programmed, drawn, modelled and developed for their eventual construction. Design parameters included a maximum plan proportion (and height restriction) based on the limits of the forklift which would eventually load the pubs onto a flatbed trailer for transport from the school of architecture to the final destination. A recommended material palette was also set along with a program definition for the individual pubs; one would serve draft beer, another wine and soft drinks, while the other would serve as central storage and dispensary for the other two. All pubs shared general design elements such as the ability to hinge and unfold from a compact transportable state to an open state, the accommodation of electrical and plumbing needs, a robust, yet ephemeral material construction, dramatic lighting and efficient usability. Their differences lie in the interpretation of the general problem by the three individual student teams. The resulting three unique, yet related, architectural characters stand as comfortably in their autonomy as they do in their triadic relationship.

2000 Design-build workshop

Sponsored by: Royal Architectural Institute of Canada
Supported by: Merkeley Supply and Ottawa Builder's Association
Instructors: Dino Di Sano and Yvan Cazabon
Primary Investigators: Gulzar Haider (Director) and Yvan Cazabon
Students: Bartek Bielny, Norman Chin, Michael Conway, Trevor Houghton, Mark Huang, Carolyn Jones, Stephane Lacroix, Jay Lin, Vram Malek, Kevin Martin, Jason McIntyre, David Pritchard, Kevin Thomas, Vanessa Valladares.

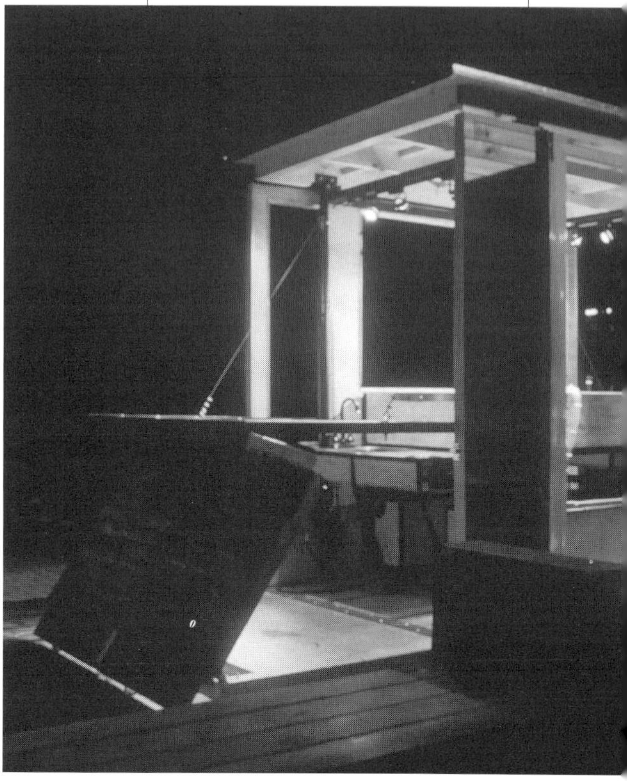

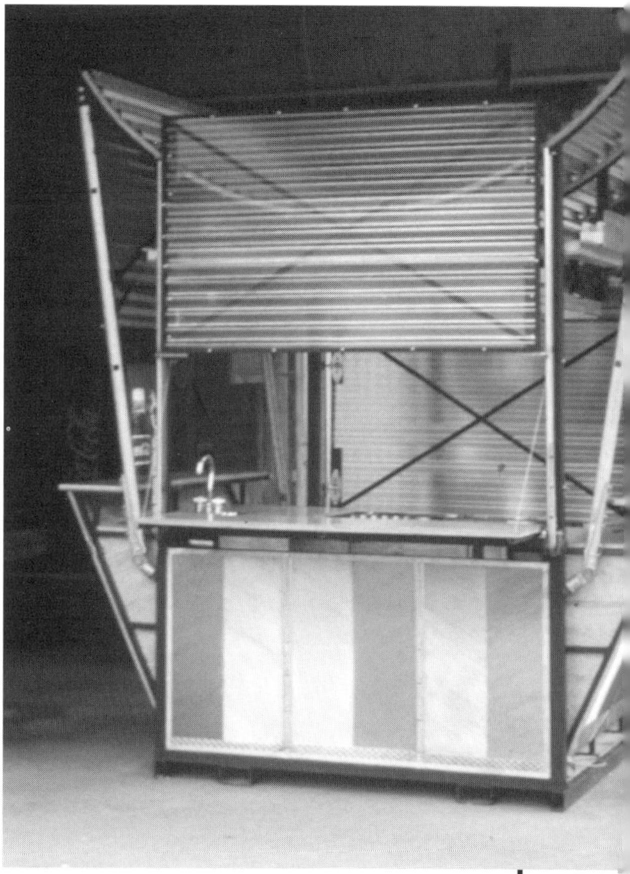

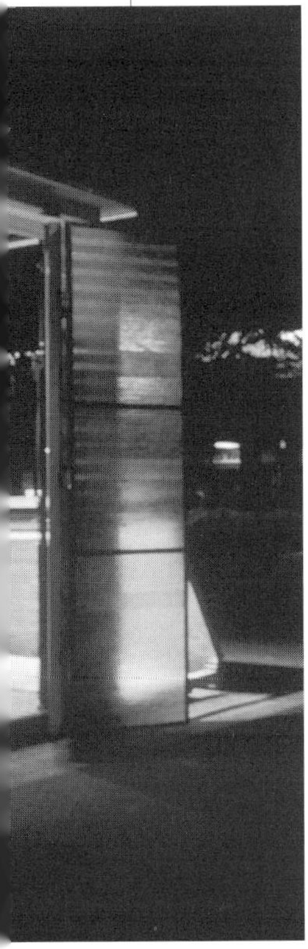

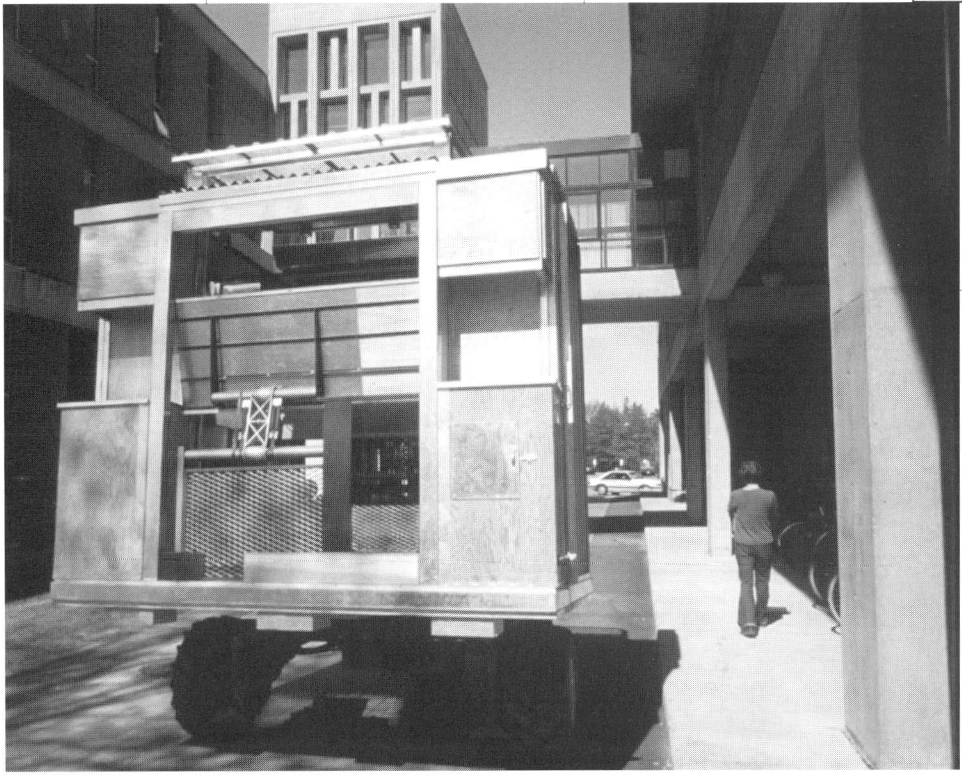

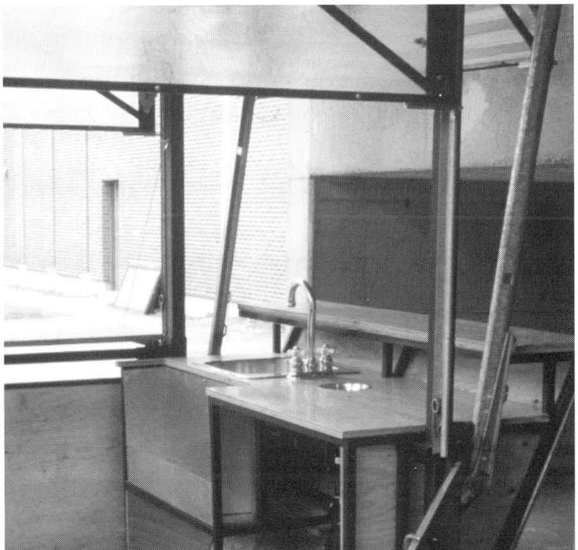

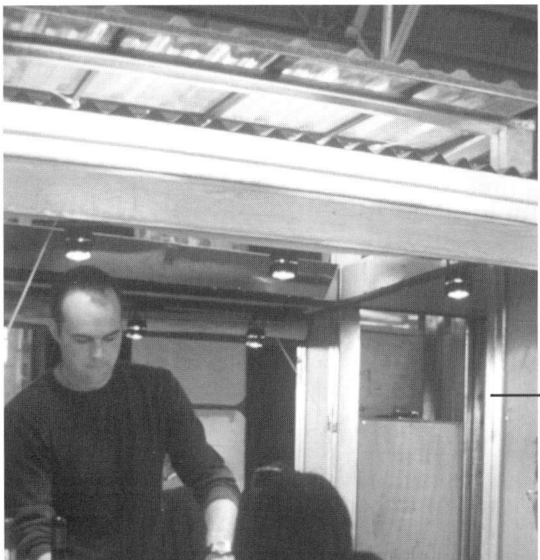

"Tamara's House: Research into a [hi]Story of African Dwelling"[1]

> "The problem is this: mankind as a whole is on the brink of a single world civilization representing at once gigantic progress for everyone and an overwhelming task of survival and adapting our cultural heritage to this new setting. To some extent, and in varying ways, everyone experiences the tension between the necessity for the free access to progress and, on the other hand, the exigency of safeguarding our heritage."[2]

Along with the present pressures of globalization, numerous developing / recovering African nations are struggling with the remnants of a recent release from colonial occupation. In the case of Zambia in southern Africa, this struggle includes an attempt to secure political and economic self-determination along with reviving a fragmented cultural identity. The term *recovering nation* is perhaps more appropriate to Zambia's situation than the more commonly used term *developing nation*. With the latter comes the biased perception of incremental progress and gradual accumulation of techniques, tools, and knowledge-whether applied to politics, economics, science or engineering. Following Paul Ricoeur's assessment of the conflict between universal development pressures and the need to re-establish cultural identity, I would propose that Zambia as a recovering nation defines her identity from the deepest roots of cultural history. One example of this rooted stance is demonstrated by the co-existence of seventy-two tribal languages officially recognized by Zambia's constitution (English being one of them). This is not to say that Zambia, as she lays claim to her cultural origins, does not recognize the necessity of access to an international modern civilization. In fact, Zambia's future depends on her ability to engage in a complete dialogue and exchange with the international community.

The House as Human Right

Architects throughout the Northern Hemisphere are beginning to respond to an urgent call—to build millions of houses for communities lacking in the most basic of human comforts. Architecture in the context of international aid and development is seen as a generous act of helping less privileged societies attain a basic standard of living. From the point of view of international aid agencies, this represents a significant part of the foundations of basic human rights which include health, education, freedom of speech, access to income, etcetera. Numerous architectural interventions however, while based on noble intentions, often present concepts and techniques foreign to the cultures within which they operate. Inevitably, along with the

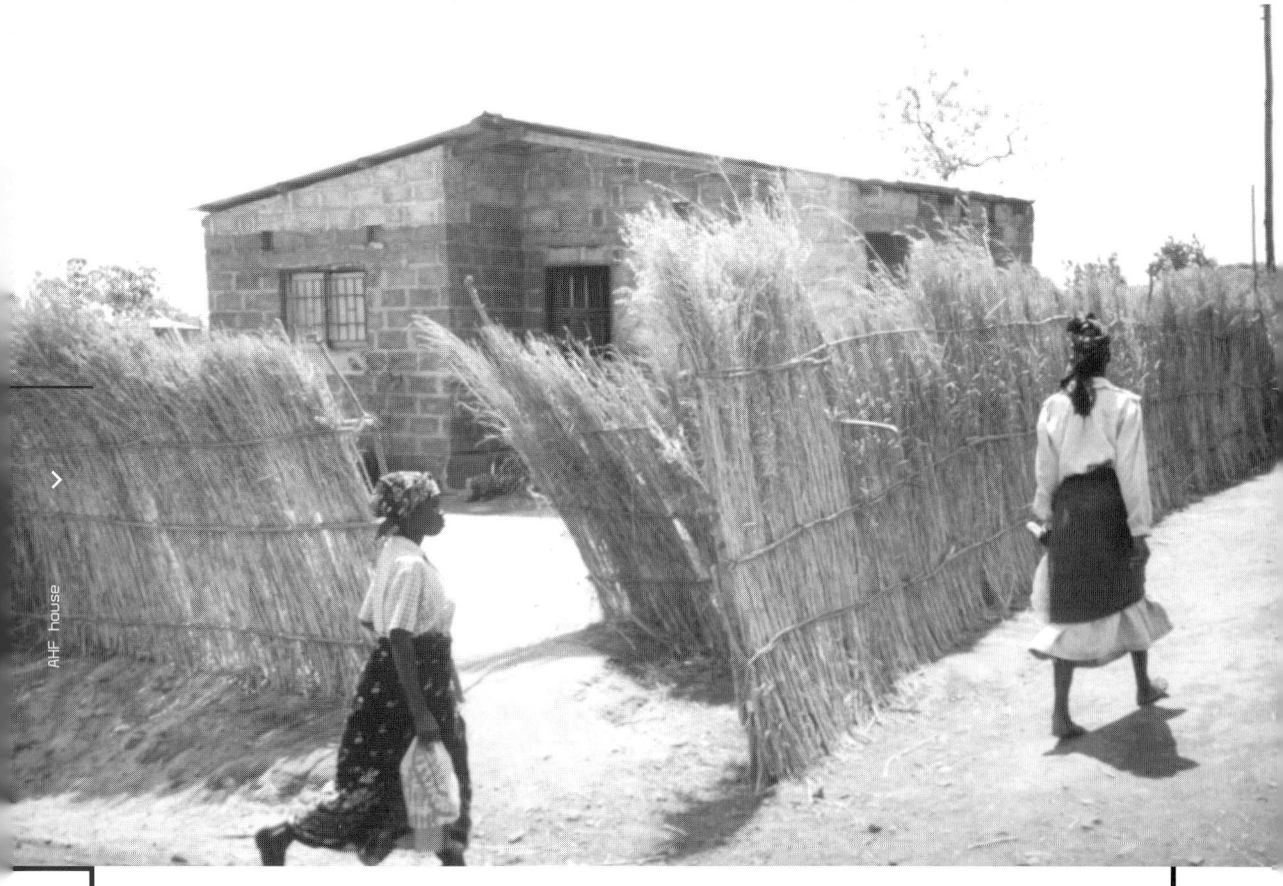

architectural project comes the western (northern) bias of practice over theory-driven by definitions of progress as cumulative betterment. Practical questions of technique and *how-to* often override theoretical concerns of cultural perception, tradition and world-view. Herein a balance must be stricken.

International Non-Governmental Organizations (NGOs), like Habitat for Humanity, Builders Without Borders, and Food for the Poor, are already making significant inroads in developing low-cost quality housing alternatives with improved design characteristics. Private-sector firms also have highly-developed programming and technical skills in this area. From a critical standpoint based on direct experience however, projects like these operate at a distance from the community's full potential. Standardized plans and community layouts using *efficient* materials and methods make it possible for numerous shelters to sprout up instantly while personalization, family adaptation and specific programmatic needs are left wanting. More importantly, the potential of community-based management to ensure the gradual evolution of houses and neighborhoods along with culturally defined expression are rarely components within the design process.

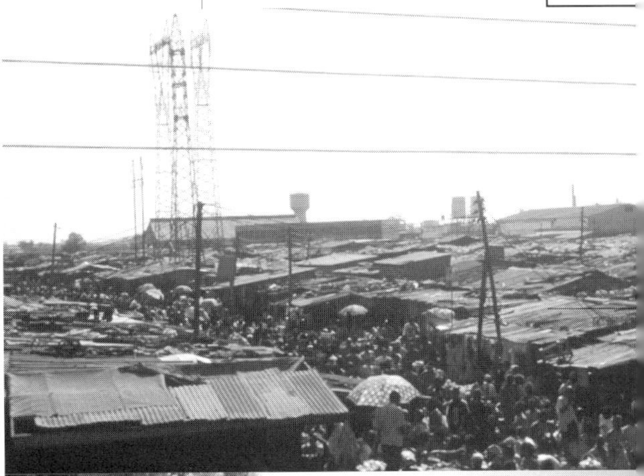

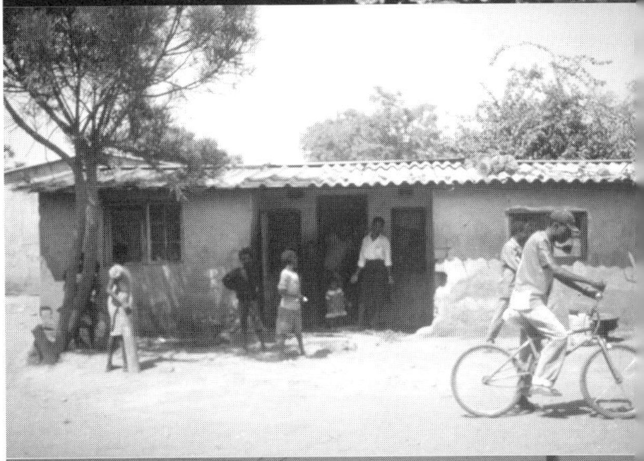

The House as Subject of Cultural Research

In order to more thoroughly investigate the African housing crisis, CARE Canada has initiated a working relationship with Carleton University's School of Architecture and the CARE International Center for Urban Development (INSAKA in Zambia). The primary objective of this collaboration is in researching and developing practical skills and knowledge that would contribute directly to the collective's competitive advantage in obtaining and implementing large-scale donor-funded urban housing projects. More importantly however, in seeking out an academic center for its housing research, CARE anticipated a *cultural exchange* that would reciprocally benefit both the host country and the research team. CARE representatives understood that students of architecture, our future international architects, could afford a more profound research extending beyond the *real-life* limitations of normal architectural practise. *In-the-field* investigations culminating in architectural proposals would benefit from a prolonged contact with Zambian communities with the likelihood of personal experiences with deeper meaning. Indeed, students were quick to observe the superficial evidence of internationalization. Strewn amongst the fabric of a *culture not their own*, the young architects could discern the all-too-familiar discarded remnants of a universal consumer society as they walked past the smoldering garbage heaps of plastic Coca-Cola bottles and package wrappers.

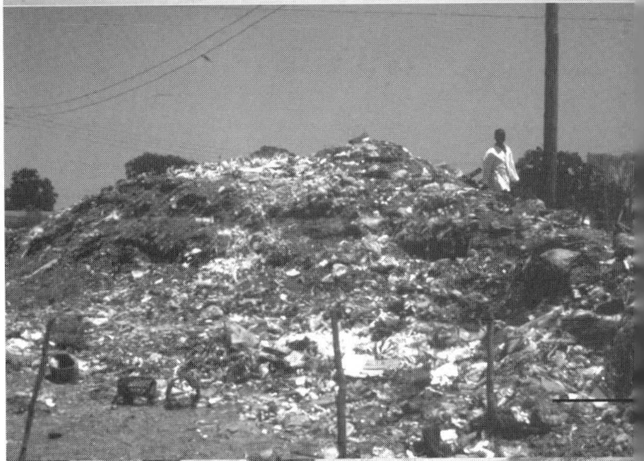

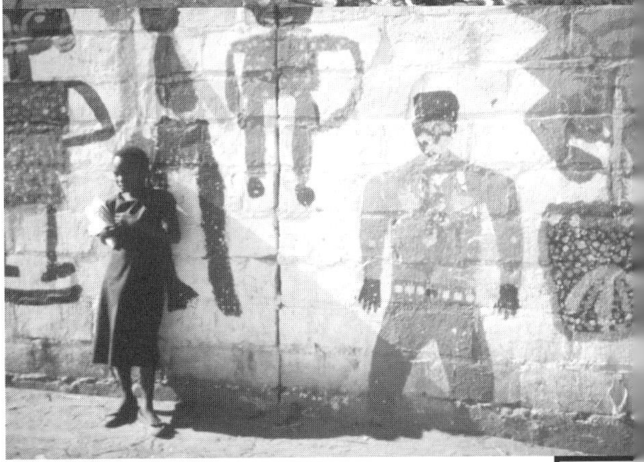

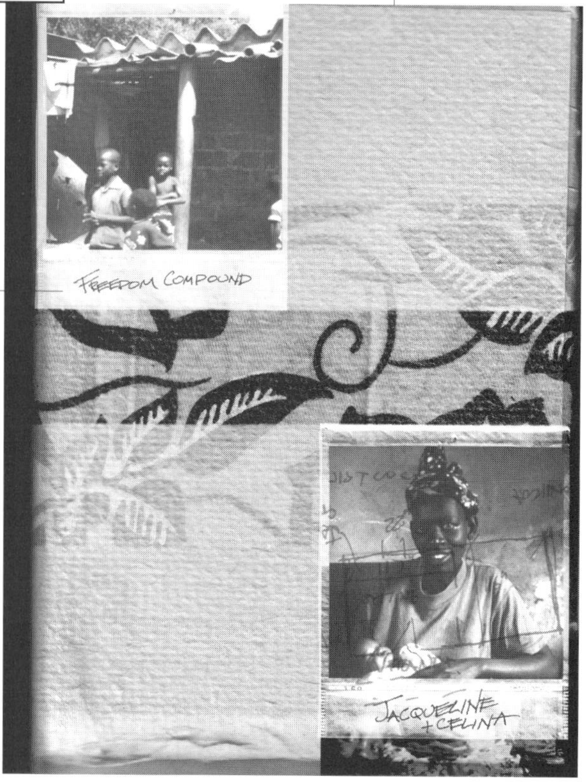

But with a deeper, penetrating glance and intense inter-personal exchanges, the research team would eventually begin to appreciate that below the superficial signs lay the creative nucleus of a traditional culture. This realization would not be possible until the displaced Canadians entered the very fabric of everyday life in an attempt to decipher the hidden stories. After spending hours with individual families in their modest homes and conversing repeatedly with merchants and craftsmen in the local markets, each and every student return with unique fragments of a cultural puzzle.

The Structure of Exchange

Students participating in the Directed Studies Abroad (DSA) program were enrolled in three required courses including a materials application workshop, a full design studio and a history / theory elective (culture). Distinct lines were not drawn between these courses. Instead, the research-based program aimed at unifying the various modes of investigation in an attempt to deliver a wider range of critical output. Students were able to align their observations with various input ranging from on-site interviews, presentations by local experts, drawing exercises, 1:1 material and methods experimentation, lectures in cultural studies and studio based design. While each course would ultimately revolve around similar issues, the mode of research and therefore the resulting assignments differed in scale, medium and focus. Each course included a survey / research component which took place in Zambia over a one month period and was followed up by design-based assignments upon the group's return to Canada.

For the first four weeks of the term (while in Zambia) participants in this course ventured into the field of community work as defined by numerous national and international programs. This first phase was one of gathering and documentation as well as a research requiring dialogue and the exchange of ideas with members of host communities. Students sought to know about the aspirations and the frustrations, the desires and the concerns of people who they met in the underprivileged neighborhoods—in short, students engaged in the exchange of stories. It is with this reciprocity in mind that the course structure for the Directed Studies was established. In addition, it became clear from the outset that the student group would experience urban Zambia in a near-nomadic way. With the exception of rudimentary sleeping accommodations, all participants made their homes within the fabric of Lusaka's urban settlements (compounds) and their inhabitants.

In lieu of a permanent studio space in Zambia, students were asked to create for themselves a nomadic portable *studio* and to continually evaluate and transform it during their stay in Zambia. All aspects of the Studio and Workshop courses-including *desk reviews*, public presentations and seminars were conducted in full mobility. Further to this, the theme of *storytelling as documentation* was set as the foundation to most course exercises.

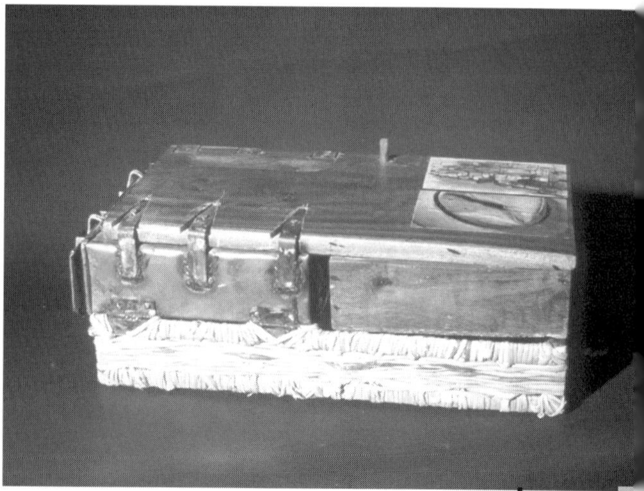

All courses in the DSA Zambia line-up (Workshop elective, Studio and Theories Elective) were conceived as inter-related and complimentary—the product of one influencing the outcome of the others. For this reason, students were asked to formulate relationships between them to satisfy their personal interpretations of the course objectives.

Workshop

The Workshop course was concerned primarily with the teaching of the architect's fundamental tools: i.e. drawing (drawing from) and documenting the experience of a place. It was a course that focused equally on drawing and making. Both modes of representation were important components for the students to be able to formalize the abstract and represent (re-present) the lived experience of new and foreign places. The architect's diary or sketceterahbook is often a juxtaposition of sketceterahes, text and images which help to inform and recollect existing buildings, cities, landscapes and artifacts. In addition to this, through this workshop (and the studio that ran in parallel), additional media investigations were encouraged: i.e. sound samplings, music, photography, video, material investigations and constructions, and eventually—upon our return to Canada—computer based media. All of these were to support the idea that layered traces of recording reflect the collage-narrative of the nomadic experience.

Although it is expected that the inclination to *put down on paper* comes naturally to many students of architecture, this course required that this be done with clarity of intention, with skill and craft, as well as with a clear attempt at inter-subjective reading and communication. Furthermore, because of the close-lived experience that DSA Zambia would provide, inter-subjectivity also involved inter-dependency and cooperation. Students were to be sharing ideas, information, experiences and personal discoveries and, through the course projects were also expected to occasionally work in groups as well as with the community in sharing stories, information, materials and resources.

The Work Table / Diary

The actual construction and development of the Work-Table / Diary was reviewed during the travel component of the workshop. In preparation for the table's design and construction, the Workshop projects explored issues of making, documentation and transportation. This was to include consideration for wear and tear, weight, weather, instructions for use, programmatic transformation, etceteraetera.

As every architect expresses different preferences for tools, layout, materials, instruments, etcetera., it became possible for each student to reflect carefully on the program for his / her portable workspace. This course asked each student to speculate on the inter-relationships between program and architectonics, as well as use and construction, by developing a program outline in narrative form while critically challenging conventions within the tradition of representation in architecture. The three parts of this project addressed separate yet similar issues all geared to a common set of questions, namely: How do the place, the objects and the intentions of making (process) affect the product and work of an architect? Can drawing conventions be challenged by questioning not their *style* but their *making*? Does a re-interpreted drawing board lead to a re-interpreted drawing? The response to these questions (if not the answer) can most clearly be demonstrated by the personal and interpersonal qualities in each of the Table / Diaries. It is in the integrated *log-books* displaying sketceterahes and text that personal intentions are best understood. Meanwhile the individual Diaries, which incorporate all aspects of observation / reflection / response,

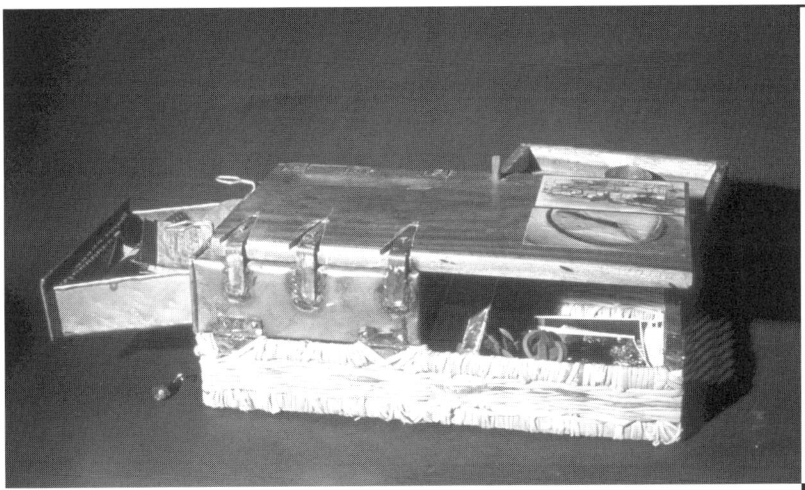

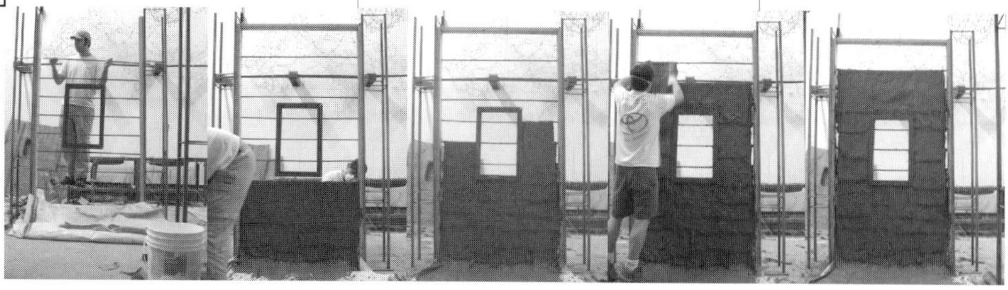

demonstrate the exchange between the students and the local tradespeople who would help them resolve their personal constructions while giving insight into local traditions and contemporary craft.[3]

The logbook constitutes part of the individual Table / Diary. In effect, the boundaries between these gradually became blurred. Students were asked to present their logbook-in-progress at each review. This logbook, a travelling diary, was to contain all aspects of their stay in Zambia. It was to be as representational as it was physical and it was to hold all that was necessary for its transformation into a vehicle of narrative. After numerous iterations and critical *renovations*, the individual logbooks, now merged with the Table / Diary can be read, touched, and interpreted. The logbook / Table / Diary are at once a studio space, a personal diary, a *cabinet of curiosities*, and a graphic novel with physical attributes.

Studio

The studio course, in direct parallel with the workshop component, was concerned with the teaching of the architect's fundamental tools: i.e. drawing and documenting the experience of a place leading to a proposal for an architectural speculation in the city of Lusaka. As outlined in the Studio assignments, the building proposals were urban interventions meant to speak to local concerns. How does architecture respond to complex urban issues that have more to do with cultural anthropology and tradition than with issues of form? With this we find ourselves in a situation where our actions, whatever they are, demand of us ethical contemplation and ethical action. Furthermore, the very idea of an urban intervention is put to question when we as outsiders *intervene* upon a physical condition with hidden underlying orders.

A significant portion of our involvement in Zambia revolved around the existing efforts of CARE Canada, CARE Zambia, Urban Insaka and other national and international groups. As part of our investigation into urban and peri-urban living conditions and our eventual proposals for housing, we were introduced to relief efforts which are more structural (in a social sense) than physical. This is to admit at the outset that housing issues are not specifically architectural issues and rarely does architecture resolve the problems of economic, political or social struggle. We can nonetheless hope that the process of community building and the direct involvement of a community in the process of architectural delineation can lead to the successful implementation of community structure-including buildings.

Our success in communicating with our hosts in Zambia, especially the communities which could most benefit from our input, can best be measured by the *documentation* of an experience as lived and the interpersonal communication of that experience. Witnessing from a distant stance can only lead to solipsism and a denial of the necessary reciprocity in the creative process of thoughtful-making. Our involvement in a reciprocal exchange was and continues to be crucial to a successful speculation.

Upon our return to Ottawa, the Zambia group set up a studio bay devoted to the continued explorations of the Africa experience. In the Workshop component, this meant a laboratory-like setting for materials and media exploration, aiming at the *complete* documentation of each participant's story-line. These experiments, in turn, were to supplement and compliment the Diary whereby exercises took on the *pure and applied* aspects of construction projects as well as the more elusive qualities of interpretative narrative. From the experience in constructing the Diary in Zambia completed with significant input from local craftsmen and women, students had gained significant insight into the ever-evolving traditions of making. It is with this knowledge that the group set out to experiment with indigenous materials and traditional methods of construction. The specific location and program for the house proposals suggests that material application experiments and construction were to consider the many facets of material inquiry, including availability, structural integrity, workability, import vs. export potential, local construction means and conventions, technological adaptability, workmanship and appropriateness. In considering appropriateness, *design* issues in response to traditional and adapted ways of life figured prominently. These were derived from an open dialogue with the community in question.

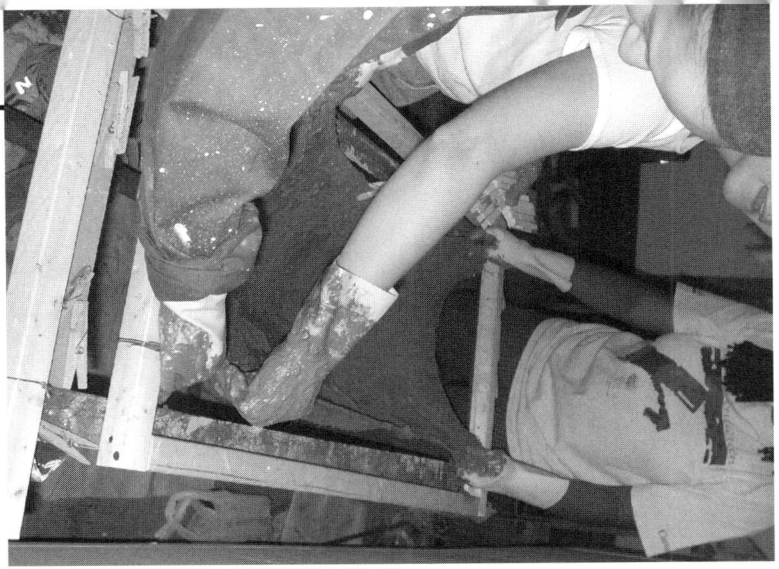

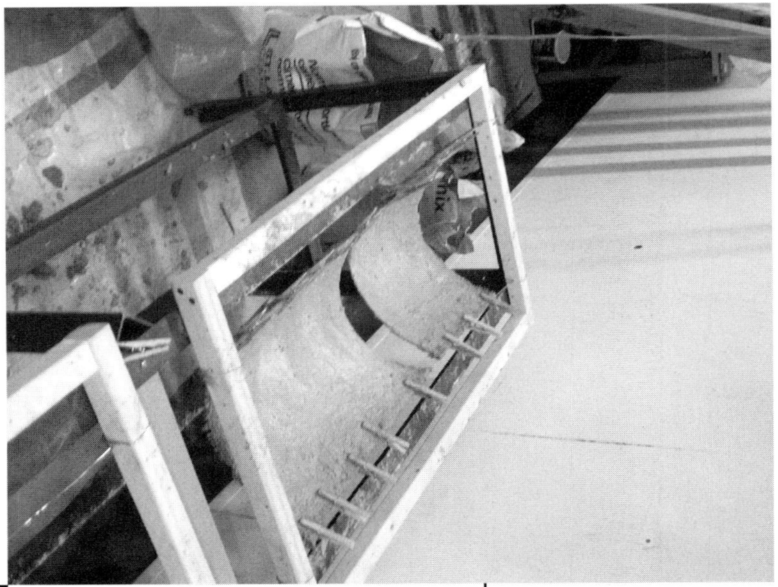

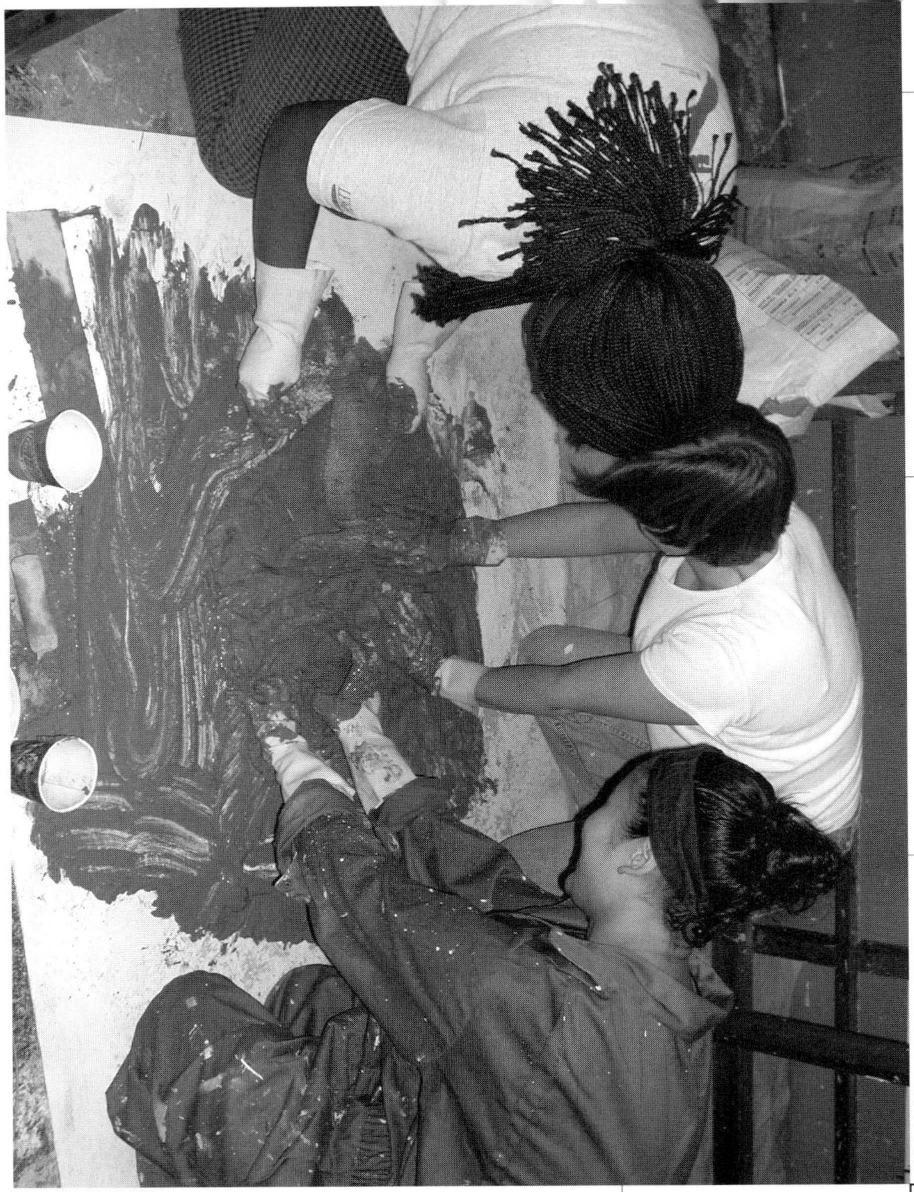

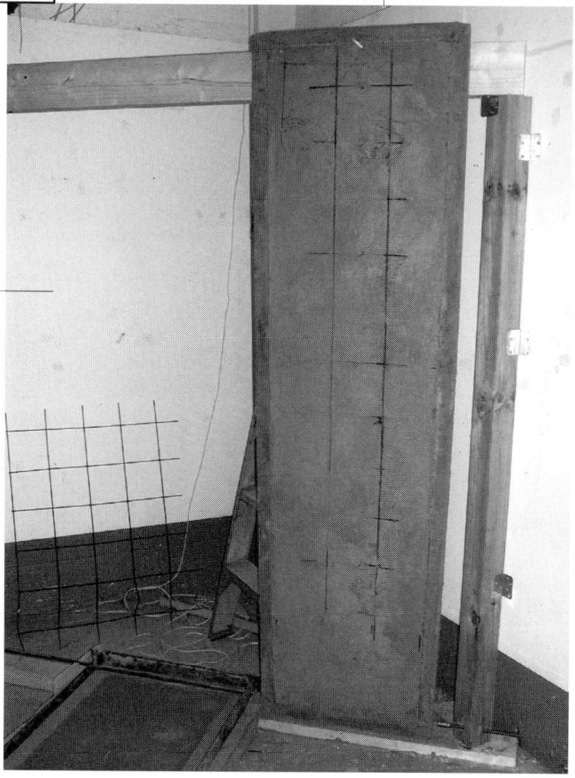

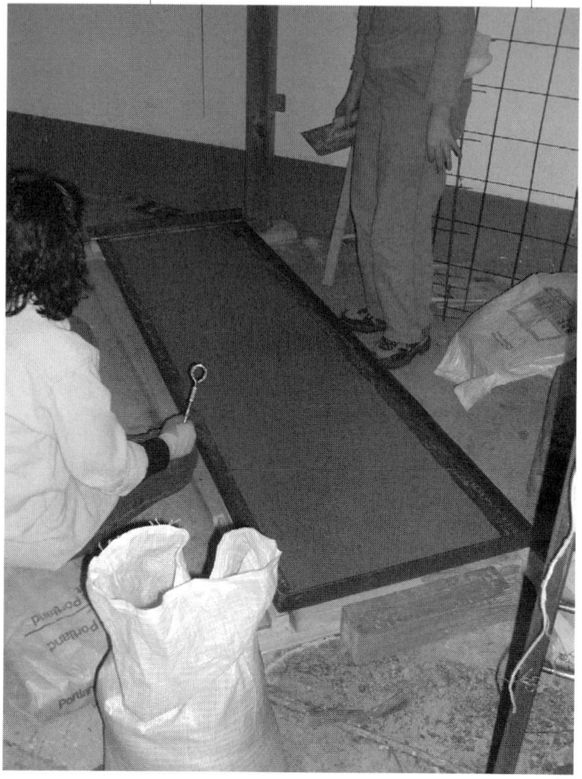

In the studio component, students were to propose a public Architecture by responding to their gathered research. The contents of their Diary, which now included notes, sketches, sound-bites, video, photographs and artifacts, would suggest a point of departure in defining an architectural program which would develop a speculative architecture focusing on urban living and large-scale housing projects for Chepata Compound, Lusaka.

The focus has been on developing a demonstrated capacity to create affordable low-cost quality housing units and well-designed communities for the benefit of poorer urban families in countries faced with rapid urbanization needs. While the central *topic* of such research can be signified by the term *housing*, greater issues of urban development, urban anthropology, urban economics, employment generation, social and cultural contexts, materials development, housing and urban area design, appropriate applications technology, community management, government relations, institutional and financial sustainability, cost structure, and potential donor interest also figure significantly.

Projects from the Design Studio were submitted using traditional and non-traditional representational techniques and depicted an elaborate architectural program (use) as well as a specification and/or speculation on eventual implementation (process). Each student was expected to propose an architectural program or a hybrid program of their own. While housing was the central focus of the studio, community infrastructure (architectural) programs relating to community, health, culture and education--or hybrid versions of these--were encouraged. The course pedagogy focused on research, observation, documentation, and especially, process.

The long-term expectations of the CARE / Carleton University partnership aim at the implementation of housing projects. At Carleton University, Design / Build Studios have, for a number of years, been structured such that students are encouraged to find alternative methods of design based on the context of the problem and with the most limited of means. While good solutions rarely come down to materials and methods, we remain optimistic that architectural solutions can be found from within the communities in which they are set. In this way, architects and future architects can find their role as members of a community (universal or national) focused on the specific and inherent problems at hand.

"A [cross-cultural] encounter has not yet taken place at the level of an authentic dialogue. That is why we are in a kind of lull in which we can no longer practise the dogmatism of a single truth and in which we are not yet capable of conquering the scepticism into which we have stepped. We are in a tunnel, at the twilight of dogmatism and the dawn of real dialogues."[4]

DSA Zambia

Instructor: Yvan-pier Cazabon (Carleton University) and John Scoggan (CARE Canada)

ENDNOTES

1. "Tamara's House" is the working title of a program for affordable housing in Zambia, Africa signifying: "Toward A Modest, Appropriate, & Responsive African House" and was inspired by a young Zambian woman interviewed by architecture student Andréa Macecek. This housing project is a collaborative effort between Carleton University School of Architecture and CARE Canada begun in 2001.
2. Paul Ricoeur, "Universal Civilization and National Cultures" in History and Truth, p. 271.
3. By *local tradition* one will instantly make associations to the historical crafts of African wood and bone carvings, basket weaving, fabric printing, drum making, et etceteraetera. Today's Zambia displays a truly *honest* creativity in the way that crafts people transform discarded materials such as wire, tin cans and plastics in the making of toys, functional objects and works of art.
4. Paul Ricoeur, "Universal Civilization and National Cultures," *History and Truth*, p. 283.

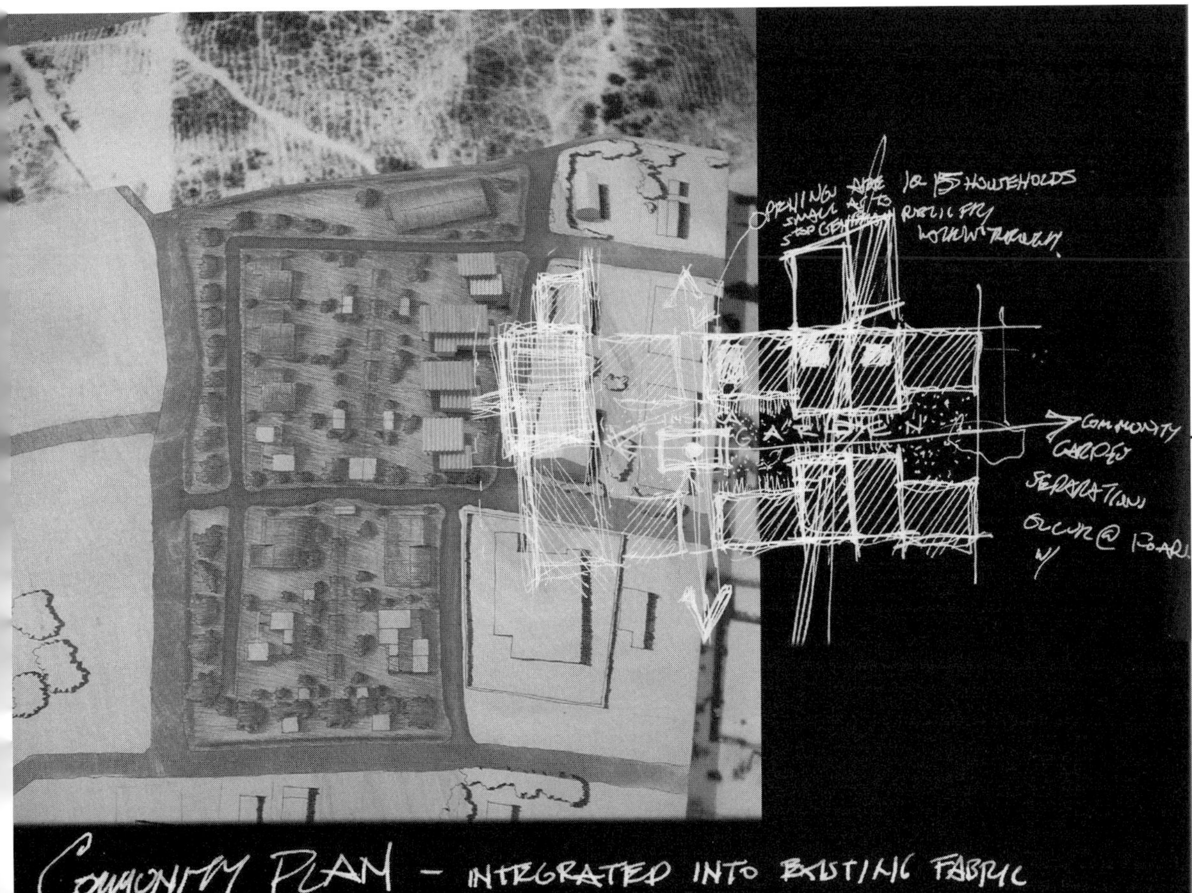

Country Description

Zambia is a southeastern African nation with five distinct topographical regions: the central highlands; the western plains, swamps and semiarid deserts; the Rift Valley of the Zambezi Lowlands; the Muchinga Uplands; and the swamps and lakes of the Northeast.
Despite progress in privatization and budget reform, Zambia's economy is struggling. With the drop in copper prices, Zambia's copper mining sector, which accounts for over 80 percent of the nation's foreign currency intake, is struggling. Meanwhile, inflation continues to be a serious concern. Adding to economic woes, many of Zambia's donors withdrew aid after political instability in the elections of 1996.

COUNTRY FACTS

Location: Southern Africa
Climate: tropical
Population: 9,508,200
Economy: agriculture, brewing, cement, chemicals, mining (cobalt, copper, lead, zinc)
Government: republic
Religion: predominantly Christian with some Muslim/Hindu
Literacy: 72 percent
Language: English; 70 indigenous dialects

Community Description

The original capital city of Lusaka, in south central Zambia is home to approximately 300,000 people. Surrounding the city are numerous squatting neighborhoods termed *compounds* with colorful names such as Kamwala, Freedom, Chiesa, Linda, etceteraetera. These dense communities, ranging from 30,000 to 80,000 souls add to Lusaka's growing urban population of 1.3 million and have recently been included in the official delineation of Lusaka proper. For the purposes of our design exercise, Chipata Compound, located in the northwestern extension of the city, was selected as the site for our housing proposals. The CARE / Carleton Group had grown fond of this neighborhood where they had witnessed evidence of gradual growth and increasing stability. Through their numerous interviews and social contacts, students had also made friends in this friendly and open community. The group recognized the potential for community involvement, labor and craft input as well as the visible desire for community betterment.

Precedents for community building and housing initiatives were documented from numerous visits to surrounding compounds including *Linda* where the Africa Housing Fund proudly exhibits its housing program.

Family Unit Description - Program

The implementation of the housing prototype was conceived with urban implementation and community development in mind. This *house-type*, a construction of approximately 24 m2, was designed based on the basic programmatic needs of an extended family living in the high-density peri-urban area. In order to identify potential user families, students spent numerous hours in difficult conditions interviewing family members of the most diverse make-ups. A life of poverty and struggle is impacted by myriad social and economic factors. The search for work drives young Africans from their villages in search for work and a better life in the city creating a continuous influx into already crowded squatting neighborhoods. High unemployment limits dreams of success and gradually affects a family's earning potential and education access while squalid living conditions invite disease and health complications. A family member's good fortune, as rare as this may be, promotes additional influx of families coming to benefit from their relative's tenuous stability. The impact of HIV / AIDS especially has transformed the African family unit. It is not uncommon to meet a grandmother caring for 5 or 6 grandchildren whose parents have recently been taken by the disease. We met a great number of young adults who were caring for the children of their siblings along with their own all the while struggling to make a better life for their extended family. These harsh realities have a profound effect on what would be considered a straightforward house program. Hence, built into the exercise of program definition was the requirement for direct contact and an exchange by storytelling. With this direct contact, students could more readily focus their designs on a real clientele while pondering the necessary flexibility of architectural programming. The house therefore was to accommodate the most basic of a family's needs while responding to cultural traditions, changing lifestyle and eventual physical or financial growth / change within the family unit.

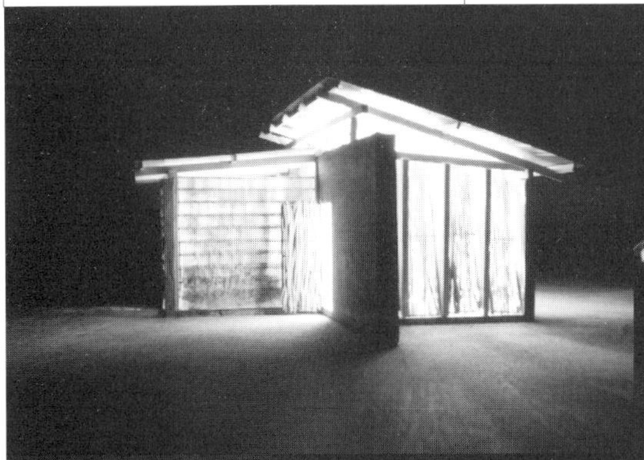

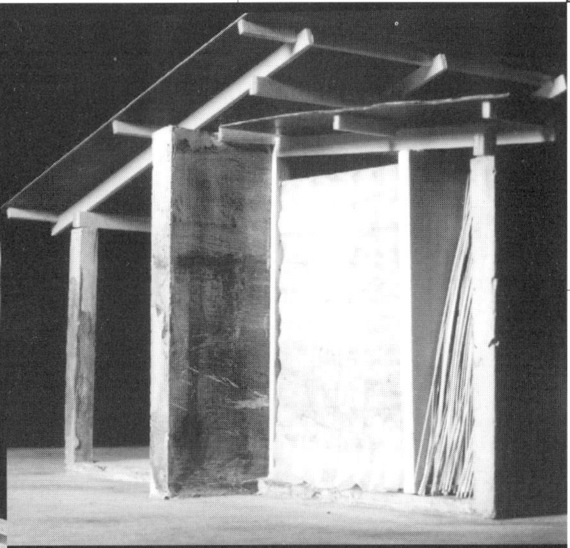

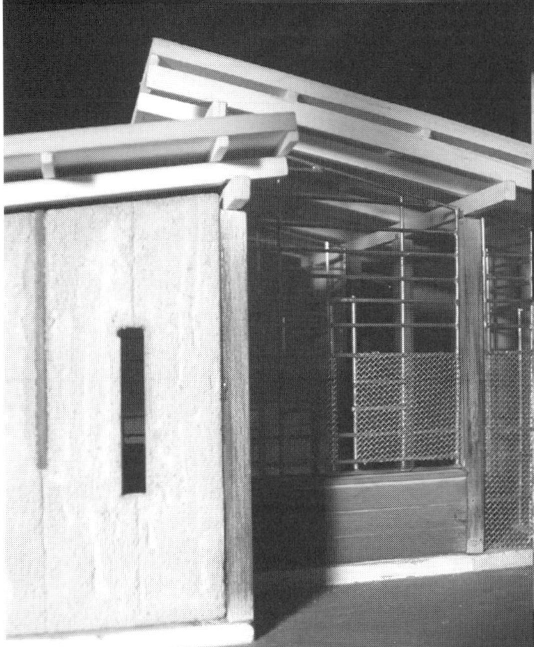

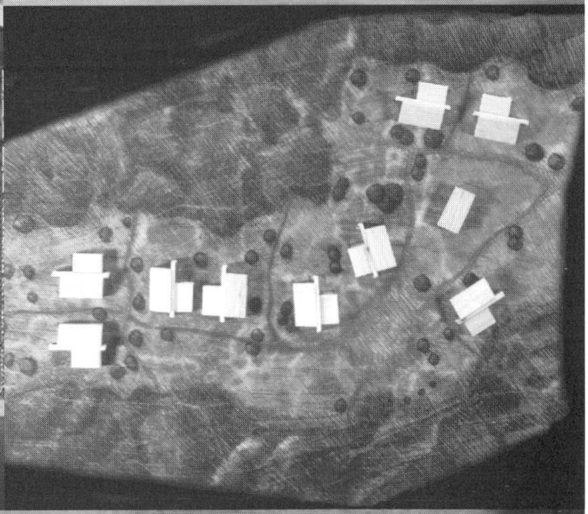

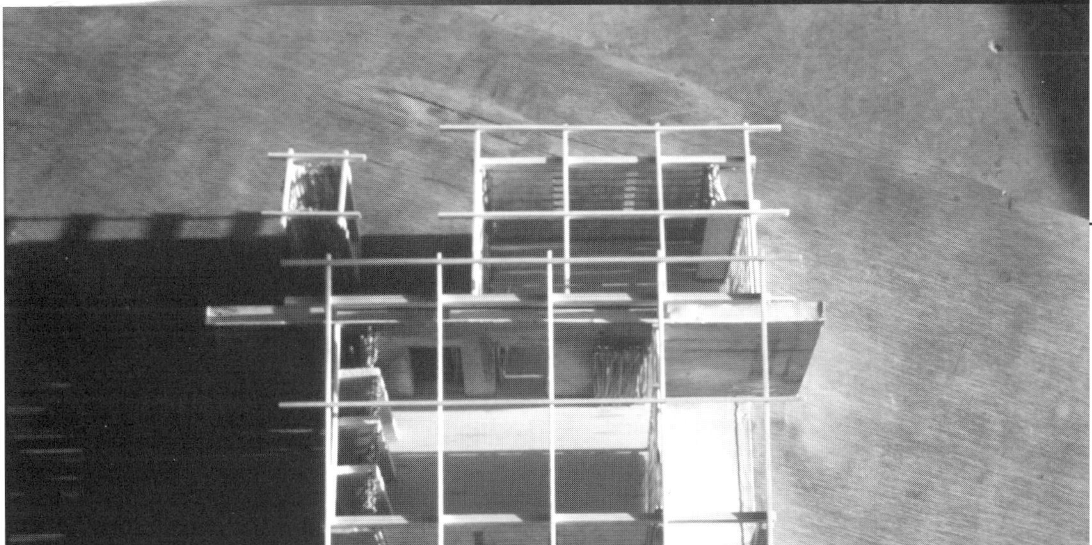

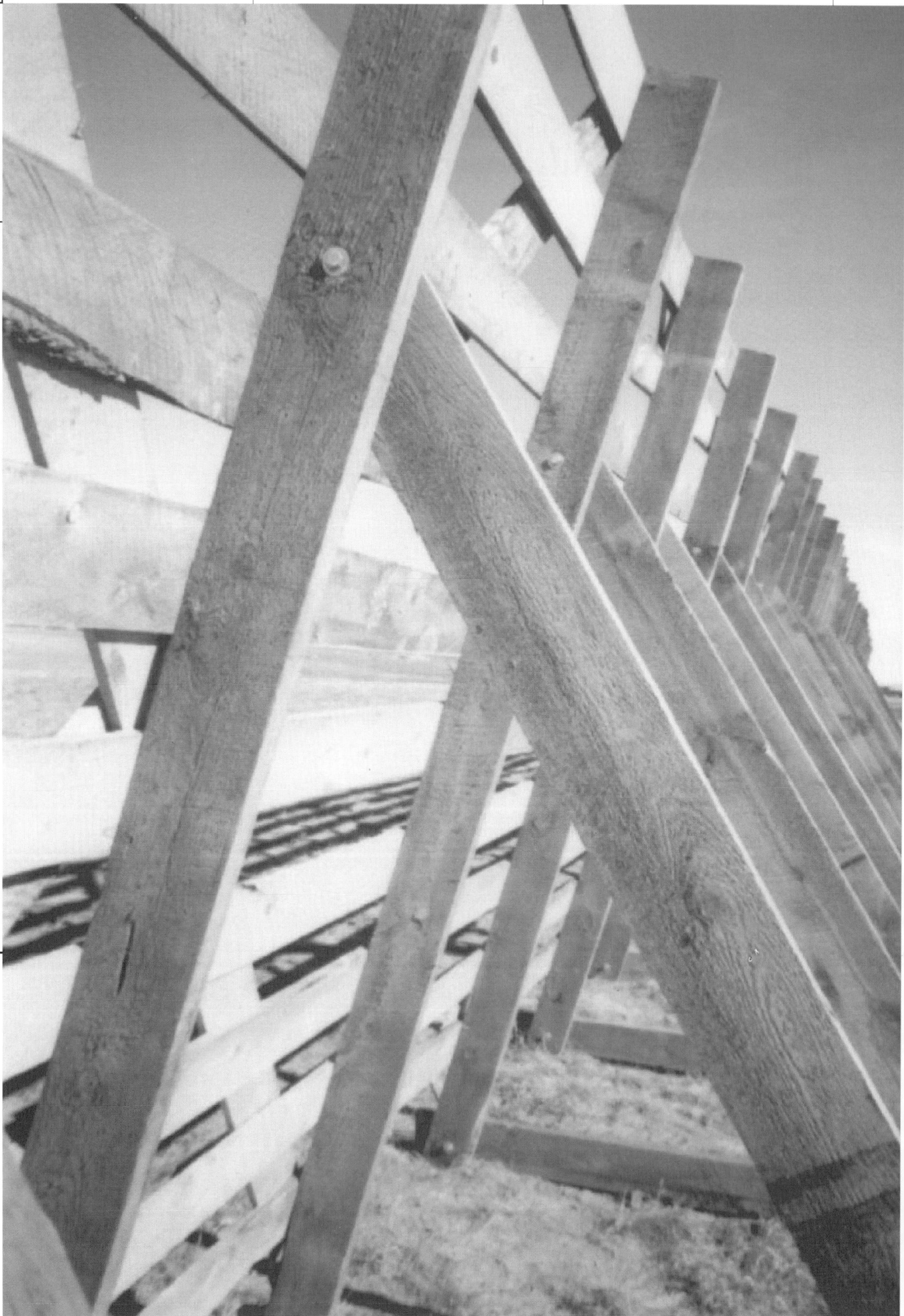

Snow fences as art space

ECO-VENTIONS

by Terry Boling and Marc Swackhamer

In early 2002 we collaborated with Sue Spaid, curator at the Contemporary Arts Center in Cincinnati, Ohio, to design and construct an exhibition of environmental art entitled "Ecoventions." We were asked by Ms. Spade to build an organizing display wall for the exhibition that was inexpensive, temporary and built with volunteer labor.

The image of a simple ecological intervention, a snow fence, provided us with a strong visual reference for the project. We proposed a variation on the snow fence that could define a variety of spaces and programmed functions as well as guide viewers through the exhibition. Closely placed fence slats created dark areas for viewing projected imagery; fence slats with large gaps created light-filled zones suitable for viewing sculptural artwork. We constructed a continuous surface that modulated from the open to the closed condition by using a variable support piece at 4-foot intervals. This allowed the slats to subtly twist from vertical (closed) to horizontal (open) along the 76-foot length of the wall.

The investigation of the relationship between design and technique was a primary focus of the project. Material limitations and availability, cost constraints, construction feasibility and schedule continually informed and revised our initial design

Terry Boling, AIA is an assistant professor at the University of Cincinnati and received his architecture degree from the same institution. Terry worked in Europe for a number of years prior to returning to Cincinnati to set up his own practice.

Marc Swackhamer is an assistant professor at the University of Cincinnati as well as a graduate of the program. Marc received a MArch from Rice University.

Terry and Marc have collaborated on a number of projects and installations, all involving students. Ecoventions recently won a design distinction award in I.D. *magazine's 2003 annual design review.*

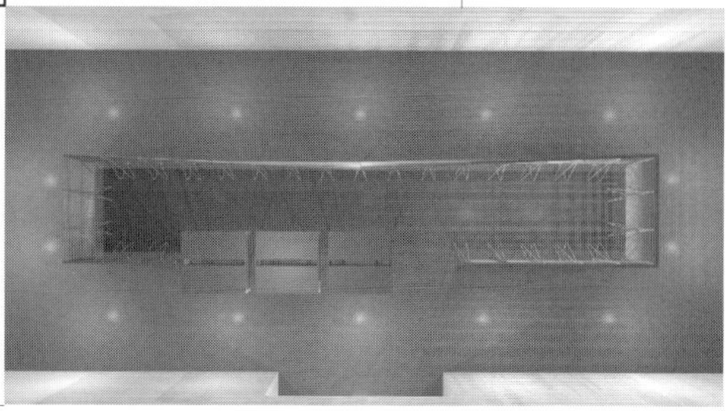

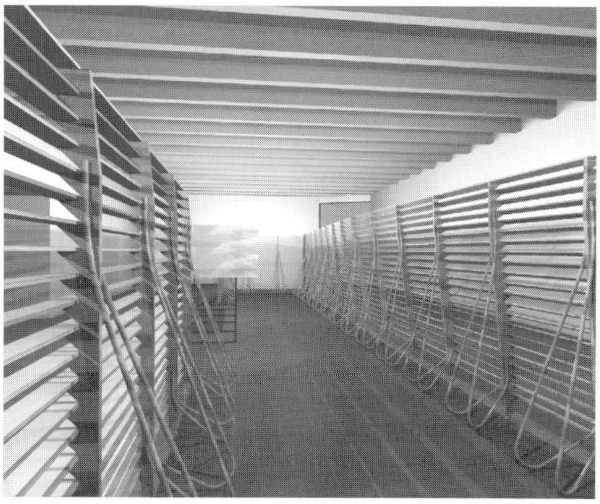

intentions. After considering and testing several iterations of the variable support pieces, we settled on a 1½" laminated plywood spline that was cut using a computer aided milling machine. This technique proved most effective in fabricating individual *one-off* splines, each requiring a unique profile.

For the splines' supporting members, the concept of repetition prompted a completely different, low-tech approach. We formed 8-foot lengths of ½" round EMT conduit using an off-the-shelf conduit bender to create the sixty supporting legs for the splines. Finally, 4'x8' sheets of ½" MDF were cut down to three-inch strips to create the fence slats.

At the end of the wall, the Contemporary Arts Center required three large light boxes to display transparencies. We constructed these of standard 3'x6'8" hollow core doors, bolted together, and supported on welded steel frames.

We recruited four graduate students to participate in the design and construction of the project; Parker Eberhard, Abby Kosky, Joshua Summers, and Matt Winter. In exchange for their work, these students gained first-hand experience with materials and construction techniques. Full-scale mock-ups encouraged the students to interact with the actual materials and methods of detailing

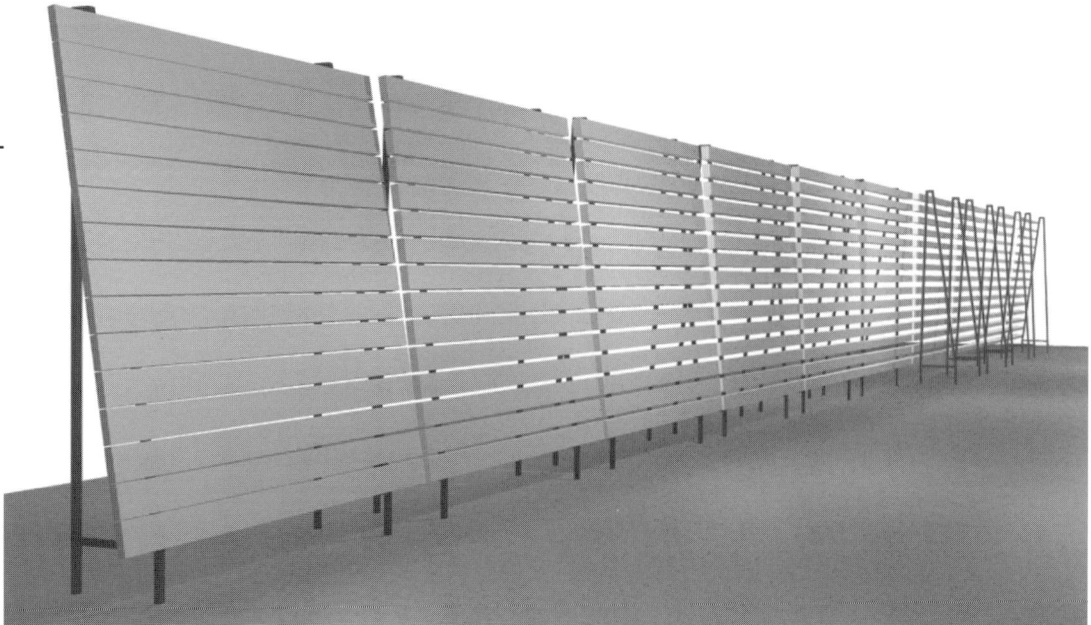

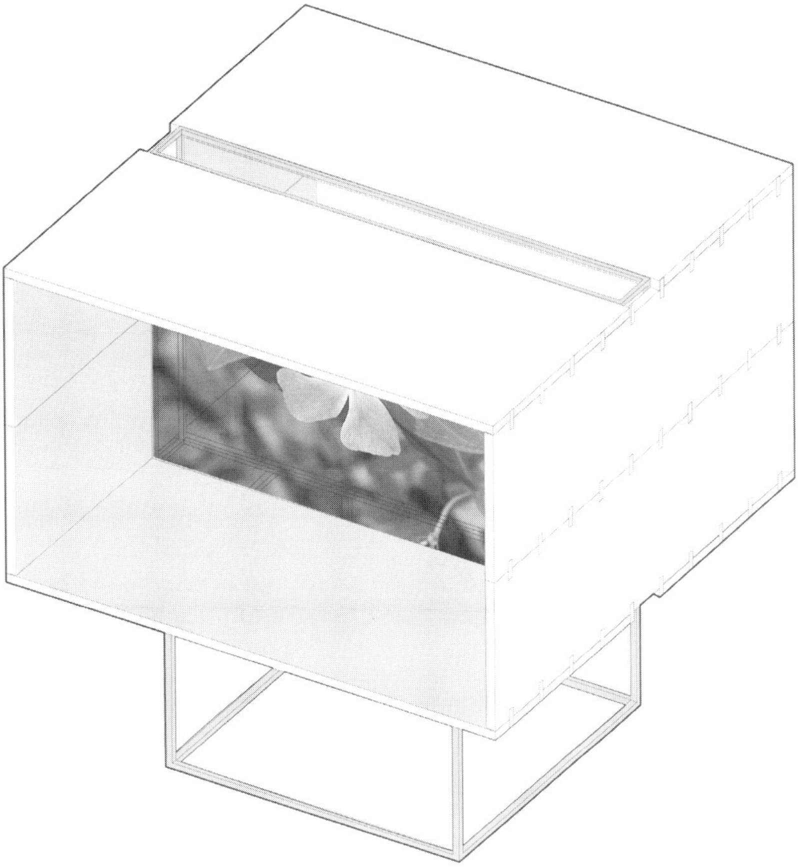

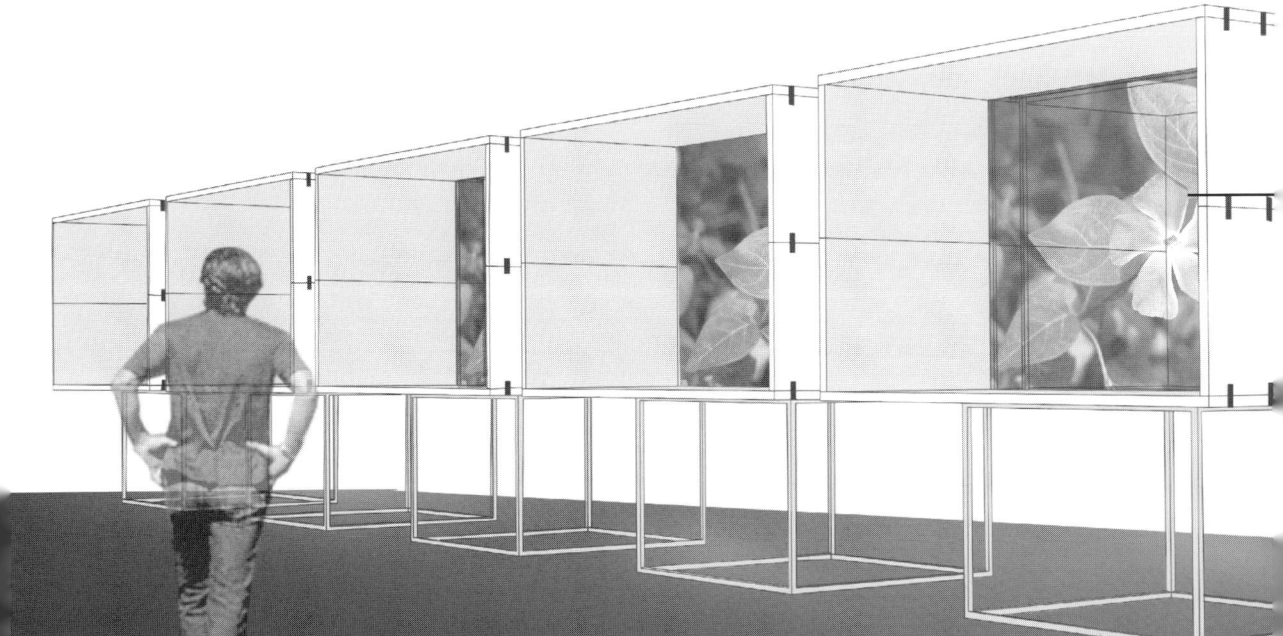

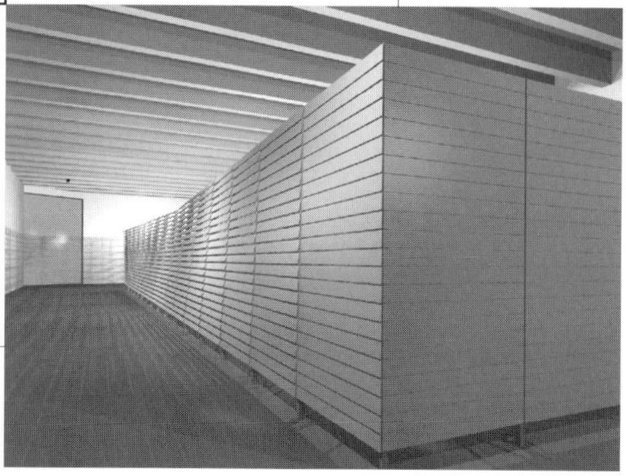

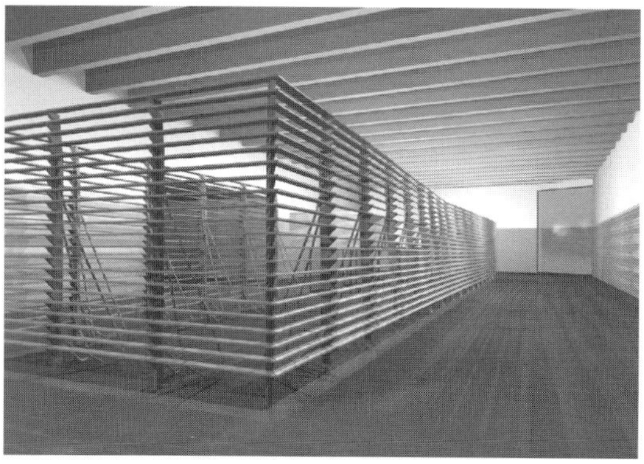

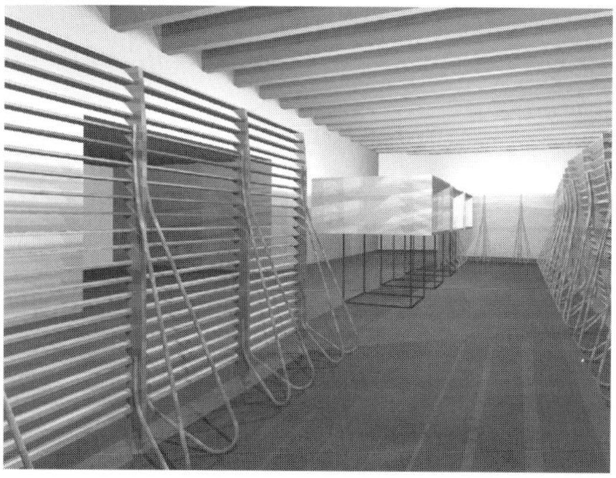

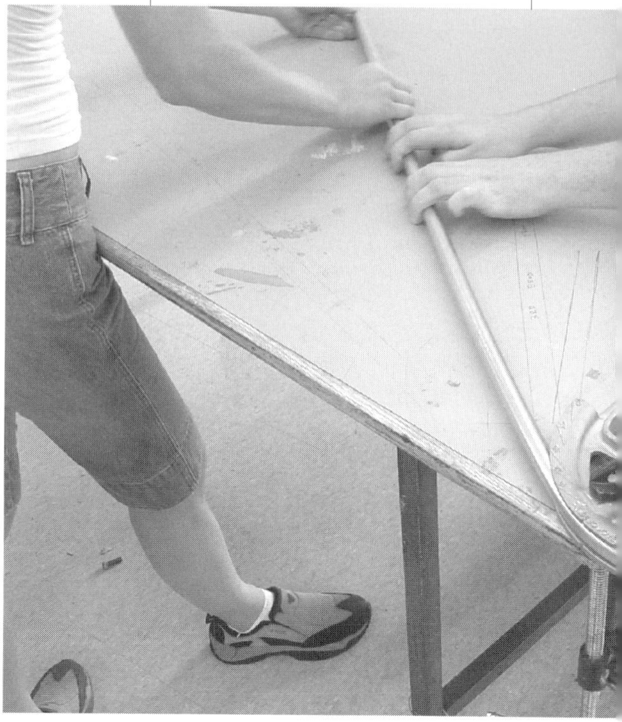

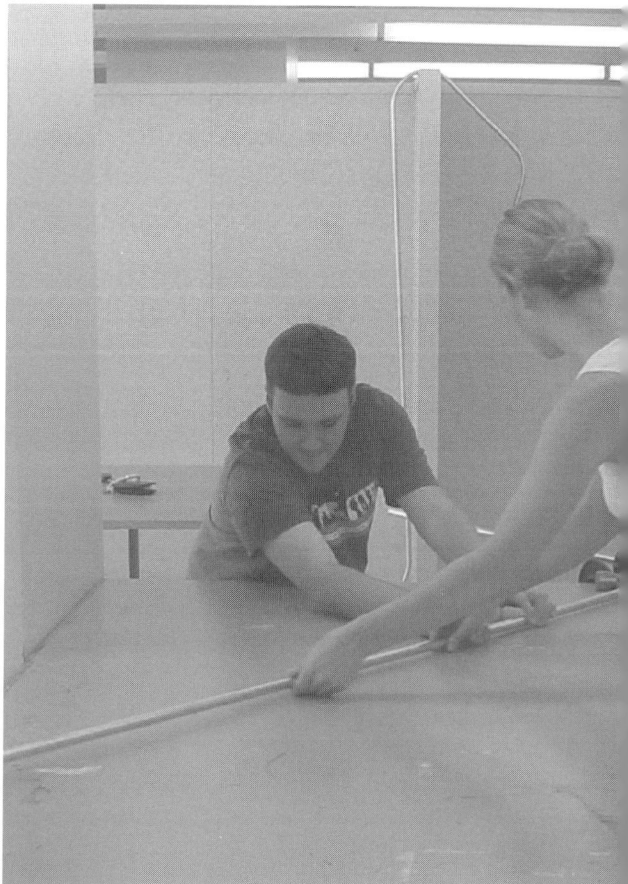

during the design process. During the design and construction process, they also began to recognize that design decisions are made at multiple scales and phases throughout a project–not just at the drawing board or the computer screen. Students dealt directly with fabricators, consultants, and suppliers for the first time. They also had the opportunity to collaborate with the curators, artists and sculptors from the Contemporary Arts Center-no doubt similar to future clients. The alternative perspectives gleaned from these outside sources yielded refreshing design suggestions that impacted the final project in a way that could not be predicted.

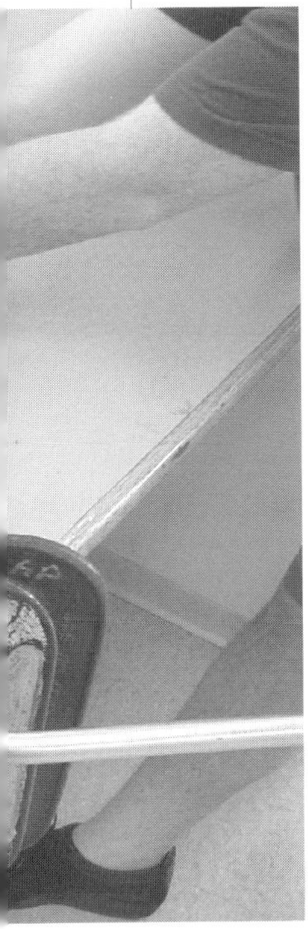

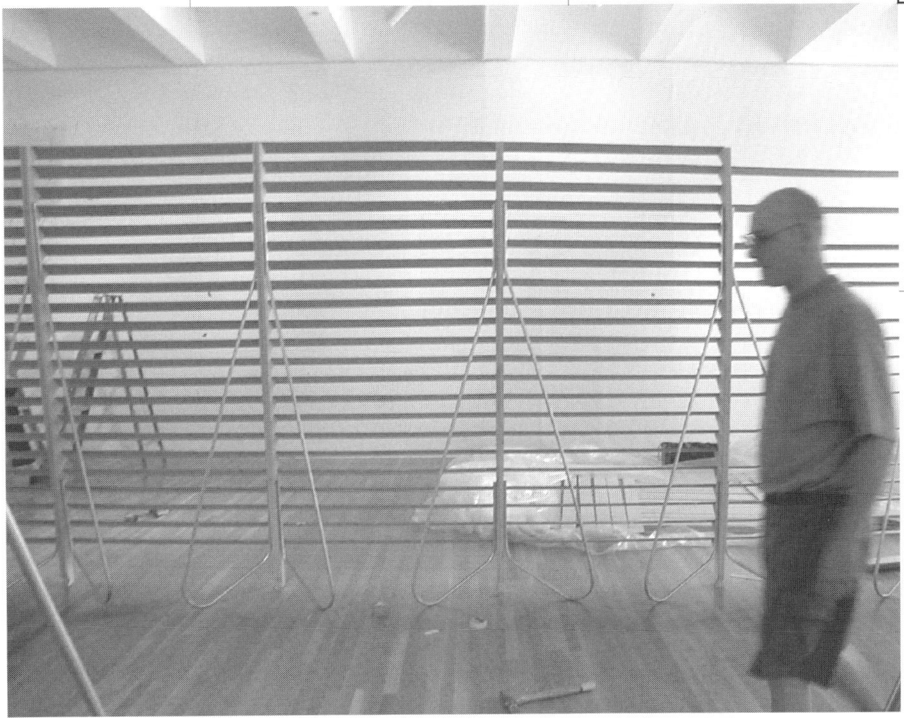

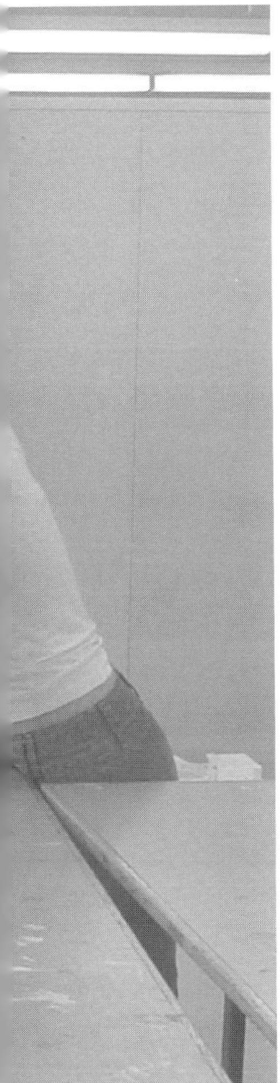

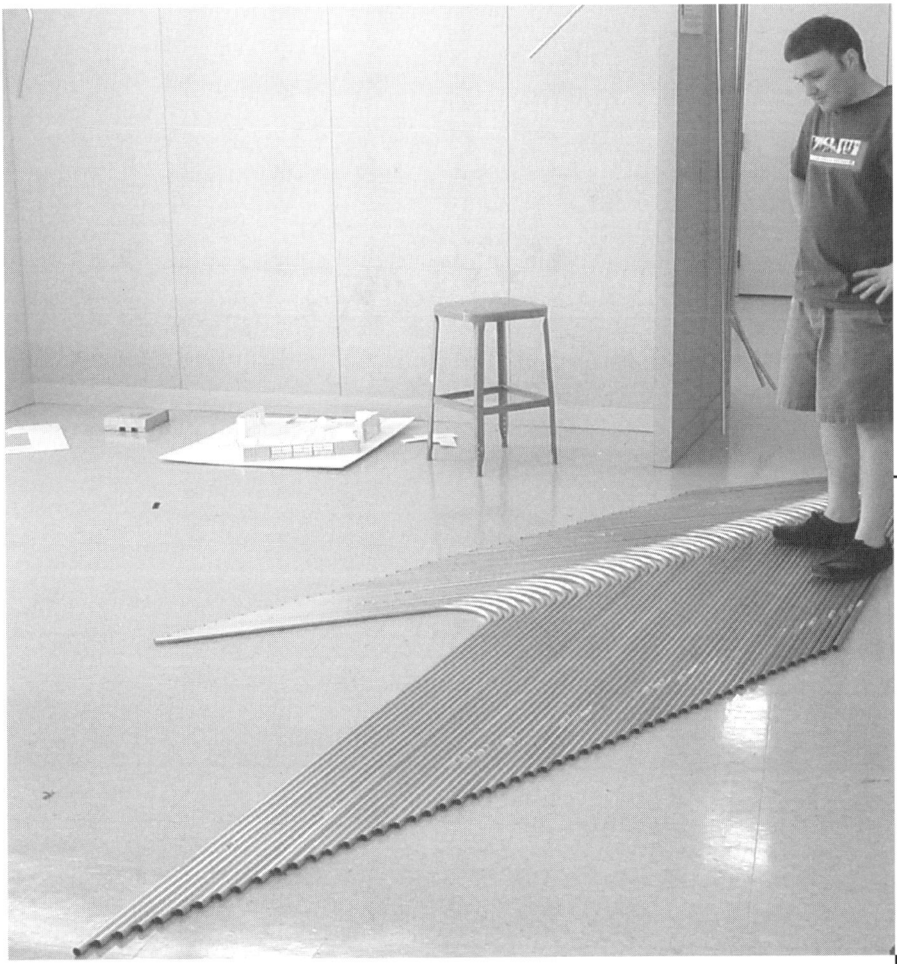

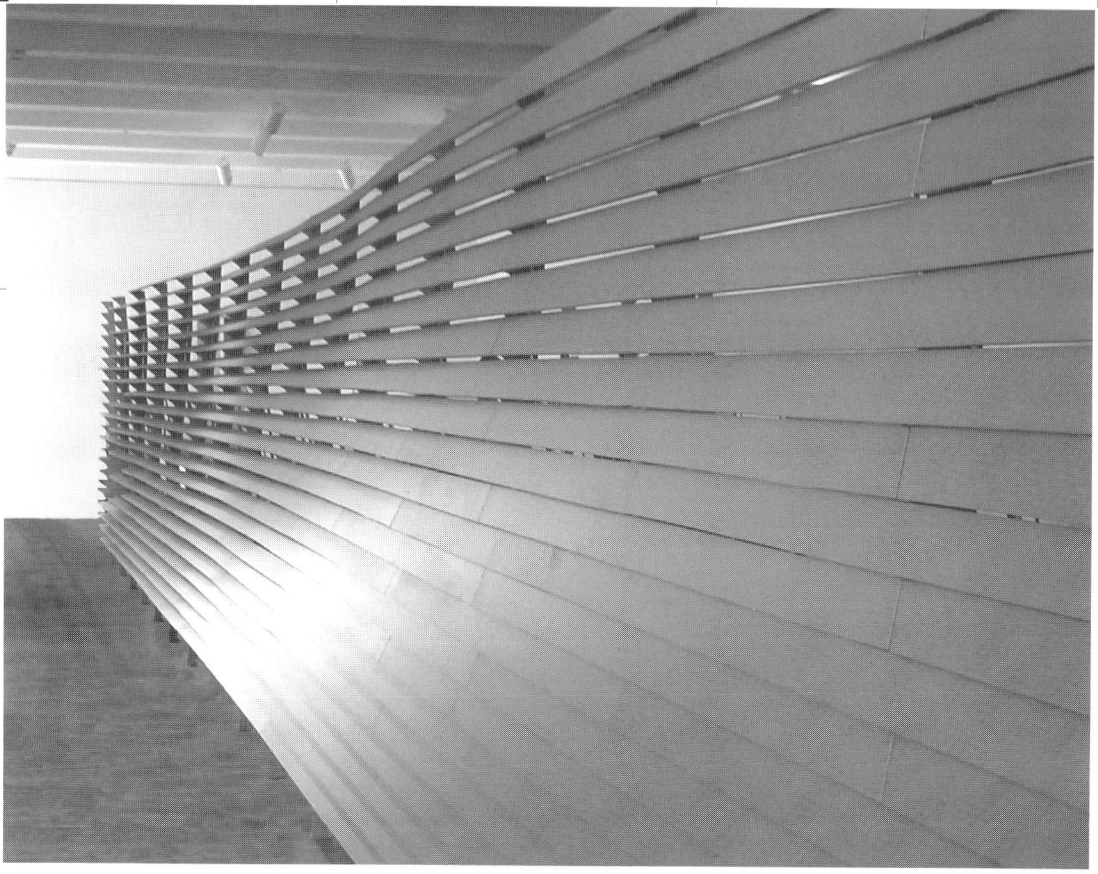

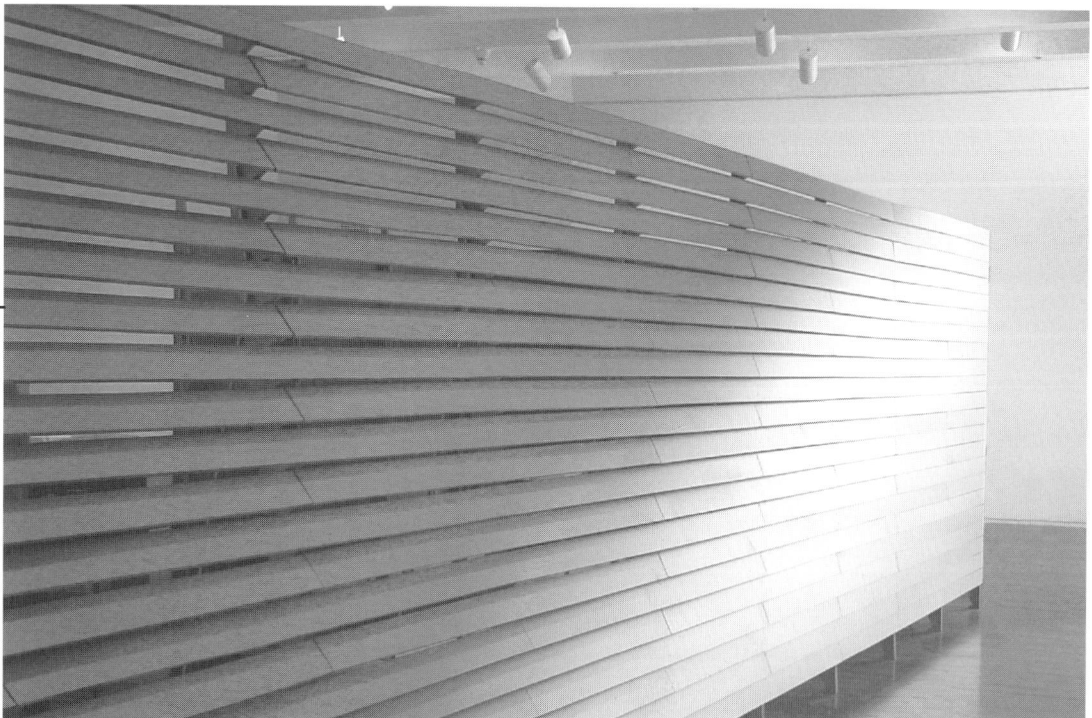

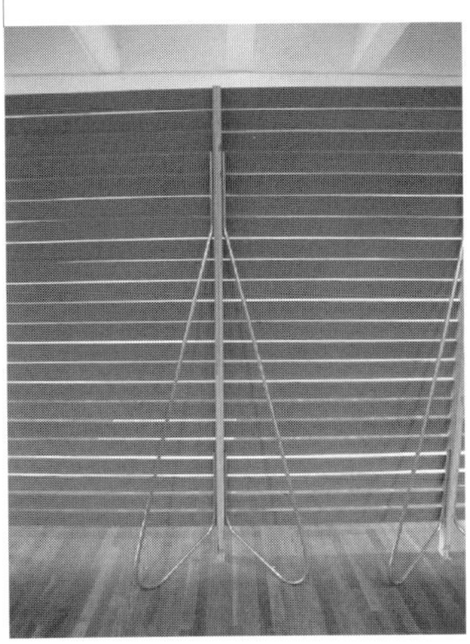
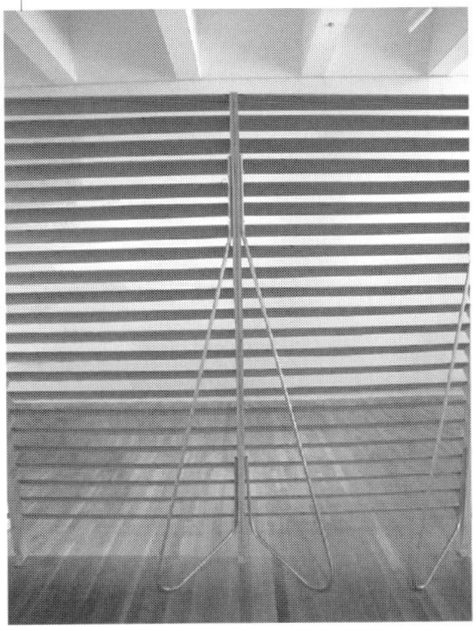
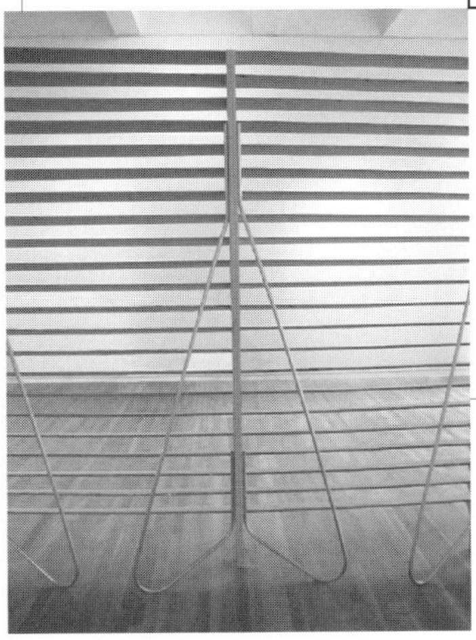

HOW TO: BUILD YOUR OWN ECOVENTION

Snow fence Construction:

1. To construct the supports for the continuous surface, use your computer-generated splines. Cut each out of 1½-inch laminated plywood using a computer aided milling machine.

2. Place these variable support pieces at 4-foot intervals.

3. Use an off-the-shelf conduit bender to form 8-foot lengths of ½" round EMT conduit. This will create the sixty supporting legs for the splines.

4. Finally, cut 4'x8' sheets of ½" MDF to 3-inch strips on order to create the fence slats.

Light box Construction:

1. At the end of the wall, the CAC required 3 large light boxes to display transparencies.

2. Construct the boxes out of standard 3'x6'8" hollow core doors. Use bolts to secure these together.

3. Using 1-inch welded steel tube frames, weld simple steel frames to support the boxes.

4. Use translucent acrylic and florescent lamps to complete the light boxes.

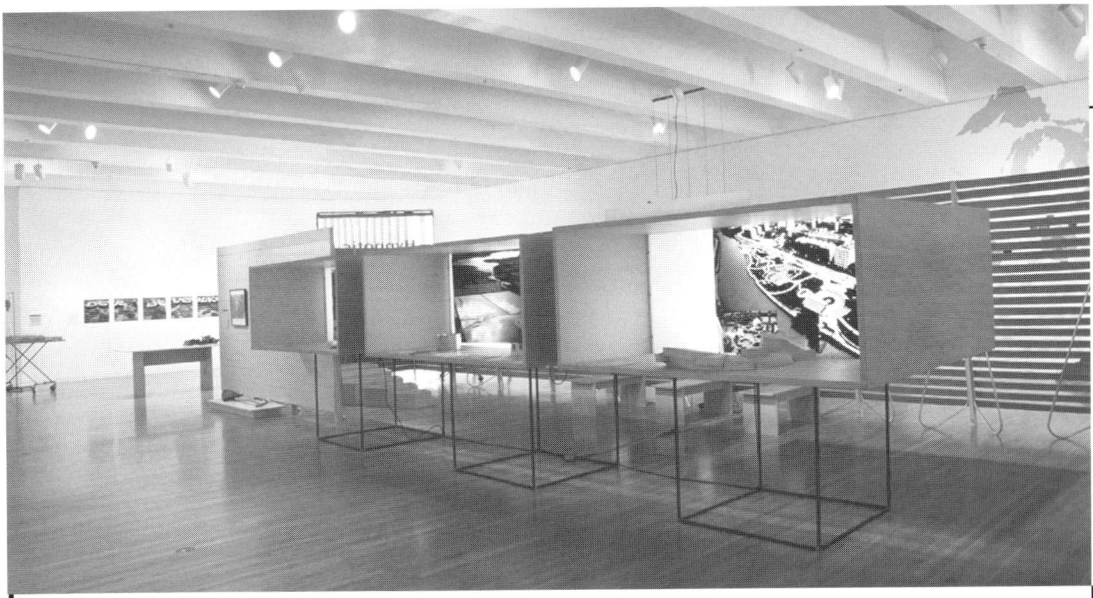

FLOATING REA

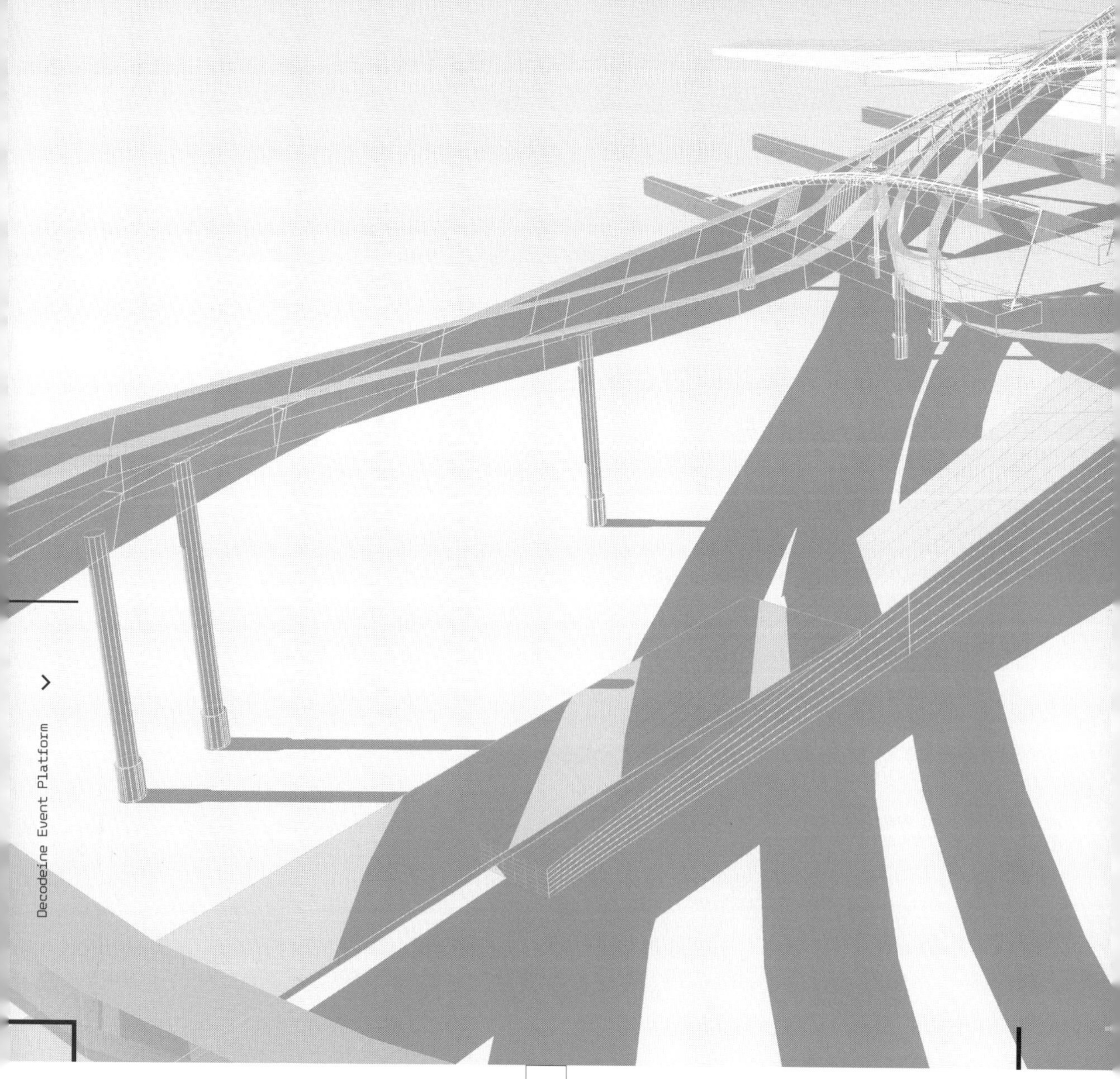

Decodeine Event Platform ›

ITIES

PATHOLOGY AND SPACE

by Margot Krasojevic

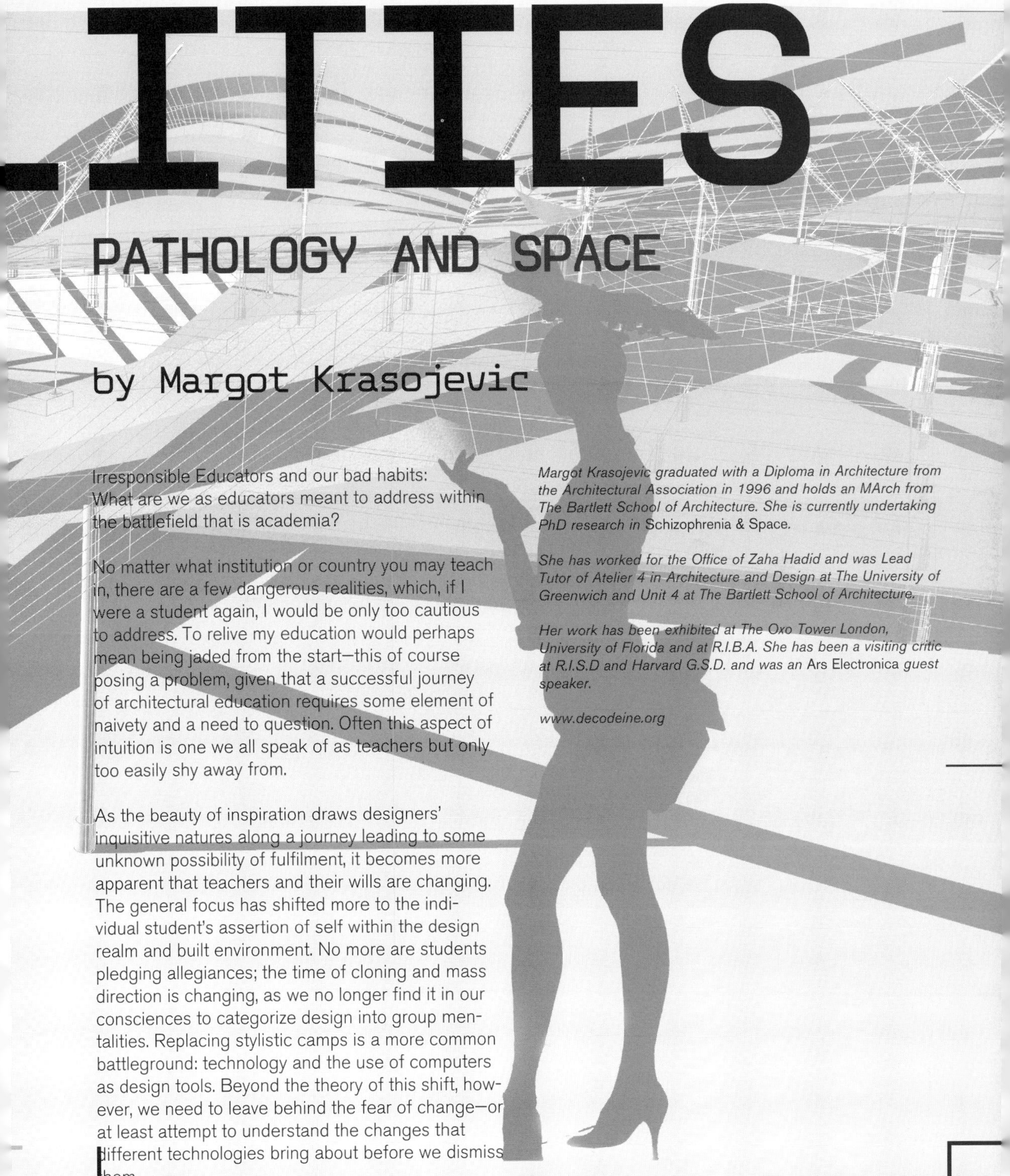

Irresponsible Educators and our bad habits:
What are we as educators meant to address within the battlefield that is academia?

No matter what institution or country you may teach in, there are a few dangerous realities, which, if I were a student again, I would be only too cautious to address. To relive my education would perhaps mean being jaded from the start—this of course posing a problem, given that a successful journey of architectural education requires some element of naivety and a need to question. Often this aspect of intuition is one we all speak of as teachers but only too easily shy away from.

As the beauty of inspiration draws designers' inquisitive natures along a journey leading to some unknown possibility of fulfilment, it becomes more apparent that teachers and their wills are changing. The general focus has shifted more to the individual student's assertion of self within the design realm and built environment. No more are students pledging allegiances; the time of cloning and mass direction is changing, as we no longer find it in our consciences to categorize design into group mentalities. Replacing stylistic camps is a more common battleground: technology and the use of computers as design tools. Beyond the theory of this shift, however, we need to leave behind the fear of change—or at least attempt to understand the changes that different technologies bring about before we dismiss them.

Margot Krasojevic graduated with a Diploma in Architecture from the Architectural Association in 1996 and holds an MArch from The Bartlett School of Architecture. She is currently undertaking PhD research in Schizophrenia & Space.

She has worked for the Office of Zaha Hadid and was Lead Tutor of Atelier 4 in Architecture and Design at The University of Greenwich and Unit 4 at The Bartlett School of Architecture.

Her work has been exhibited at The Oxo Tower London, University of Florida and at R.I.B.A. She has been a visiting critic at R.I.S.D and Harvard G.S.D. and was an Ars Electronica *guest speaker.*

www.decodeine.org

While we may be losing stylistic categorizations, another long-standing divide continues to exist now as it did when I first started studying architecture. Architects either build or think; many of the lucky few that do both seem to dilute their intentions by reducing building strategies to pure theory. As the eagerness to categorize is still present, one wonders whether we can we ever successfully fulfill the requirements of both realms.

In a studio environment, students are often faced with one option—to adapt to a certain way of design-in order to survive. On the other side of the coin is the teacher. A teacher is often faced with the frustration that his or her beliefs will not have a life beyond that very studio. The need to translate the theory into the built environment is felt—in effect strengthening and defining the physical presence of the teacher's ideas as well as his position in the eyes of the students.

Returning to the problem of technology, we tend to communicate what our tools suggest. From collage to French curves to computer modelling and simulation, the extent of our thoughts and their manifestations starts and ends with the technology that is at our disposal. In general, our profession has not so far voiced a need for exclusively defining and exploring that technology for the built environment. As a result, we have rarely been given the opportunity to actually become visionaries.

What occurs over time with the use of such technologies is a kind of dilution, resulting from adaptation to the given constraints of each tool. Often, the importance of these shifts goes unnoticed, as does the effect that the resulting work has on other disciplines—as well as the return effect those disciplines have on architecture. With architecture forever a multi-disciplinary art, we constantly monitor the media and other professions in order to define our reality. Thus, the importance of questioning technological mediation is manifold, as the choices we make here, in turn, shape our contextual response.

Further dilution occurs when architects, no longer students, attempt to build. The fact that the emotions and paranoias instilled in the research labs differ immensely from the efficiency and financial realities of the building process is often ignored or dismissed as unimportant. The eventual realization that design concepts and criteria do actually differ from their actual representations often comes as a shock, causing a revaluation of the ideals students are exposed to during their academic years. The eventual union tends to be clouded by a need for reiteration; referring to a time long gone. The resulting loss of interest in theory creates a divide between the two worlds—and we eventually strive to regain the past experiences and research approaches that were once available to us during our naïve years.

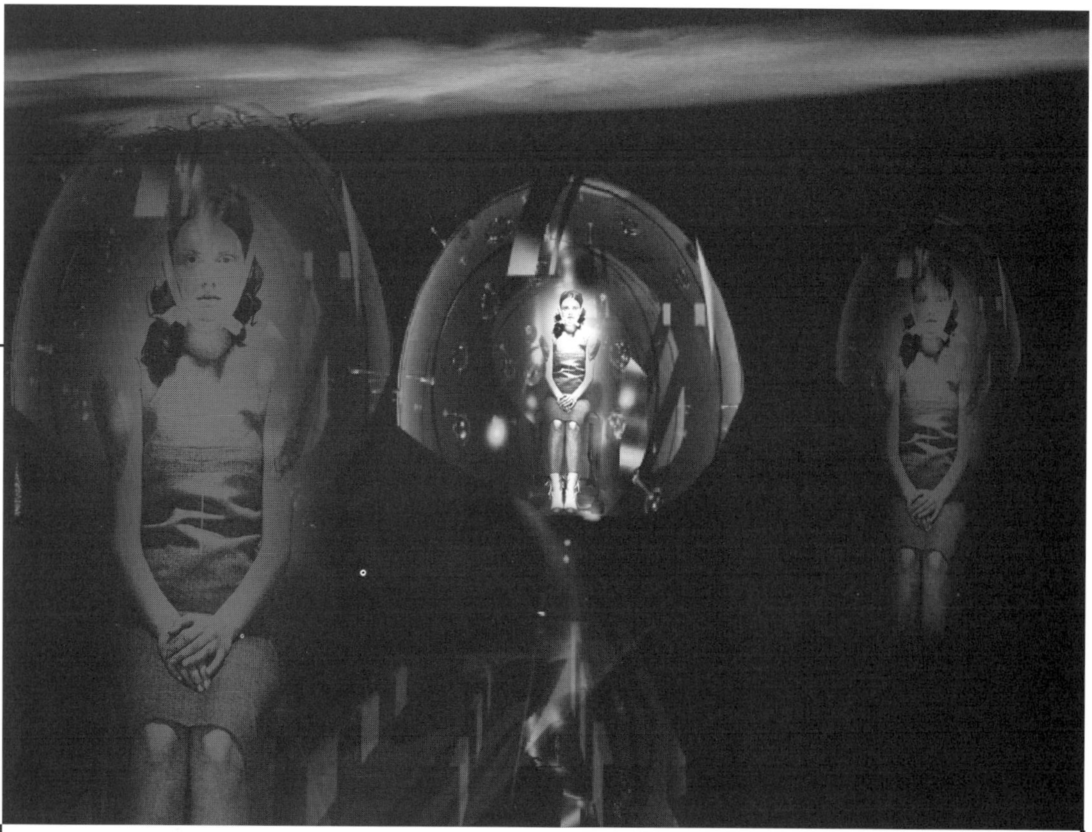

I thus find it necessary to dwell on an important chapter of my work as a teacher and architect. The focus of this work is reality and its application; that is, considering technology and its effects on society and the built environment as well as attitudes and methods of communicating visions. What follows is an abbreviated essay about that very experience. Are distinctions made between products of the unconscious or are they seen as parts of an objective, but invisible, reality? The fascination with compartmentalizing experiences into categories such as religious, supernatural, phenomenological or

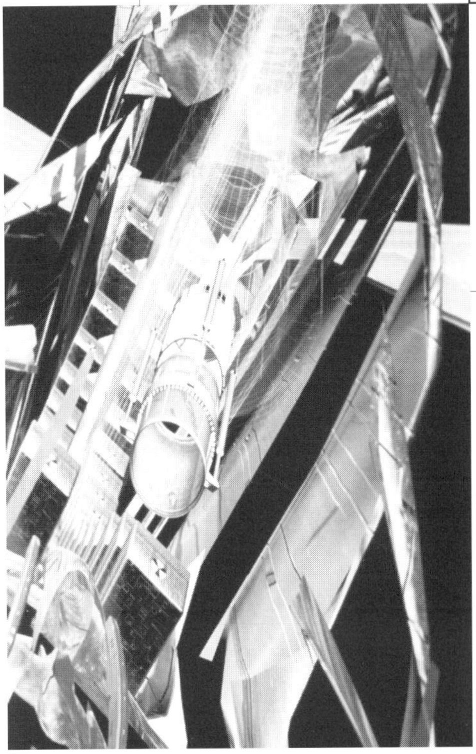

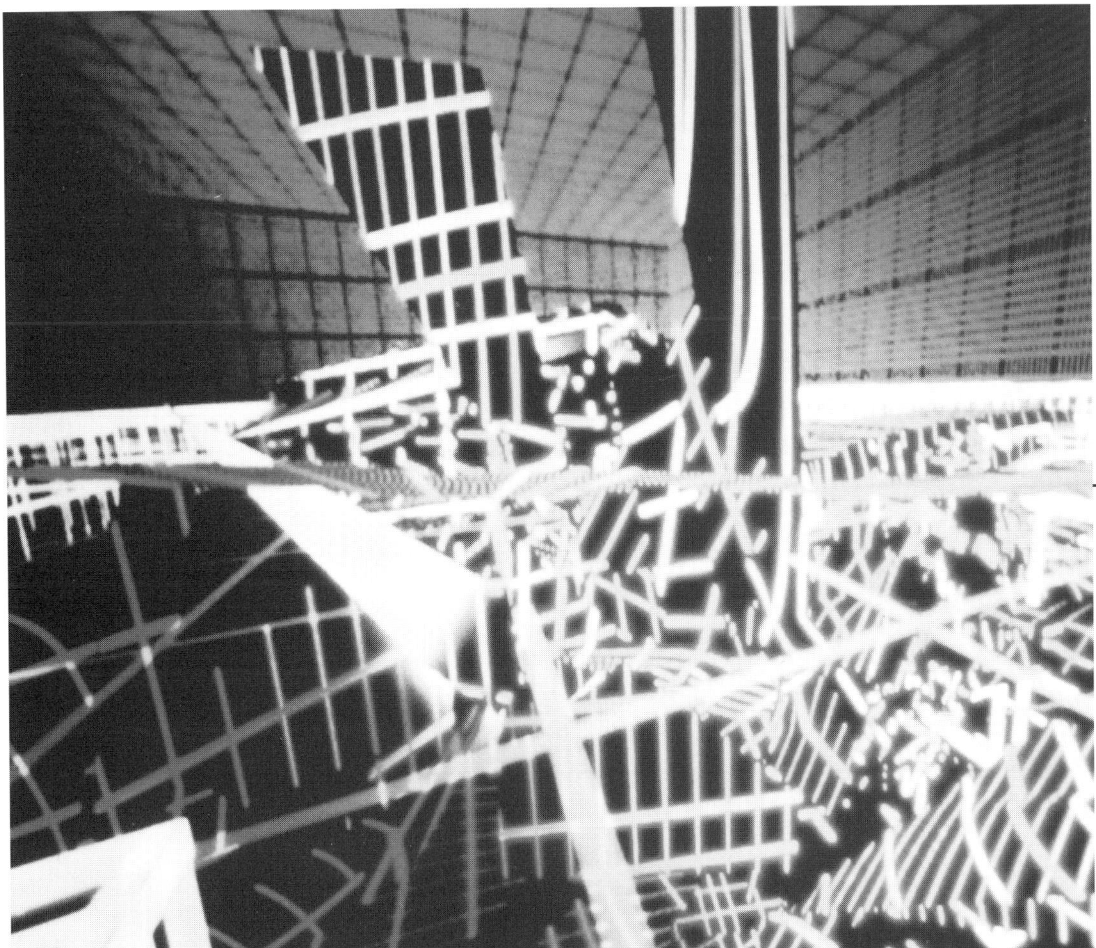

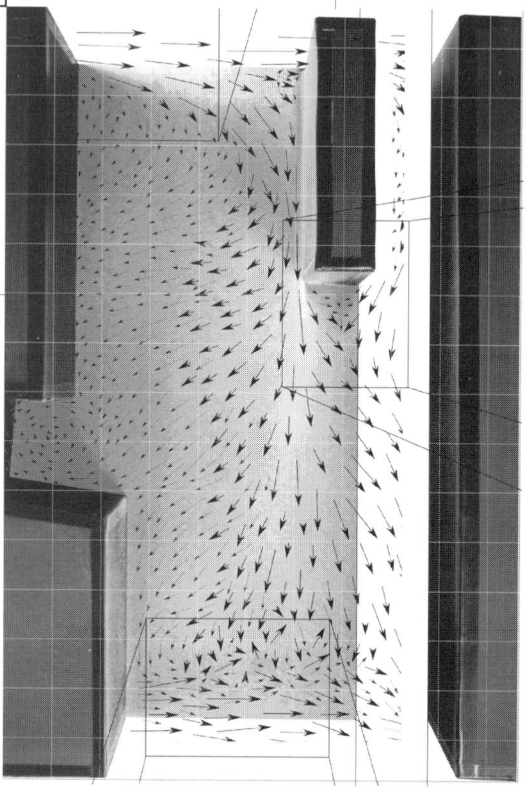

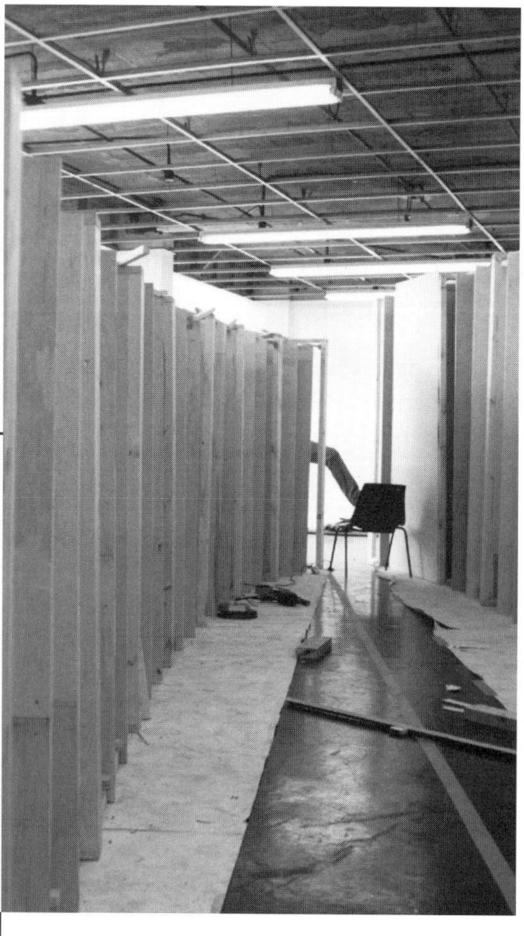

Student Installation: translation of scale

metaphysical processes is readily evident in today's society. We have all had extraordinary experiences that have left us questioning their validity. Stress, fear, exhaustion and alcohol induce emotions such as paranoia, psychosis and euphoria, yet we mostly return to our everyday repeated patterns, relying on old methods of communicating our thoughts and feelings, all the while pushing these further into our subconscious. We use inadequate symbols to describe these extraordinary forms of awareness and we muddle the metaphysical universe with all the accessories of our subconscious.

Links between the unconscious, creativity and technology are exposed in Freud's watershed essay of 1929, *The Mystic Writing Pad*[1], which presents writing as a tool for reconciling the perplexing issue of how temporary sensations and other bits of information are retained as memory and made available for total recall. The core of the study suggests that the psyche's structure is an ongoing flickering of marking and erasure, where each impression leaves a trace of itself at the moment of its vanishing-in short, a loss of context.

For Freud, the mystic writing pad is analogous to the way the psyche system—which receives sense impression from the outside world—remains unmarked by those impressions which pass through it to a deeper layer where they are recorded as unconscious memory. This memory possibly triggers panic attacks and other seemingly random behavioral processes, all non-related in our conscious lives but in the subconscious, which holds the key to recognition and in turn understanding the relationships between both realms.

Derrida claims that none of us apprehend the world directly but, rather, retrospectively; our sense of that which is beyond ourselves is the product of previous memories, previous writings. "Writing," says Derrida, "supplements perception before perception even appears to itself."[2] This appears as especially evident in evident everyday rituals such as going to work—we follow the same paths without really actually experiencing the city. Repetition is equally evident in the architecture of today, dulling the palette when a good idea is exhausted. An example of this may be evident in Renzo Piano's beautiful, yet predictably saturated, Kansai airport, where a section that is initially quite interesting is merely extruded for an entire mile.

Nox, MVRDV, Rem Koolhaas, Daniel Libeskind and Frank Gehry have all embraced new geometries. Whether these include multiple programming, non-static conditions, continuous surfaces, animation or simulation time-sequencing processes, fractals, unpredictability, or pushing the boundaries of engineering, materiality, and form, there is one

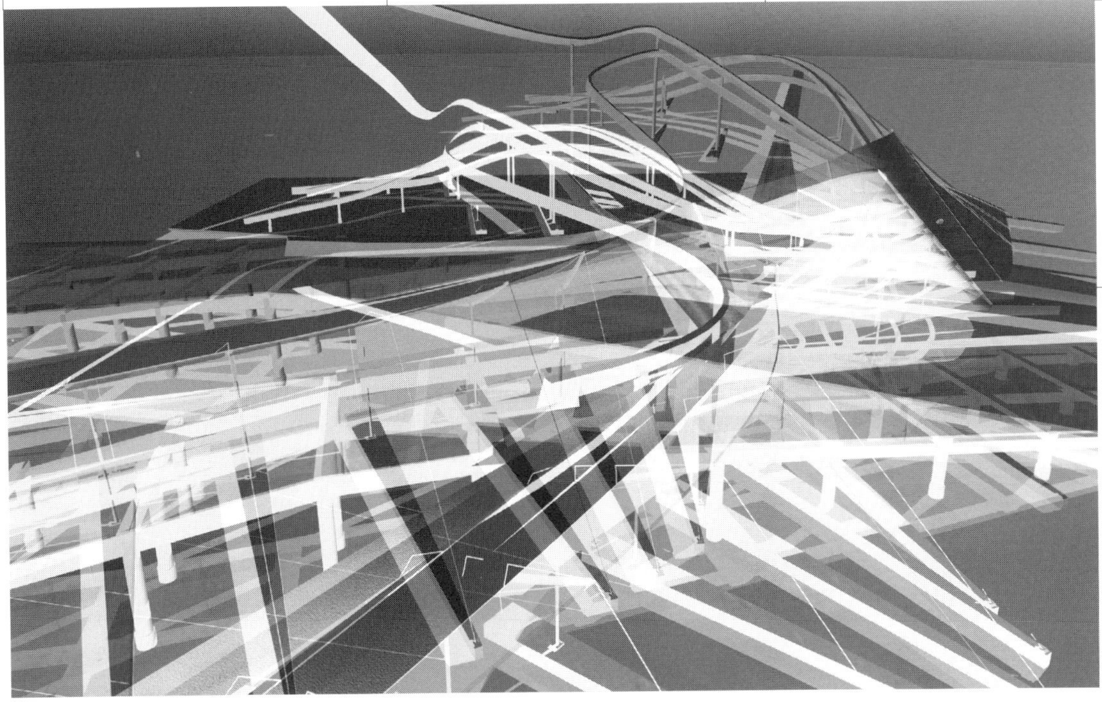

characteristic that they all share. This is the element of surprise; the architecture of multiple identities, perceptions, appropriations—of nonlinearity. In this work, the potential of non-hierarchy presents us with a new set of rules that act as the antithesis of the autopilot repetitive experiences we are continually faced with in our everyday routines.

We are contributing to the cult of distraction—once only expressed through cinema—the optical fairy-lands, shrines to the cultivation of pleasure. Architecture today sees us looking to these picture palaces and applying similar social parameters to all programs—be they work related, residential or cultural.

Walter Benjamin's observations about distraction, usually associated with a discussion of the concept of aura, refers to the distracted state of mind of the urban dweller—jaded, bored or swamped by the flood of visual and social stimuli of the modern city. While usually only a tourist would arduously focus in order to attempt to understand his or her new surroundings and explore that new physicality, there is another character who does the same on a regular basis: the student.

Many students approach projects as tourists approach cities. Yet more of us are experiencing other cities in an anesthetized way. We go to places that remind us of where we came from and take our own rituals with us, an identity to superimpose within the newest of conditions only drawing out of them similar experiences; a comfort blanket cocooning us in a familiar and protective set of circumstances.

Benjamin was one of the first to think about how technological reproduction alters the way we look at ***reality***. He saw that the new media of his day was fundamentally altering the relationships between signifying systems in society and reality by a process of simulation. We are still experiencing a type of this, one in which the tools are more advanced but the principles are very similar. In relation to critical / cultural theory, simulation is the process whereby representations of things come to replace the things being represented. In other words, we perceive the representations as more important than the *real*.

Someone like Baudrillard, for example, would likely argue that we, as a society, have lost touch with reality and are instead hooked into a simulation of reality, made up of television and the Internet. This new ***reality*** supplants the real thing, and we feel comfortable in our new simulated world, feeling a little unsettled if we stray away from it far too long. It is important to remember that this simulation is not really a fake; a mere copy of something real. It is, instead, another reality that has a power and a meaning that is, if anything, greater than that of the *real* real.

A phenomenon important to this discussion is that of *Forward Masking.*[3] This occurs when our brains forward mask (i.e. anticipate) certain feelings and responses, allowing most bodily sensations to be conditioned, their responses automatic and able to occur in split seconds. To summarize this process, when we touch something with the end of a fingertip it takes a greater amount of time for that signal to reach our brain and in turn allow us to be aware, make a decision and finally, respond to the stimulus. Since this process may take too long for our bodies to protect themselves from harm, our bodies instead (through conditioning experience) anticipate the response—the brain having an expectation of various stimuli—and *forward masks*, responding automatically through repetition.

Modernism and The Unnamed Movement:

Modernism can be thought of as a radically altered aesthetic form and perspective; the modernist stress upon art as a self-referential construct instead of as a mirror of nature or society. If this is true, we may anticipate a future disagreement with psychologists concerning the effects of the city and its perception.

Modern architecture puts economic and sociological issues above those of style as the imperatives of architectural progress. As such, surely modern architecture should accept a relationship between itself and the number of psychological diseases exposed during the Modern movement.

Modernism has acknowledged, and for some theoreticians is responsible for, symptoms of agoraphobia—significantly defined as a spatial disease—seen as the effect of life in the modern city. Other similar metropolis-induced illnesses exposed during the modern movement included vertigo, amaxophobia (fear of carriages), hypsophobia (fear of elevated places), hydrophobia, pyrophobia, anthrophobia (fear of social contact) and so on.

Modernists dismissed these new psychological definitions (from the 19th century as primitive regressions) introduced to social awareness by counter-Modernists and latter-day Ruskinians. The fact that urbanism might not be the mother of these psychological conditions, but instead genetics, is as influential a part of the argument as the actual fact we are more likely to survive and adapt to new environments. Thus, psychologists' and psychoanalysts' concerns with phobias are replaced by anxiety attacks, multiple personality disorders, attention deficit disorder (short attention spans), schizophrenia, depression, de-realization and depersonalization.

Skyscrapers, elevators, reinforced concrete, glass curtain walls, roof spans, floating walls and the open plan all contribute in exercising the technology of the architectural modern movement.

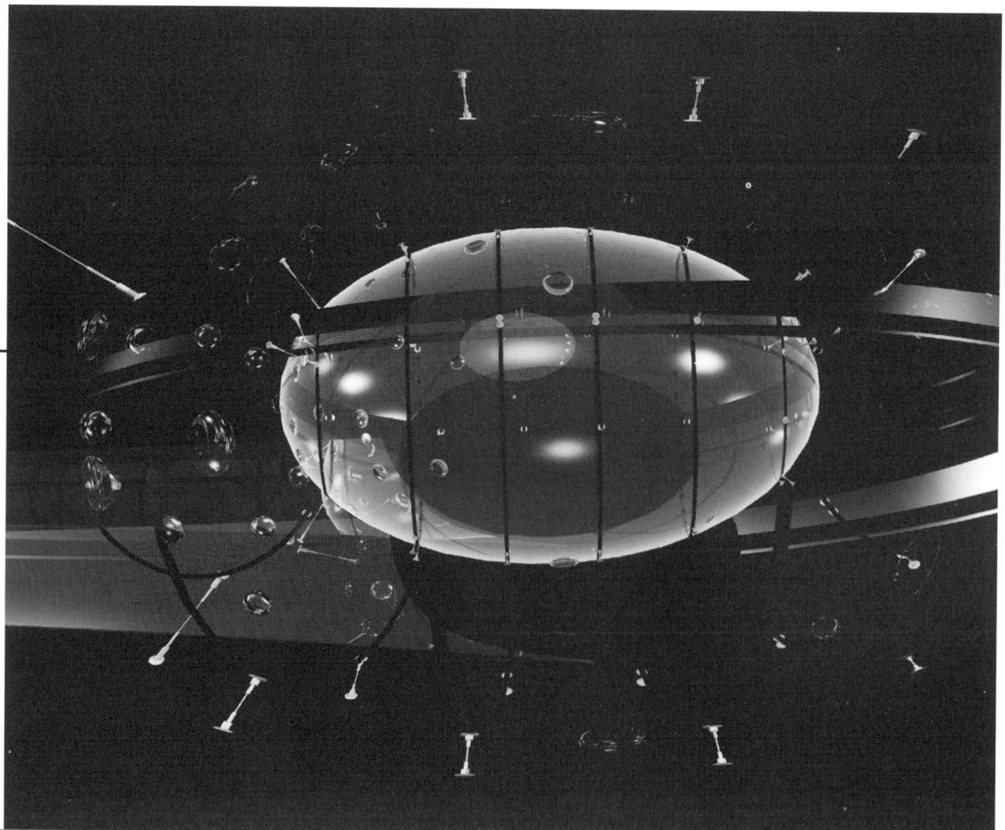

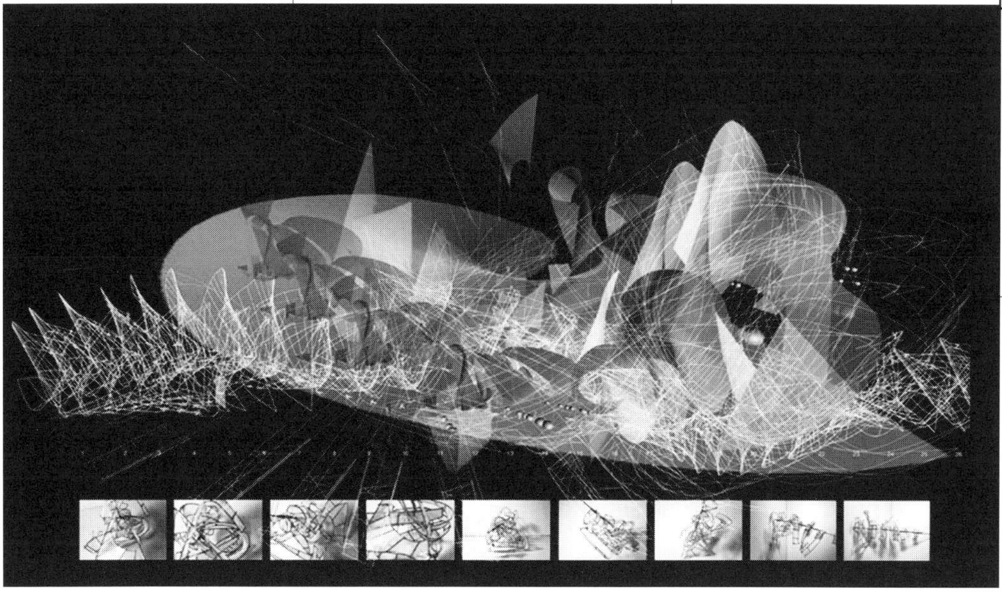

What do we consider as the most influential technological changes in relation to architecture? The effects, some would argue, are precisely these and other new brands of psychological conditions. Today's architecture, however, needs to address the fact that these conditions are a part of society—whether truly pathological or otherwise.

It is obvious that, over time, we do not live, work or love in the same way—let alone relate to others in the same way. Information overload should not be blamed but accepted and understood; equally, our superficial connection to technology and altered psyches needs to be discarded in favor of a more precise understanding. Thus we will be able to adapt and appropriate, because we are born to modify and survive.

With this increased understanding, we will find that the disappearance of the city through information overload is not necessarily true. We edit and have learned to speed-read, we have designed methods for staying awake and alert for longer (artificiality now more of a way of life than a natural state). Our options are becoming broader and broader and it is up to us where we position ourselves within this framework. Occasionally, we short circuit—as our brains and bodies are in heightened alert, putting the entire body in anxiety mode, or, over stimulation. Selections of multiple personalities are presented to us in the form of E-mail chat rooms, where we change our bodies and minds either to keep up with or to define our identities. The endless realms and possibilities for identity change asks: whose reality is it, and, can we no longer clearly define the boundaries?

Adapting to the changes around us makes us rely more on our intuition and memory to guide us. Similar to a series of deja vu remnants of the previous trace experienced, this reflects the characteristics of a blind alley with the bored, jaded inhabitants of the city simply existing. This is one direction in which the excesses of information technology can lead us.

Alternatively, we can introduce new realities that question our previous experiences. As reality is never experienced twice in exactly the same way, this reality is not synchronized but liquid. It does not depend on our body's forward masking. Surprise occurs when forward masking does not synchronize with the actuality of that half-second response time that it takes longer for a signal to be processed. Perhaps this is what we are now seeing in buildings by Nox, MVRDV, Daniel Libeskind and Frank Gehry. Referring back to the non-repetitive or the unexpected, this is an architecture that is the antithesis of forward masking.

Whose reality is it? I believe that architecture should support the social need for diversity and liquid identities. We must understand that non-static conditions are not purely environmental but exist within social, political and technological disciplines affecting monumentality, permanence, typologies, awareness, intention, experience and availability.

The world we inhabit and appropriate via our body's relationship to these parameters must also begin to realize the connection between the body and the mind. The intimate connections between emotional diseases affecting the psyche also influence the body's relationship with its context as a result of this communication.

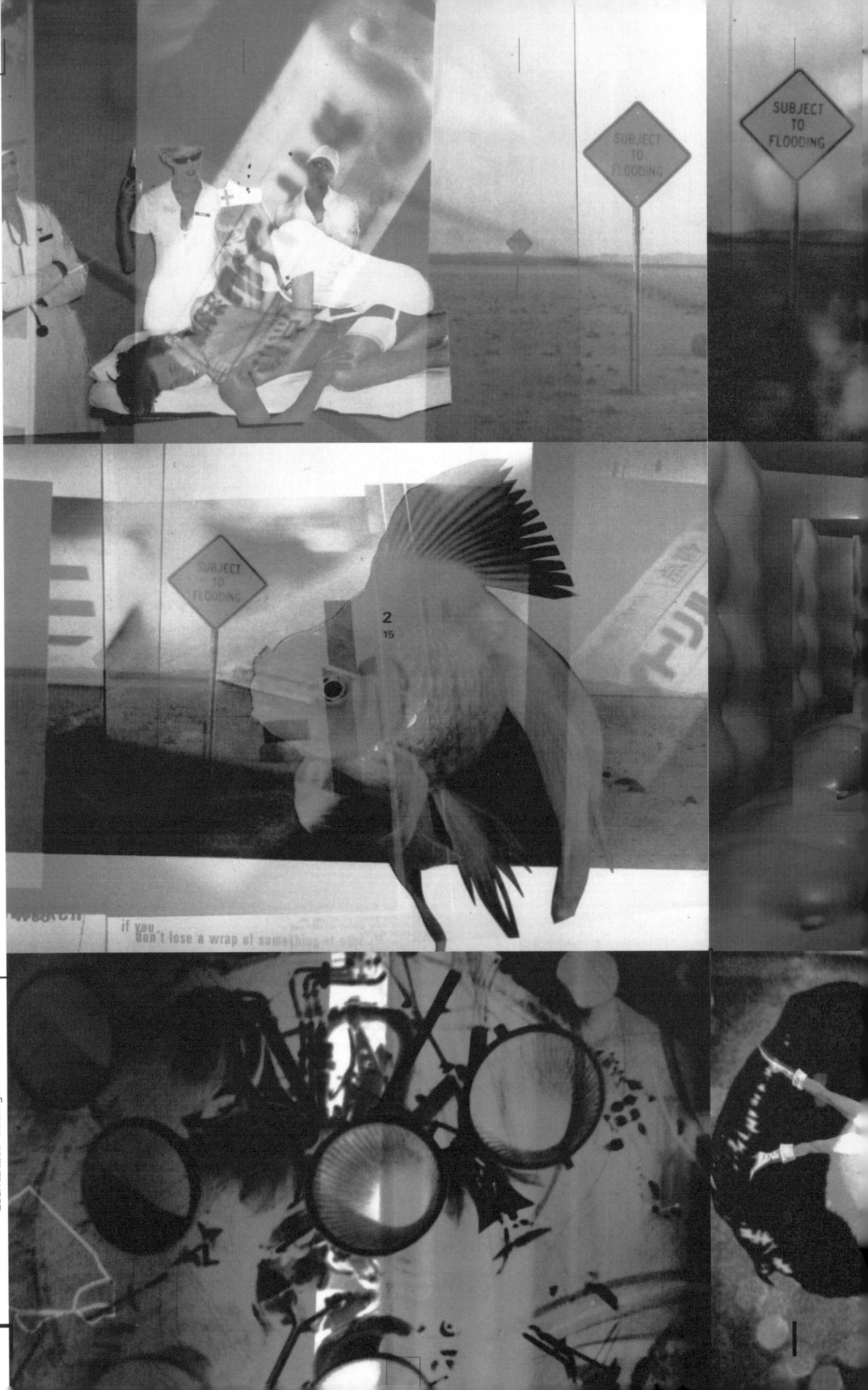

Multiple Personalities: online identities collage

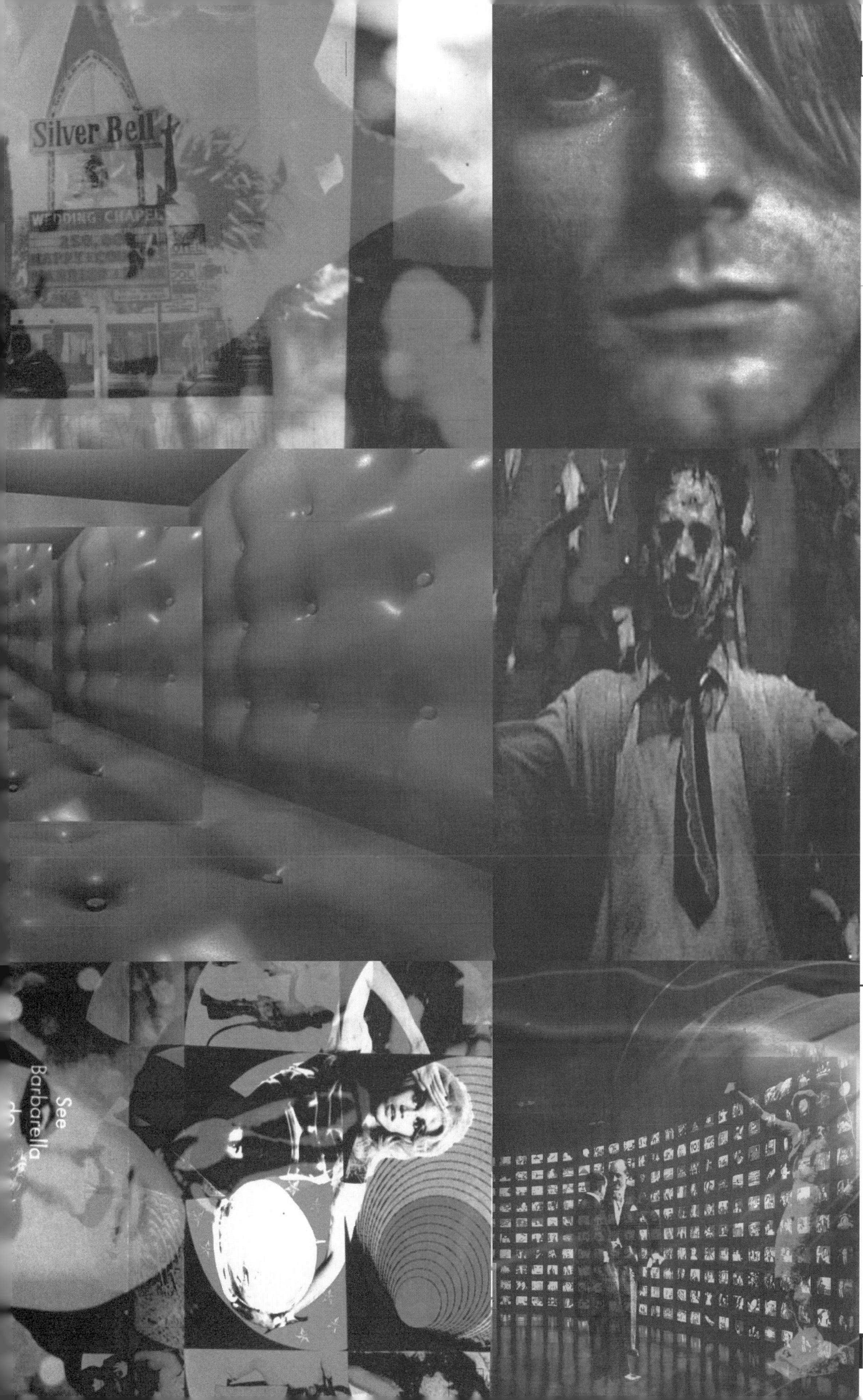
Silver Bell
See
Barbarella

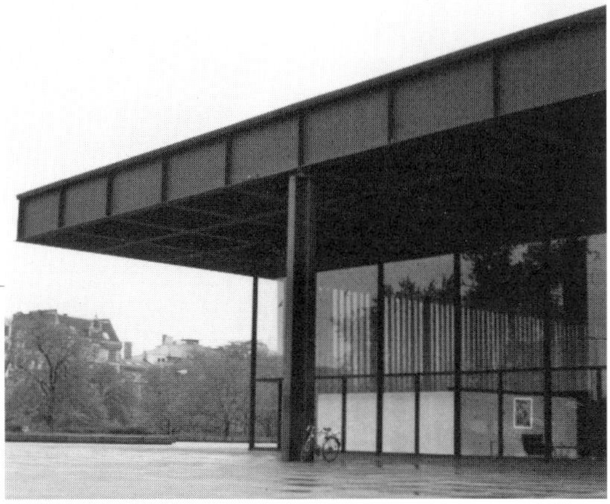

Mies van der Rohe's National Gallerie, Berlin

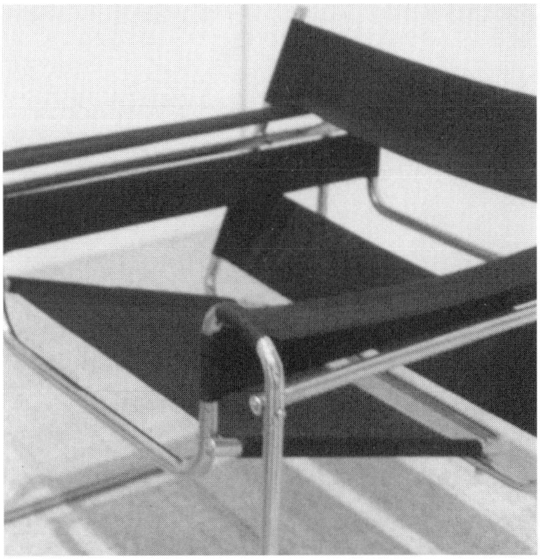

Marcel Breuer's Wassily chair

Mind and body, psychologists and neurologists now agree, aren't that different. The thoughts and emotions that seem to color our reality are the result of complex electromechanical interactions within and between nerve cells. The disembodied voices of schizophrenia, feelings of panic and depression-although they seem to be based on reality and certainly are exorcised or exercised within the physical world, alas are no more than distortions in brain's electrochemistry. Researchers are learning how these distortions evolve and develop, how to lessen their severity and, in some cases, how to correct them. Scientists are realizing that not only is the mind like the rest of the body, but that the well-being of one is intimately intertwined with that of the other. They share the same systems: nervous, circulatory, endocrine and immune.

If this belief of mind and body exchange is becoming more popular and supported by more disciplines, how can we as architects reflect the growing concern for society's psyche? If we suffer within our mind's eye and unleash the results of our fears and anxieties in the physical world, it also becomes a problem for the built environment.

It is important to note that not all feelings are negative; there are many positive euphoric emotions that we present to the world. The one thing that both extremes have in common is a comparison to social conditioning in that neither play by the rules. Is this why they are deemed unworthy?

If we believe that the built environment should reflect not only technology's influence on society but also, in turn, society's response to that continually

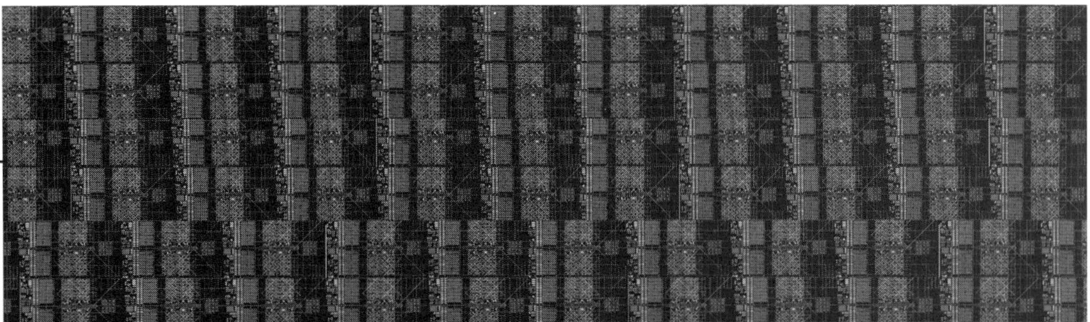

Le Corbusier's Ville Radieuse

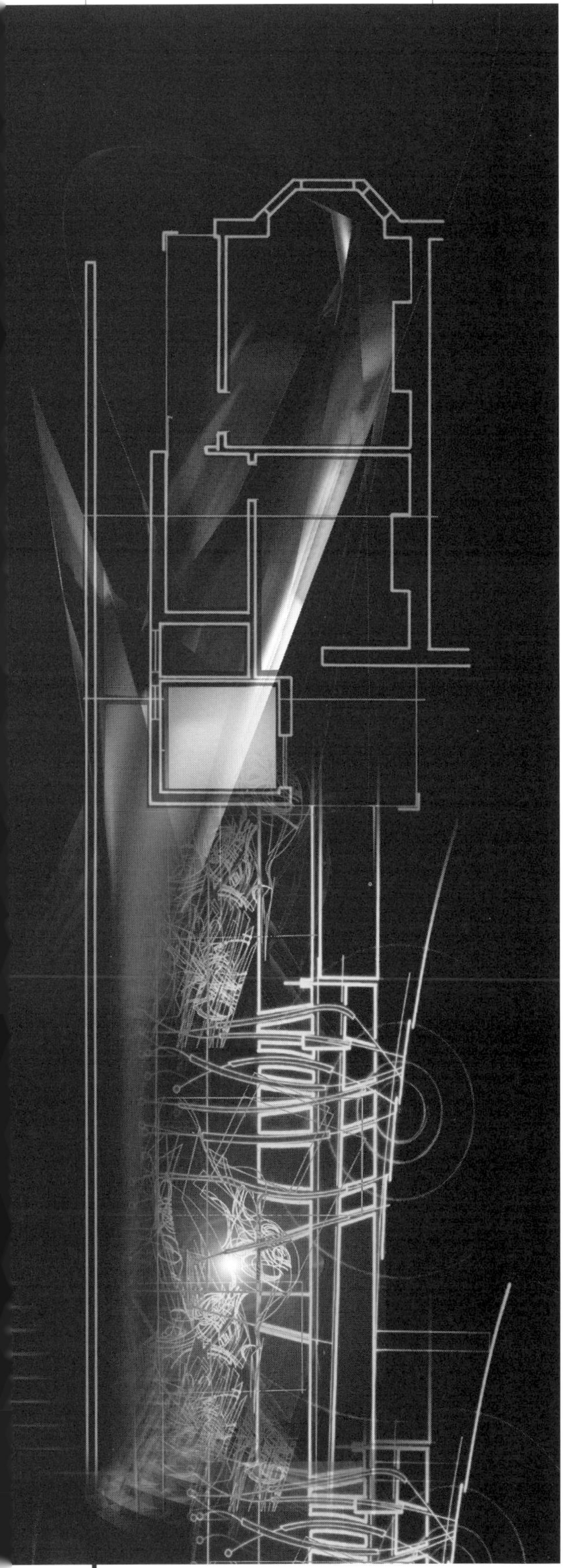

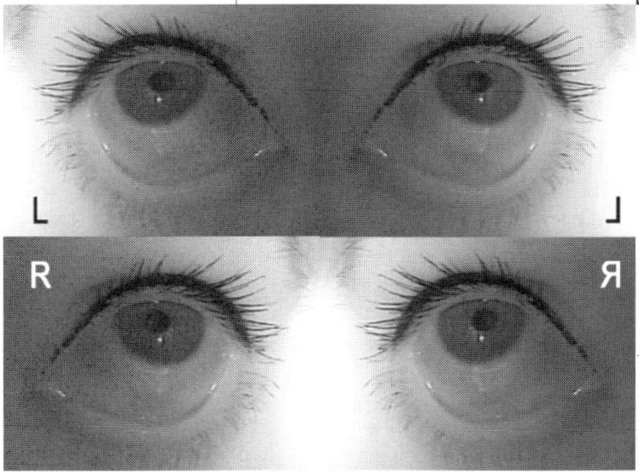

changing Ritualscape[4] how, then, do we deal with the increase in the numbers of mental diseases? Even when the antithesis of these is presented to us with the multiple ways in which we can dislocate and leave behind our ritualistic reality, we condone and support the de-realization of events. However, when our identities blur these edges of virtual and actual, we are pigeonholed as having a mental disorder.

Surely there is a gray area somewhere that does not group the many symptoms of the age we live in with disorders whose influences are not a result of direct exposure to technology and the options presented to us.

"Man's desires are limited by his perceptions. None can derive what he has not perceived."[5]

ENDNOTES

1. Sigmund Freud, A Note Upon The Mystic Writing Pad, Vienna, 1925.
2. Jacques Derrida, Writing and Difference, 1967.
3. Nicholas Zurbrugg, Transit Lounge: An essay on Forward Masking, edited by Ashley Crawford and Ray Edgar, Thompson Press: India, 1997.
4. Ritualscape: A term given to a repeated formulaic gesture and its effects within the physical environment, the appropriation and transition of this social conditioning.
5. William Blake, Songs Of Innocence and Experience, Oxford 1789.

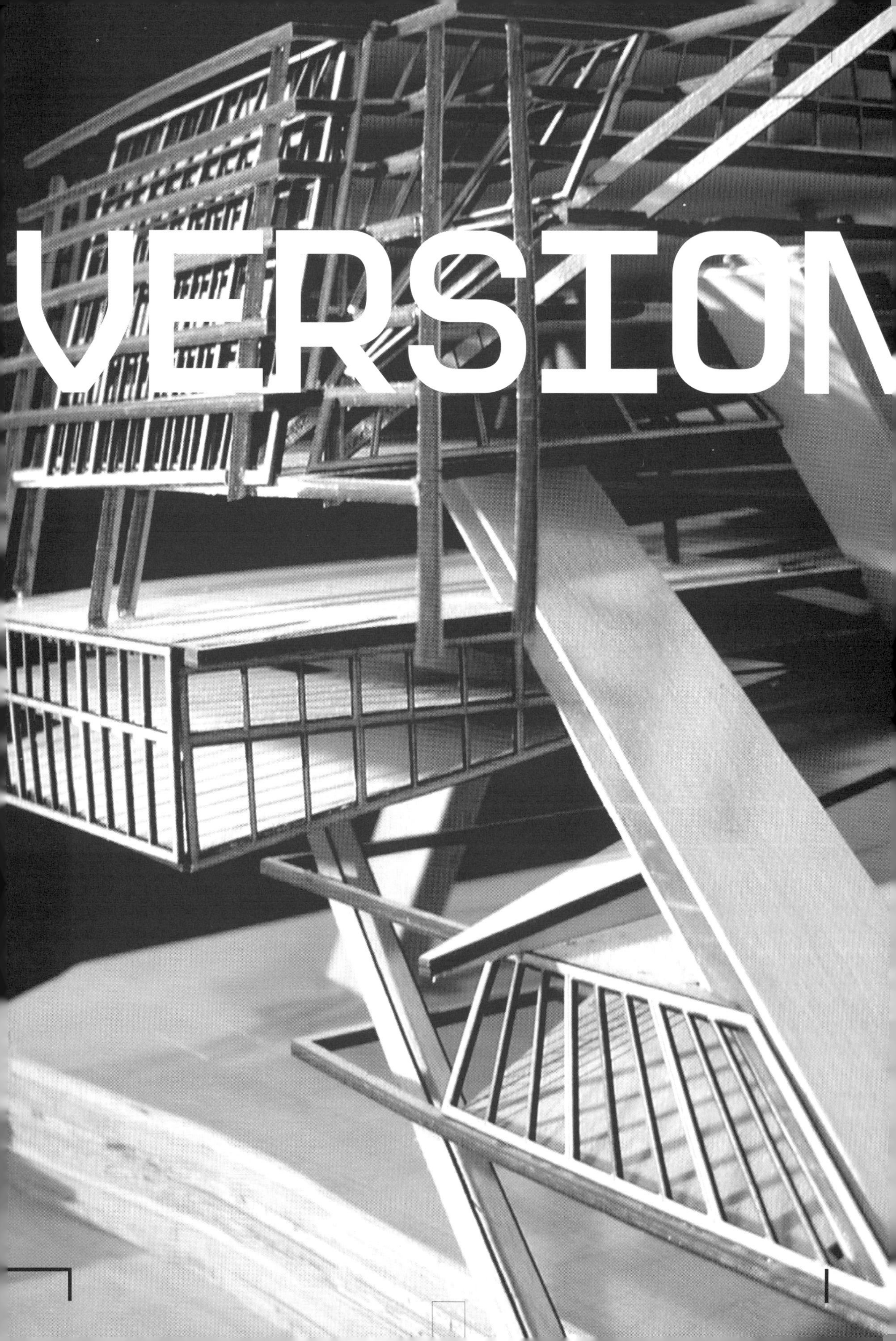
VERSION

A Los Angeles district school's proposal that the developers can't refuse

ING L.A.

by André Soluri and Dieter David Schoellnberger

Over the next ten years, the city of Los Angeles needs to build several hundred new public schools, but does not have the resources to pay for them. As a result, the body that controls the school system (the Los Angeles Unified School District, or L.A.U.S.D) is looking for alternative methods of developing and paying for the new schools. One possible alternative method would be to integrate the schools into commercial or residential development. Under the direction of Gregg Pasquarelli and Richard Garber, we developed a project that proposes a large scale, mixed-use development that integrates a given high school into a series of nine clustered mixed-use structures that include residential, commercial and office uses.

The project's viability is dependant upon the flexibility of these clusters, which are designed to re-allocate floor area for different programs as their specific rental values fluctuate based on the movements of real estate and financial markets. An analysis and mapping of this fluctuation generates a striking architecture that is complex and dynamic. By using this dynamic programming strategy, the building is able to consistently generate a profit, even during drastic market fluctuations, making the project more viable for a potential developer. At the same time, the additional revenue generated by this strategy adds 22% to the overall construction budget, allowing for greater design freedom in the built architectural expression.

André Soluri received a MArch in Advanced Architectural Design from the Columbia University Graduate School of Architecture, Planning and Preservation. He holds a Bachelor of Architecture from the Cooper Union and has been a regular juror at Pratt Institute. He has been the principal of Soluri Design Group and has recently formed a new firm with Gregory Okshteyn. The firm is currently working on four major projects including a 7,000 sq foot loft in Chelsea, a 40,000 sq foot dance club in Chelsea, a go-kart amusement park in Boston, and a penthouse in TriBeCa.

Dieter David Schoellnberger holds a MArch from Columbia University.

Financial Development Consultant:
George Petrides

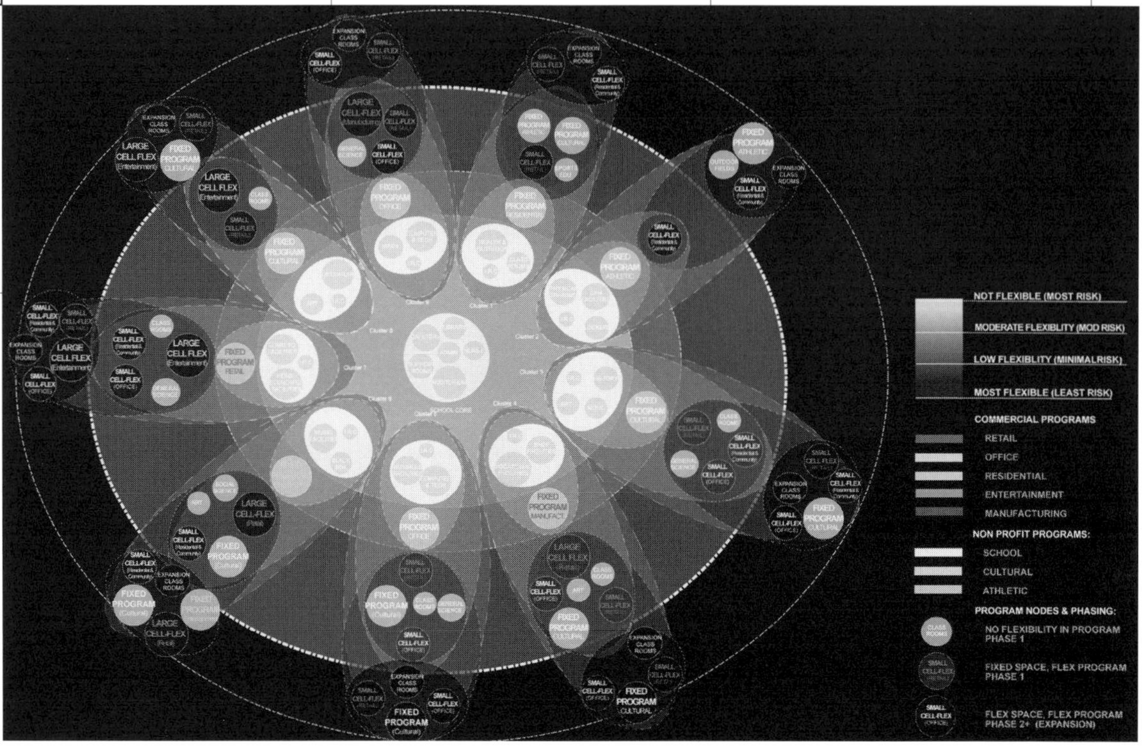

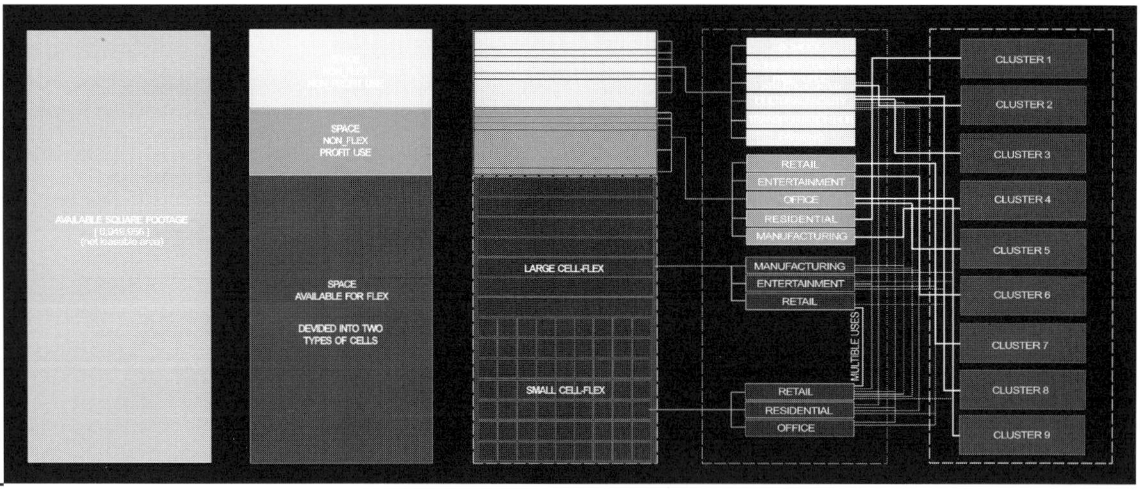

The project focused on generating an architecture that could pay for the high school and various cultural / community programs as well as providing a convincing argument to the city and to developers that the project was not only viable, but profitable. The work of a Financial Development Consultant, George Petrides, was thus incorporated into the team to help us analyze the project from the financial development perspective. Finally, the project sought to prove that the profitability of development could be a positive and generative aspect of the architecture.

An initial zoning analysis of the site and an examination of the Los Angeles Zoning Code revealed a series of Floor Area Ratio (F.A.R.) incentives for mixed-use projects located near public transportation. These incentives allowed an additional 30% of floor area, potentially increasing the profitability of the project. A mixed-use development not only allowed a greater F.A.R., but could also have a more positive impact on the community by integrating cultural, recreational, retail and office programs into the project. We also realized that a mixed-use development created additional opportunities for architectural and programmatic hybrids.

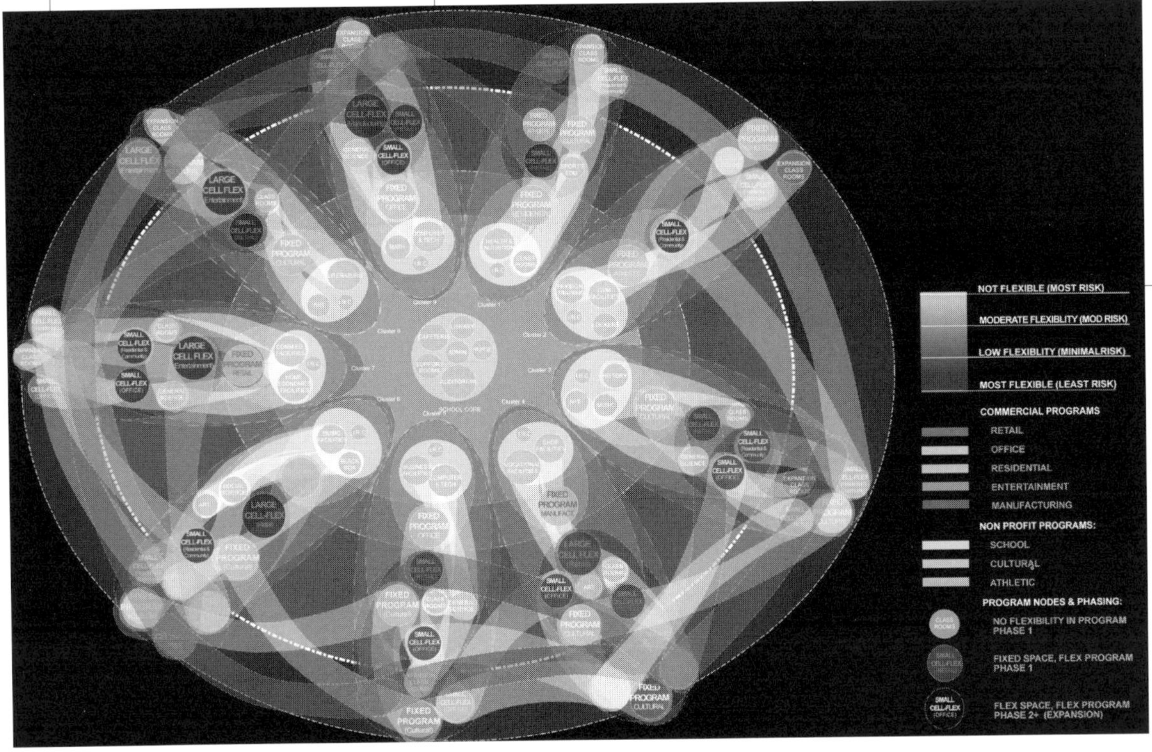

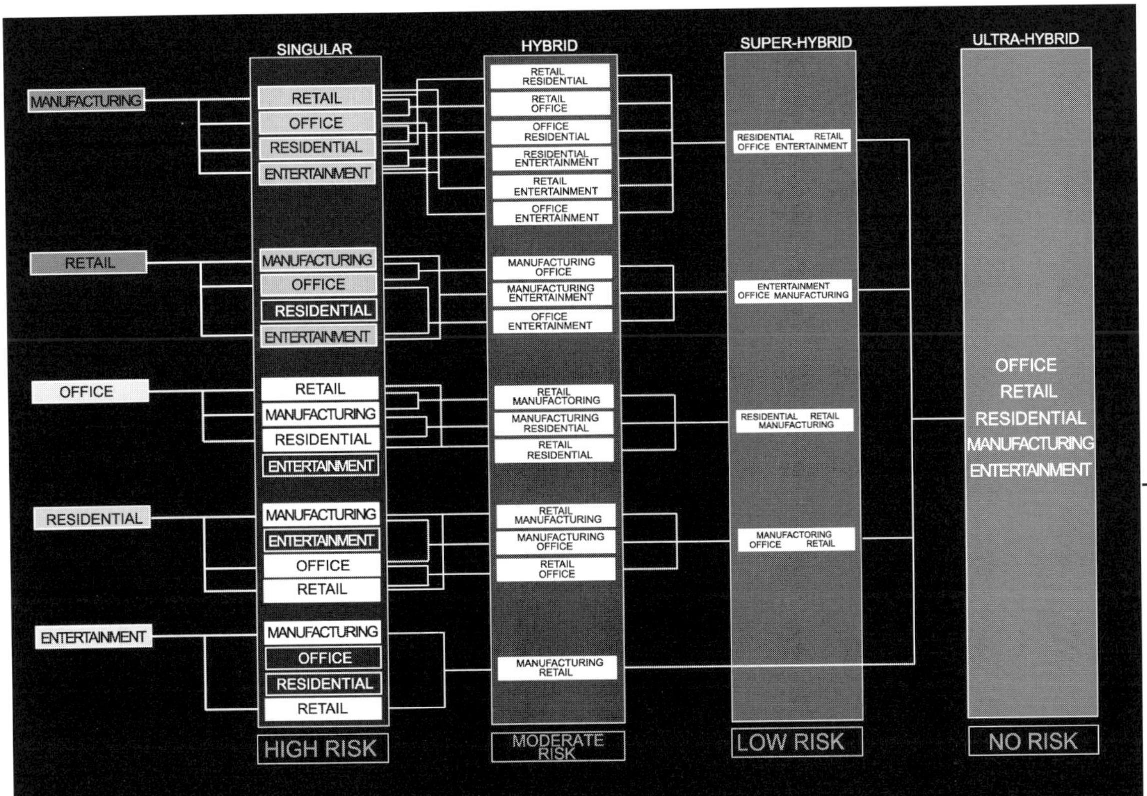

RISK MATRIX BY PROGRAM: MORE HYBRID PROGRAMS = LESS DEVELOPMENT RISK

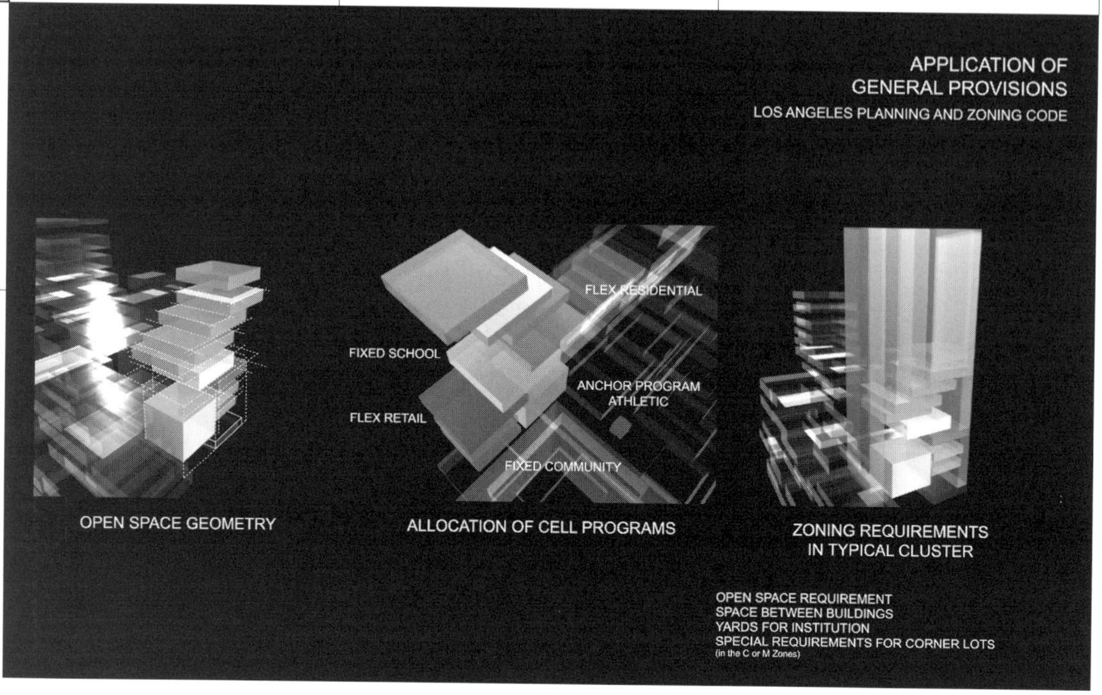

A dozen programs were then selected in the mixed-use scenario, some of which would function mainly to generate a profit, and others, including the high school, which would benefit the community in other ways. The proportion of area allocated to a specific program was based on a financial spreadsheet that automatically reallocated floor area to the most profitable programs while maintaining pre-determined quantities for the community and cultural programs. These programs and their associated floor areas were ***versioned*** (see the accompanying interview with Gregg Pasquarelli for an explanation of this term) throughout the project to arrive at optimal mixes.

Based on research into existing educational models, the high school was divided into nine clusters, each associated with a proportional segment of the school based on a multi-disciplinary, project-oriented pedagogy. A clustered program diagram examined how the programs could co-exist in this clustered format. Via a continuous diagramming process, an analysis was created that charted the relationship between the risk inherent in real estate development and the building's program. The diagram entitled *Risk Matrix by Program* illustrates that a diversification in programs due to a hybrid condition less financially risky than a development with a singular program.

In order to test how this clustered system would respond to the financial requirements of the project, we used a process of *Financial Versioning* to determine how the building would respond to fluctuations of market-rate rent per square foot of a given program. Through extensive research and analysis, five market cases were chosen as benchmarks to test the viability of the project. [Case A represents actual projected rents for 2007 and is considered the base case; Case B represents a 15% drop per year for three years in retail rents from Case A; Case C represents a 15% drop per year for three years in commercial entertainment rents from Case A; Case D represents a 15% drop per year for three years in office rents from Case A; and Case E represents a 15% drop per year for three years in residential rents from Case A].

By testing the project through these five cases, we determined that if a building was able to re-allocate its programmatic matrix as the markets fluctuated, the project would pose less risk to potential investors and developers, thus making it more viable in the long-term.

We developed a series of spreadsheets, diagrams and dynamic architectural models that showed what would happen if a building could conceptually re-allocate programmatic areas in conjunction with major fluctuations in rents. To simplify the architectural and financial analysis of this dynamic system, two basic area units were devised. The large cell of 300,000 sq foot could accommodate either big-box retail or entertainment uses, and the small cell of 30,000 sq foot could accommodate residential, small-scale retail or office uses.

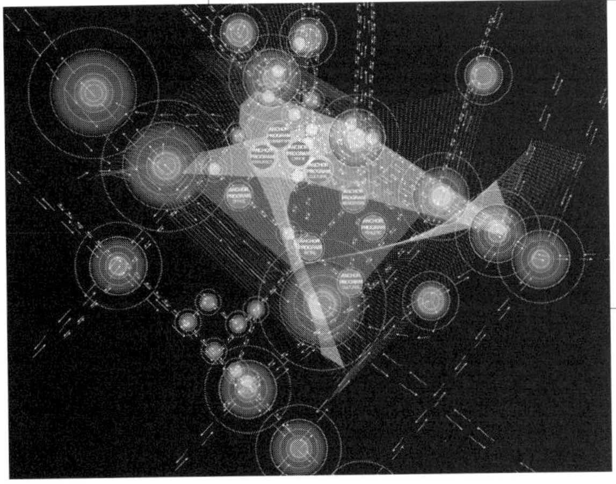

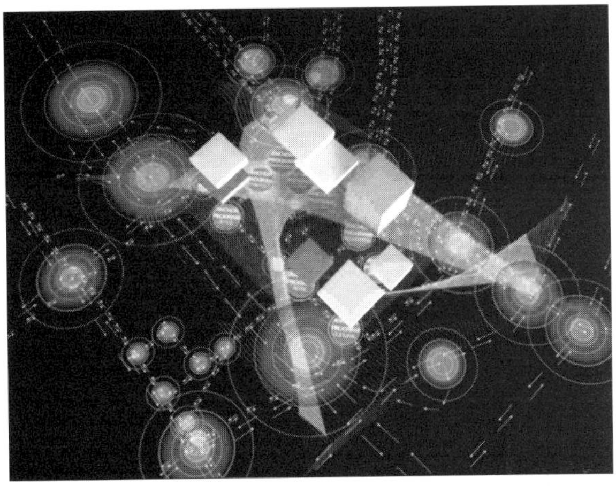

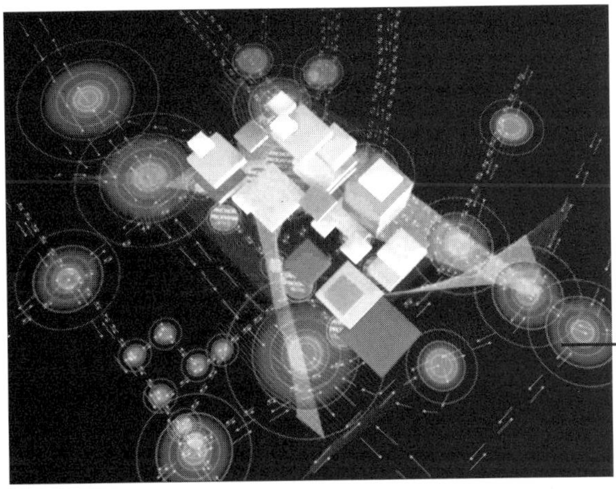

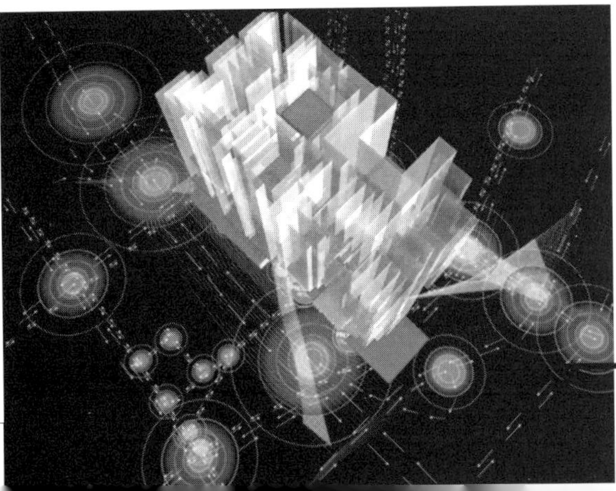

With the application of the open space requirements in the zoning code and an extensive site analysis, a massing study we generated that indicated how each cluster was arranged through a series of anchor programs, community programs, commercial programs, and school programs. (This initial massing study represented Case A.) We discovered that as a self-organizing system, certain programs would be attracted to each other. To test this overall scenario, a new massing study was generated for each of the market cases, producing a dynamic animation of Financial Versioning as the project reallocated areas to different programs based on market fluctuations.

The form of the building was generated by simply tracing the movements of the programmatic cells as they were reallocated and displaced by the Financial Versioning process. This formal massing study, which greatly exceeded the maximum area allowed by zoning, was then trimmed to reveal only the overlapping conditions [Entire building: {Image 18 (montage), 18A (trace) & 18B (trimmed outcome)} and in Cluster 3: {Image 19 (montage), 19A (trace) & 19B (trimmed outcome)]. The original Clustered Program Diagram was then modified reflect these overlapping conditions and co-citations.

To resolve the paradox of flexible floor area within a static, preexisting building, a ***Circulation Codification*** was derived to provide an internal zoning matrix govern how the floor plates within the building could be divided and re-allocated. Internal geometries generated by the intersection of overlapping forms provided the divisions between these areas. Degrees of compatibility between programs were derived and then projected onto designated circulation routes. The width of these circulation routes varied according to their compatibility, providing a scalable buffer between programs as they changed over time. To further articulate the flexible programmatic nature of the building, the façade was designed as a curtain wall with a unitized glass system on the exterior and interchangeable façade inserts on the interior. These five-foot wide panels are installed from the interior and can be easily changed when different tenants move into a given area. The panels are each articulated to correspond to the various glazing needs of the programs represented within the project.

The final financial analysis produced by George Petrides compares the proposed flexible mixed-use development (flex) against a single-use building (fixed). The analysis revealed that although a flex-building may initially cost more to construct, it could nevertheless be considered a ***superior investment*** (for details, please see the adjoining article). One of the most important discoveries

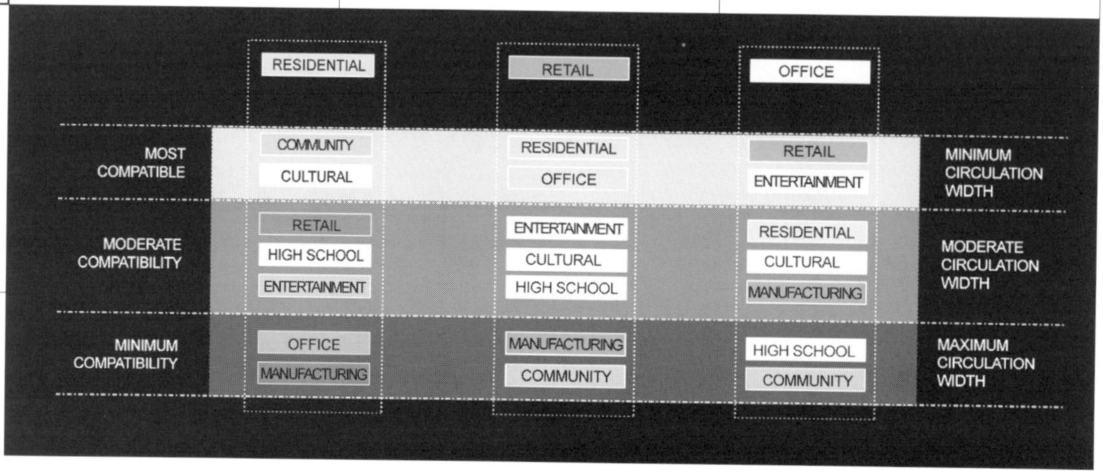

PLAN AT LEVEL 148'-0" ABOVE GRADE

FLOOR PLATE AT INITIAL BUILD 14,680 SQ FEET

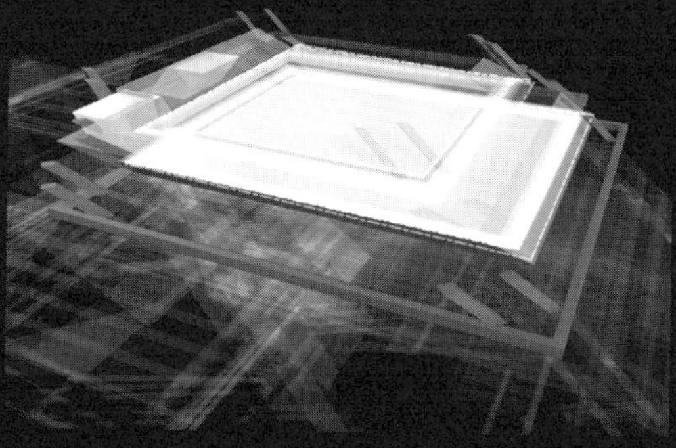

RENDERING LOOKING NORTH

CIRCULATION:

MIN. REQ MOD. REQ MAX REQ

PROGRAMS:

OFFICE RESIDENTIAL CULTURE

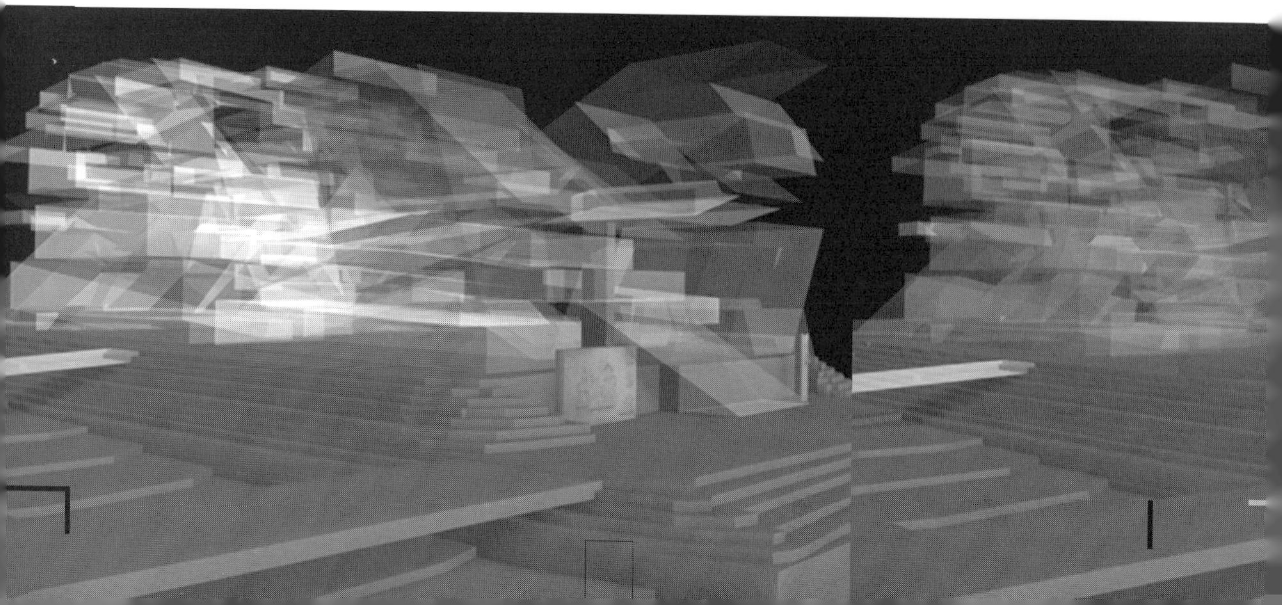

gleaned from Petrides' financial analysis was how higher architecture-related construction costs affect a project's overall profitability (Return on Equity). It was shown that if a flex-building were to cost the same as a fixed-building, it could potentially generate a 35% Return on Equity. The challenge in building this project is to devise methods of fabrication that can reduce costs on site without sacrificing the design goals of the project.

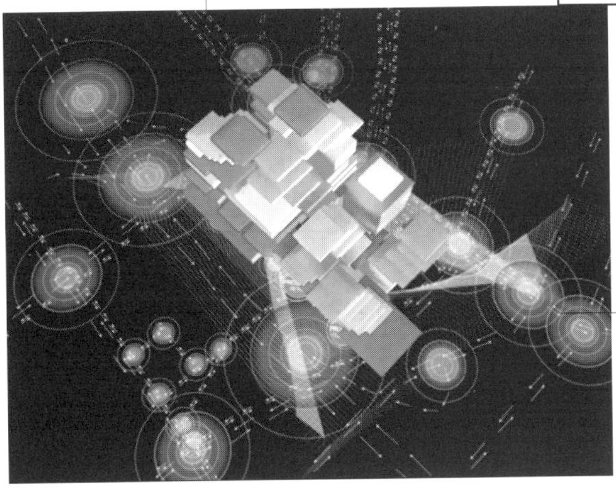

To determine the optimal methods of fabrication, the project was again *Versioned* to produce a final physical model. The simple, flat surfaces generated in the design process were initially assumed to be easily fabricated; however, the multiple intersections of these forms, all at varying angles, proved to be more difficult to fabricate than initially believed. Three fabrication techniques, each using a two-dimensional laser-cutter, were tested before a method was found to be accurate and fast enough for rapid prototyping. The final method utilized a series of structural ribs, support, and slabs that were modeled three-dimensionally in Maya with all the required notches and holes for assembly. These pieces were then imported into AutoCAD, labeled and aligned onto a two-dimensional surface for laser-cut fabrication from sheets of aircraft plywood. This technique allowed all the pieces of the final model to be cut from 12 pieces of 3/16" aircraft plywood. The fabrication of the final model proved that it was possible to extract and construct the complex forms generated within the computer. Ideally, these techniques could be deployed on a larger scale of fabrication, and, as technology continues to advance, it may be possible to construct a flex building as proposed in this project.

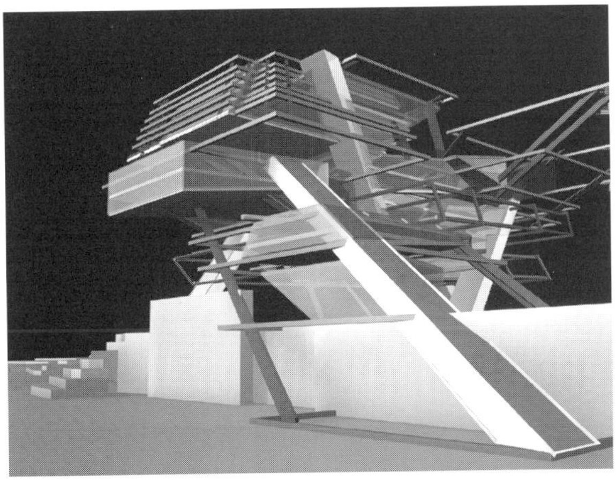

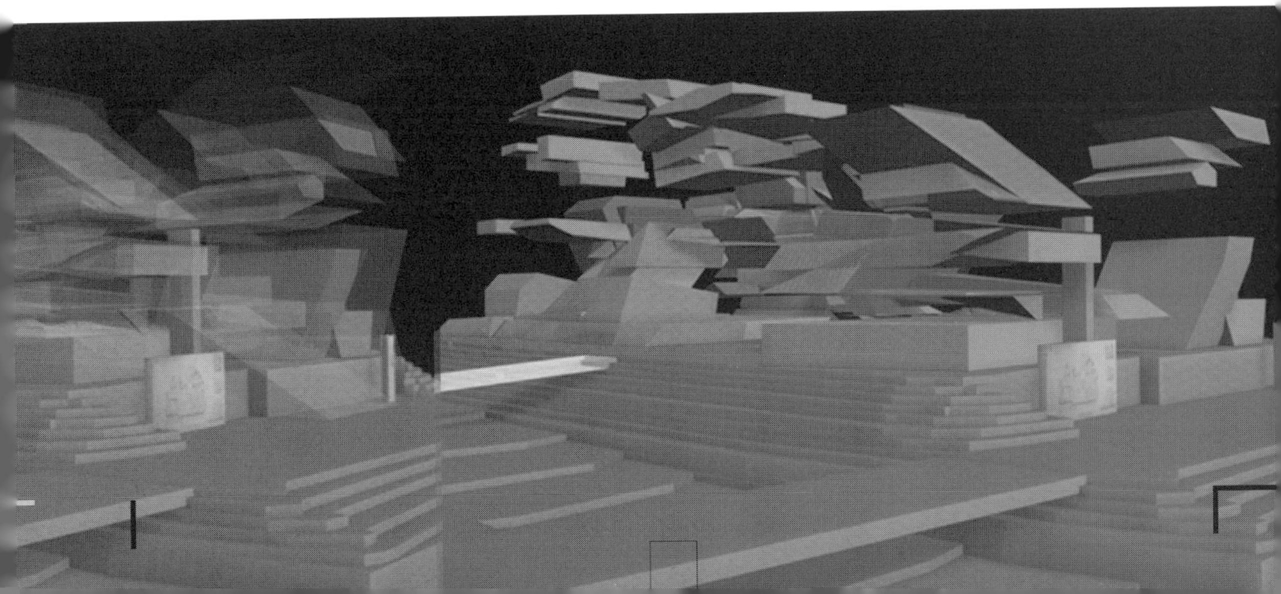

FABRICATION TECHNIQUE 1

UNFOLDED AS A 2D SURFACE

STRUCTURE WITHIN SURFACE

EASY TO BUILD SINGLE ELEMENTS

LIMITED ARTICULATION

SLOPPY CONNECTIONS

NO MATERIAL THICKNESS

CORNERS NOT PRECISE

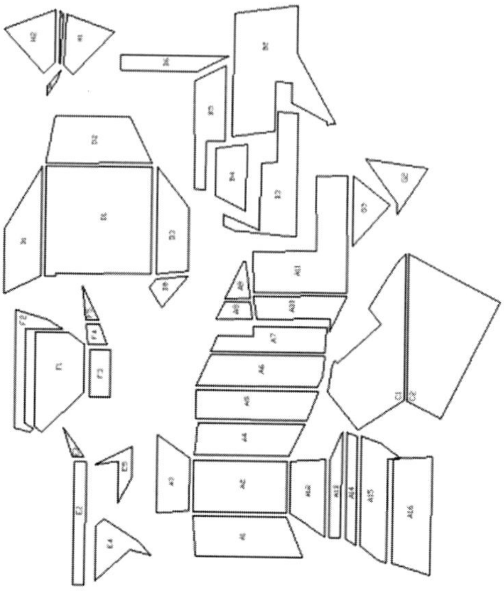

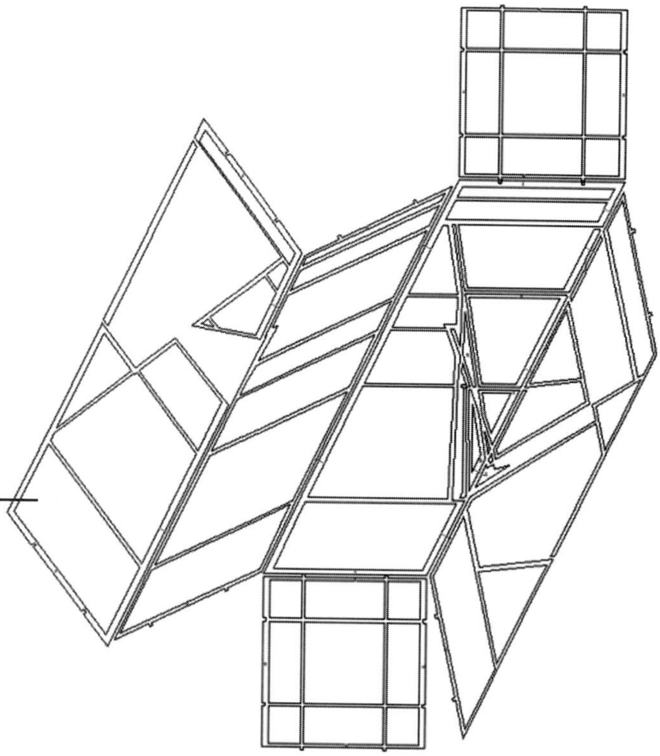

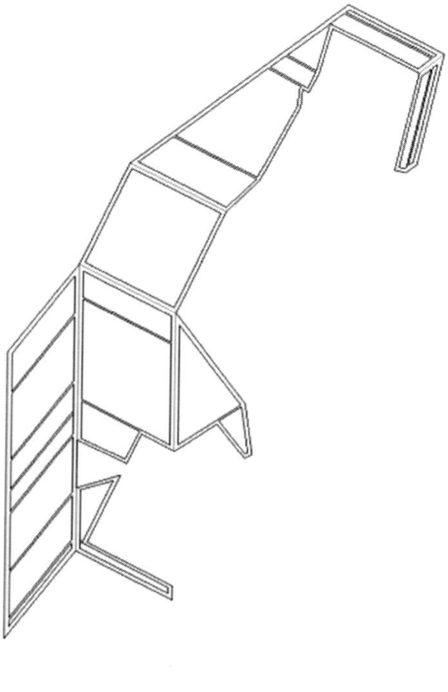

FABRICATION TECHNIQUE 2

SECTIONS CUT THROUGH 3D MODEL
ALLOWS FOR CONNECTION DETAIL
CONNECTS MULTIPLE ELEMENTS

TIME CONSUMING
2D METHOD
NO IRREGULAR CONNECTIONS
DIFFICULT TO VERSION

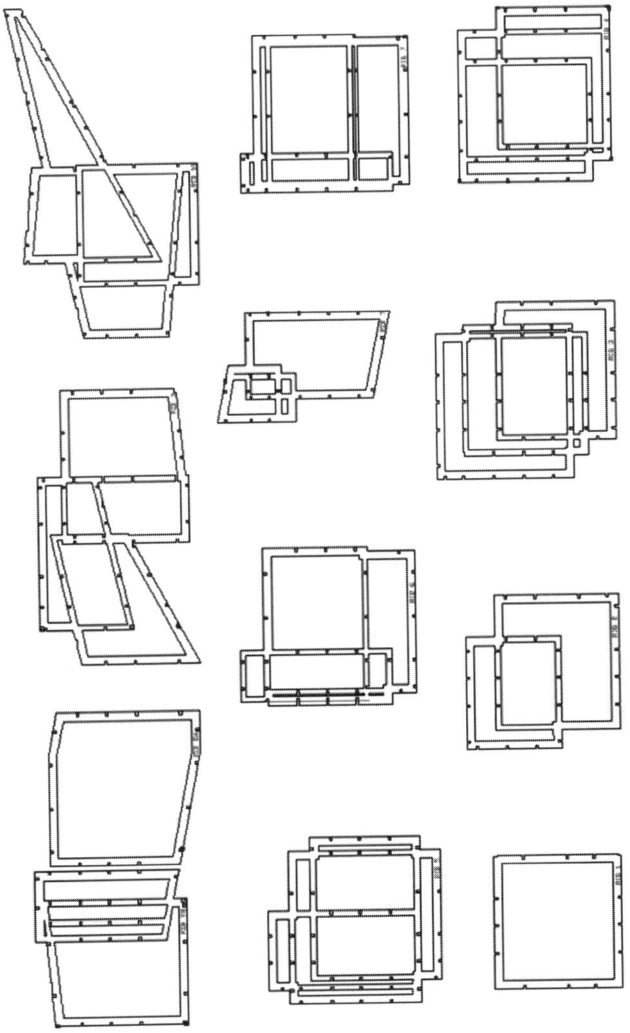

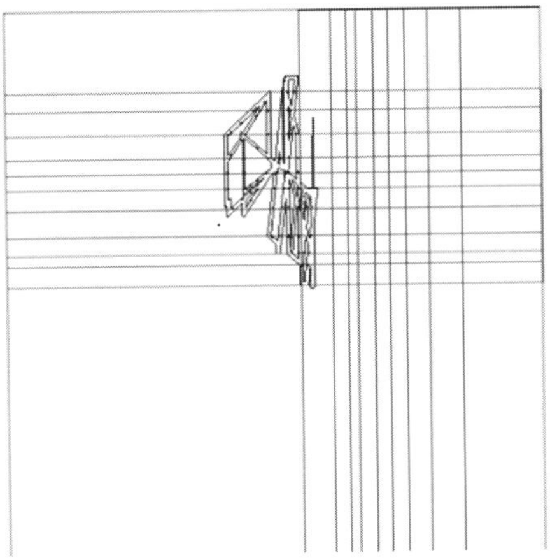

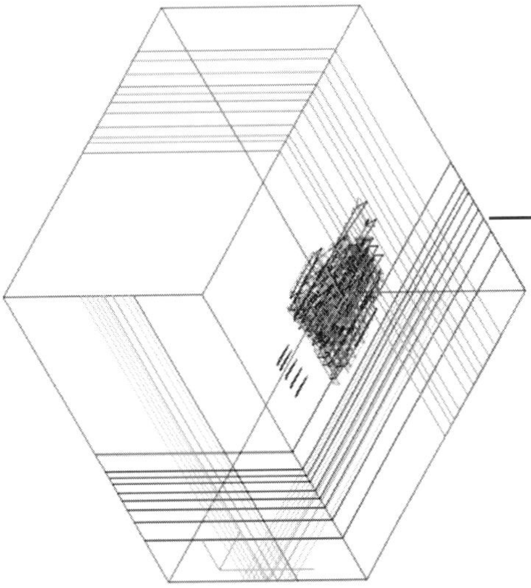

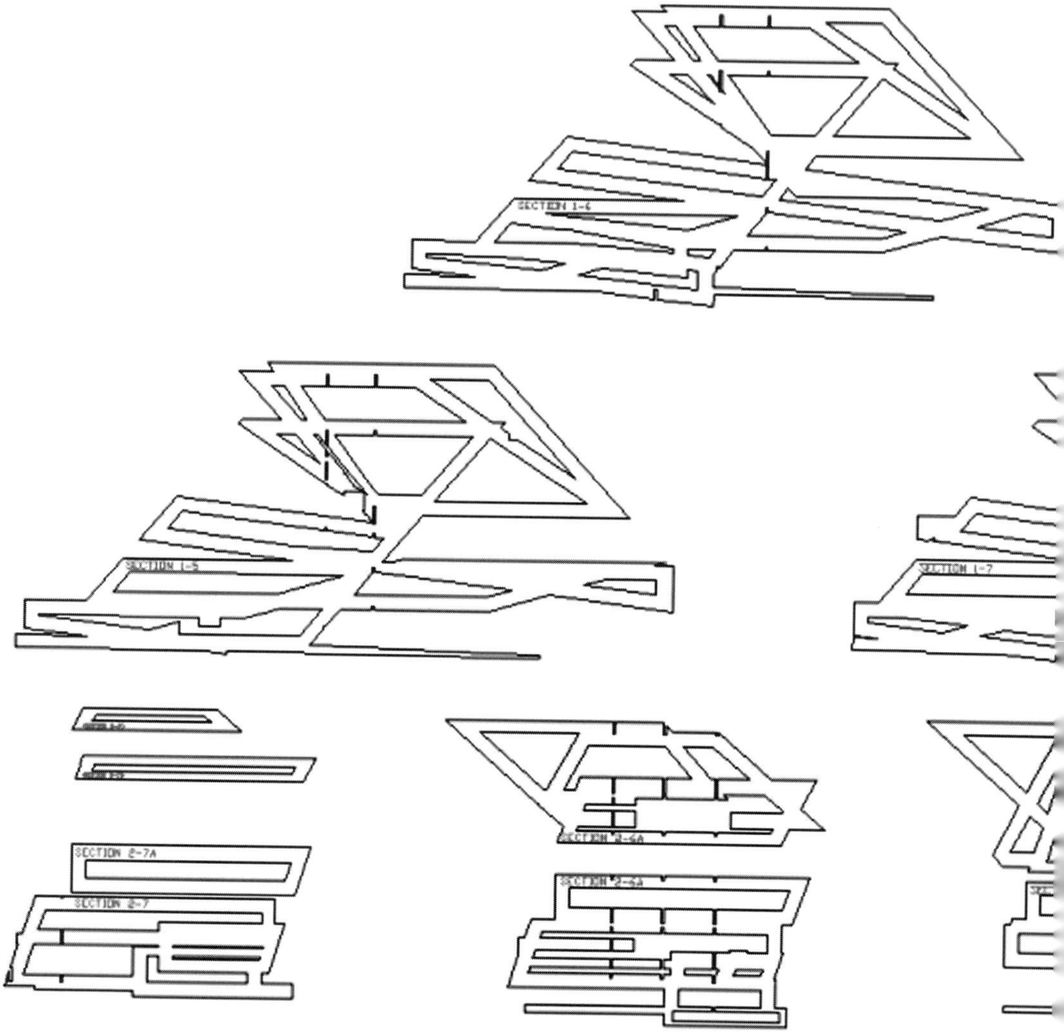
SECTION 1-6
SECTION 1-5
SECTION 1-7
SECTION 2-7A
SECTION 2-7

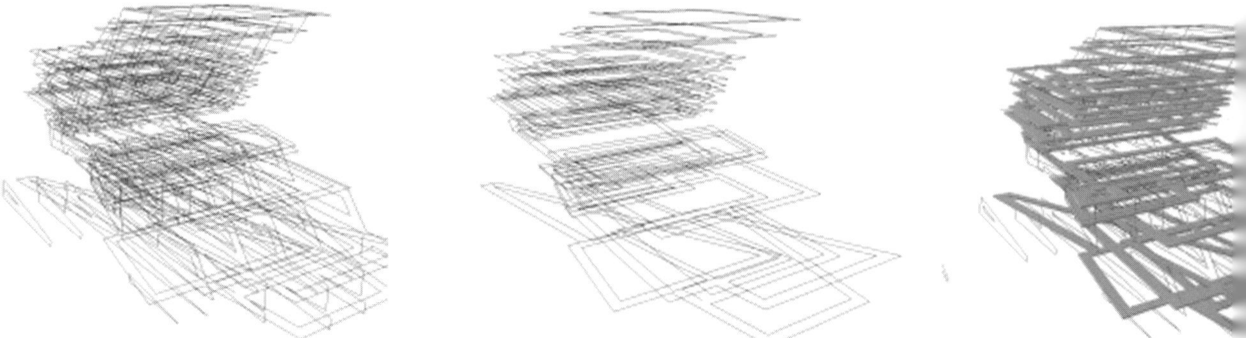

FABRICATION TECHNIQUE 3

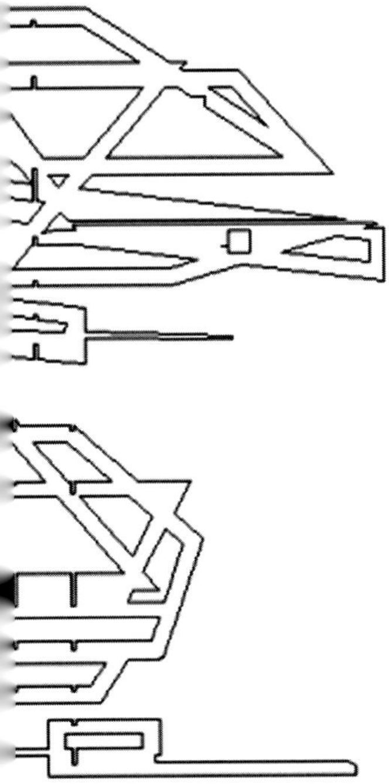

FRAMES CONSTRUCTED IN 3D MODEL

BOOLEAN OPERATION FOR JOINTS

ACCOMMODATES IRREGULAR JOINTS

CONNECTS MULTIPLE ELEMENTS

EASIER TO VERSION

COMPLEX 3D COMPUTER MODEL

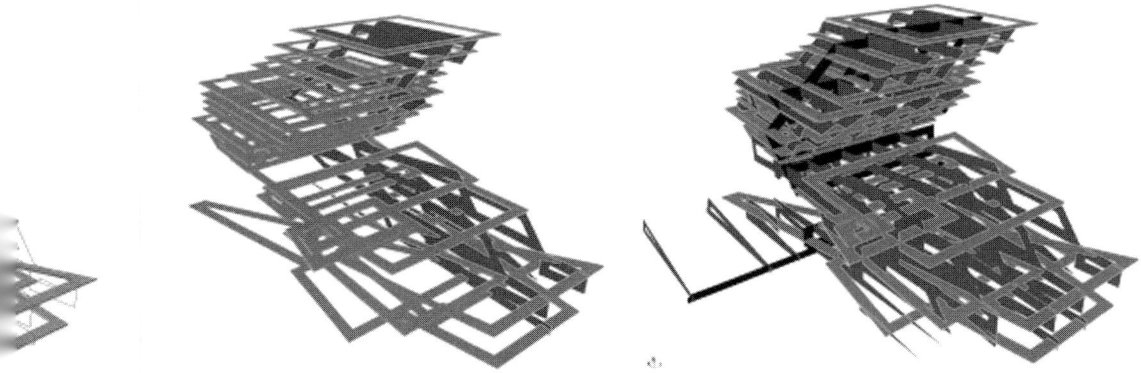

L ST T ME WE G
T IS A RY

cr ics: Gr Pasqua
Ric
Unive GSA
Advanced Studio VI
Spring 2003

.abstract

"And if all else fails, put on side two of Led Zeppelin IV"

Versioning is an operative term meant to describe a recent, significant shift in the way architects are using technology to expand, in time as well as in territory, the potential effects of design on our world. Versioning can be seen as an attitude rather than an ideology. It allows architects to think or practice across multiple disciplines, freely borrowing tactics from film, food, finance, fashion, economics and politics for use in design, or, reversing the model and using architectural theory to participate in other problem solving fields. Digital technology has enabled architects to rethink the design process in terms of procedure and outcome in ways that common practice, the construction industry, and conventional design methodologies cannot conceive of. This, in turn, has had an equally profound impact on legal practices, insurance liabilities, and design/production partnerships, thereby initiating a restructuring of the traditional relations of power, responsibility, and accountability in design. Versioning implies design's shift away from a system of horizontal integration (designers as simply the generators of representational form) towards a system of vertical integration (designers driving how space is conceived and constructed and what its effects are culturally). Versioning is important to architects because it attempts to remove architecture from a stylistically driven cycle of consumption.

This studio will continue our recent exploration of new processes of extraction that develop other languages to transpose forces into the making of space. The project will begin with an intensive series of design charrettes that will focus on understanding the external influences that shape a design strategy. The legislative, programmatic, and economic forces will be modeled as abstract rule based systems whose positions and influence on the resultant architectural insertion can be radicalized through a re-writing of those rules. Each student can change their field of play by repositioning and re-scripting the engines driving the design. By understanding the array of relationships between multiple programs located within the same site, the resulting architecture will move away from image based systems of representation and towards a vertical integration of making and effect.

.program

"Dude, don't worry, my old man's a television repair man, he has an awesome set of tools."

The project will be to design the first in a series of Central Los Angeles Area New High Schools. Students will choose between two available sites in the downtown Los Angeles area for the complex. The first site is in a relatively dense portion of downtown LA, located on Grand and Cesar Chavez Avenues, separated from Rafael Moneo's new cathedral by the Santa Ana Freeway. The second is East Hollywood, bounded by Sunset Boulevard and Van Ness Avenue. Both sites have a very different character. The city hopes to subsidize the development of the school(s) by building an unspecified amount of mixed-use space within the school complex, thereby requiring the design of a large-scale, programmatically blended complex whose aim is create a new kind of economic infrastructure for a rapidly changing clientele. The project will look for methods of integrating the necessary spaces for residential, commercial, community facility, and manufacturing programs *with* the high school typology and *within* a series of heterogeneous structural systems while redefining the zoning envelope. This mandates a strategy for multiple symbiotic relationships to create a layered, vertical, urban machine for mixture. These relationships and resultant hierarchies will lead to a final architectural proposal. While there are no precedents for this program, it is expected to lead to a visionary new urban typology of economic and structural possibility.

A CONVERSATION WITH GREGG SQUARELLI

Emily Abruzzo
Can you tell me a little bit about the studio brief?

Greg Pasquarelli
Well it was the last time I knew I was going to be at Columbia and it was the last time I was going to teach with Rich, which we had done for five or six semesters in a row. The concept of *Versioning* was clipped on three years ago; so this is really a three-year program. We probably did a variation of it about six times to perfect how it worked. "Last Time we Give This a Try" was what that was about.

The meat of the text is pretty important. It actually is very much about the way we work in the office; the program comes directly from the way we think here. It's set up in a way so as to give the students a performative model of how to think about design but also to get them to understand very quickly the influence their design moves on the computer have on the notion of building. *Versioning* came from a critique of the blob and the (slightly) older generation's notion of what using the computer as a design tool is about--let's call it the baby-boomer generation. As a second-generation computer savvy firm, we started to see a difference in thinking. The notion of Versioning came from the question that arises when you draw something: how do you pull it out; it's all about ideas of extraction. Then you draw it once and are then forced to build it.

The first couple of versions that the students make are along the more traditional model—let's make the image and then try to figure out how to build that image. When they first start its still about the image and then they try and make it. And what this is really about-and what happens here with all these thousands of models that are in this dust bin of trying things out—is, once you actually pull the information out and you figure out a material and a way of building it, you have to redraw it. So the drawing becomes more intelligent as it leads to a construction or a materiality. Then you pull it out again and you build it and you realize, 'Wow, if I had had this information, I could have built it much faster,' or, 'If I had used this material, I would have gotten this different effect.' Then you redraw it again . . . and that's the Versioning. There's this kind of continuous back-and-forth between an idea, an effect, a design, a drawing and a method of organizing information so that it can be built.

I tell the students that they will never click the same thing again because they will never be clicking without automatically having that presumption of asking, 'What does this click mean?' When I put that first line and another line and I draw a vector, what does that vector mean? Is it the image of a vector on the screen? Or is it the edge of a material; is that where two materials join; is that where they're fused? Or is that the path of the laser cutter; is that describing the surface for a stereo-lithography model; is that describing the surface for a 3D milled object? And suddenly you get an intuitive understanding for that connection between here, the screen and the object. And that's how we really work here and that's what this program was about.

EA
It always seemed to me that the kinds of materials and methods of making are very important at SHoP. You talked about many different ways—especially computer-assisted ways-of creating models. Maybe you could talk a little bit about that and why that's important to the work.

.procedure

"Then I'm gonna call Mick and wing it on over to London to jam with the Stones"

The extraordinary amount of work to complete this project successfully requires the students to work in teams of two to develop their proposals. All students are expected to use dynamic modeling, animation, sketching, rendering, drawing, and physical model building wit[illegible] ec[illegible] assi[illegible]ll [illegible]e [illegible] zo[illegible] env[illegible]onm[illegible]tal, and/or [illegible]an mode[illegible] bas[illegible] on one [illegible] the tw[illegible]sites di[illegible]sed a[illegible]. wil[illegible] lea[illegible] to an urban [illegible]ping of [illegible]tr[illegible] perform[illegible]e. The [illegible]ond ass[illegible]ment wil[illegible] foc[illegible] the [illegible]ns[illegible]tion of prog[illegible]matic a[illegible] fi[illegible]ncial (development[illegible] data an[illegible] how spec[illegible]ic[illegible]on spe[illegible]fic[illegible] a c[illegible]tical ele[illegible]nt [illegible]al success[illegible] The thi[illegible] assignme[illegible] wi[illegible] be to [illegible]uc[illegible]ation[illegible]ip pote[illegible]als [illegible]e schoo[illegible] and add[illegible]onal pr[illegible]am[illegible]tic pr[illegible]osal[illegible] Once these [illegible]s" are comple[illegible] it will [illegible]e up to [illegible]e teams [illegible]ti[illegible]ly c[illegible]lleng[illegible] the nature [illegible] the [illegible]stems [illegible]d to ex[illegible]imental[illegible] re-posi[illegible]n their [illegible]oj[illegible]'s [illegible]entia[illegible] outcome as an [illegible]chite[illegible]al p[illegible]osal.

VERSION

The projects will require the use of organizational disruption and efficiency rather than an aestheticized or image based presence to create effect. They should engage the effects they have on urban organization and density and the reciprocal forces that influence the complex itself. The final seven weeks will be dedicated to the design of systems of construction, drawing, extraction, and fabrication that can accommodate the requirements of the first assignments. Some of these models will be constructed by hand, others will use automated rapid prototyping technologies available here at the school or through outside service bureaus. A series of large-scale final models will be executed demonstrating the transposition of potential form into an actual, buildable proposition.

.rapid prototyping

"Make up your mind, dude, is he gonna shit, or is he gonna kill us?"

The use of the school's Thermojet 3D Printer and new laser cutter is highly encouraged but not required. At least three of the models made during the semester will be executed using rapid prototyping technology such as laser cutting, stereolithography, three-dimensional printers, or milling machinery.

.trip

"First he's gonna shit, then he's gonna kill us…"

The class will take a field trip to Los Angeles to study the sites and tour the Diamond Ranch High School by Thom Mayne and C-TEK (Creative Technologies), a rapid technologies firm that has produced a variety of installations for Hollywood and has collaborated with Frank Gehry on a variety of projects.

.required viewing

The viewing of the following films will be helpful in the understanding of California high school culture:

Fast Times at Ridgemont High
Orange County
Clueless
Swingers

GP

As architects we're building prototypes. And whether its 6 inches by 6 inches by 6 inches or 6 feet or 600 feet, it's still a prototype. What we found is, the same place that you have trouble building a model is the same place the contractor has trouble building the building. That spot where those two sticks of basswood—and you have to really hold it there for a long time for it to dry—is the same place where two cranes can't get those two pieces of steel together. So we really find that by being really precise about the model building and understanding it, you can presuppose the problems that are going to occur on the construction site. I also think that as architects we don't really build, so the model is actually the closest we come to really building. So if you can determine what the issues are going to be and can learn where to focus your energy, and you bring them up to the contractor immediately, you get on a very different playing field with them. They're expecting you to say, "This is my vision-figure it out for me." But instead, you walk into the meeting and say, "This is what were after, here's the theory behind the building," and at first they kind of roll their eyes—but simultaneously you've said "Here's the machinery that will do it and here are the shop drawings already done (because we don't need shop drawings) and here's one series of drawings that we think will help you assemble this. Are there any other kinds of information that you would like? Tell us what it is and we'll produce it for you." And, "Right here-this is going to be your tough point. So we have three ways that we think you could do it." And suddenly they're in there with you and you get a completely different relationship on site.

Did you see the issue of *AD* that we did? There's this discussion about the vertical and the horizontal in integration of design processes. This is really important. The baby boomer generation over the past decades had given away—and I don't know if it's because it's such a litigious society—architecture has become so image-oriented that they've given away all of the territories that we used to figure out and they've reduced themselves to composers of elevations. The elevation is the one drawing that we don't really do in this office and the drawing that I pretty much do not allow people to do in my studio. It's the most worthless drawing that an architect has. I call that the thinner and thinner horizontal band of the design process-when its just about the image and just about the composition. The developer does all the financing and then the code consultant figures out the massing and the engineer does the core and the shell and then you end up looking in a *Sweets* catalogue and you pick the materials and you compose an image; and the interiors person does the furniture and you are just one of these people. What Versioning gets you—what's really interesting about the technology—is not the blobs and not the renderings and not the fly-throughs, but the fact that it gives you control that you can think, "What does that vector mean?" and make a direct connection to construction. And you can now mass-produce custom parts so you do not have to go to *Sweets* catalogue to build the building. This is the power-and you are also able to do so many different versions of a building so quickly that you suddenly are helping the developer again—or the client, or the city, or the town you are working in. Now its really returning us to the Renaissance—to the master builder. That's what's interesting about the technology—we are regaining back the territories that were given away over the years. So I guess the studio is to try and teach within 15 weeks what that power is; how do you control all aspects of it.

With Dieter and André's project—since I was an investment banker before I became an architect—I've always been really interested in the connection between the financial model and the physical model. The problem is, most architecture students are just not equipped to pull off a decent financial model. These guys were really smart and did exactly what you should do—they hired a consultant, basically. They teamed with a business school guy who had an interest in architecture. Here they were, architects with an interest in the financial model . . . and they got really close. They really made a breakthrough. Whatever the project looks like in the end is completely irrelevant; what they learned to do is make a vertical argument. I believe they will never build a building that looks like what they designed in my studio, but they will use that argument every day for the rest of their careers. And that's exciting to me as a teacher.

They understand now more about how to convince a client to build an avant-garde building than the most beautiful rendering ever made, because if you just show a rendering, the guy either likes it or doesn't like it. But if you can construct an argument to convince somebody—and an argument that's open and fluid . . . What's that old expression? "Give a man a fish and he eats for a day; teach a man to fish and he eats for a lifetime?" Something like that. I think that that's what's exciting about the emergent technologies and that's what exciting about a studio like this. I'm really proud of those guys.

Greg Pasquarelli received a BS from the College of Commerce and Finance at Villanova University, and a MArch from Columbia University. He was a designer, project manager and site architect at Greg Lynn FORM. He co-founded the architectural firm SHoP / Sharples Holden Pasquarelli in 1997 and has lectured, exhibited, and been published internationally. He is currently on the faculty of Yale University's School of Architecture.

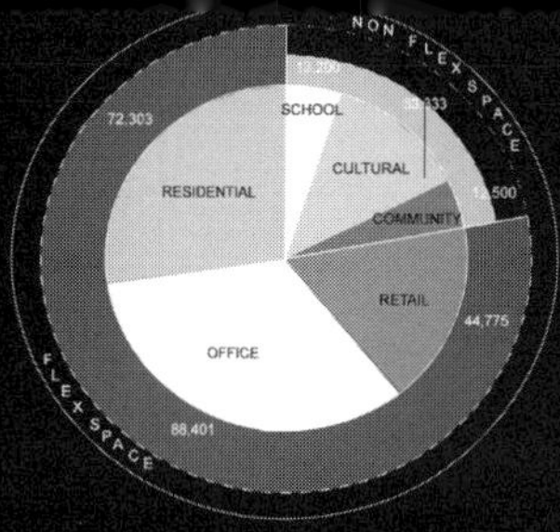

INITIAL ALLOCATION OF SPACE (IN SQ. FEET) BEFORE FLEXING

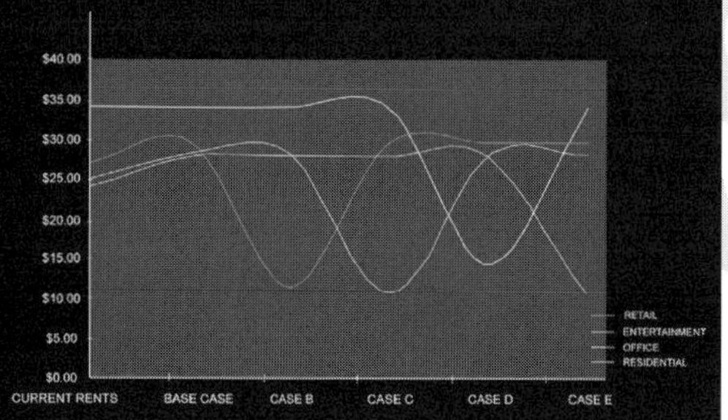

RENT BY USE UNDER DIFFERENT SCENARIOS

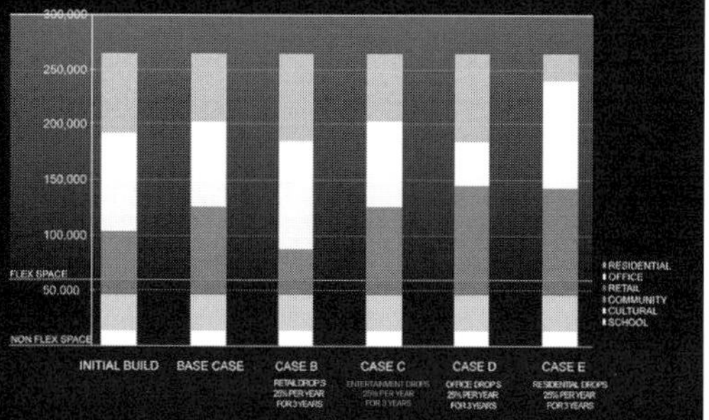

CHANGING ALLOCATION OF SPACE AS FLEX BUILDING RESPONDS TO CHANGING RENTS

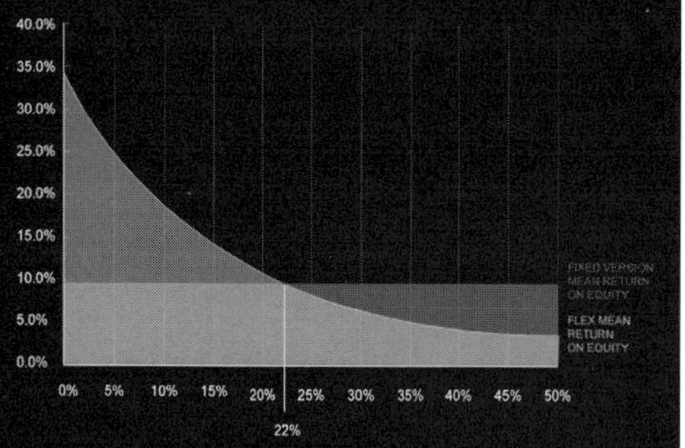

CROSSOVER RATE OF RETURN FOR FLEX AND FIXED BUILDINGS

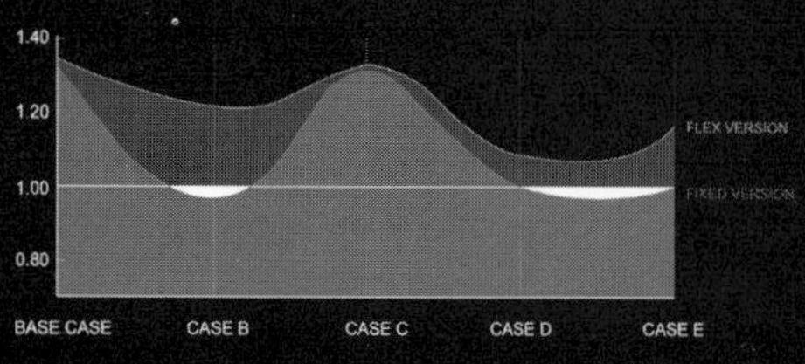

DEBT SERVICE RATIO BELOW 1:00 IS FIXED'S INABILITY TO SERVICE DEBT

André Soluri and Dieter-David Schoellnberger approached me in early 2003 with the idea of using financial analysis to support the design of a Los Angeles high school complex for a studio led by Gregg Pasquarelli and Rich Garber. I assisted them by conceptualizing a financial framework and designing a financial model that would dynamically allocate square footage among different uses in order to capture the highest rents for the building's developer as those rents changed over time. Such a building might be termed a Flexible Use Building or, in short, a Flex building. This is in contrast to a conventional fixed-use building, which can sometimes be adapted for another use (*e.g.* office or manufacturing buildings being transformed into apartments or residential lofts) but only with expensive reconstruction with each change of use.

Perhaps the best example of an existing Flex building is Moneo's L'Illa complex in Barcelona, a large commercial mixed-use complex (www.lilla.com). Viñoly's Tokyo Forum and the Berlin Free University also have Flex aspects, but they are less relevant to this exercise as they are not commercially oriented. At the corporate Seagram complex in Los Angeles, Koolhaas altered designed uses frequently in response to the client's program changes, resulting in a flex-friendly system, if only partially visible in the final designs. Piano's projected New York Times building in New York has some Flex aspects, including expensive raised floors that can accommodate frequent space alterations (individual user HVAC outlets can be easily reconfigured, as can computer and electrical systems).

Given that Flex will always cost more to design and build, the goal of this exercise is to estimate how much more in construction cost a developer can pay for a Flex building and achieve a return on investment comparable to that of a similar size fixed building, judging return both with regard to level of return and risks of achieving it.

The Flex building is most financially attractive relative to the fixed building when rents for uses change dramatically in relation to each other, for example, the softening of the Manhattan office market in 2003 while the residential market stayed relatively strong. In such a scenario a Flex building would have allocated space away from office use in favor of residential. By contrast, when rents decline for all uses more or less in proportion to each other, the whole real estate market suffers and in that case the Flex building suffers too as there is no better rent to *escape* to.

A Flex building's income is not only generally greater than the fixed building's but it is also more stable over time, as the latter will be tied exclusively to a particular use's rent cycles. As a result, the value of the Flex building relative to a fixed building of the same income level is greater because investors prefer higher certainty of outcome and are willing to pay more for a stable cash flow than for a variable one, all else being equal. A resulting benefit of the Flex building's increased value is the ability to secure a larger mortgage, which will often allow for less of the developer's equity to be invested in the project and so improves the rate of return on that investment.

However, the Flex building is not always better financially: the rate of return on investment has an inverse relationship to the premium of the construction cost of Flex over the construction cost of the

FLEX IN DETAIL

by George Petrides

fixed building. That is, as the cost to build Flex increases, the return on investment declines so that there is a *crossover* point where the two building types' rates of return are equal. Given the set of assumptions made in this financial analysis, that crossover point would be around 22%: when the Flex building's construction costs are 22% more than the fixed building's, the return on investment for the two projects is similar—but the Flex building delivers those returns with lower risk (defined as variability in return). Furthermore, with the same assumptions, a Flex building could cost 50% more than the fixed building to construct and deliver returns that, although lower than for the fixed building, might be acceptable to a developer as they would be substantially less variable and therefore be less likely to cause bankruptcy in the usual boom-and-bust real estate cycle. By staying afloat during the lean times, the developer might survive long enough to enjoy the rents of the next boom.

There are a number of conditions under which the Flex building will have better financial performance than a fixed use building:

- When the Flex construction cost increment over fixed is small
- When there are substantial fluctuations in rents of different uses or there are frequent desired changes in use for other reasons
- When the switching cost between uses is low
- When zoning allows for more uses and combination of uses on a lot
- When tenants' uses are compatible, or incompatible uses can be kept apart
- When lease lengths can be synchronized so that large areas of the building can have their use changed without confronting issues of incompatibility with tenants whose lease is still running
- When interest rates are lower, so that future benefits of higher Flex income have a larger present value to offset higher Flex current construction costs; in contrast, when interest rates are higher, it may be more sensible financially to build and use a fixed building for a period of time and then demolish it and build one dedicated to a different use when that use's rents justify the cost of doing so

Generally, some of these positive conditions will exist and they will be balanced out by the negative effect of others which are not present—so that the net effect may or may not indicate that a Flex building is a better financial proposition.

Current trends favor the creation of more Flex buildings: construction technologies increasingly allow them to be constructed and at the same time there is increased need for them as societal trends feature larger scale and more rapid changes, movements of people and new ideas.

George Petrides is a developer focusing exclusively on multifamily residential projects. Petrides received an MA in Economic Development and a MBA from Stanford University and has also attended Harvard College. He serves on the board of the MIPC research center at NYU School of Medicine.

PLAYING WITH

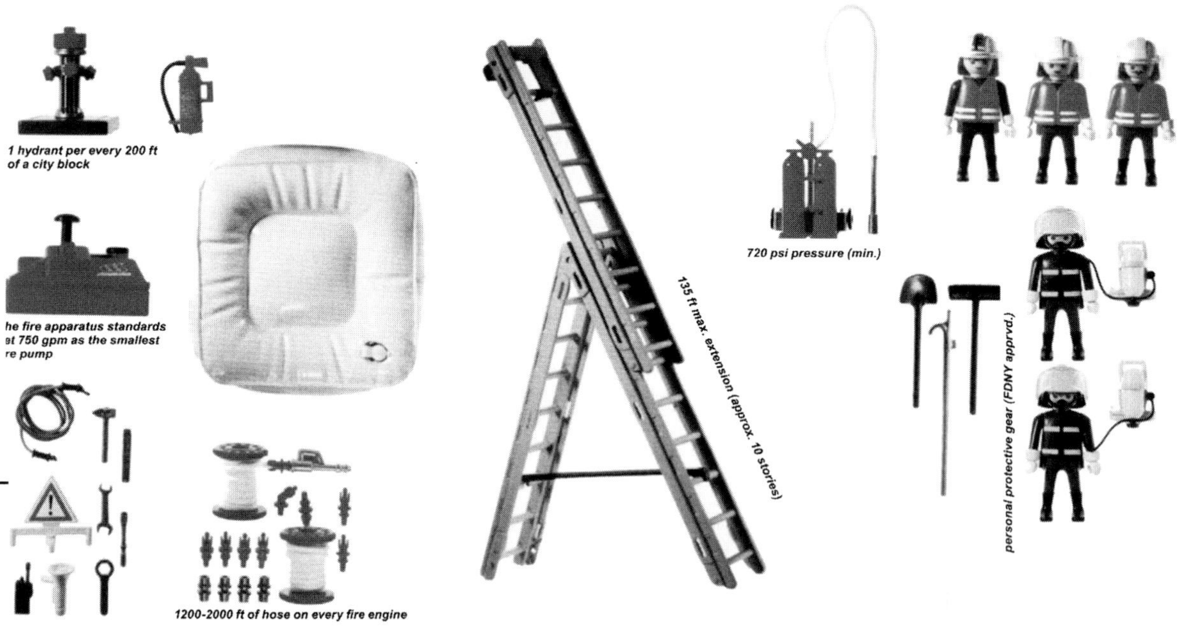

(Suitable for children)

FIRE

by Aleksandr Mergold

...a dream

One way to enter this project is from the standpoint of a child. Remember? You too wanted to be a firefighter. Recall the big rubber boots, shiny couplings, the red truck and gleaming brass sliding pole in a fire station? Oh, the fire station! That mysterious, often antique looking, unlikely hybrid of a doll house and high-tech command center: firemen's home, your play site and toy storage . . . but that dream never materialized. It wasn't meant to be—just one of the many ideas you had as a kid. The old toys are rusting away in a closet. And instead you became something else—an architect . . .

Aleksandr Mergold was born in the former USSR. He holds a BArch with honors from Cornell University—where he received the NY AIA and Charles Goodwin Sands medals—and a MArch from the School of Architecture at Princeton University. He has worked for Perkins Eastman Architects and Swanke Hayden Connell Architects. Alex is currently a senior architect at Pentagram and a partner in MeRa Design, a multi-media collaboration.

www.meradesign.com

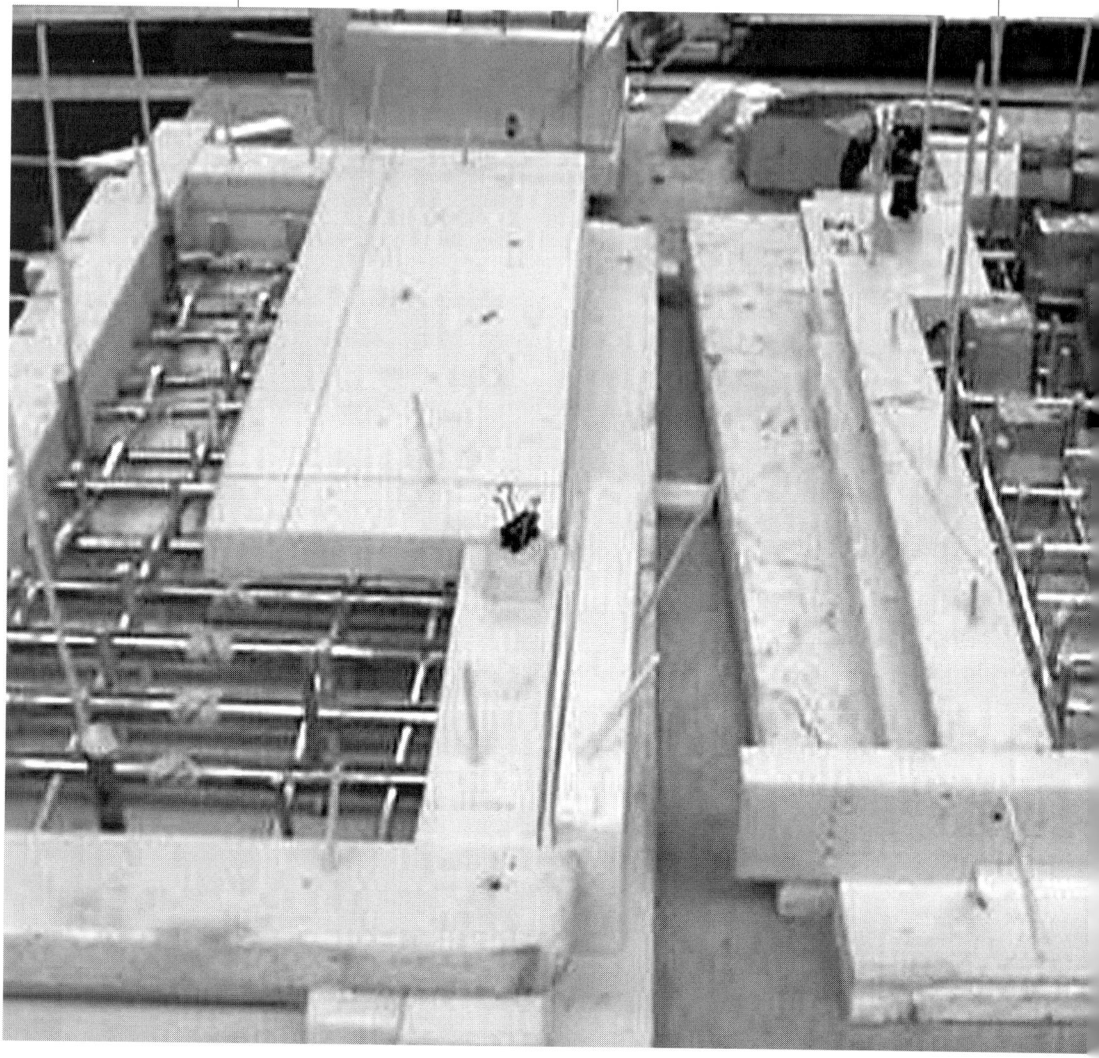

...reality

This is the second path for following the project: that of an architect, who investigates an urban problem—a proposal for a fire academy campus. It is only five miles away from the city which will become the very object of protection for today's students of that academy. How are they trained? Fires have been devastating cities for centuries, spreading rapidly house to house, destroying property and oftentimes human lives in a matter of minutes. Therefore firemen have to be well prepared to effectively counteract the blaze, be able to contain it and quickly prevent its further spread. This requires training; but to practice in a real city with open flames is reckless and dangerous. Thus, historically it has been in the nature of firemen's professional education to simulate real conditions and represent actual settings elsewhere, establish conventions, make believe, assume and imagine—play! Here the architect remembers that he, too, played firefighter. And the project becomes a toy—a reality in itself—with aspirations to suggest real architecture—an urban proposal. After all, toys are reflections of life, but simpler, and oftentimes, more fun.

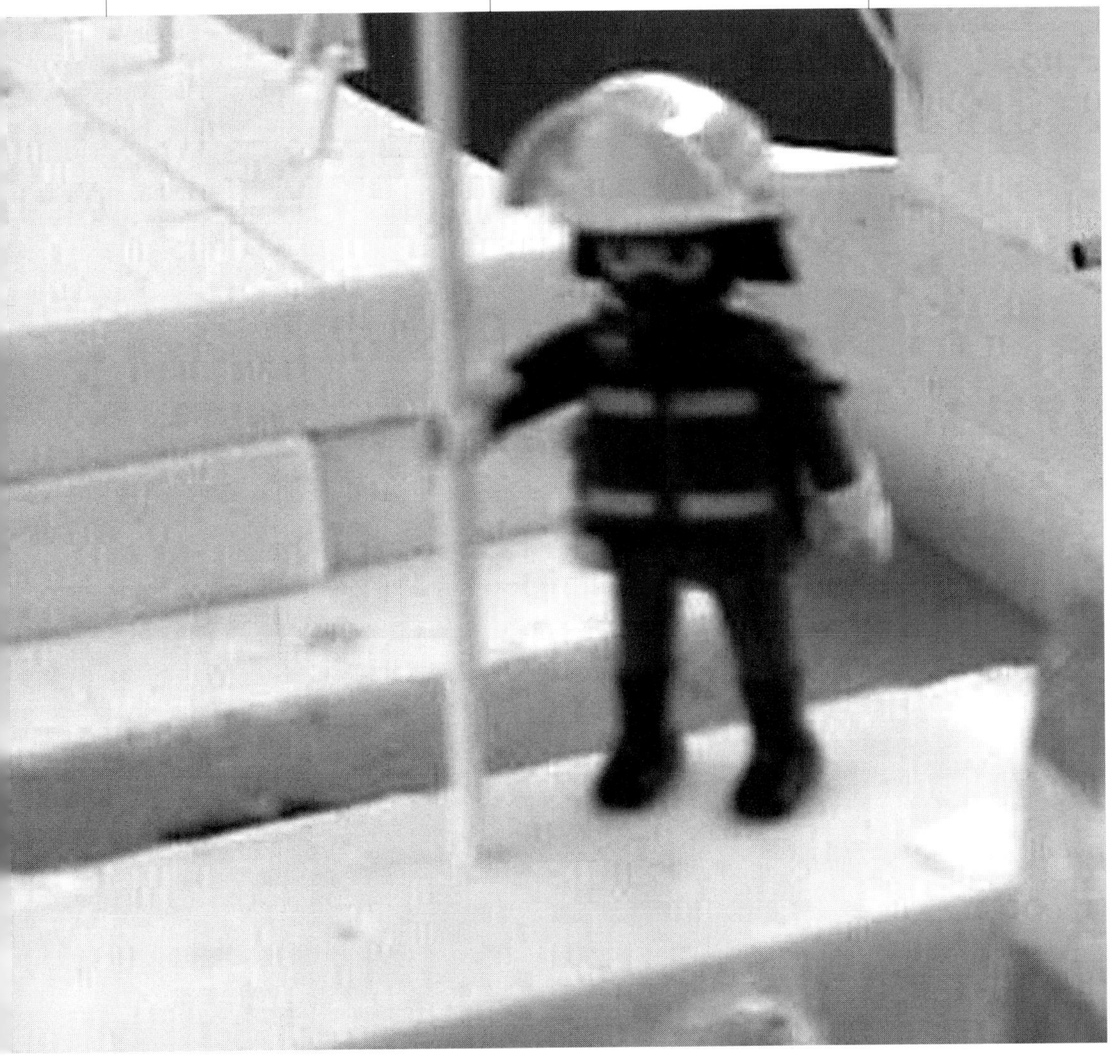

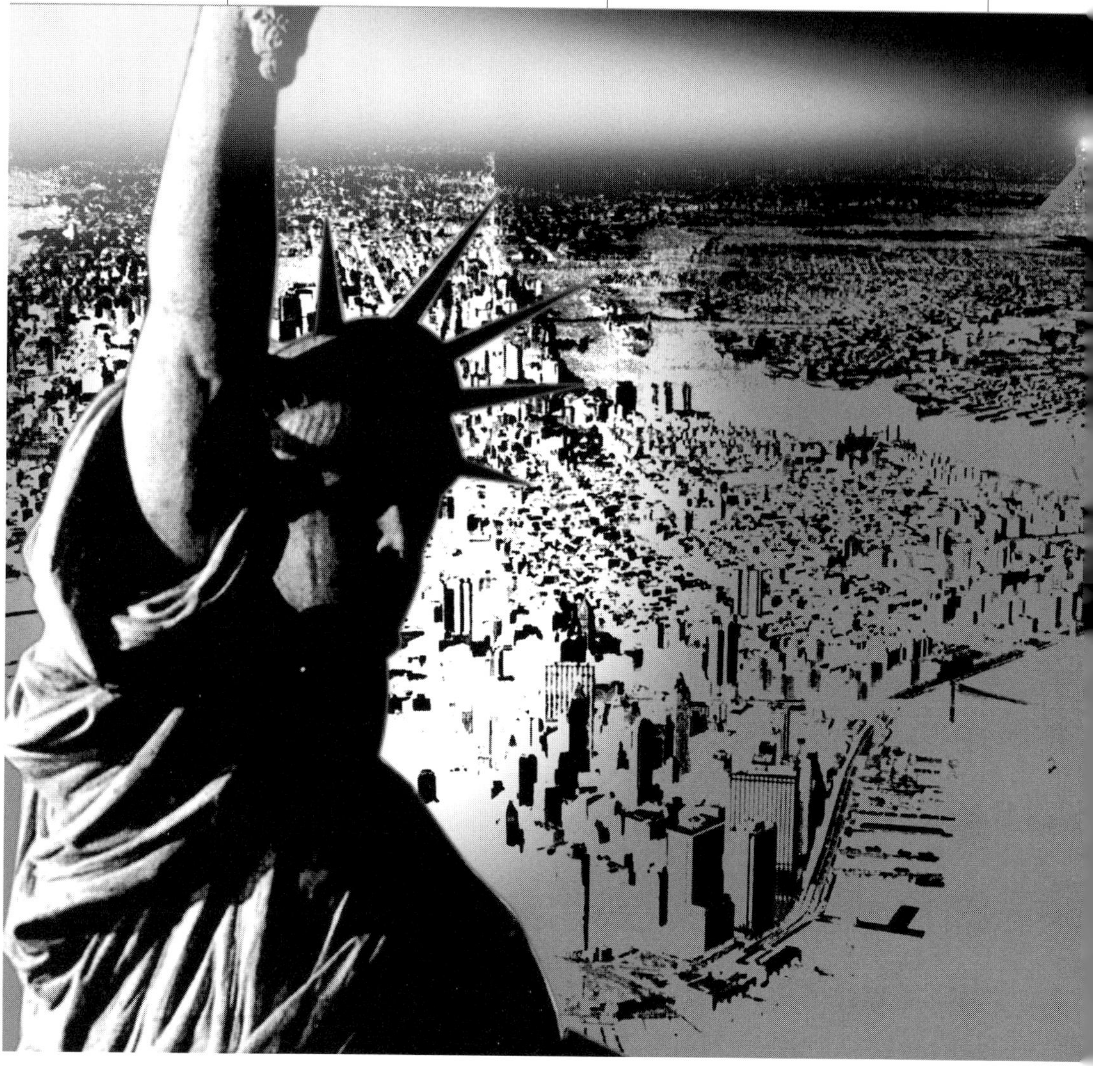

...the unexpected

This proposal for the new FDNY Training Academy was completed in May of 2000. Yet September of next year called for an amendment to the very purpose and idea of the project. The memory of those firefighters who stood up to the challenge on that fateful day must be kept alive. The architecture that serves as training ground for aspiring firefighters should also become the memorial to their heroic predecessors, giving a greater significance to the whole educational process. To the people of New York, the Fort Totten Fire Academy shall become, like the Statue of Liberty in the south, the great monument at the northern sea gate of the city.

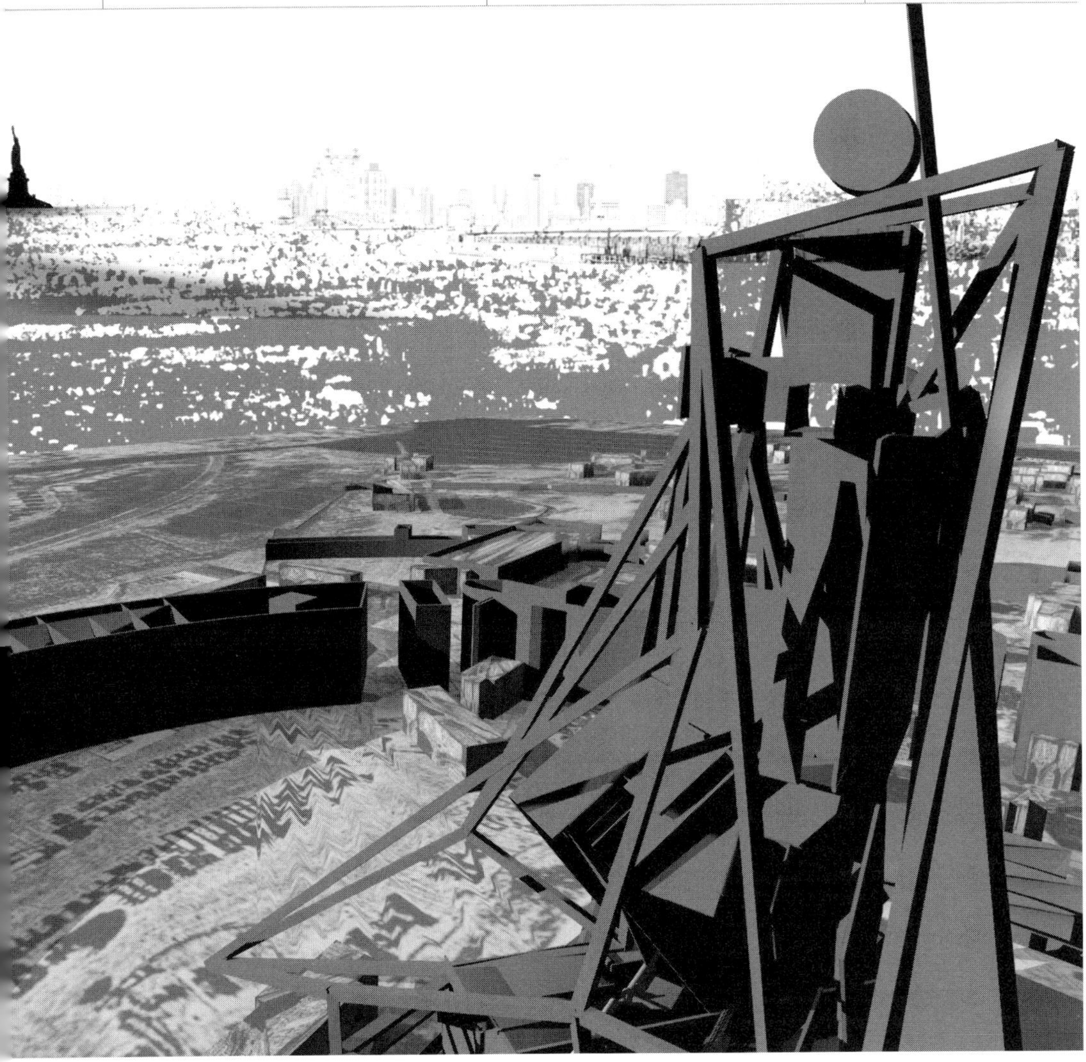

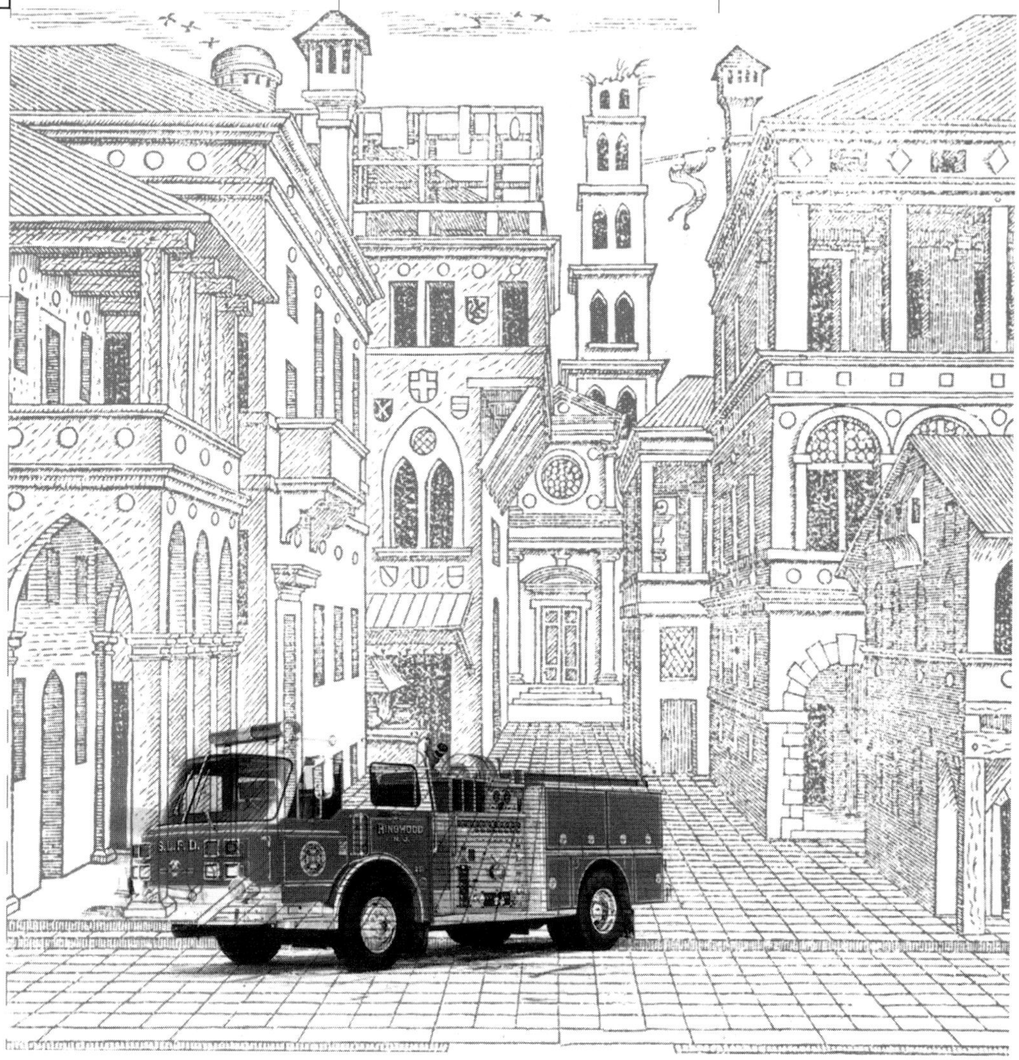

The real project:

During the last decade, the New York City Fire Department has been upgrading its existing training facilities at Randalls Island. When the land at Fort Totten in Bayside, New York, was made available by the US Army to other agencies, the idea for an entirely new training center emerged—the Fire Department Academy campus. This project has been taken up in succession by a series of large New York City architecture firms and is still in development.

This project is not what architects would usually consider to be a dream job. The budget is tight and the technical aspects of the project are extremely complicated. The new Burn Building (otherwise known simply as *the Simulator*) has to meet a multitude of construction regulations, fire safety and zoning codes and still be able to accommodate the training program of the Fire Academy courses. To add to the challenge for local residential communities, these types of facilities are equally as undesirable as waste processing plants; therefore despite the formidable expanse of *the Simulator*, it has to be kept low-profile to remain virtually unnoticed.[1]

The imaginary (but real) project:

Historically, the fireman's profession has had an affinity towards theatricality, regalia and paraphernalia. Being a fireman is still a romantic first choice for a 5-year old (along with policeman and astronaut), and the sheer number of firemen-related toys manufactured each year attests to this popular status of the profession. Even the process of becoming a fireman, in spite of the grave necessity and seriousness of the intent, can nevertheless be described to a large extent as playing a game—*fire in an imaginary city.*

An FDNY training session is a theatrical performance with its own techniques of staging the make-believe reality as well as its own set of actors and on-lookers (ranging from fire marshals inspecting the site to, potentially, crowds of tourists). Why not then, instead of a traditional sprinkled shed for burning hay and old furniture and where fake smoke is produced, make the *Burn Building* a theater with multiple machines and stage sets accommodating different training procedures outlined in the FDNY curriculum: one house for many plays, one building for the whole city?

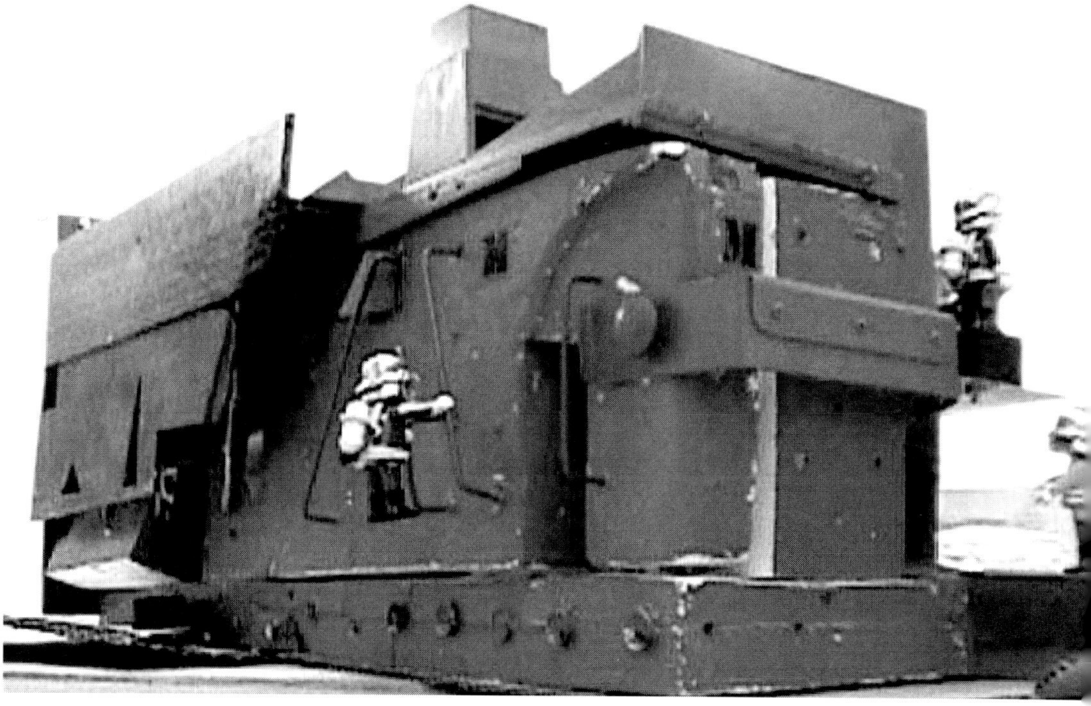

The practical (but imaginary, yet real) project:

At the turn of the 20th century at the Coney Island amusement park, a popular attraction, *The Fire in the City*—complete with pyrotechnics and other special effects—allowed the virtual experience of that very real and ubiquitous occurrence for New York at the turn of the Century. Ironically, the lessons of fire safety were not derived from this exercise, and the attraction eventually burned to the ground.[2]

The wild and un-predictable *training* flames have become a thing of the past; gone are the days when firefighters burn old furniture and trash to hone their skills. Contemporary fire simulation equipment includes burners and smoke outlets controlled by computers. Yet given the space limitation of one building that is meant to represent the whole city, the question remains—what urban essentials are in a Burn Building? How to distill a city into a building? What to include and omit in the process?

The way to approach that problem is through an attempt to understand how a firefighter sees the city from a professional stand-point. The FDNY academy handbook contains some of the answers—a list of necessary courses that deal with hands-on training in the urban environment. Those range from *basic emergencies* to complete *structural collapse*, broken down by building types and building materials.[3] How can this be accommodated in one building complex?

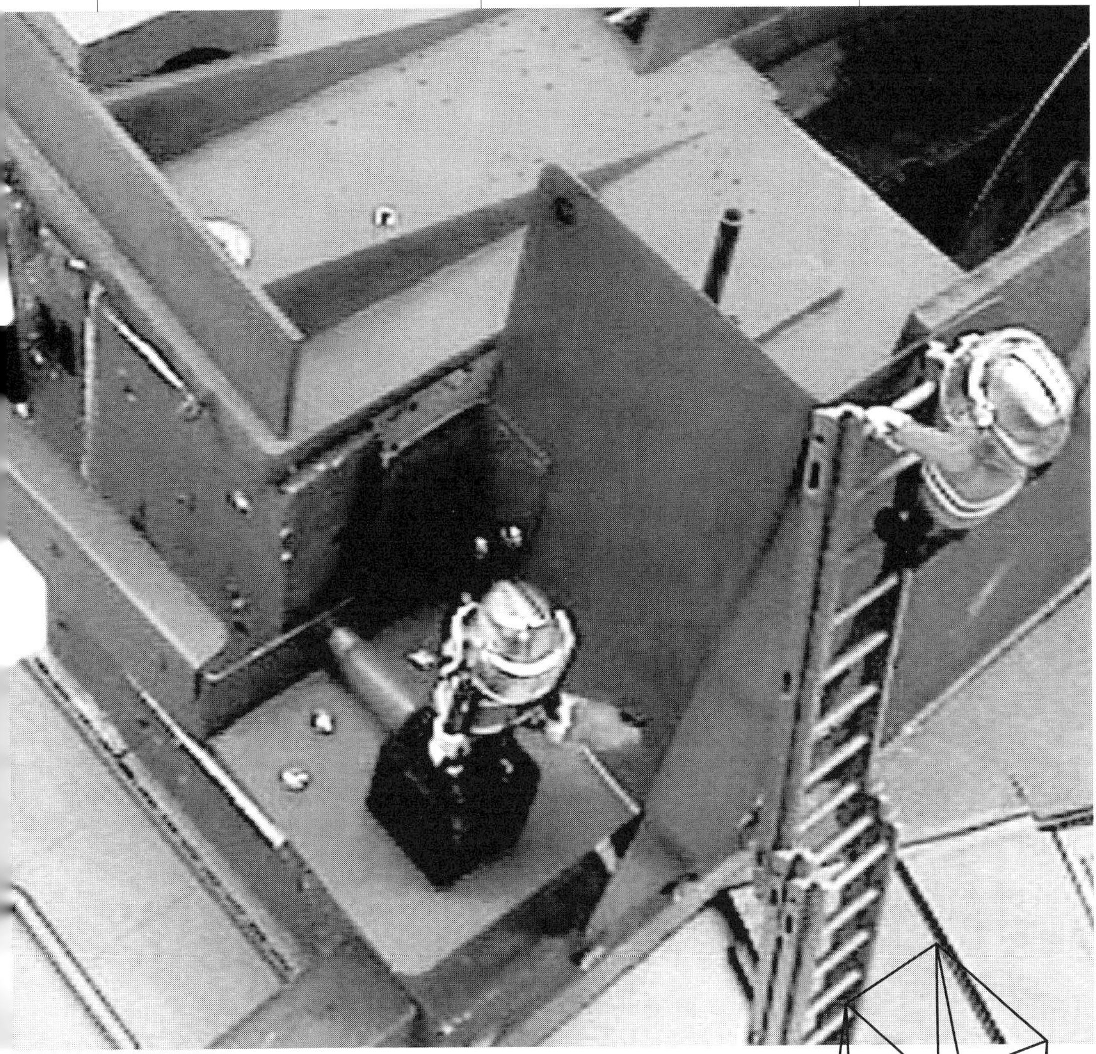

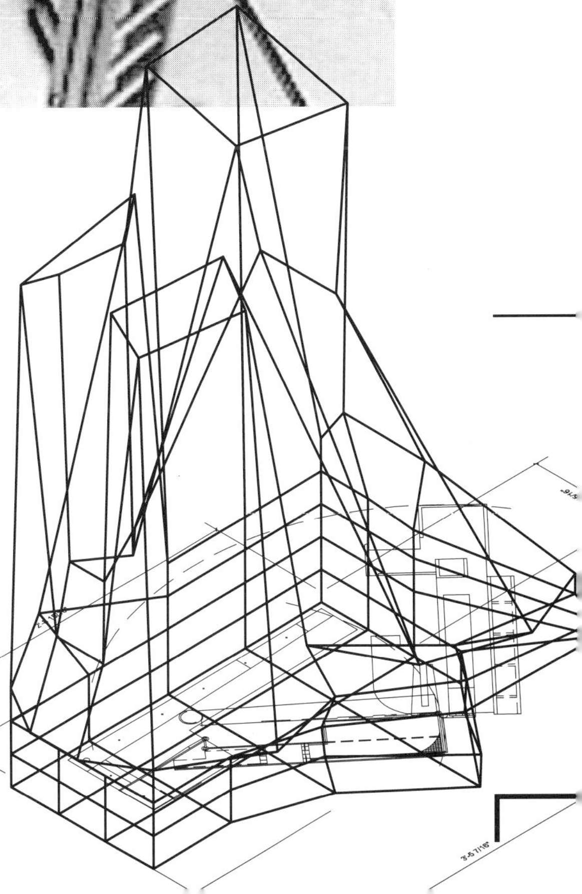

A manual of equipment available to firefighters specifies the building height as the key limitation. A standard ladder reaches to a maximum of 135-feet—roughly 10 stories. Tall buildings virtually do not exist as architectural entities for firefighters—every skyscraper is simply several 10-story buildings stacked on each other with a standpipe after every 10th floor. The only document that deals with and regulates building height at the urban scale is the Zoning Resolution. Regulating the height of buildings translates into controlling their purpose, which also involves construction materials, combustibility and *fire-ratings* that are governed by more specific sets of local regulations. From these codes, a city can be translated from its geographical representation (the map) into a list of zoning regulations (the code), and then remapped again into a Simulator diagram.

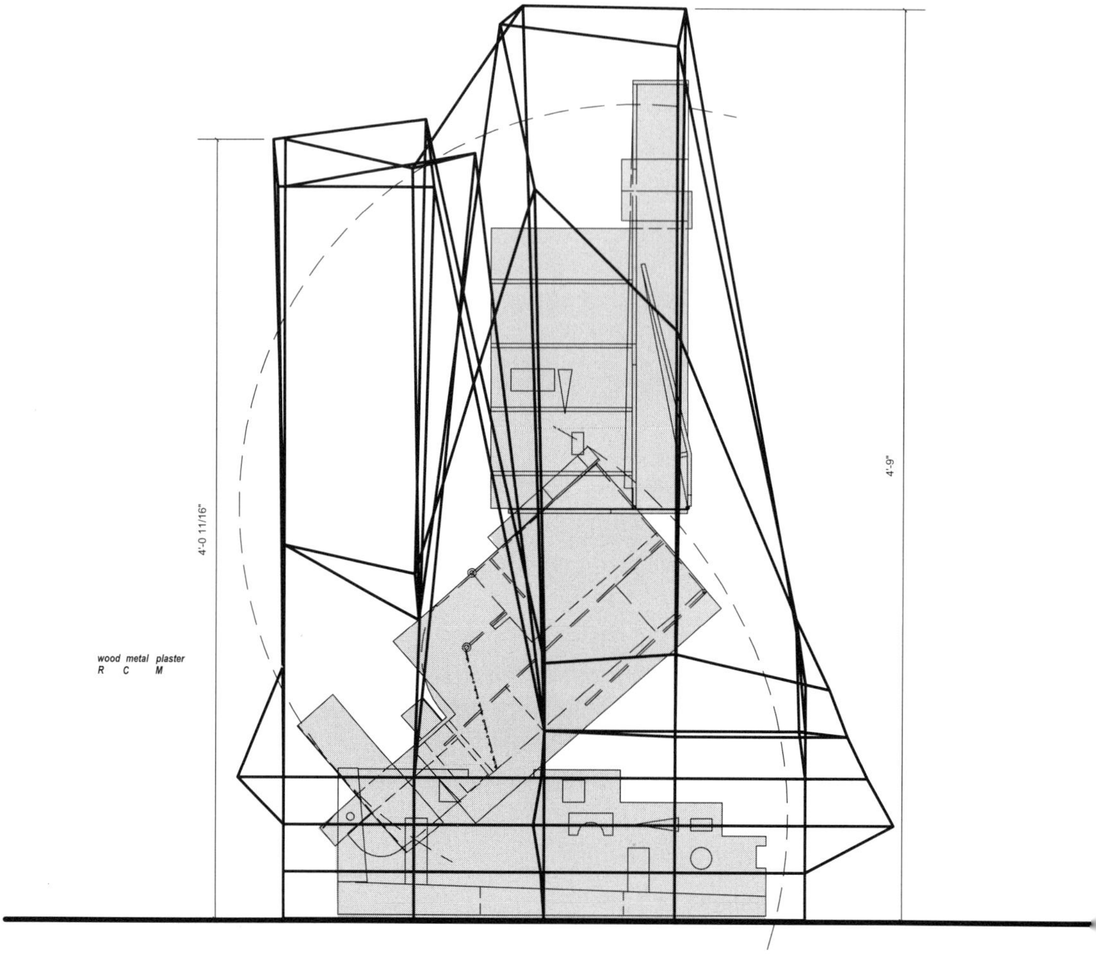

elevation

The three major zoning types—residential, commercial and manufacturing, with numerous variations within each one—must be reflected in the Burn Building. Given that the training procedures of the FDNY require flexibility and frequent reconfiguration of the Burn Building, it has to be mobile, much like a Transformer toy.

In its closed position, the Burn Building is ideally suitable for the *structural collapse* exercise—a maze of overlapping shapes and materials. As it opens up, the opportunities to play out other urban situations—fire in a brownstone, manufacturing facility or on a roof of a high-rise—increase dramatically. Burn Building itself is assembled of concrete, metal, wood and plastic elements to illustrate material combustibility. The maximum height of the expanded Simulator is just over 135-feet. In order to accommodate the transformations, the building must be surrounded by a structural envelope that acts as a supporting skeleton, a crane, as well as infrastructure carrier for the Simulator. This structure is the Burn Building's own *zoning envelope*.

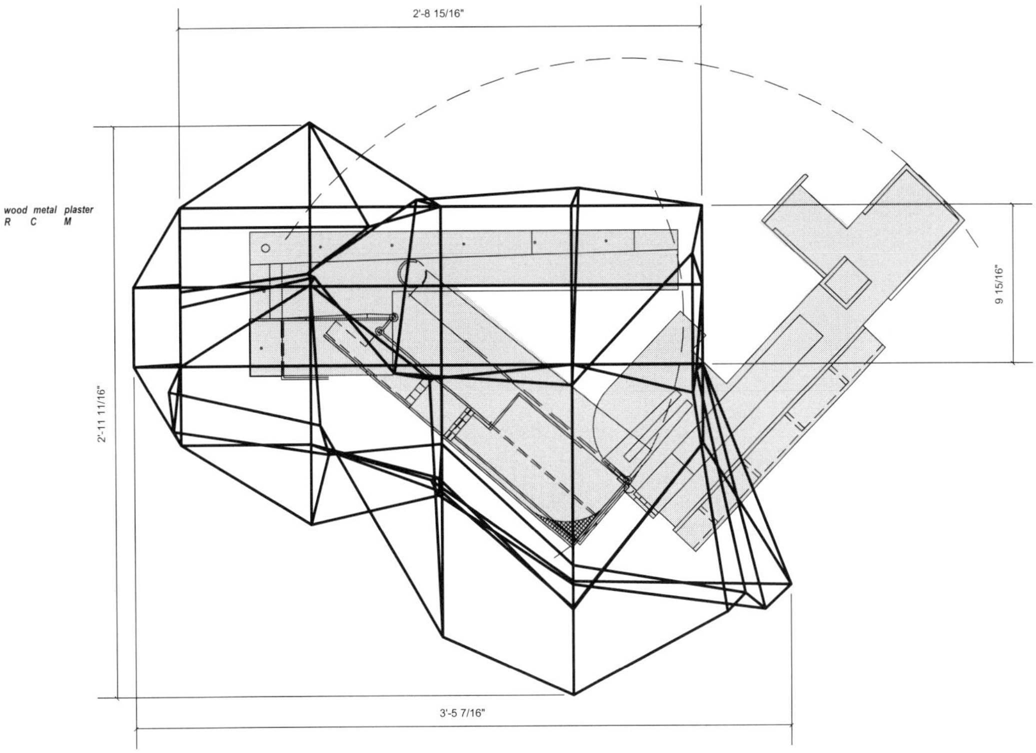

1ft = 1in

top view

The representational (but practical, imaginary yet real) project:

Representing the idea of a toy that simulates a building that is in turn a reflection of a city is a challenge. The solution, in keeping with the initial theatrical premise of the program is a kind of a performance. The audience is introduced to a set of zoning regulations and building fire codes, and then assistants bring in a box . . .within a box . . .within another box—a large toy, much like a fire-truck, wrapped as gift for one's child . . .or one's childhood. The first paper box unfolds to reveal a series of urban development drawings of the Academy's campus. The second box is the Zoning envelope that supports the third box of plaster, steel and wood as it is transformed into all of its possible configurations for the purposes of training firefighters. Thus the practical training considerations, theoretical curiosity about transforming a city into a building and sheer enjoyment of children dreaming to be New York's Bravest—all come together here. Welcome to Burn Building Manhattan!

ENDNOTES

1. The project is currently being developed by Swanke Hayden Connell Architects Ltd., New York City.
2. Rem Koolhaas, delirious new york, Monacelli Press: New York, 1997.
3. FDNY Academy Courses of Instruction, 1999.

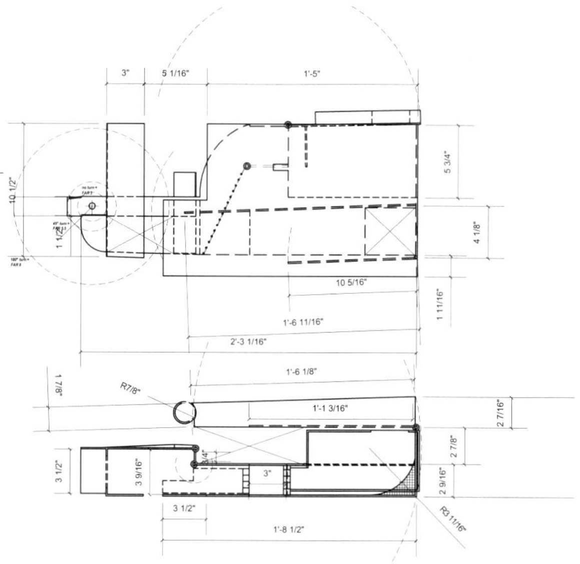

C - commercial METAL

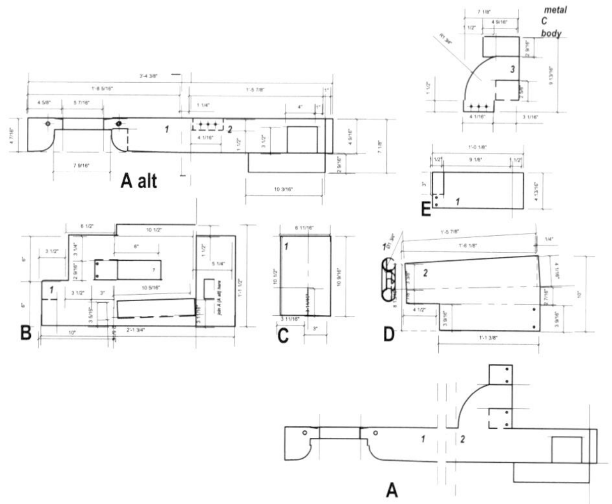

METAL fabrication

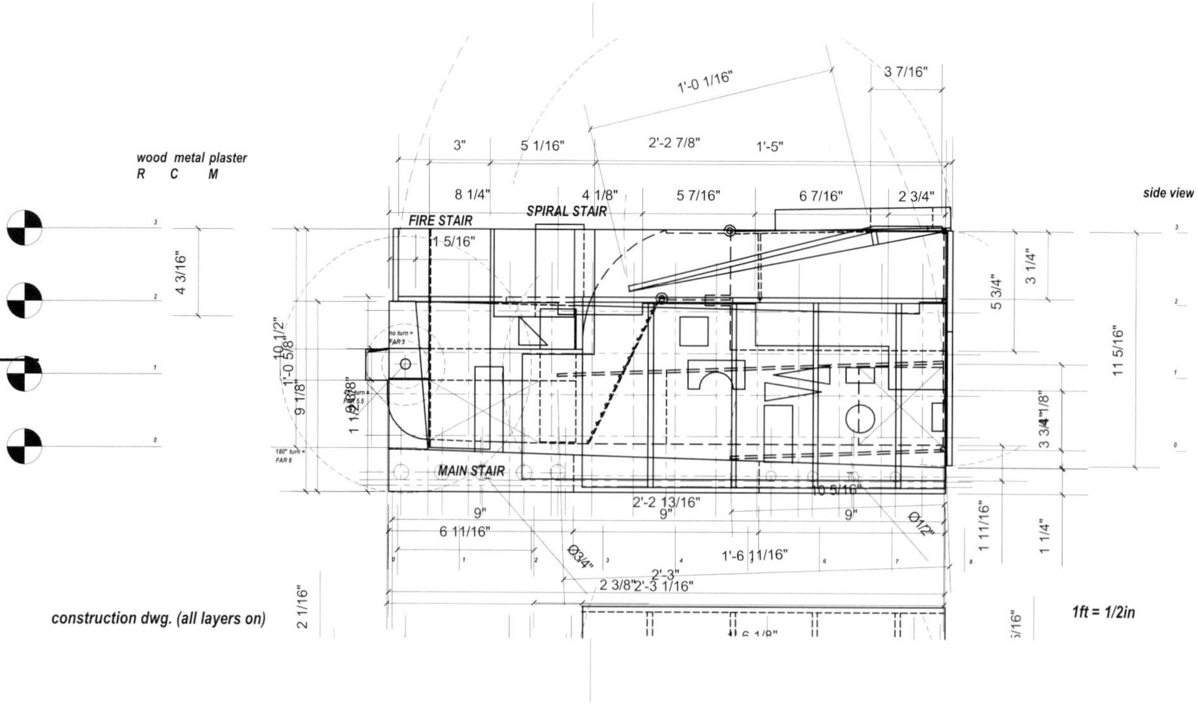

construction dwg. (all layers on)

1ft = 1/2in

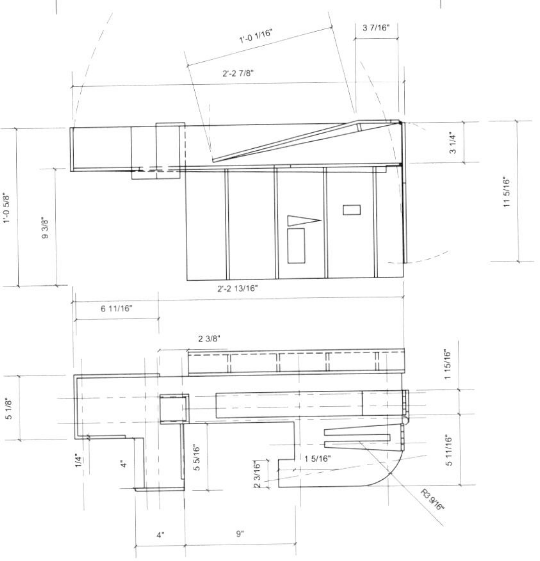

R- residential WOOD assembly

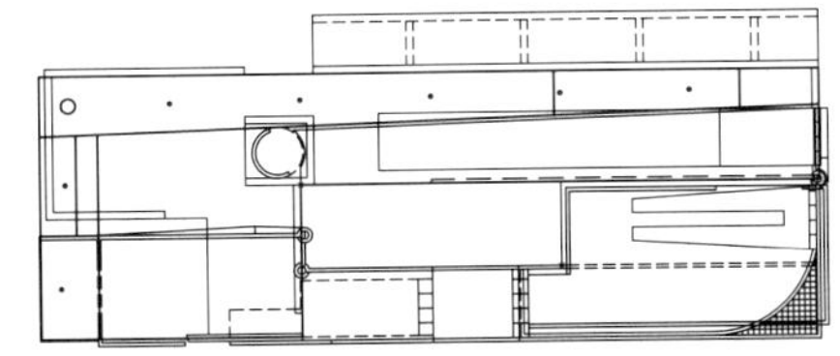

plan

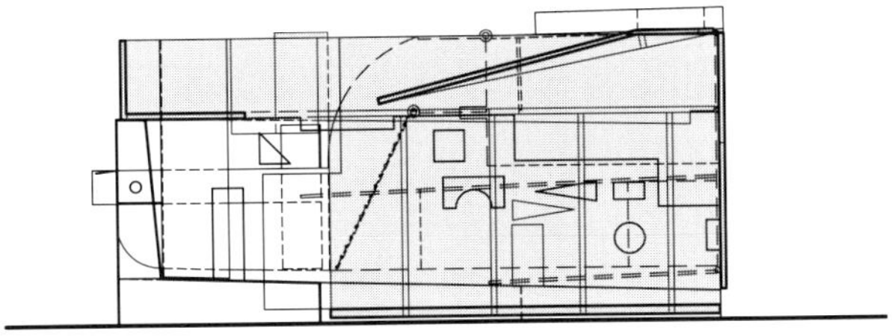

combined M C R - metal, concrete, wood

section

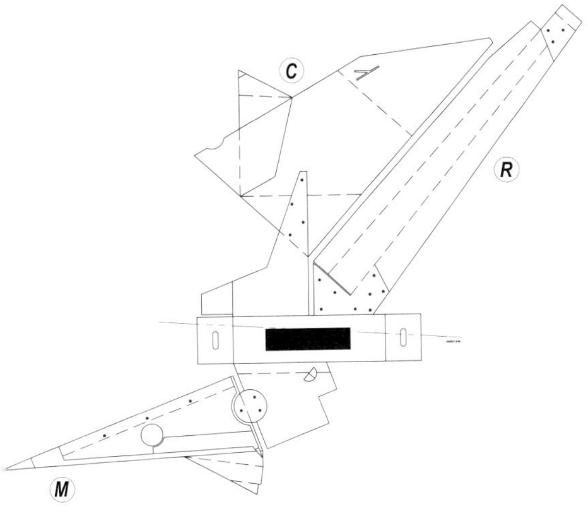

cardboard box

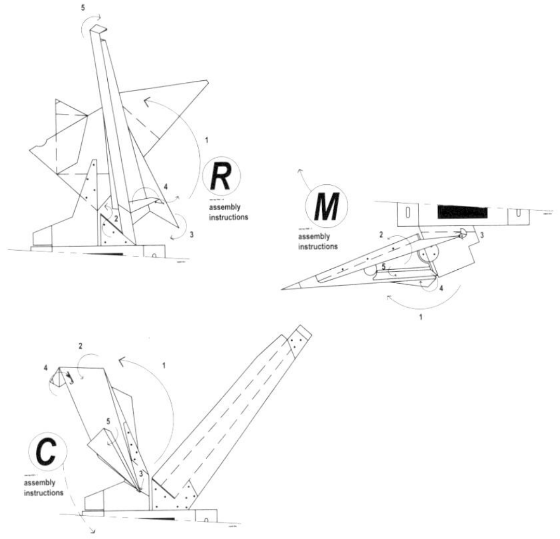

assembly & functions

plaster
M
foundation

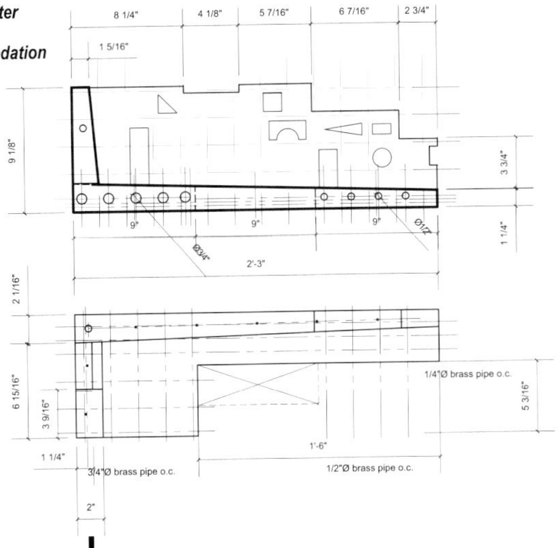

plaster
M
foundation

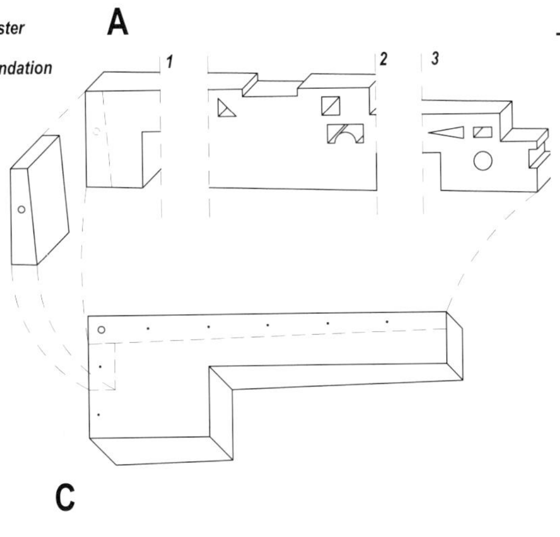

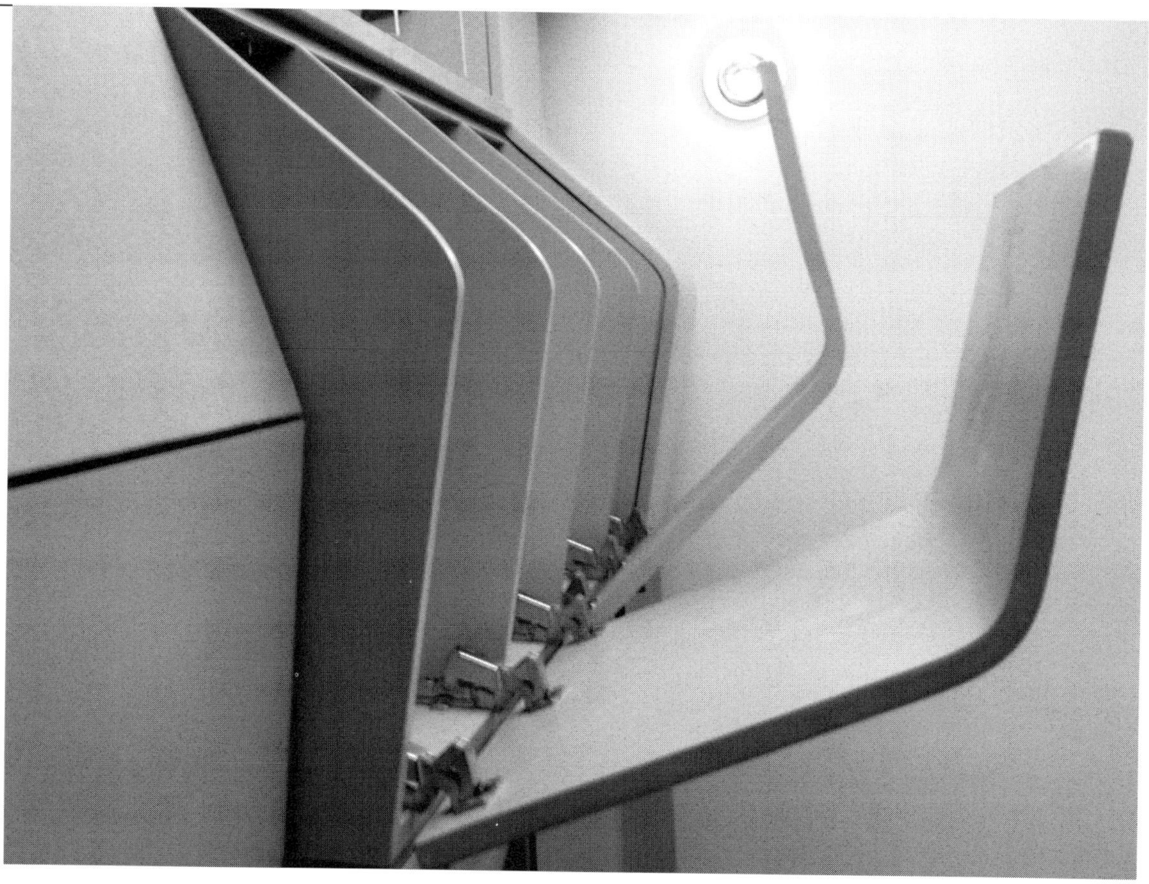

All images courtesy of *emerymcclure* Architecture and Frank McMains

Small Scale
Blum ROOM

1,444 cubic foot installation into the historic Blum House. The Blum ROOM is for an adolescent girl. It is to accommodate her teen-age life and her 21st century accumulation of necessity. It sits within a Victorian container registered as a National Historic Place; it must be semi-permanent and not damage the site, yet it must also withstand the activity of a young girl. Our task is to design the event: to create order in chaos and to design the antithesis of the Victorian room where she spent her childhood. The inefficiencies occur in the difference between the existing house and the new inserted skin. The skin mediates between outer bedroom events and inner skin storage necessity.

Heterologous learning and building in Southern Louisiana

GUMBO PRACTICE

by *emerymcclure* architecture

As teachers and practitioners of architecture, we ask our students and ourselves these questions about our region:

1. Can a contemporary practice / investigation be critical and/or relevant within the *culture of congestion*, specifically a viable heterologous landscape?

2. What type of practice / investigation can relevantly negotiate any of the infinitely unique landscapes?

3. Can a practice / investigation, like the region, be simultaneously local and global?

"It's buildings that give cities their identity, especially in New Orleans."[1] Southern Louisiana finds itself in a contemporary heterologous contradiction of preserving and promoting its *languid spaces* of tourism within an atmosphere of convenient and immediate speed. One of the greatest commodities of the lower Mississippi river valley, from Natchez to New Orleans, is its build environment and they too perceived cultural meaning that this environment holds for those who live outside of it. Our challenge is to both teach and practice in a way that understands the contradictions, never relying or forgetting the influence from both.

Ursula Emery McClure is an Assistant Professor at Louisiana State University, and Michael A. McClure is an Assistant Professor at University of Louisiana-Lafayette. As partners, they have won regional and state AIA awards and have been featured in Dwell *and* Southern Living Magazines.

www.emerymcclure.com

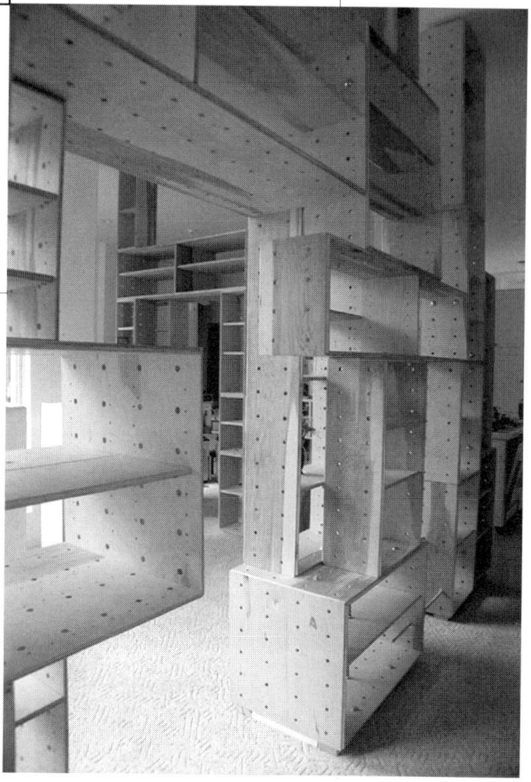

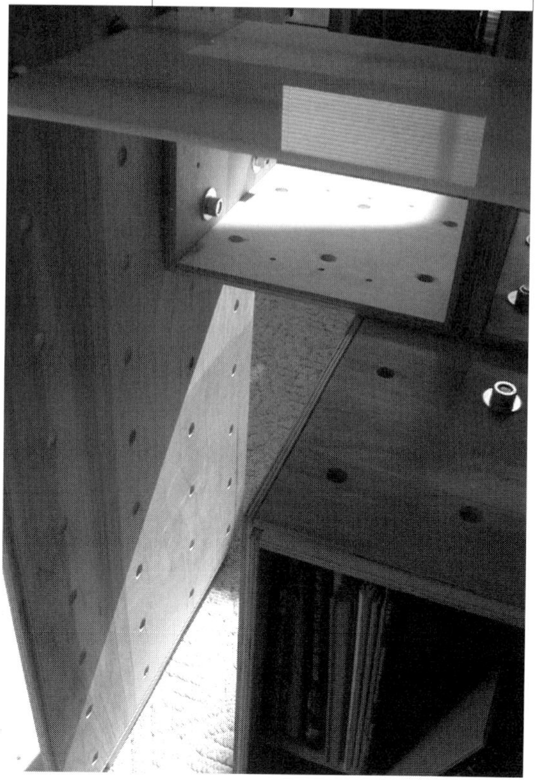

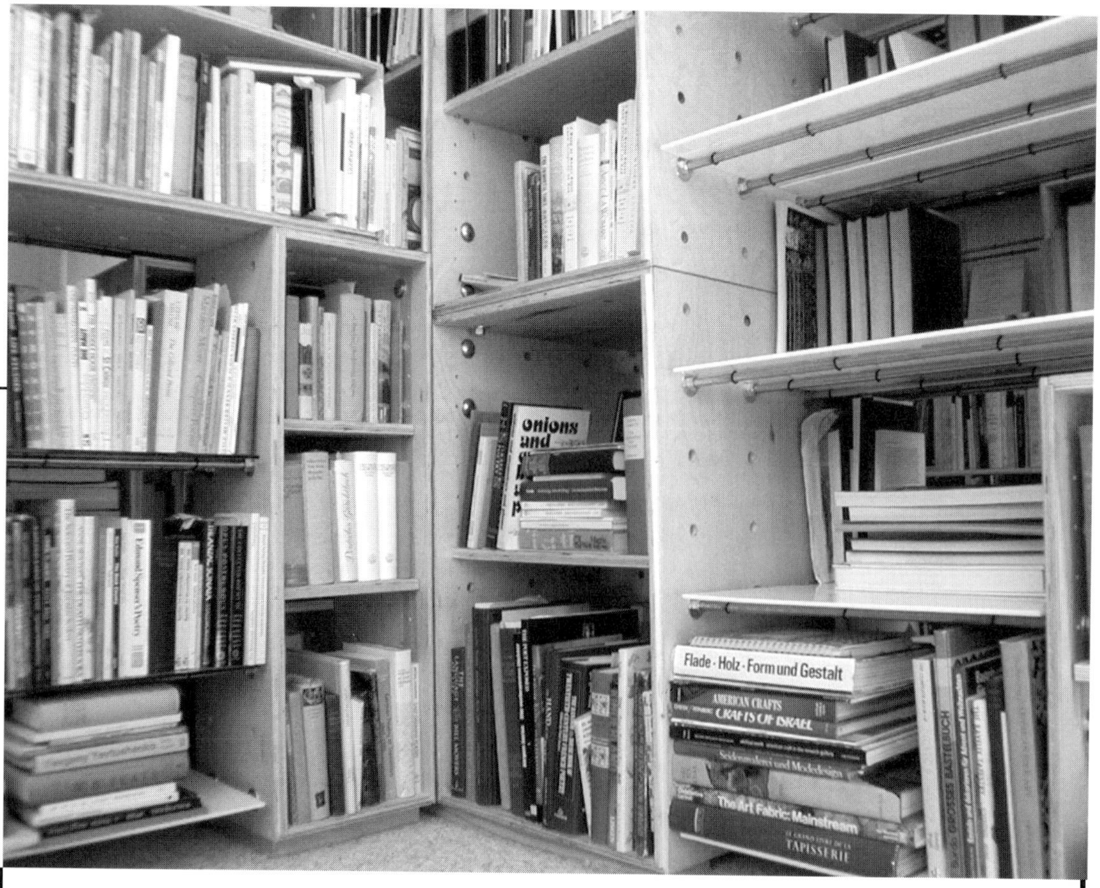
onions
and
Flade · Holz · Form und Gestalt
AMERICAN CRAFTS
CRAFTS OF ISRAEL
The Art Fabric: Mainstream
TAPISSERIE
GROSSES BASTELBUCH

We define Southern Louisiana's *languid spaces* by their differences from what is seen as the American norm. If the efficiencies in communication, convenience, and accelerated obsolescence define normative American space, then the opposite is the inefficiencies, which define unique *languid space*. Inefficiencies in communication are mostly spatial and historic: porches, porticos, and plazas. These tangible places in turn encourage inefficient human interaction—chatting, lounging, and strolling. Inefficiencies in spatial convenience decrease acceleration: pedestrian districts, meandering byways, and tree-lined, residential thoroughfares. They encourage, and sometimes force one to stop and observe. Delayed obsolescence has value in a *languid space*. We measure the value of these spaces by the difference from what is progressive.

The New York historian Kenneth Jackson draws comparisons between modern-day New Orleans and turn-of-the-century Venice, Italy. He asked the question of whether or not New Orleans had given up its role as a vital progressive urban environment, or if, like Venice, it had become an artifact frozen in time, valued only as a past thing. Many similarities exist between the two cities regarding the value of architecture, urbanism, and space within its economic viability as something other. However, New Orleans and Southern Louisiana differ from other historic tourism centers such as Venice. The difference exists in the vast compression and complexities of space, economy, time, culture, and tourism. The overlay of inefficiencies with efficiencies and inconveniences with conveniences demands unique hybrid buildings, practices, and academic investigations.

Southern Louisiana has kept its architectural detritus. It is not a zone or area separated from modernity. This detritus is its own unique progressiveness reliant on ideas of regression. The two co-exist simultaneously. It is not a simplified and sanitized version of entertainment (Disneyland) or a regressive capsule of the past (Williamsburg, Virginia) yet neither is it a vibrant contemporary cultural and economic center (New York, Chicago). It is partly all of these, and not really any of them.

> "Art requires a delicate adjustment of the outer and inner worlds in such a way that, without changing their nature, they can be seen through each other. To know oneself is to know one's region. It is also to know the world, and it is also, paradoxically, a form of exile from that world."[2]

This investigation into notions regarding the complexities of space, economy, time, culture, and tourism stems from a desire to teach and practice relevant architecture in Southern Louisiana. This region presents a unique microcosm of the conditions found in contemporary global environment. Its *languid space* is a progressive space that capitalizes on the idea and the experience of the regressive, while its built environment consists simultaneously of adaptive reuse, preservation, contemporary industry and replication. It is landlocked by the Mississippi River, the Gulf, the Atchafalaya Basin, Lake Pontchatrain, and numerous swamps, rivers, and bayous. The compression and overlay of these infinite influences and their lack of clear hierarchy epitomizes the contemporary "culture of congestion."[3] If we are to contribute to the built environment and cultural identity of Southern Louisiana (or anywhere), it is necessary we understand the constant influences of everything and nothing at all. An understanding of oneself and ones environment is dependent on these influences vying for relevance. The process is fluid, dynamic, and non-hierarchical. In a time when hierarchies are fluid, should not the practices and pedagogies that attempt to translate them into the built environment be fluid as well?

The projects presented are part of a larger investigation into relevant practices. We hope they act as the lever to pry open an understanding of relevant responses in practice and education. The projects are essentially referential to the contradictions of their physical site, function, cultural place, precedent, event, personality, economy, and tectonics.

ENDNOTES

1. Whitehead, Ingrid., "Patricia Gay: Working Hard for preservation in the Big Easy," *Architecture Record*, September 2002: p 256.
2. O'Connor, Flannery., *Mystery and Manners*, The Noonday Press: New York, 1997.
3. Koolhaas, Rem, *delirious new york*, Monacelli Press: New York, 1994.

Minute Scale

316 Shadylake Drive. Deployable / adaptable shelving/ wall system.

316 Shadylake is the addition of a deployable / adaptable library into a suburban tract house. It must create a room where there is none. It must be both storage and display, both furniture and structure. It cannot physically modify the existing house yet it must read as a permanent installation. The inefficiencies are constructed through offsetting the measurement system of the boxes and support holes. This misalignment insures spaces for framed views and storage / display of personal items: pictures, vases, and art objects.

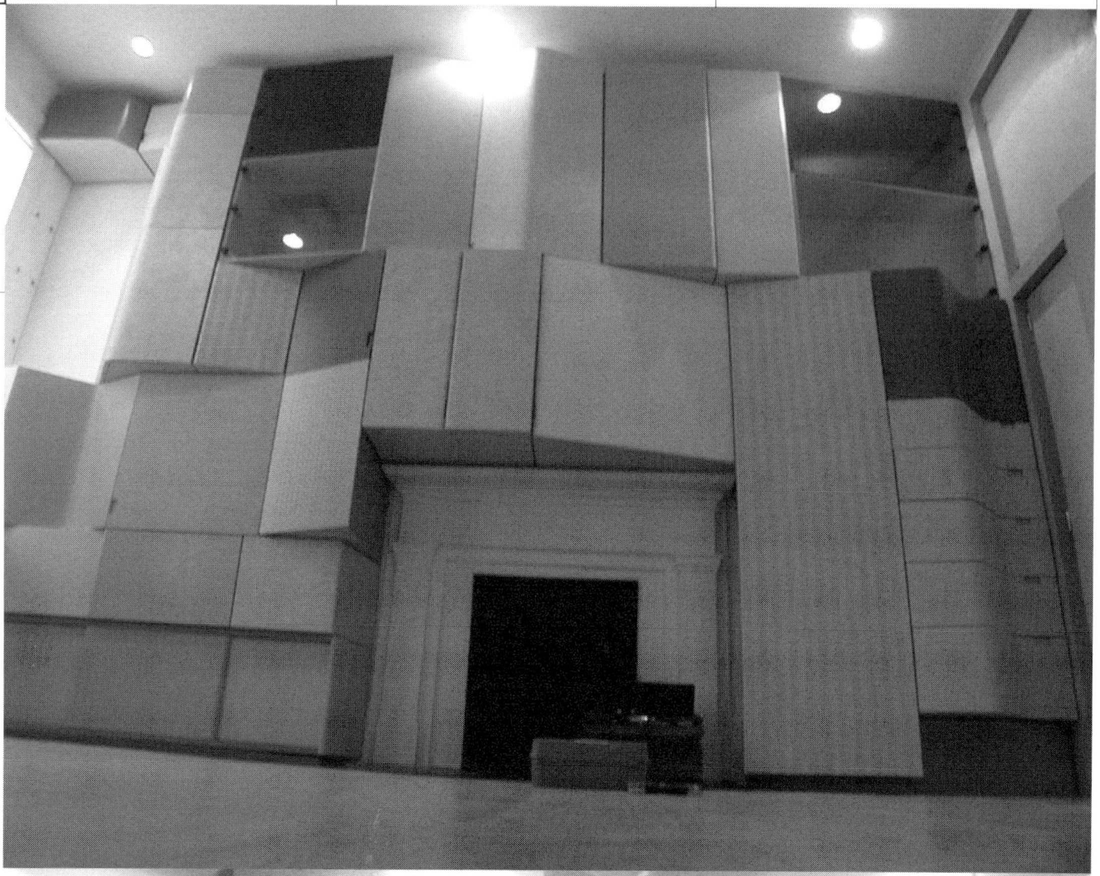

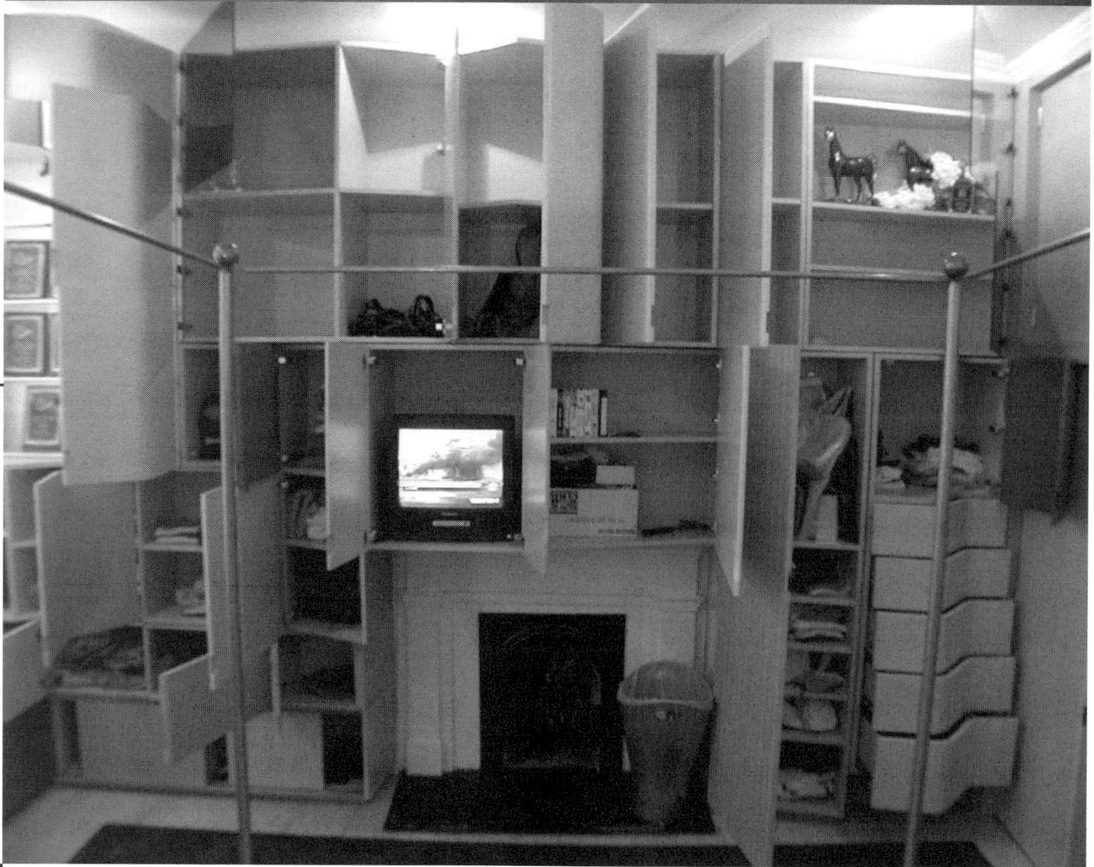

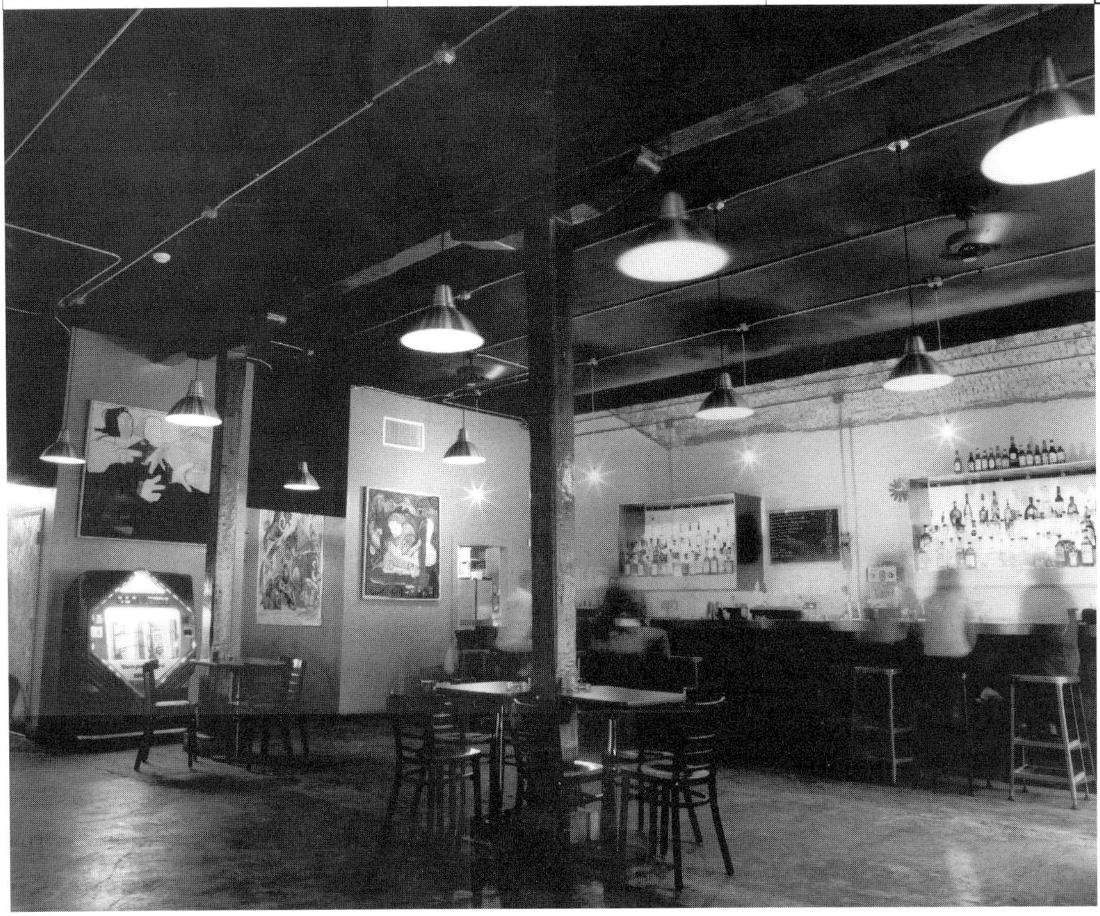

Medium Scale

Red Star Bar: 1,200 sq. foot cocktail lounge

The Red Star Bar is first an urban insertion of event into a dead downtown. It will be one of three downtown spaces open to the public past 6:00 PM in a city of 300,000 people. Secondly, it is an insertion of minimal budget into an existing storefront space. The programmatic functions are placed into boxes. The events take place between and within them. The events take place between the lit steel display boxes, the cypress service box, the gray evacuation boxes, and the translucent façade boxes. The inefficiencies that are necessary of a social space are allowed to take place as required.

> Red Star Bar

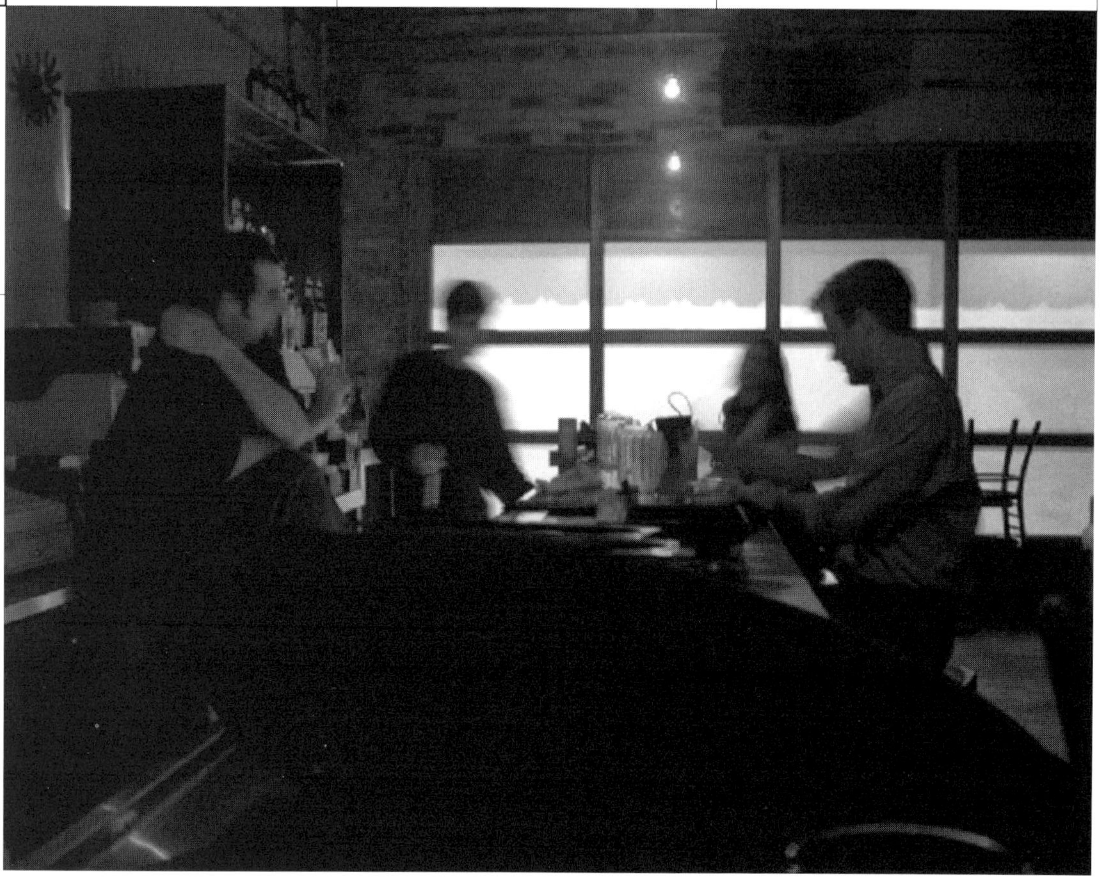

> ABF Barn

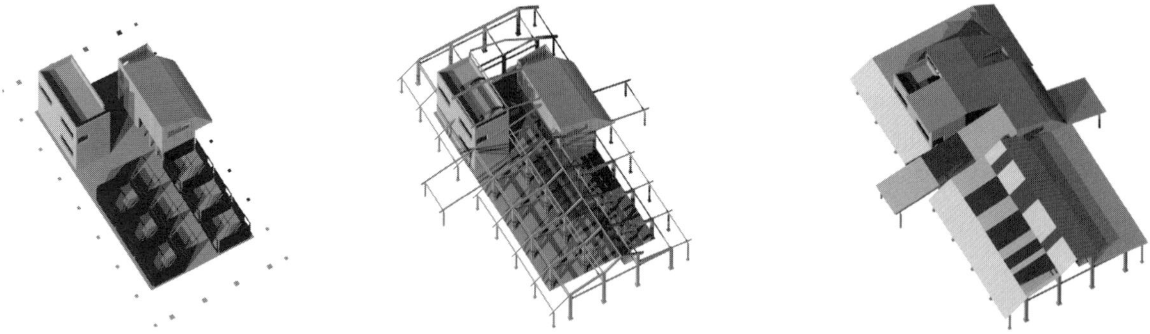

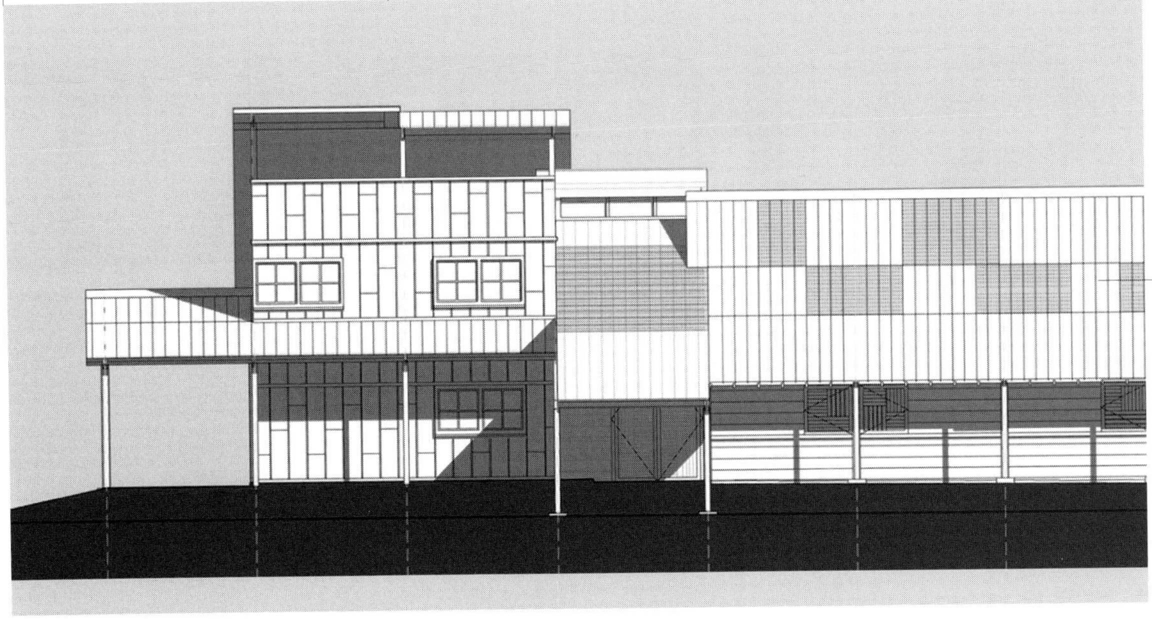

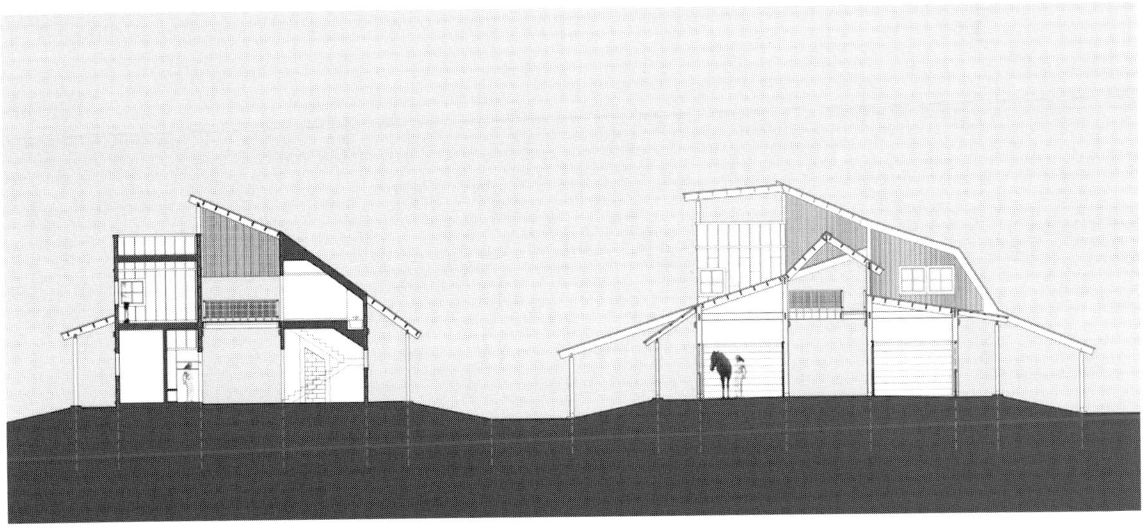

Large Scale

ABF Barn: 3,400 sq. foot Arabian horse breeding facility

ABF Barn is an Arabian horse barn and veterinarian laboratory. There are three unique and contradictory clients: a rider, a landowner, and a landscape architect. The physical site is a rural Southern Louisiana landscape. The function requires simultaneously both rough and finite finishes (stall and laboratory respectively) and must allow for two varied scales of occupants (horse and human). Lastly, but most importantly, there exists the loaded architectural precedent: BARN. The inefficiencies occur where these disparate functions, materials, and scales meet.

SUSTAIN

V

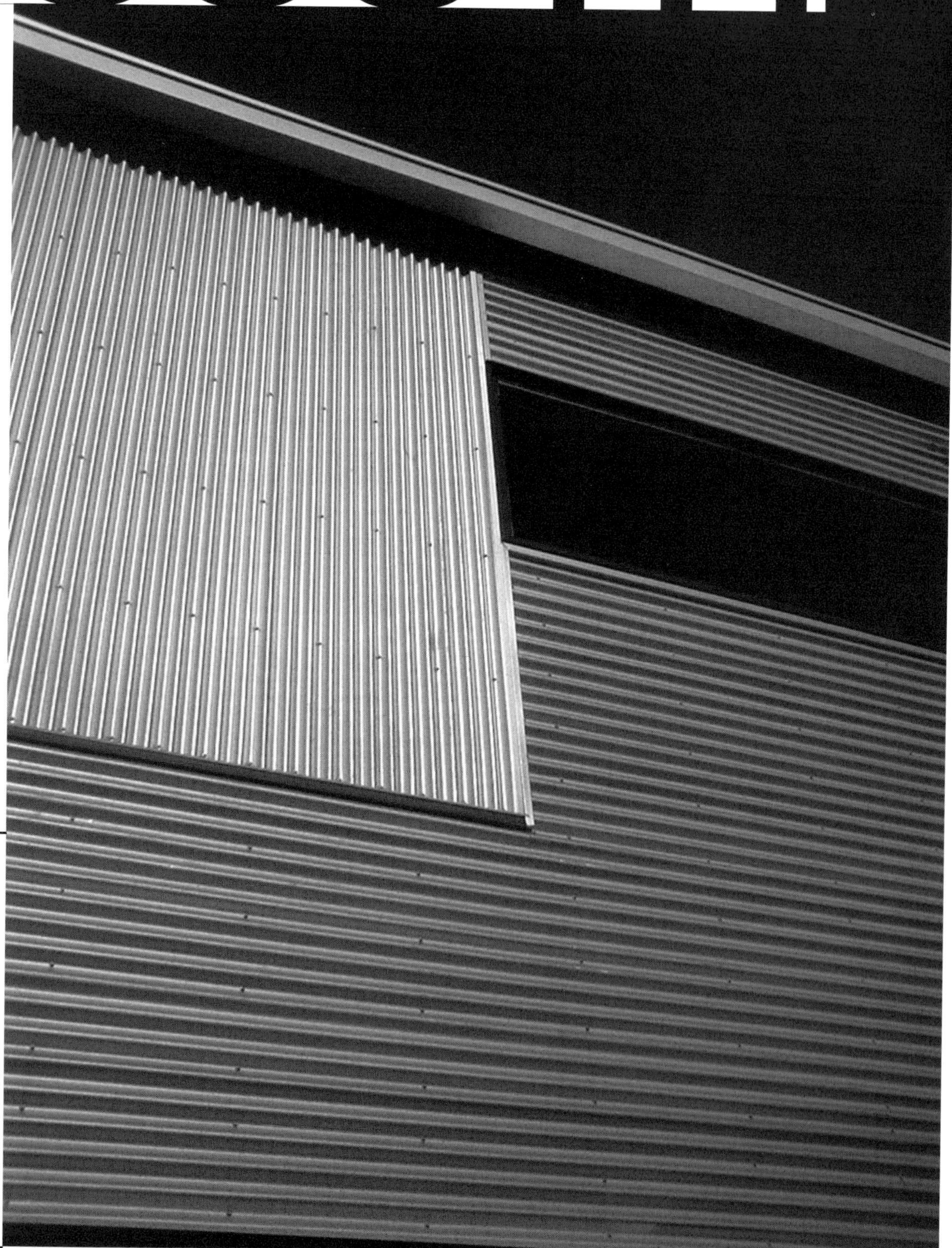

East Elevation ›

A sustainable home for the director of recycling

IABLE ORPHOLOGY

by Tonino Vicari

It is difficult to establish a position against sustainability in architecture when it is defined as a set of design decisions that allow one to arrive at a more cost-effective design solution, which in turn consumes less energy over the life span of a building and does not impact the environment in negative ways. Put into these terms, sustainability becomes a logical design philosophy. In this instance, the development of a sustainable home for the director of recycling for the city of Ann Arbor becomes a case study in passive solar design, the vehicle for the formulation of a body of research that has helped in developing the concept of sustainable morphology.

Sustainable morphology invokes the notion that a building can work like a natural organism: the theory states that its design, including formal qualities, window placement, mechanical, electrical and passive systems, can work with the environmental characteristics of site, place, and time as apposed to working against them. The response is a technological vernacular in that it addresses the specifics of climate, place and culture with contemporary formal strategy, new materials and intelligent systems. Another important lesson from nature is that an organism's evolution is based on its ability to adapt; thus the design of any cultural artifact, be it a home or other structure, must have the ability to adapt to both its environment and its energy sources.

Tonino Vicari received a MS in Environmental Technology, a MArch and a BArch from the University of Michigan. His independent projects include residential and urban projects that focus on sustainable considerations and adaptive reuse.

www.konstruct.us
www.tectonic-design.com

Daylight Analyses

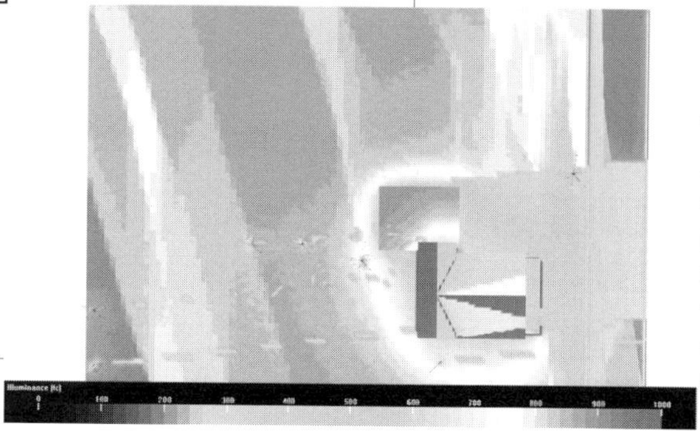

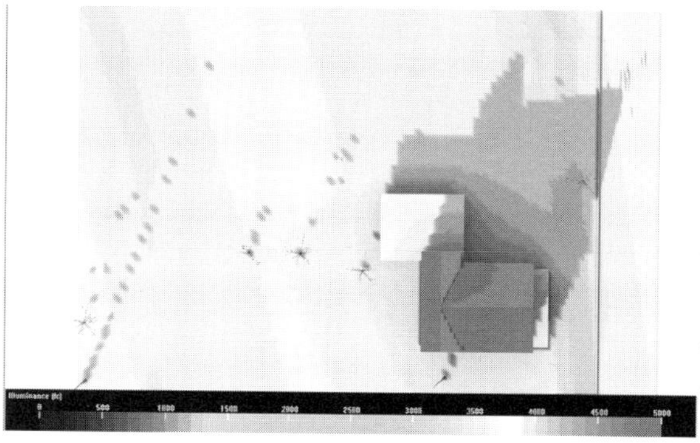

Designing a single-family residence has become an exercise in the integration of research, simulation, design, production and postproduction validation. Through this process of design, one can develop a more technologically responsive process that can yield a positively performing, environmentally responsive structure. Also integrated into the concept of sustainable morphology is the idea that the design approach progresses beyond dependence on a building's mechanical systems to a consideration of the performance of the structure as it relates to the overall design. The shape, form, and massing of the building are informed not only by intellectual concepts but also by a desire for an environmental response. In the same way that a car is designed in a wind tunnel to achieve minimal drag and optimal fuel–consumption performance, so too is the design process of buildings to be synthesized with formal considerations for sunlight patterns, wind patterns, and energy performance. In the case of the McMurtrie residence, it is the particular shape of the structure that allows it to capture light for heat energy.

This dynamic solution is similar to the way a sunflower responds to light through the mechanism of phototropism, both interacting with and reacting to the sun's light throughout the day through movement. Following this theory, so too should a building transform itself to react to these

Diagram: Solar Absorption

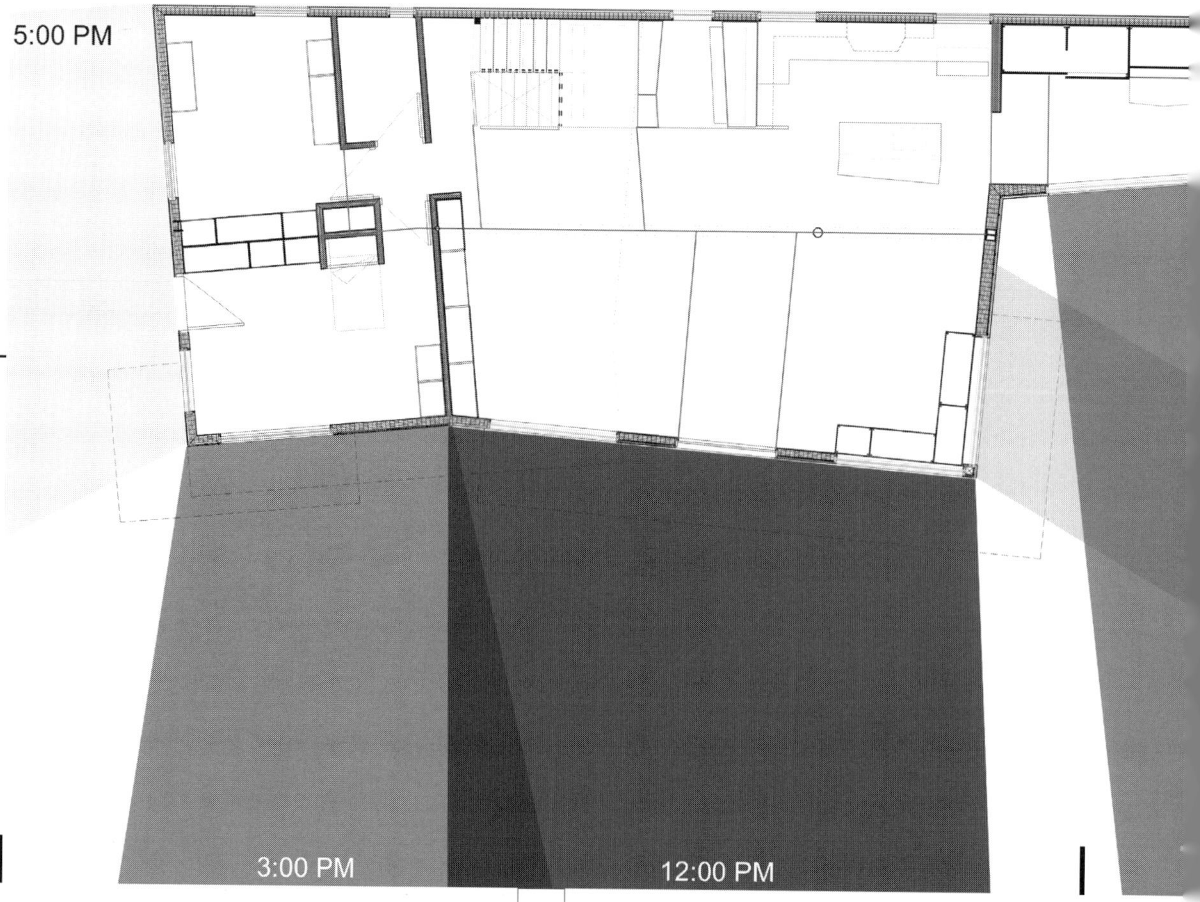

changes. Before the process of design begins, site and climate research—coupled with pre-design simulation—are essential to analyze in gaining a clear understanding of environmental factors.

Research is not an isolated exercise; on the contrary, it directly impacts and informs the process of architectural production by opening up the possibility for more design tools, thereby generating new solutions for the client as well as the building's environment and context. Specifically, research into weather patterns (such as rainfall, wind patterns, temperature ranges, and cloud coverage percentiles) can uncover vast differentials in how these factors impact the building across geographic regions. Since the city of Ann Arbor endures extreme cold temperatures in the winter months and experiencing hot humid summers, it becomes necessary to analyze and design for both ends of the environmental and climatic spectrum. Specifically, research into weather patterns and extreme seasonal conditions related to resulting data can serve as preparation when designing for specific environmental variables.

Simulation differs from research in that it is able to predict certain environmental and naturally occurring patterns through the use of computers or conventional tools. This gives the designer a range of scenarios to respond to in their design, as

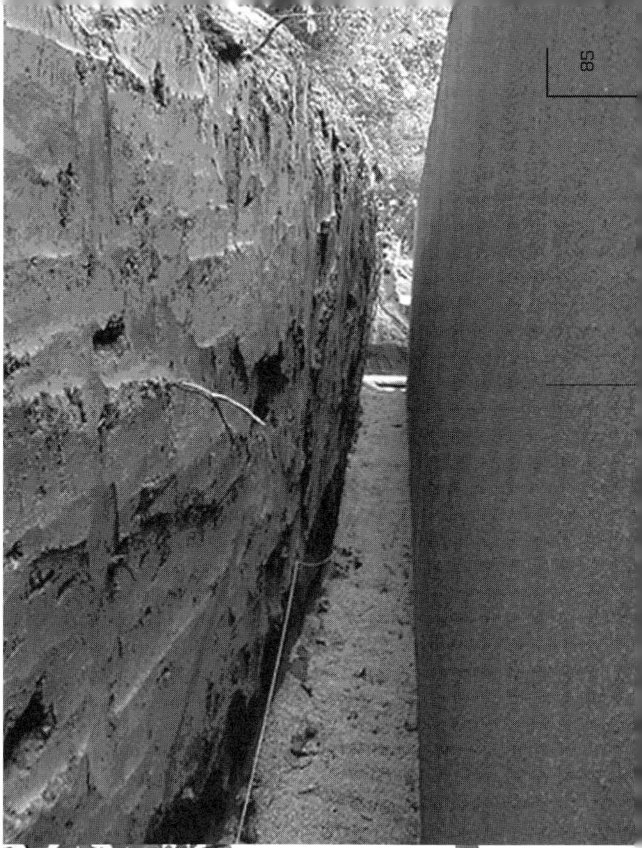

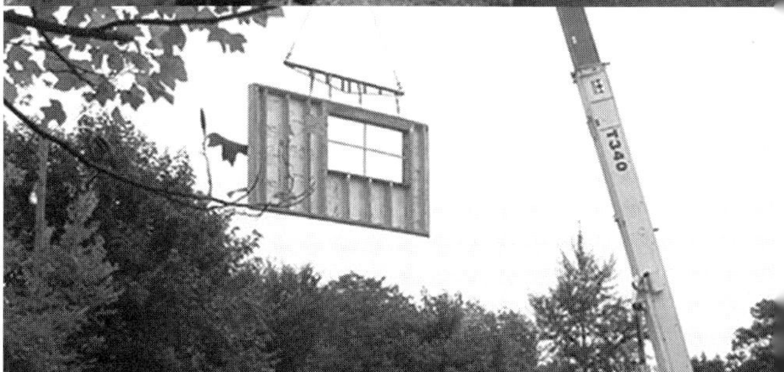

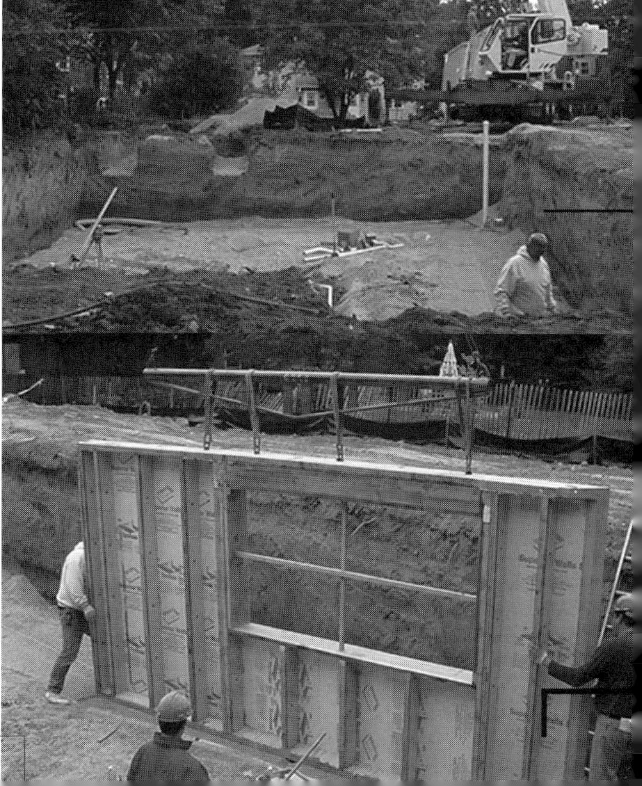

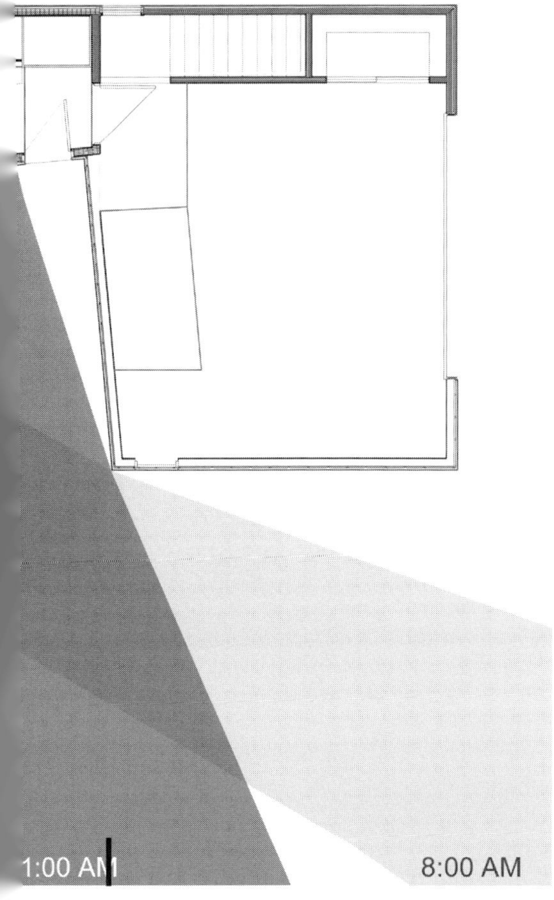

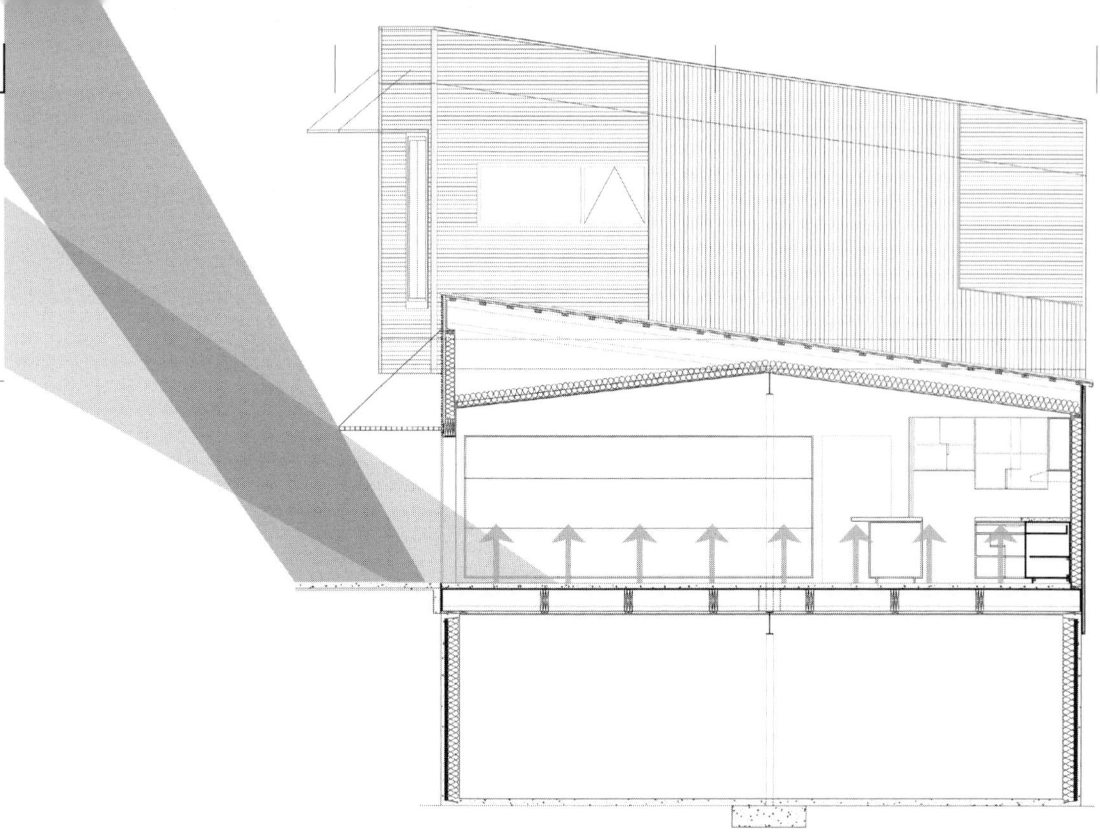

opposed to relying solely on impressionistic data or experience based on a single site visit. Through the use of simulated studies of daylight distribution over the course of a year, an architect can have 2, 3, 12 or 356 site visits depending on the specificity of the data desired. This information can also be computer-generated within a few hours. Utilizing simulation as a pre-design tool gives the architect and designer a wider range of site experiences to which to respond architecturally. In the case of the McMurtrie Residence, the upper, lower and median dates of solar movement were analyzed at its extreme conditions on the dates of June 21st (Summer Solstice), December 21st (Winter Solstice) and March 21st (Equinox) at varying times throughout these dates in order to determine the sun's over the course of a day. Another element to consider in this simulation exercise is the distribution of light in and around the site, including interaction with adjacent structures, as well as with natural elements such as trees—both with and without leaves. These considerations will again be dependent on the time of year being considered as part of the digital model.

These site and environmental considerations ensure that the building form will help to optimize its energy performance, as well as providing maximum comfort and aesthetic appeal.

Using this method the building shape will necessarily become a dynamic part of the environmental response instead of an aesthetic whim or style. The preliminary simulation (using the software Lightscape) analyzed solar movement, which assisted in determining the location of the sun at various times of the year. In the given situation, the modeling and simulation have directly informed the geometry and window location for the south façade. Since the south facade is the primary vehicle through which light will enter the building, the solar mapping was instrumental in determining the described geometry.

In the daylight studies, the objective was to determine the specific path of the sun on the site in relation to contextual elements; the reason being the determination of the location and time of shadows located on the site. Since the residence seeks to gain its heat and light-energy through passive solar methods, it becomes absolutely essential to know and understand the behavior of the sun through these simulations, allowing a process that would traditionally take a year of physical solar mapping on the site to be done much more quickly and efficiently. In addition to being more time-efficient, this method allows for a plan view perspective of the site, further aiding a design process that is difficult, if not impossible, without digital methods, suggesting that in this case daylight simulation is an essential tool in the design process.

As illustrated in the site plan and building floor plan, not only the building's form but also the room distribution has been informed by sun tracking throughout the day. The spaces that require little or no daylight are placed at the east of the site, the garage and breezeway are the only spaces that fall in the shadow of the adjacent structure. The rest of the spaces in the home—such as the bedrooms and living spaces—receive maximum solar exposure, thereby inducing maximum solar heat absorption. Employing the same strategic approach, elements of the home have been scored and folded to create facets, the purpose of which is to achieve maximum exposure to the sun at a perpendicular angle over the greatest number of times throughout the day, given that the maximum absorption a surface receives is through a perpendicular surface to the sun's rays. By folding the surface of the building skin, we have maximized the potential for areas to receive optimal solar exposure and therefore increased the possibilities for using solar absorption as a heat source.

Passive solar absorption, a main feature in the sustainability of design, occurs here through light penetration of the large windows on the South façade. In this instance, when the light penetrates the space of the home, it warms a 4-inch exposed concrete slab, which—throughout the day—absorbs the heat created by this transformation of energy states. When the light energy from the sun comes into contact with the slab, it is converted to heat energy, thereby charging the slab with thermal energy. In the evening, these large windows are covered with specially designed insulating panels so that the heat collected therein throughout the day can be conserved and dissipated back into the space of the home, reducing the dependence on mechanical systems. In this instance, the exposed concrete floor acts as a thermal mass to absorb the heat energy of the sun.

Along with passive solar heating, the active system of radiant tube heating has been incorporated into the design. A much more efficient, comfortable solution when compared to forced air, this method provides even warmth distribution, while the concrete slab, acting like a battery, conducts the heat in the tubes into the space, and is *charged* by the heat of the sun throughout the day. Relying on both passive and active systems reduces dependence on the active system and therefore requires less energy, burns less fossil fuel and reduces negative impacts on the environment. Since buildings consume over 40% of the earth's energy, it is essential to consider energy consumption in any (sustainable) design project.

Conversely, the design must also be flexible, responding not only to cold weather but to extremely hot and humid conditions as well. To address these concerns, the material used to clad the house is a corrugated metal; while the desired solar radiation penetrates through the large

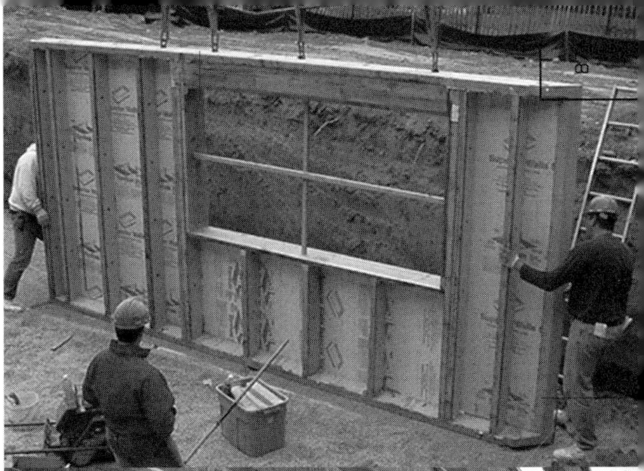

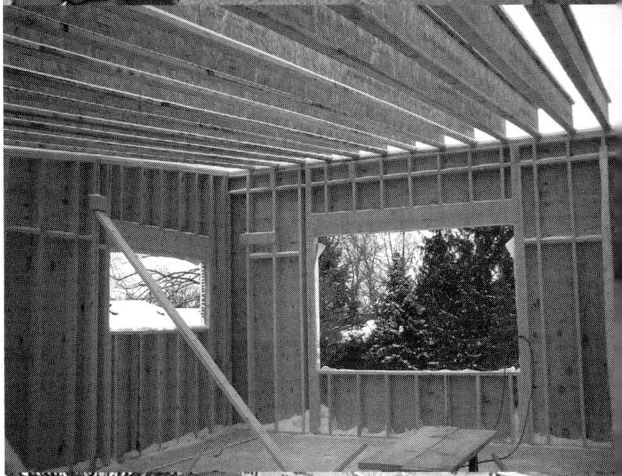

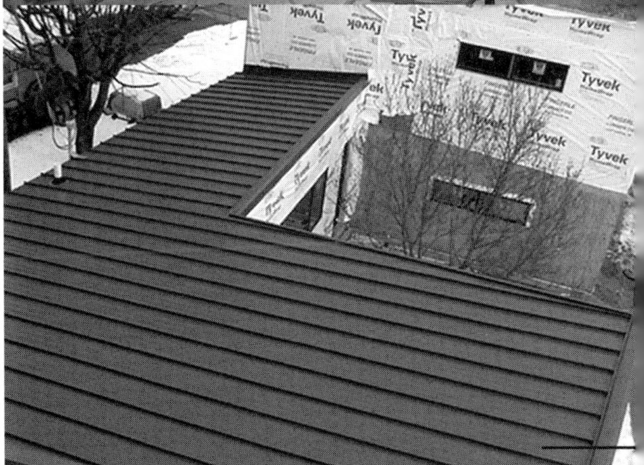

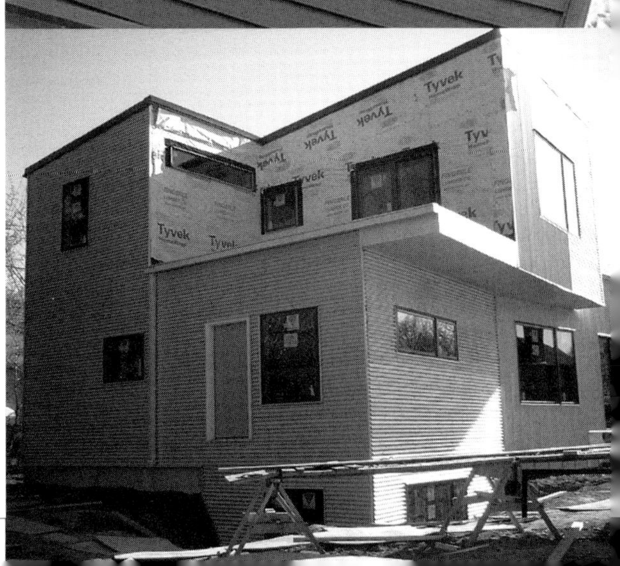

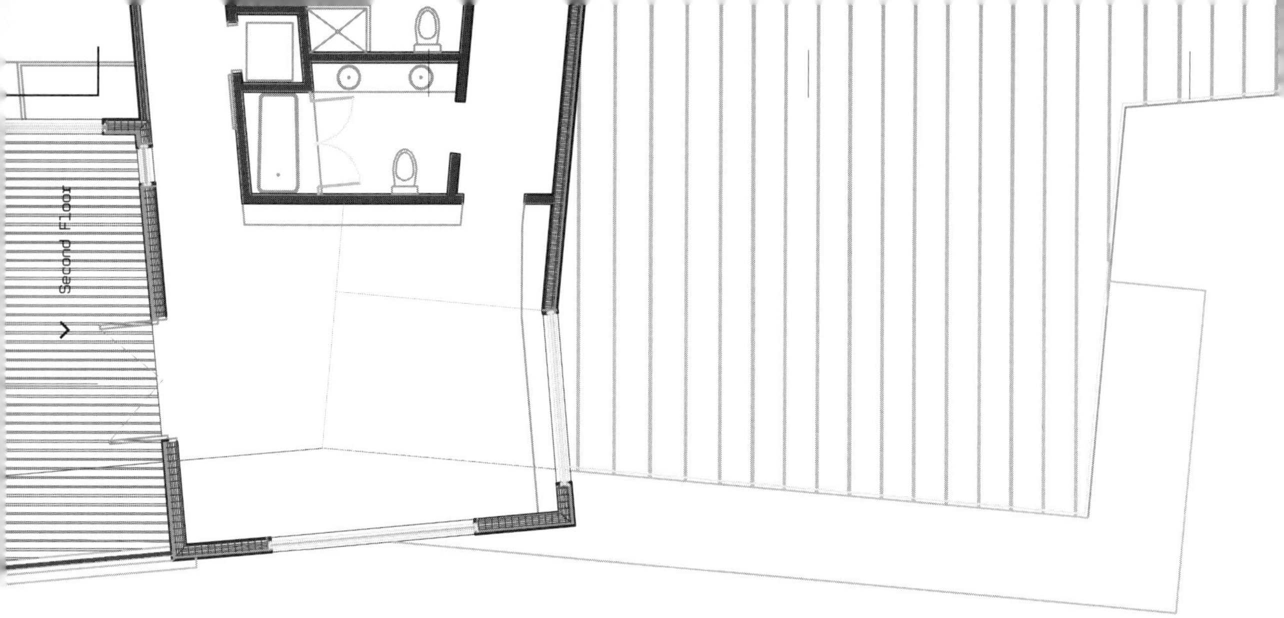
Second Floor

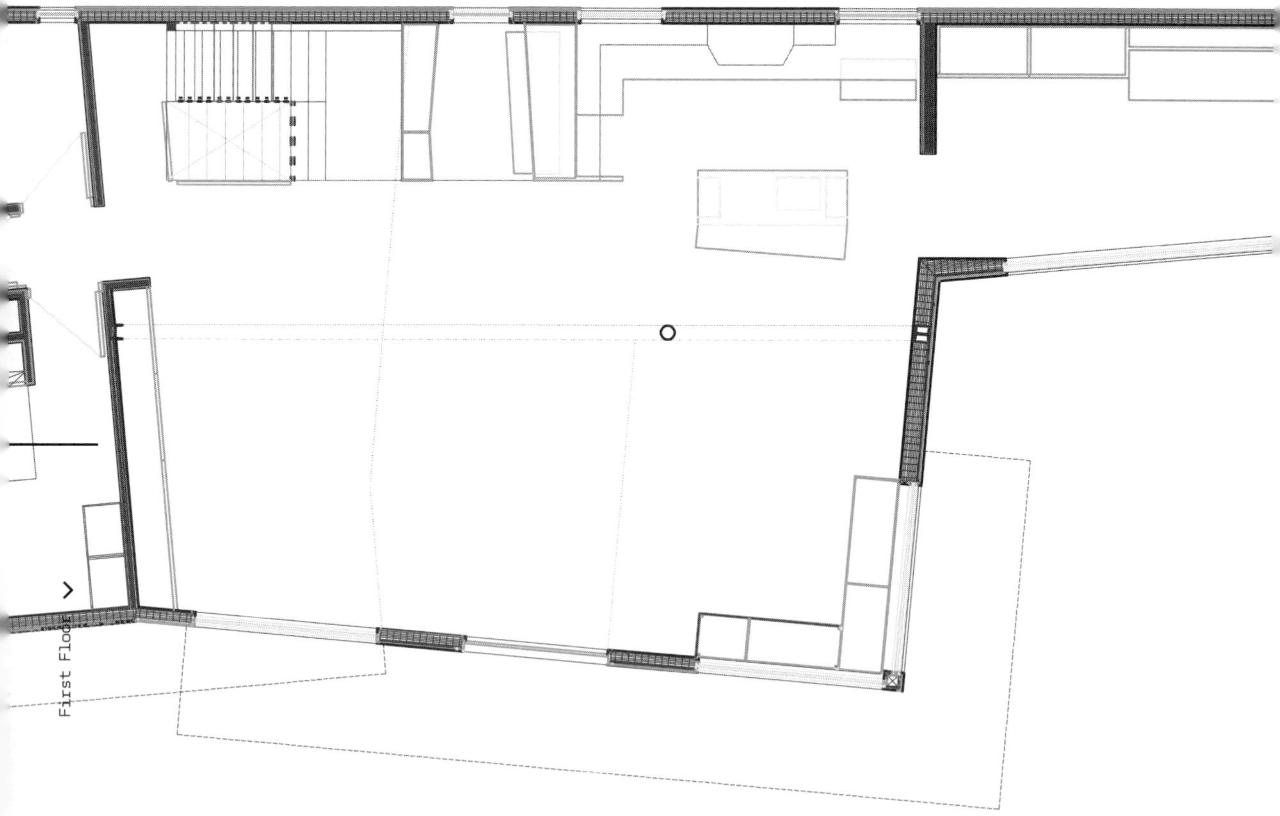
First Floor

insulated glass windows in the winter, in summer it is reflected by the metallic skin, while the home is shaded by using large metal sunshades.

Placement of windows across the space to allow for natural air circulation, along with the incorporation of a whole-house fan on the second floor, encourages strong cross ventilation, while a relatively open plan of the main living spaces further allows for maximum air movement. In a sense, the lack of partition walls is a form of aerodynamic design, allowing breezes to move excess heat out of the space. Through the use of natural and cross ventilation systems, coupled with sun shading devices, the level of dependency on mechanical systems—specifically electricity consumption through air conditioning—can be greatly reduced.

Daylight solar analysis finds the angle of the sun, allowing for the design of maximum shading in the hot summer months. 6-inch exterior walls along with cellulose insulation buffer the elements in both heating and cooling seasons.

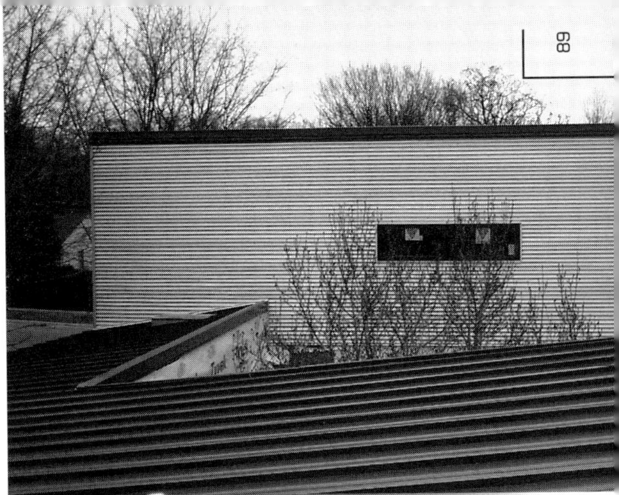

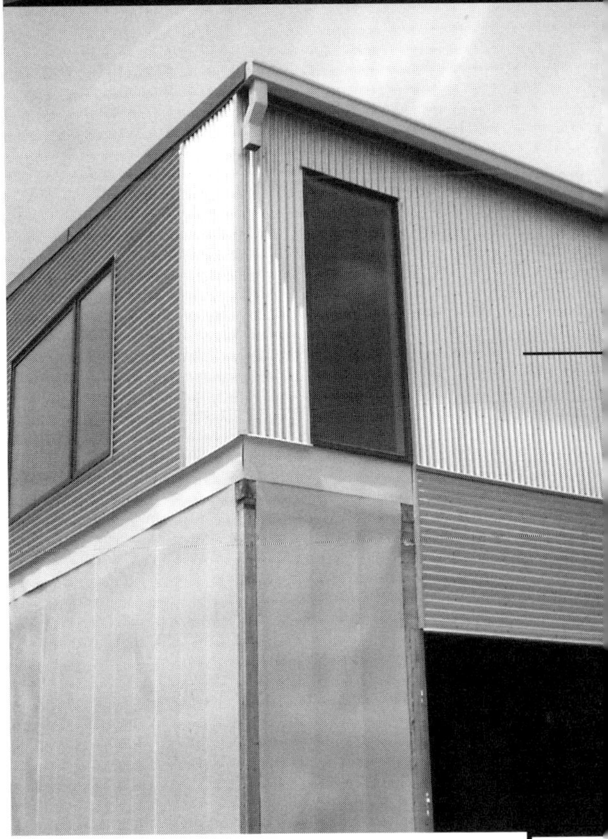

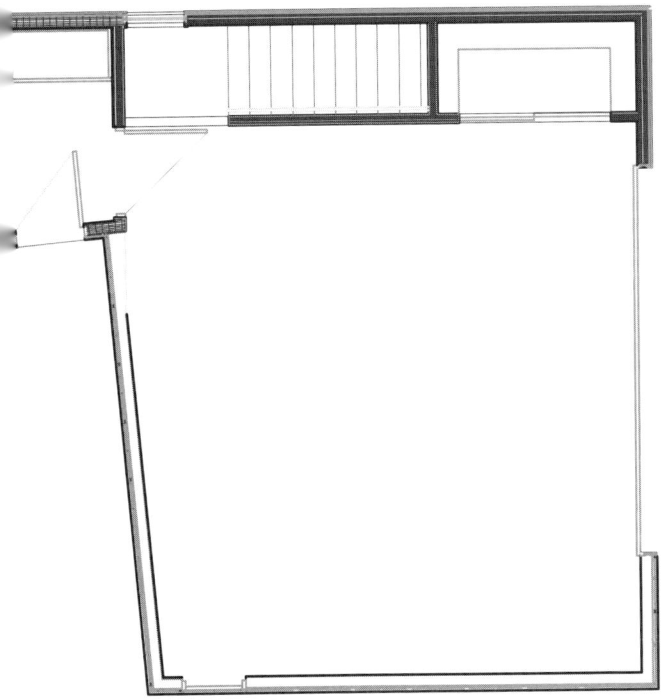

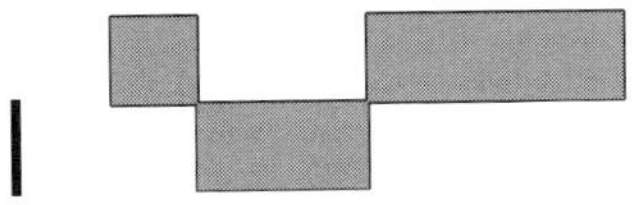

Throughout the design process, certain decisions needed required validation through simulation research. For example, certain construction systems were specified to yield the most efficient energy configuration. While some of these decisions were made through experience, all the elements acting together as a system potentially have a different performance level than each of the elements acting in isolation. In this post-design process, simulation is again utilized to verify that the collective systems—including insulated windows, 6-inch wall construction and cellulose insulation as well as the variety of materials and systems used in the building—act properly in concert with one another to provide the most environmentally responsive solution.

Energy simulation will play an increasingly important role in the design process as new tools and resources equip architects and academics with real-time data to assist in decision making. The objective to create more comfortable, safe, and environmentally friendly buildings will always inspire progress in architectural design and construction. Subsequently, this project—in the context of a body of design, design research and design simulation—seeks to position itself at the interstice between the natural landscape and the artificial landscape. Creating space for both to successfully coexist will serve as a template for future projects and approaches to design, buildings and the city.

The relationship to academic ways of working and thinking are always crucial to keeping a practice fresh, ideas young, and responses nimble. The most important element that our pedagogical system can bring to design training is critical thinking: the ability to analyze history, technology and current architectural practices in order to formulate your position within this matrix can only be generated through research, study, time and reflection, which occur naturally in the academic setting. This environment provides an individual with the opportunity, and ability to formulate architectural attitudes, beliefs and preoccupations. It provides exposure to technologies and simulation tools, as well as allowing time for experimentation and familiarizing with these tools and systems before the rush of project schedules, client demands, budgets, site constraints and the construction process occupy time and thought.

Having a design approach, series of steps and tools already formulated before the first project begins construction is crucial to success in architecture. In this sense, the formulation, testing and streamlining of the design process that happens in the academic environment is crucial for the transition to the construction site. An effective education exposes one to concepts of design, research, simulation, and computer tools and provides a forum for working with these tools in a fashion that prepares one to implement such strategies in the process of design and construction. The development of these requisite tools and attitudes fostered in the academic process through learning and teaching helps to embrace the open-ended nature of architectural design and practice.

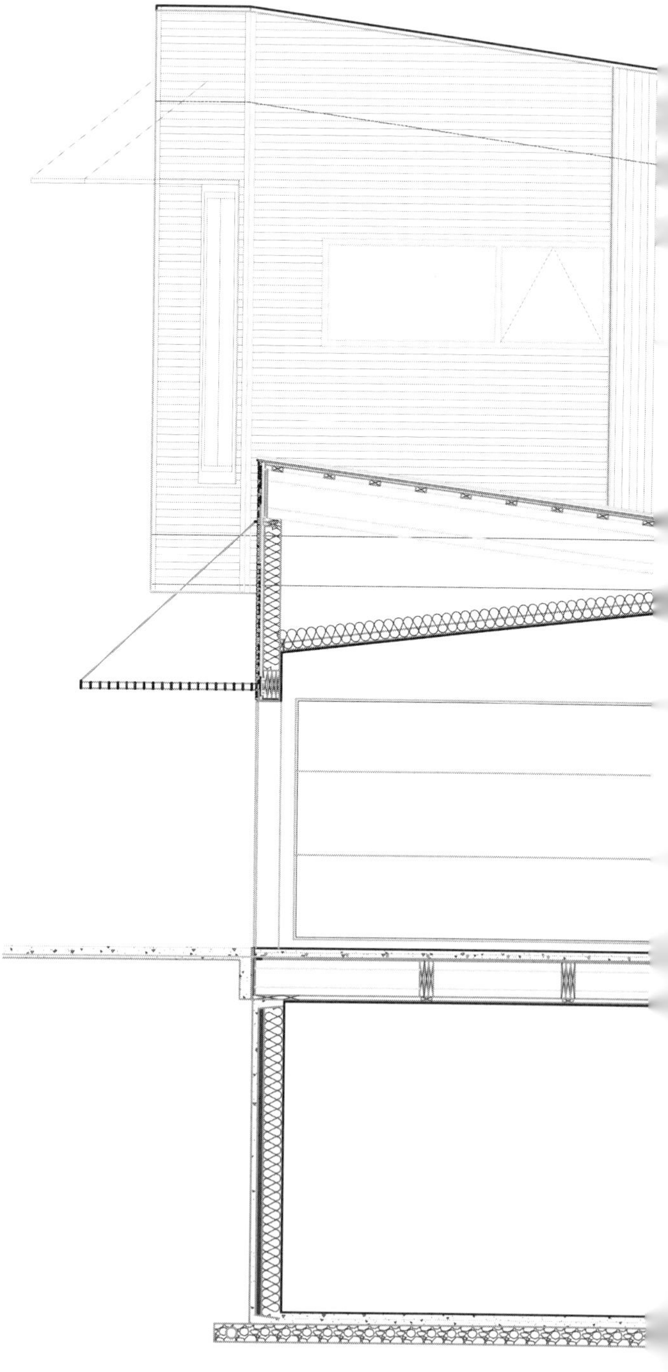

> Section With Suncatcher

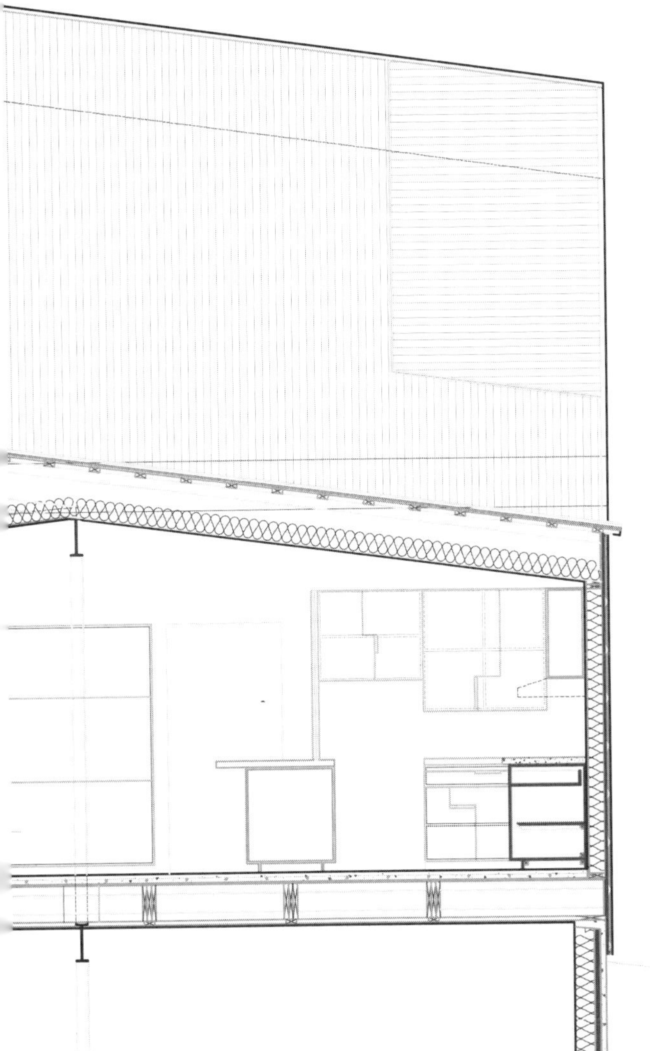

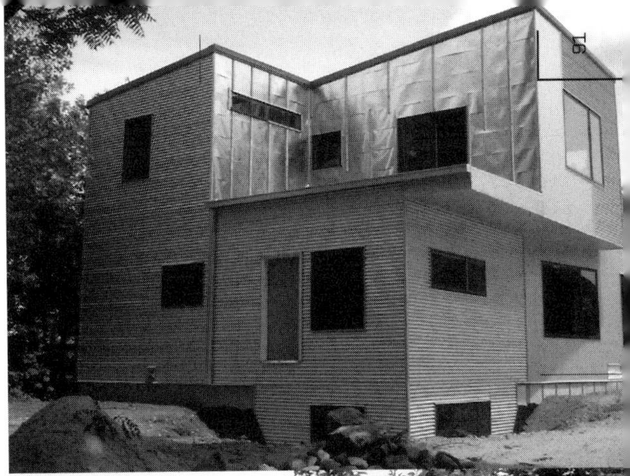

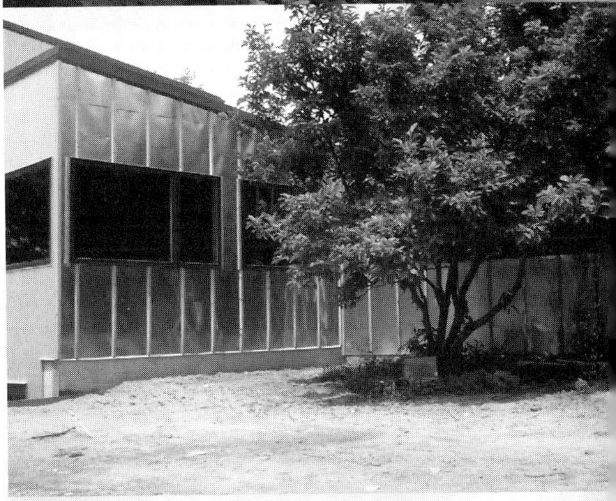

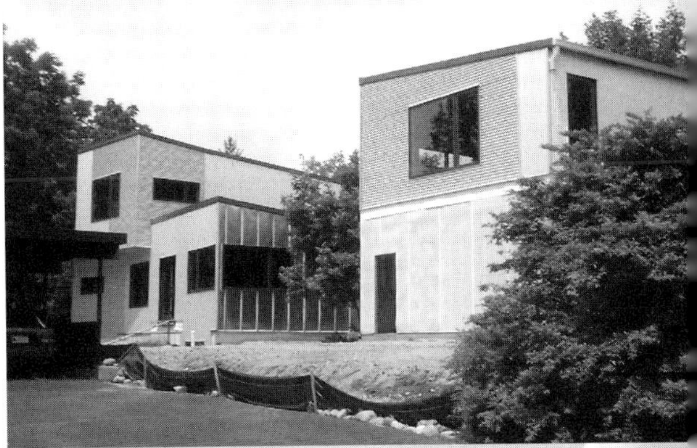

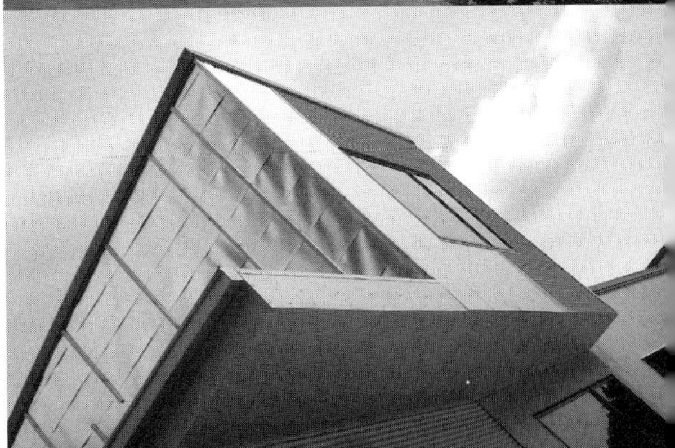

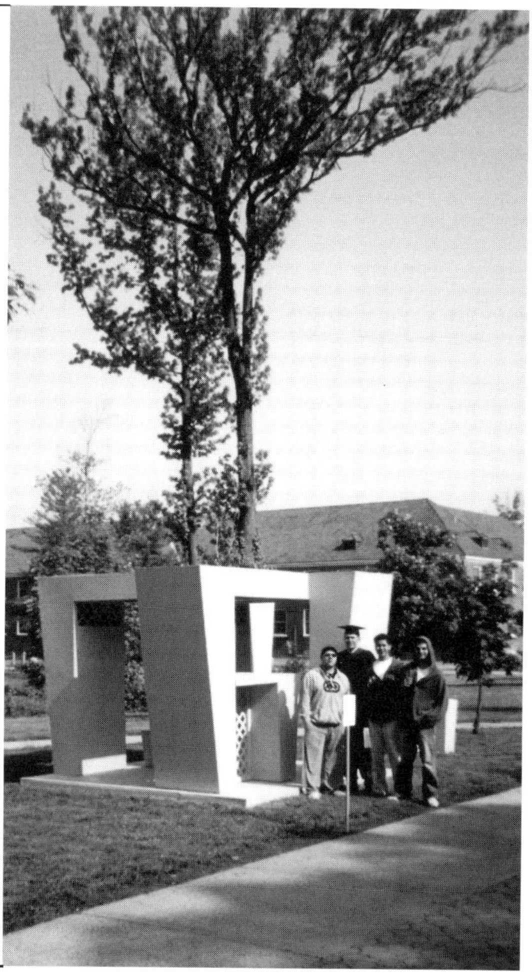

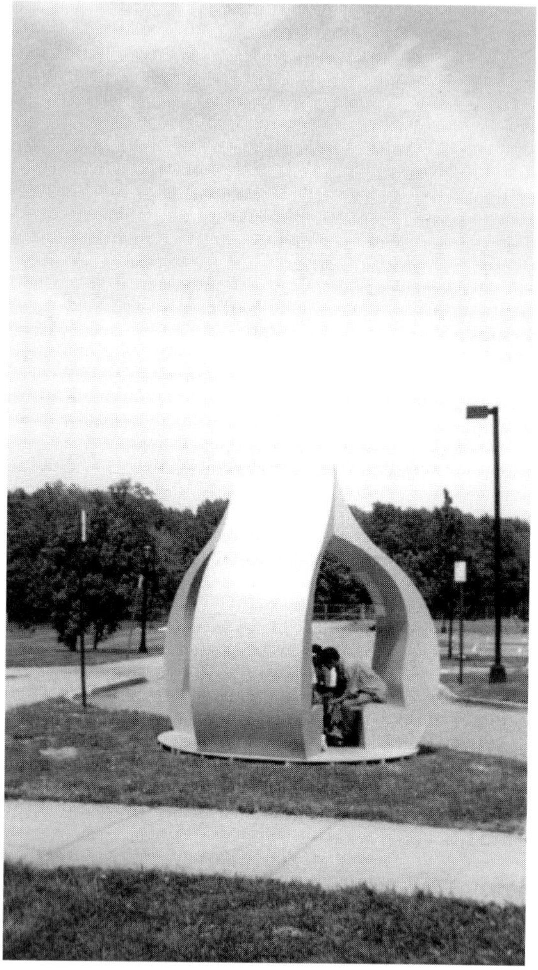

"What is this, and why is it here?"

DESIGN-WHILE-BUILD

by Andrei Vovk and Abe Argibay

After two weeks of hard work in our new woodshop and a night on the site we managed to meet our deadline—graduation ceremony. Around 7:00 AM, when the blue paint, heavily infused with morning fog, was almost dry, a service car approached. A man carrying a bundle of signs mounted on long stalks came out and asked: "What is this, and why it is here?" We were too tired to answer right away. He picked one of his signs and put it right in front of the Pavilion. The sign read "Business and Administration."

By 9:00 AM the campus was filled with crowds of people dressed in black robes. Our new pavilion went unnoticed in all the excitement. At least that's how we felt in the morning, before going home to finally get some rest. Weeks later I heard people talking about kids playing inside, parents taking graduation pictures using the pavilion as a sort of surreal blue frame—some liked it, others didn't seem care, no one seemed to complain. But that early morning unanswered question remained in my mind—"What is this, and why it is here?"

The name *Blue Pavilion* didn't exist before the structure was installed on the site and painted overnight. During planning and design it was called an *Information Kiosk*. We never even considered such questions as—who will operate and maintain it, open and close it, turn the lights on and off. For

Andrei Vovk was born in Moscow in 1962. He received his architecture degree from the Moscow Institute of Architecture and has won several awards in Architecture and Urban Design including the Grand Prix of the Union of Russian Architects. Vovk has worked for almost 10 years with the Michael Sorkin Studio. He has taught at the Moscow School of Architecture, Pratt Institute, CUNY City College and the College of Staten Island. Currently he is working on his own projects and teaching a Design and Build Workshop at CUNY.

Abe Argibay graduated from the architecture program at the College of Staten Island in 2002. He is currently enrolled at the City College of New York. He has a background in construction and architecture.

The authors wish to thank the chair of the Performance Arts Department, Charles Thomas, and Architecture Coordinator, Professor Frank Galati, at the College of Staten Island.

The following students in CUNY CSI Arch400, Design and Build Workshop, 2002 / 2003, contributed their time, energy, cars, trucks, and tools to the completion of this project:

Spring 2003:
Lek Jani, Hysni Duka, Roberto Molina, Anthony Palmiero

Spring 2002:
Abe Argibay, Mark Schneider, Hugh White

graduation it was unmanned—though passersby brought use to it of their own accord, despite the fact that it did not bear any information.

Two years ago I went to the Campus Planning Department and learned that without the signature of a licensed engineer we were not allowed to build and install on campus anything except for street furniture pieces: benches, tables, and trash containers. I don't have this kind of license and don't know anyone who does.

The first pavilion we built, the yellow pavilion, was given the code name *Bus Shelter* in the hopes of avoiding the Campus Planning Department. In fact, it even operated as bus shelter for one day. The campus loop bus pulled over and let some passengers out. Some passengers stepped on the shaky floor of the pavilion, but most walked around it with some trepidation. The next day, the bus driver was reprimanded for changing his route, and never stopped at the pavilion again. Later on the *Bus Shelter* was transformed into a *Pick-Up Place*, conveniently located as it was on the side of a parking lot. Whenever people called for a ride, that was the place to wait for a car. *Pick Up Pavilion*—another name.

At the beginning, I too, thought that the students needed some directions in their design process. A little bit of function, some program—I guess I was wrong after all.

Weeks after the installation I realized that yet another alternative to *Information Kiosk* or *Blue Pavilion* could be *The CSI Campus Entrance*. Sitting right in the center of the campus, this sculpture challenged the existing entrance somewhere far away. Indeed, at the very beginning of the design process we made a sketceterah model of a pavilion in the shape of a spiral staircase and talked about the space under the stairs; what it feels like to sit on the steps or under the steps of some staircase climbing into the blue. The idea was abandoned because the model grew dangerously high very quickly. Nevertheless, I guess we subconsciously kept working with the idea of the stair. In retrospect, looking around, I noticed the lattice we used for our interior space was a very common element in the single-family home entry stair. When the stair went up high, the lattice would cover exactly that under-the-stairs-place.

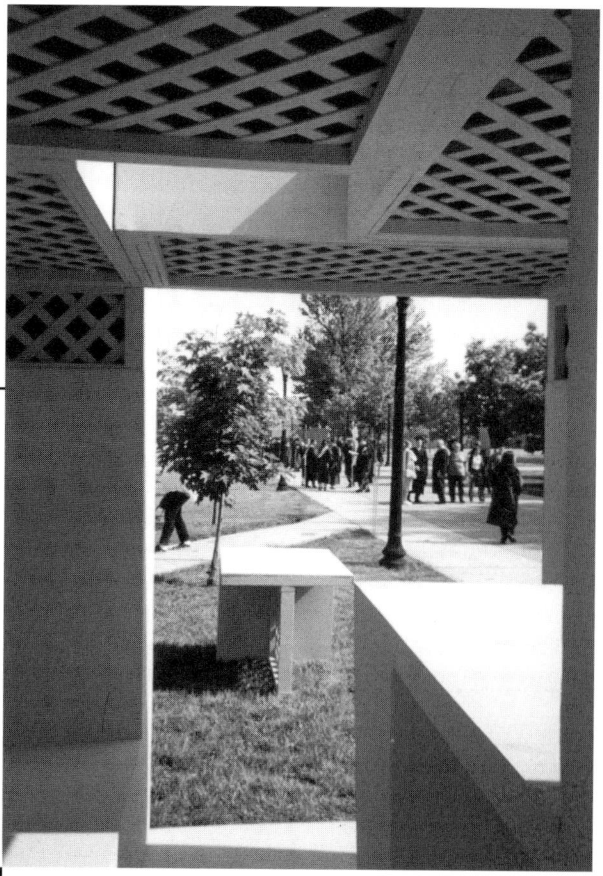

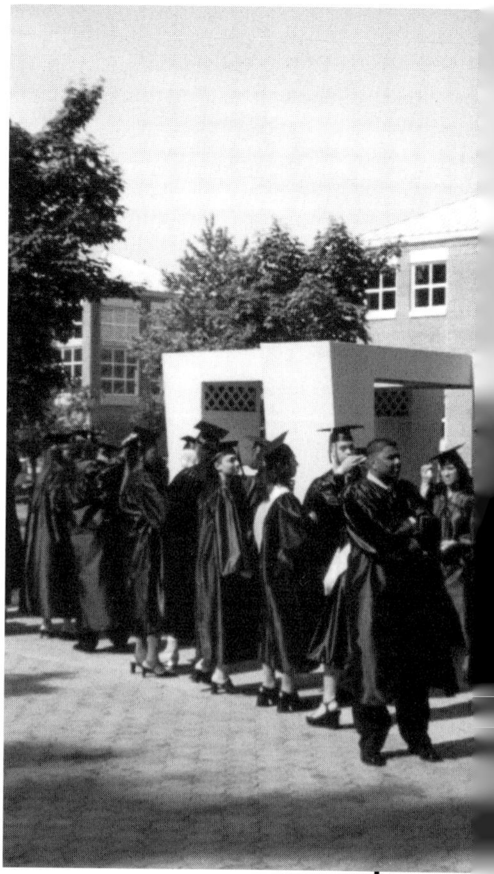

The lattice we used in the interior of the pavilion served a double purpose: to lighten the structure and to visually enlarge the interior space letting us see through the ceiling. From the beginning I wanted to use at least two different material types. One solid and the other translucent. Lattice was an affordable choice of ***translucent*** material. Among all other uses of lattice in buildings around the greater New York City area I noticed the one which all of a sudden matched our abandoned spiral stairs theme—lattice was a common element in a single-family house entry stair. When the front door of such a house is high above the ground level the lattice would cover sides of exactly that under-the-stairs-place. Domestic entrance stairs—could it be the language of our pavilion? It was certainly foreign to that no-kidding-style of campus architecture. Like a ***Stargate*** portal in the wilderness of some unknown planet. Our portal connects the very center of the campus with a very ordinary American suburban image. Imagine, once you step inside the pavilion a magic force that brings you right home. Assuming you live in that suburbia. And most of the students do.

Like the largest of projects, there was a lot that was unknown and unexpected at the very beginning. It was only after the preliminary design for the *Blue Pavilion* was done, drawings ready, and material costs calculated that we got the keys to a large, empty room downstairs.

The room had direct access to a loading dock, through a door merely 3½' wide X. 7' high. This space was to be our woodshop. Suddenly, we had to adjust our pavilion design to the workshop space. The size of the door and height of the ceiling changed everything. We had to reconsider size, weight, and even the number of parts.

We decided on one of two possible sites just at the entrance into the student center. To the left was a badly paved area; to the right, dirt and grass. The structure couldn't have any foundations. That was out of the question—so we had to have a base. Frank Galati, the Architecture Program Coordinator and I would talk about pirate methods of making such installations on the campus. The methods were supposed to beat the endless bureaucracies and internal politics of the college. We thought "Make something first and then let's hope that everybody likes it." We did it—at least the first part—we made the pavilion. The other part—where everybody likes what we did—I am not quite sure. Fifteen minutes after the yellow pavilion was removed I asked a security guard—is it better now? He replied, "I think it's better without it."

We began our studio with studies of the Public Transportation System on Staten Island. It didn't seem to go anywhere until we discovered a bus shelter competition: the program was simple, the sites were given, and there was a promise to build the best entry. We decided to work on bus shelters, and submit our projects as entries for the competition.

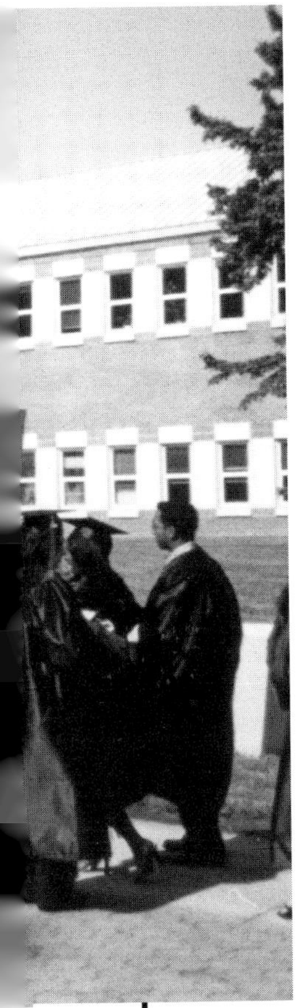

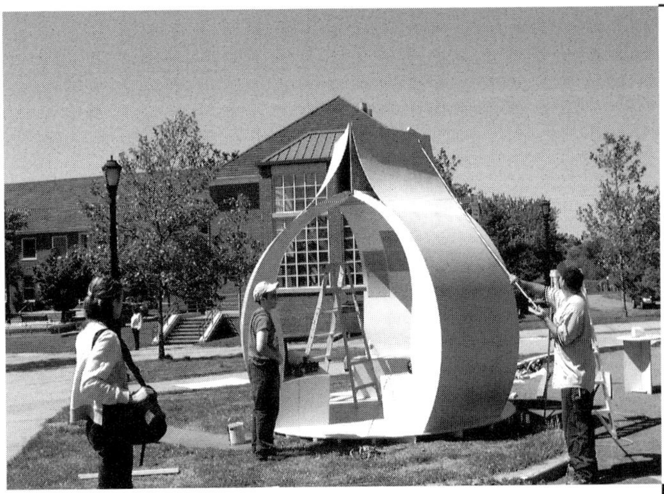

At the same time we tried to concentrate on our own campus loop bus and the bus shelters along its path.

Being a commuter campus, most students arrive at the campus by car. Large parking areas are attached to the main loop road. Those who use the campus bus must traverse large lots to reach the existing bus shelters. We proposed to change the existing bus route—bringing it as close as possible to the buildings on campus—design some new bus shelters, and build one.

At that time we couldn't count on any support from the school. Our budget was limited—less then $1,000. Towards the end of construction, we ran short of materials and time. As a result, the base was not reinforced properly, which led it to pop up in a few months. Another weak spot was the roof, which was constructed with scraps and had no skeletal structure. This was an important area to secure because it takes the brunt of the weather. As we were preparing to build the pavilion we had to determine what kind of materials we wanted to use within our budget. We went to Home Depot—which seems to have a little bit of everything. But, despite of the size of its stores and the quantity of materials and tools to choose from, Home Depot imposes surprising constrains on how and what you want to build.

Most of the products they carry are very traditional. Our desire to explore wider possibilities of materials and to experiment with alternative ways of assembling structures in that environment brought on frustration. In the end, we used 1/4" plywood wrapped around a 3/4" enforced plywood frame to construct the desired curves.

What is a Pavilion anyway? In the beginning of the summer of 2003 I removed the damaged yellow pavilion, which had been struck by a lawn mower, and carefully inspected the parts. To my surprise, everything was in good condition. A structure built with a $1000 budget survived a tough Staten Island winter and if properly patched up could last another few years. Inside, I found a wasp nest. The insects inhabiting the pavilion were buzzing around my head.

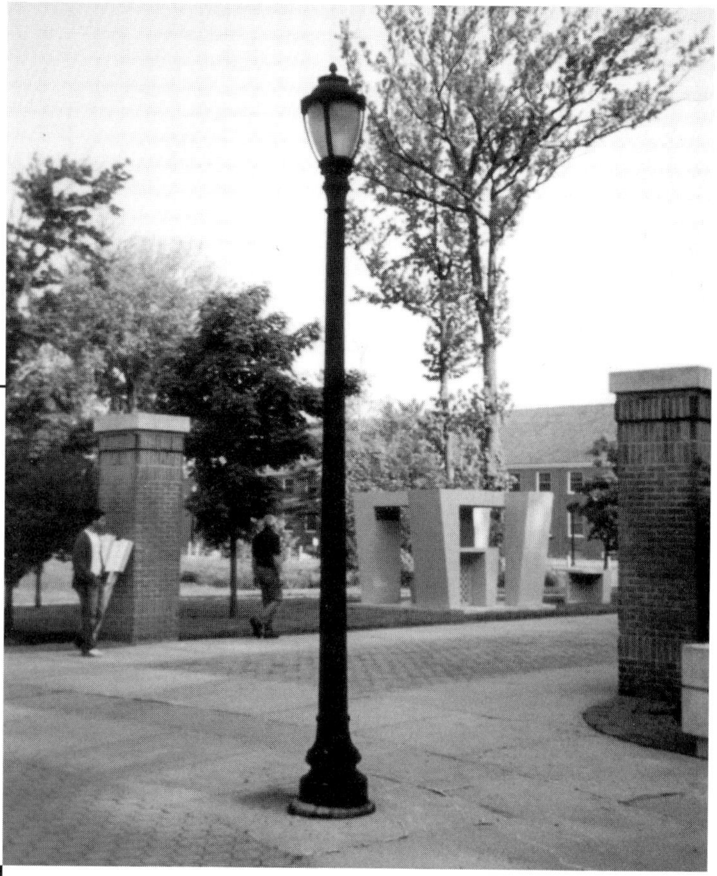

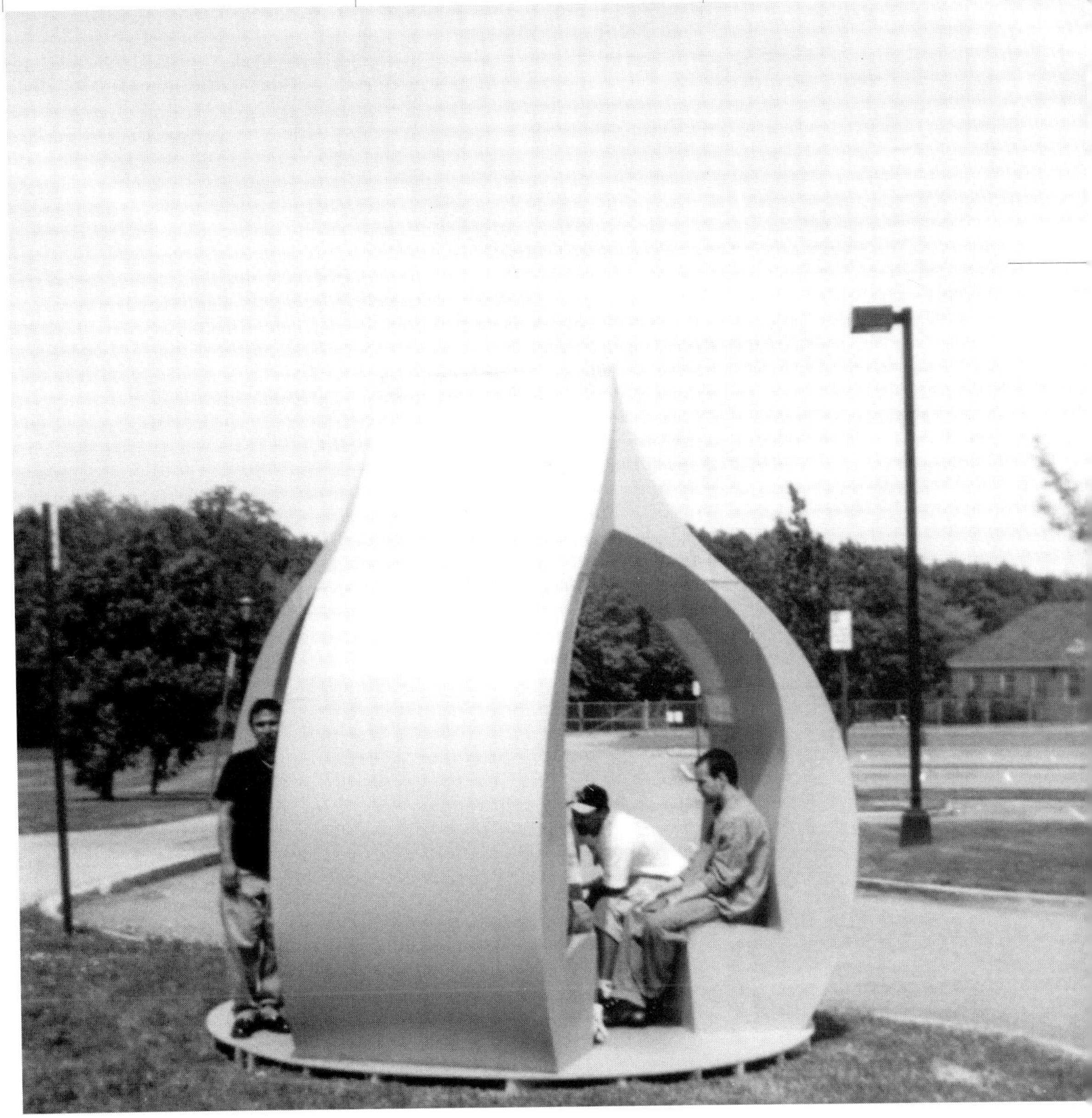

HOW TO: BUILD YOUR OWN PAVILION

Yellow Pavilion Spring 2002
Budget: under $800

Blue Pavilion Spring 2003
Budget: under $1000

All materials are available at the Staten Island Home Depot.

Basic materials:
¼" and ½" plywood, outdoor paint, 2"x3" and 2"x4" pine
Tools:
Hand held power drill, screw drivers, hand saw, and power jig saw.
Life span:
The pavilions are temporary with a maximum 1-year life span, and no maintenance required. Produced in sections, each part can be manipulated by 2 to 3 people and fit through a 3½'x 7' door opening.

Assembled on site in less then 6 hours.

PULP

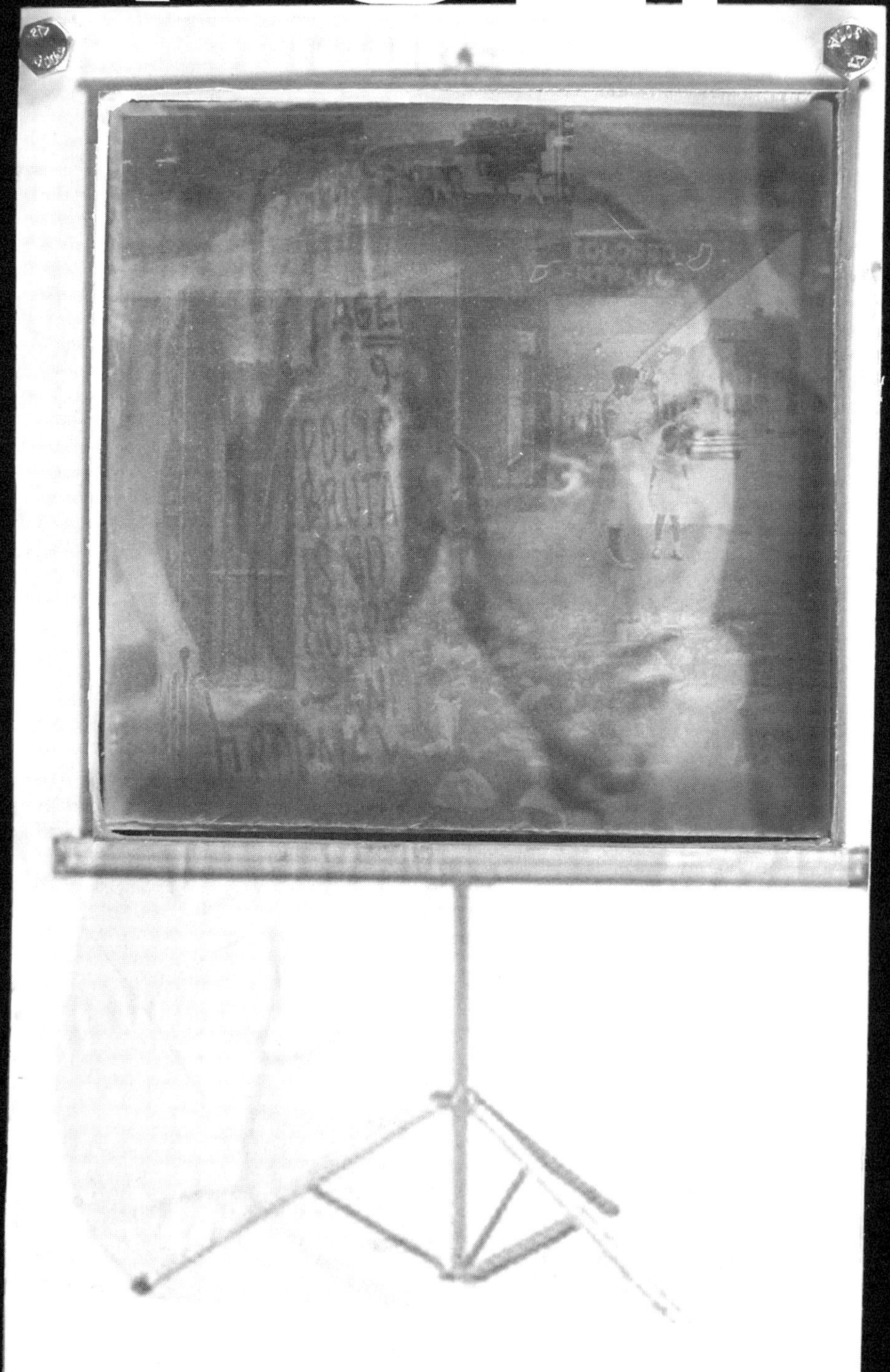

The imagined and built: social constructs and the pedagogy of the "Interrogative Design" studio

ANALYSIS

by colman a. jordan (ebo)

"Design as a research proposal and implementation can be called interrogative when it takes a risk, explores, articulates, and responds to the questionable conditions of life in today's world, and does so in a questioning manner. Interrogative design questions the very world of needs of which it is born. It must respond with a double urgency to such a world. First, it should function as an emergency aid in the process of survival, resistance, and the healing of social, psychological, or physical wounds. Second, it needs to increase and sustain the high level of ethical alertness that creates, in the words of [Walter] Benjamin, a state of emergency understood not as an exception but as an everyday ethical condition, an ongoing motivation for critical judgment toward the present and past to secure a vision for a better future."

Krzysztof Wodiczko [1]

Can architects use design as a tool to interrogate our culture and formulate social critiques? This question is answered in the affirmative if the "education of an architect"[2] embraces what Krzysztof Wodiczko calls interrogative design. Too often there are academic projects that patronize, offend or misrepresent marginalized communities through exclusionary approaches or traditional design conventions that are disconnected from these communities. In this context, non-responsive or non-interrogative design lacks *ethical alertness* and contributes to

coleman a jordan (ebo) is an Assistant Professor at the Taubman College of Architecture and Urban Planning and the Center for Afroamerican and African Studies at The University of Michigan. He holds degrees from Ohio State University and Clemson University (MArch) and has conducted research at the Arkitektskolen i Aarhus and the Royal Academy of Fine Arts in Copenhagen, Denmark. He has spent eight years practicing in the profession, and has been a full-time scholar and academic teacher since 1994.

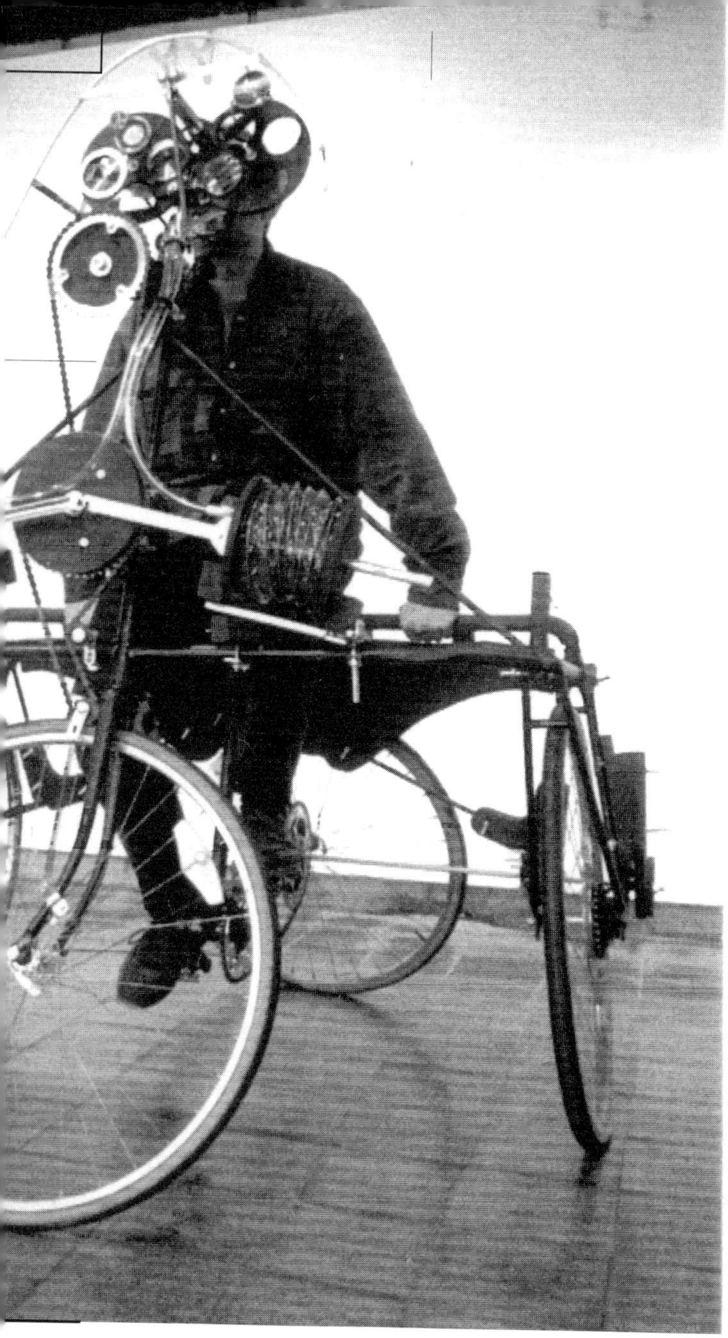
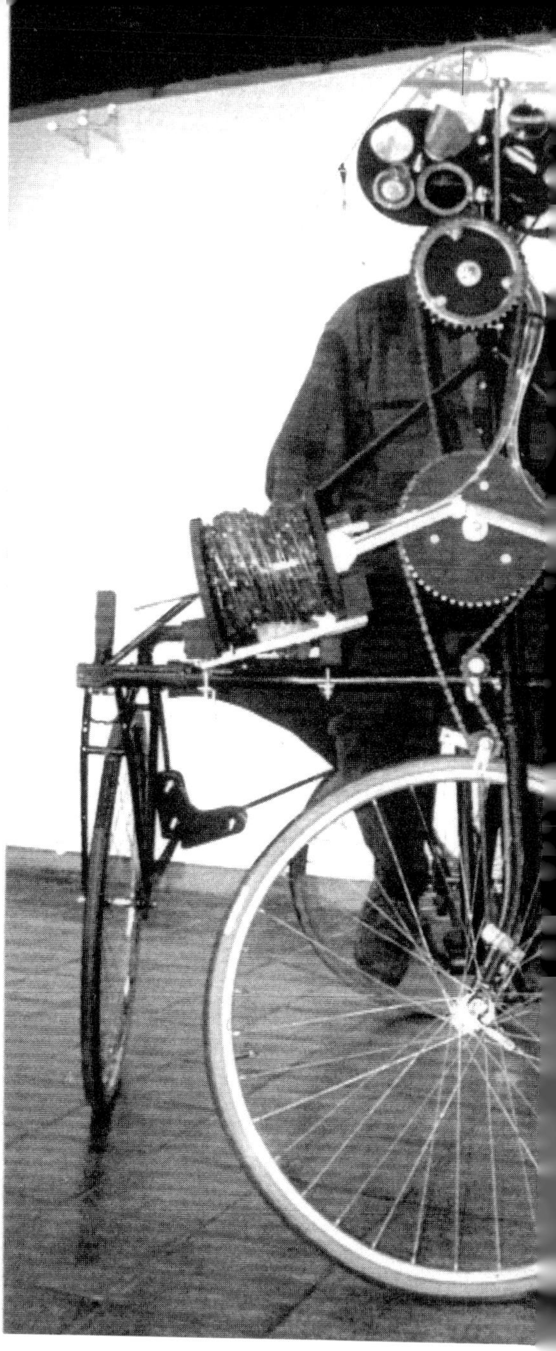

Allen Thornsberry's project mimics American mall culture by creating a spectacle, the 4-wheel bicycle. The apparatuses attached to the bicycle affect the riders experience through rapid breathing mimicking the excitement of consuming products. It disorients the rider by progressively going in circles, accomplishing nothing but anxiety. The bicycle was used as a measuring device to record mall-goers' experience of the American mall culture as spectacle. The goal was to take the information he documented and use it to critique and create the conscious consumer shopping space.

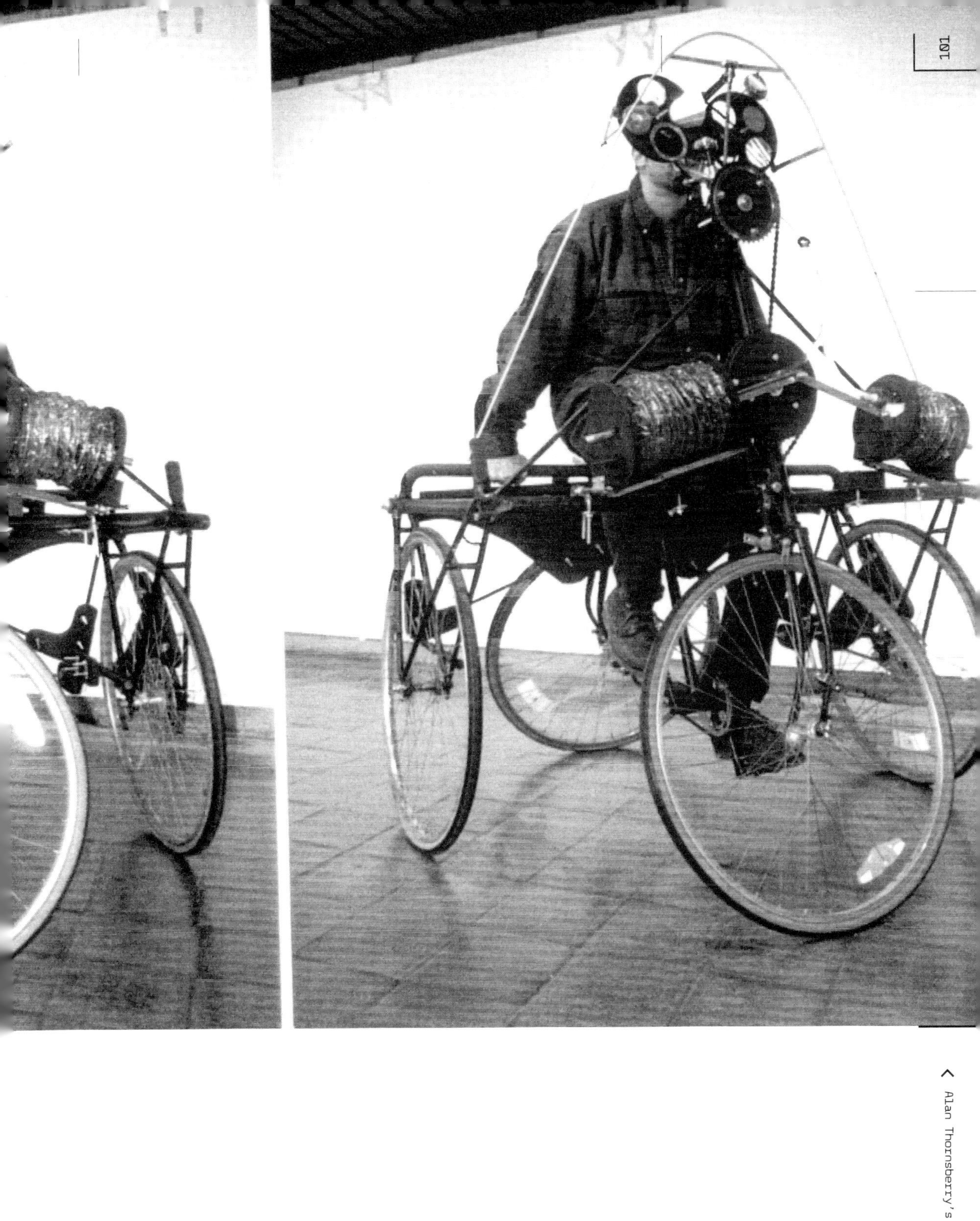

Alan Thornsberry's 4-Wheel Bicycle

> Early Study Model
by Jay Gorman

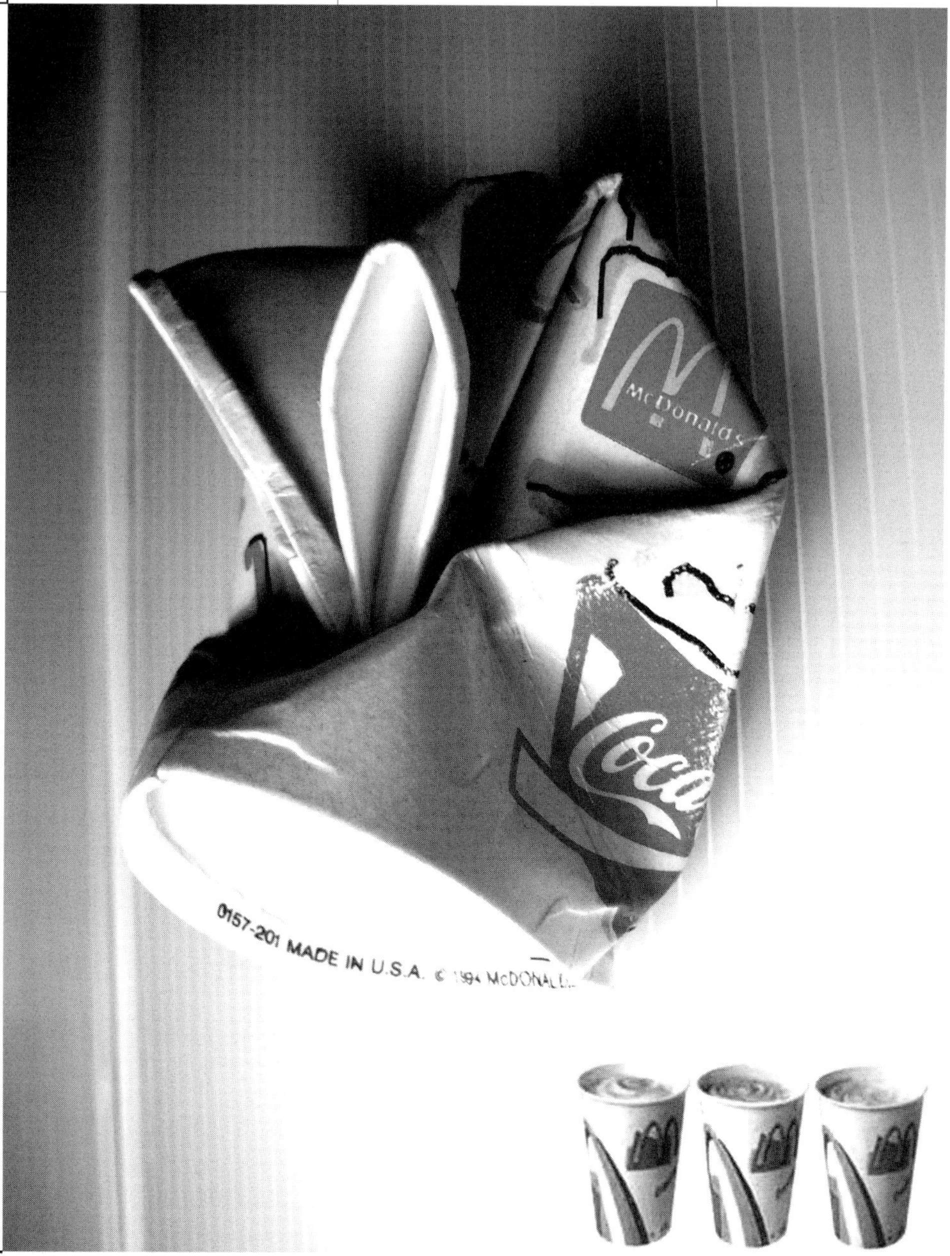

Stemming from the Pulp Analysis studio, Jay Gorman's early study model responded to the consumption of consumer products. Here, the product turns in on itself becoming a useless but dynamic gesture.

"the power of some groups over others and the maintenance of human inequality," stressed by Leslie Kanes Weisman.[3] Design studios are an opportunity to make students examine and critique culture both directly and indirectly and by so doing train them to embrace interrogative praxis and foster social change. The studio work presented here uses the platform of art installation scale-projects to examine ways of bringing interrogative design into the realm of the architecture/design studio. By using a thesis approach to questioning design in studio, the opportunities are open for students to explore social (race, class, gender, sexuality...), communal or functional issues. These projects challenge the space between art and architecture as installation work tends to do.

At the University of Michigan, it is my attempt to break the traditional approach to architectural education via interrogative design—to question beyond the realm of the *building / object*. What is then reated is a product that communicates at many levels and assists students in developing critiques of his or her environment and the tools that architects/designers have at their disposal. Although non-traditional, the projects produced foster the language of architecture/design through materials, connections, spatial interrogations, interaction, and integration. The scale of the projects is manageable and addresses the scale of the human body.

Pulp, Love, and X-istence: Three Studios and Three Agendas

The studio process presented here embraces interrogative design, asking students to propose an interdisciplinary thesis on the basis of spatial analyses of everyday cultural environments. The projects come from three separate studios taught at the University of Michigan and are concerned with redefining the *education of the architect. Pulp Analyses: (...?)*, critiques American popular culture within social contexts of identity as race, gender, class, and sexuality.

The second studio, '*I LIKE TO WATCH': Politics and Cultural Landscapes of Strangelove and Chance*, uses film as a springboard to critique American culture and encouraging the student to situate projects within physical landscapes that reflect American historic, political, and social developments since the 1960s. The third, *This studio does NOT X-ist: Deconstructing the Politics of (In)Visibility* brings praxis and theory together by developing projects with the client—the American Indian Family Health Center in Detroit, Michigan—by critically examining the implications of cultural identity through the built environment.

Each studio emphasizes that the projects assume that the architect has a social / political role to play through the design process, posing this question to the student: where does the designer draw the line between theory and praxis? Assuming that a socially engaged designer does not resolve these issues on his or her own, each student is paired with a faculty member from a discipline related to the student's specific theoretical approach (e.g., a psychologist, sociologist, philosopher, etc.). The projects discussed below also respond to the issues and concerns related to the challenges and limitations faced by design in a contemporary, political, and social climate.

The goals of the projects are as follows. First, to design full-scale projects that communicate at every level—materials, client, graphics, and verbal presentation. The design outcome is to have the students develop a design language of their own that would assist them in both constructing the physical manifestation of and communicating the argument behind their project. Second, the projects are spatial: the scale is relative to the design communicated by the student. Third, the students are to be critical of the outcome of the design process and finished product.

Last, the studios engage larger issues raised. Is it building or not? Is it architecture or not? The projects are critical and spatial, exploring the realms of the body within social space. The most important outcome is that each student can bring an issue to the table, a table that becomes a platform for discourse and spatial interpretation.

Pulp Analyses: *Thing-ifying* Space in *Cult*-ural Fiction

Thing-ifying is a process wherein elements acquire significance or meaning only in relation to their functions over time.

The springboard for this studio's pulp productions was Quentin Tarantino's cult classic film, *Pulp Fiction*. The projects arose from scenes in the film that were identified by each student as most important to communicating issues central to American cultural identity. The scenes were then analyzed based on social and theoretical concerns related to topics such as gender, race, religion, addiction, violence, power, chaos, and order.

> HONEY BUNNY
> *So you don't want to be a bank robber?*
> PUMPKIN
> *Naw, all those guys are goin' down the same road, either dead or servin' twenty.*
> HONEY BUNNY
> *And no more liquor stores?*
> PUMPKIN
> *What have we been talking about? Yeah, no-more-stores. Besides, it ain't the giggle it usta*

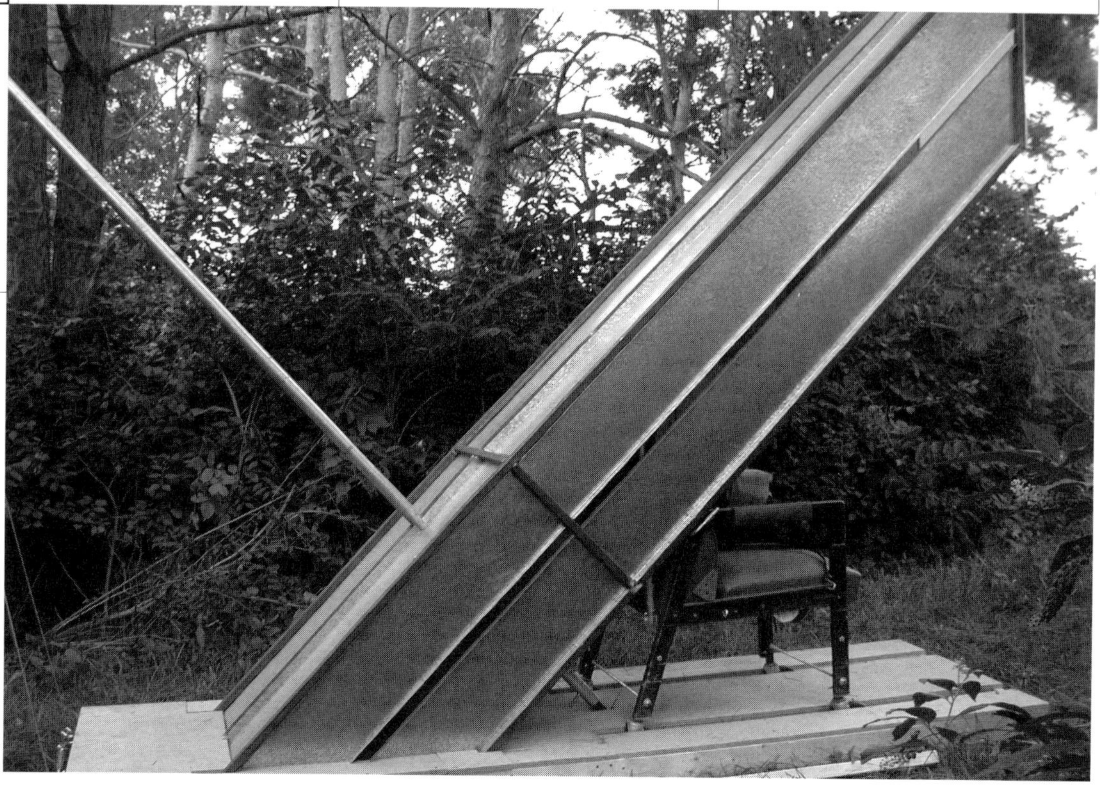

to be. Too many foreigners own liquor stores. Vietnamese, Koreans, they fuckin' don't even speak English. You tell 'em: 'Empty out the register.' They don't know what the fuck you're talkin' about. They make it too personal. We keep on, one of those gook motherfucker's gonna make us kill 'em.
HONEY BUNNY
I'm not gonna kill anybody.[4]

In this scene Quentin Tarantino has two soon-to-be robbers, complete with thick Australian accents, play out a xenophobic and conflicting scene of racist, sexist, and foreign commentary. This discussion takes place in a general/non-descript coffee shop in Los Angeles that HONEY BUNNY and PUMPKIN are about to rob. Pulp Fiction is layered with similar scenes that combine lurid text with Tarantino's spectacular display of American cultural stereotypes (*e.g.*—women as possessions, the threatening black male and his de-masculinized, non-threatening nemesis, the meek black male, foreigners bewildered by America, etc…). The film's ultimate racial statement for the 90's comes when the *BIG* black male is sodomized by a police officer (dare I say, the justice system) in the back room of a pawnshop. The spaces where the film takes place are very generic but the characters are socially dynamic; a perfect setting for architectural studio projects to critique space and the implications of cultural stereotypes.

In the students' projects the cinematic spaces were transformed and reconstructed to capture spatially-through built material forms—the social issues they addressed. The studio reified / *thing-ified* these cinematic spaces by having students make/build their own spatial responses while using multimedia forms of representation to create objects that we later on referred to as *spectacles*. Therefore, the narrative of the studio progressed from a reaction to the spectacle of *Pulp Fiction*, through the design process of student response-interpretation, to the spectacle of displayed objects they produced. All objects were then put on display as a collective exhibit/spectacle at the end of the semester, against the backdrop of the film.

I LIKE TO WATCH: Politics and Cultural Landscapes of Strangelove and Chance

'I LIKE TO WATCH': Politics and Cultural Landscapes of Strangelove and Chance, combines film analysis with interpretations of the built, un-built or imagined environment as a means to interrogate undercurrents of power and control in our society. The films used for analysis are: Stanley Kubrick's 1964 masterpiece, *Dr. Strangelove, Or: How I Learned to Stop Worrying and Love the Bomb*, a satirical, provocative black comedy/fantasy regarding doomsday and Cold War politics and featuring an accidental, inadvertent nuclear attack; and the

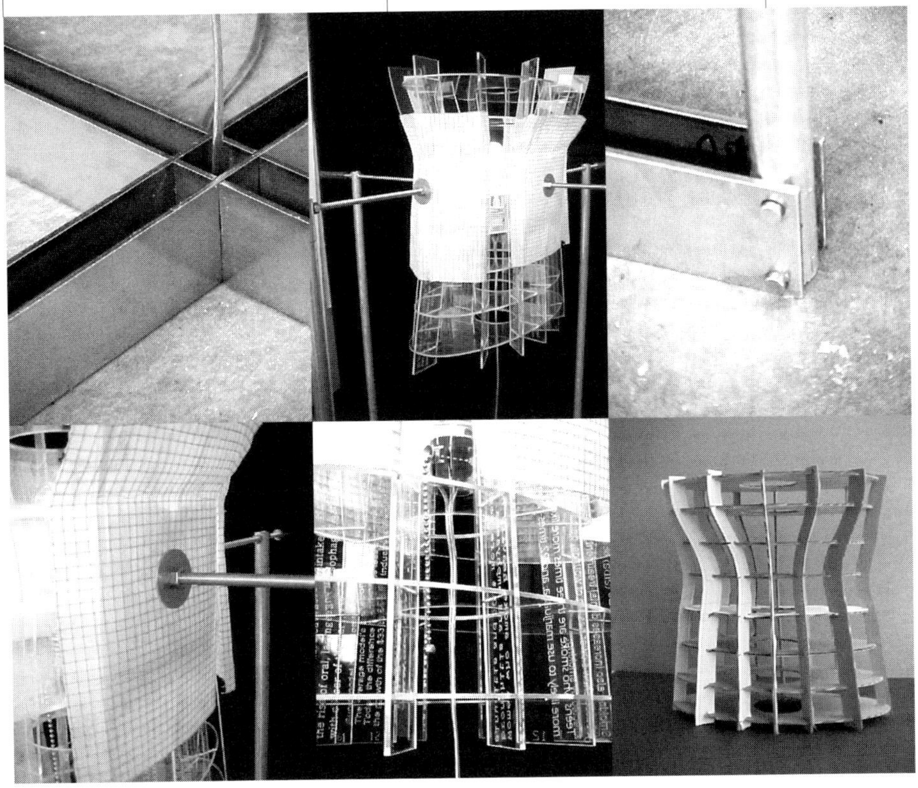

Corset Space: Take Back the Night, Light by Nikki Ross

> "If we think about boundaries from the point of view of the new sciences, the boundaries of our bodies are not edges of three-dimensional containers into which we put certain things (food, air, and water) and out of which other things emerge (food and water wastes, air, blood, etc.). The boundary is an event-horizon, in which one form (myself) meets the potentiality for transforming itself into another form or forms (the not-self). Such a body-boundary neither entails containment of internal forces nor repulsion of/protection against external forces. Those who are aware of themselves as centered inside an insulated container–free from contamination by the threatening other which is located outside are captured by an illusion generated by the mechanisms of ego-protection, as well as by spatial models inherited by a classical science which is now outmoded."
>
> Christine Battersby[5]

Christine Battersby argues that the Western concept of body as container is masculine in nature. The feminine body is not constructed as a container, but is rather defined by the boundaries constructed around it. In response to Battersby's theory, this project interrogated commercial landscapes of feminine images and values, as reflected in advertising and commercial images, in relation to historical concepts of the feminine form. The project re-imagines the feminine body, represented by the dissipative energy of a light bulb, and constrained by the boundaries of the corset within which the light is placed. The torso is a translucent shape/constricting garment molded by socially constructed masculine values.

Take Back the Night, Light is two-fold. A light at pedestrian (such as a street light) level brightening dimly lit streets, buildings, and allies to lead the paths of women "taking back the night." Secondly, it exposes the conflicting implications of gender "equality" and exploitation of gender-biased advertising by reminding women to reclaim both the night and their bodies.

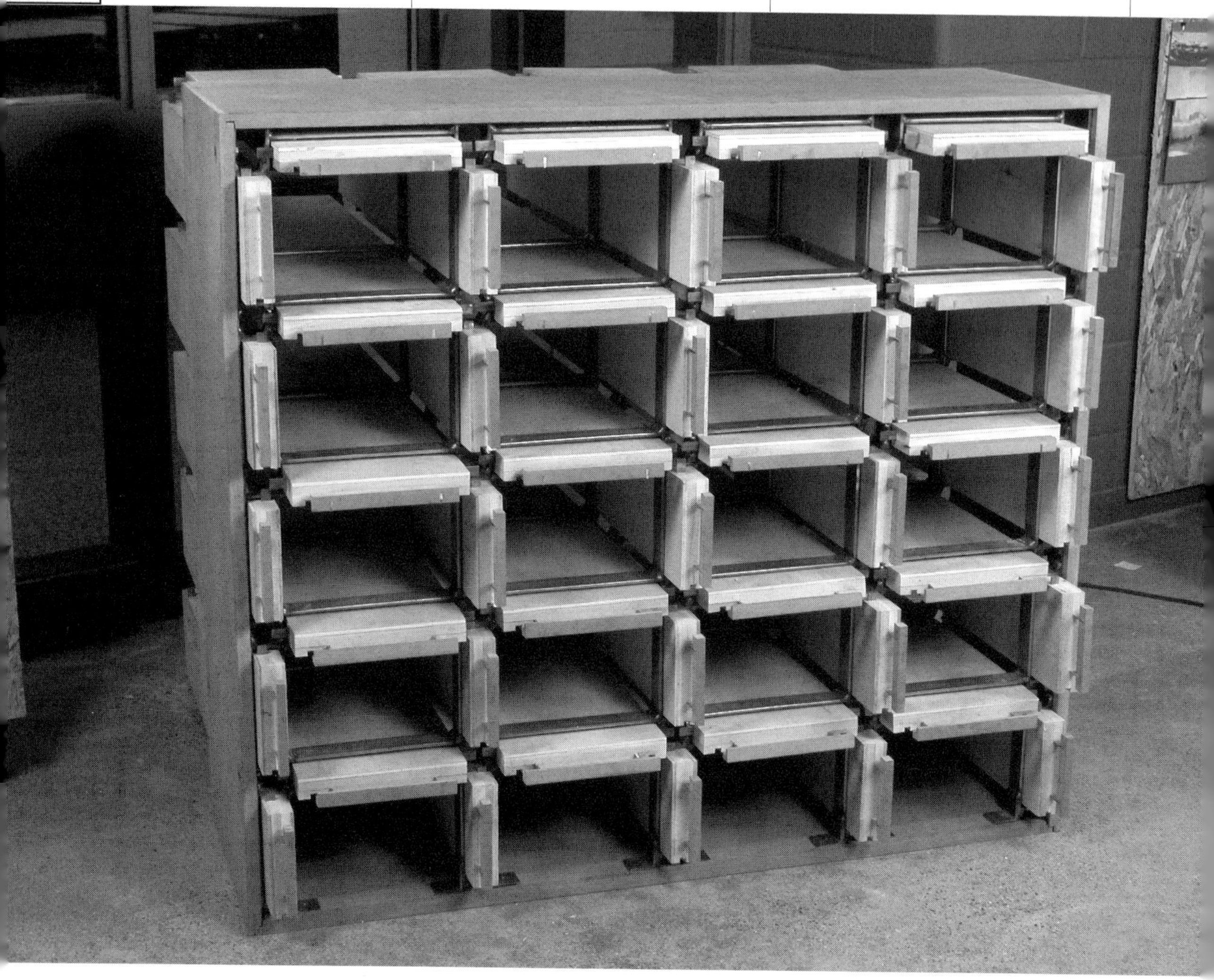

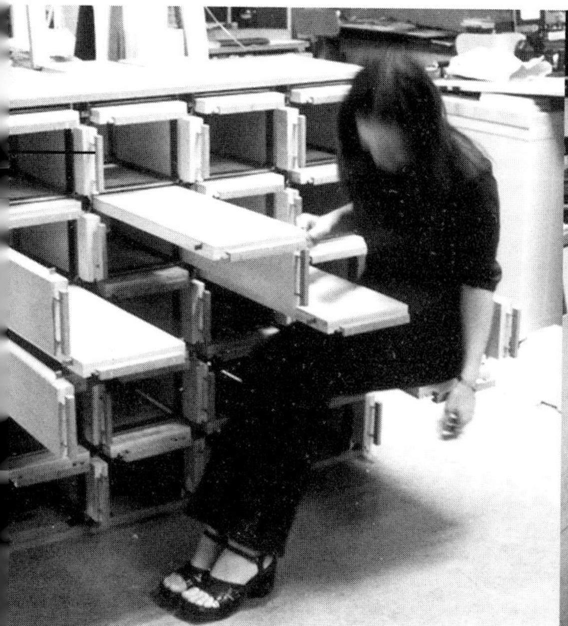

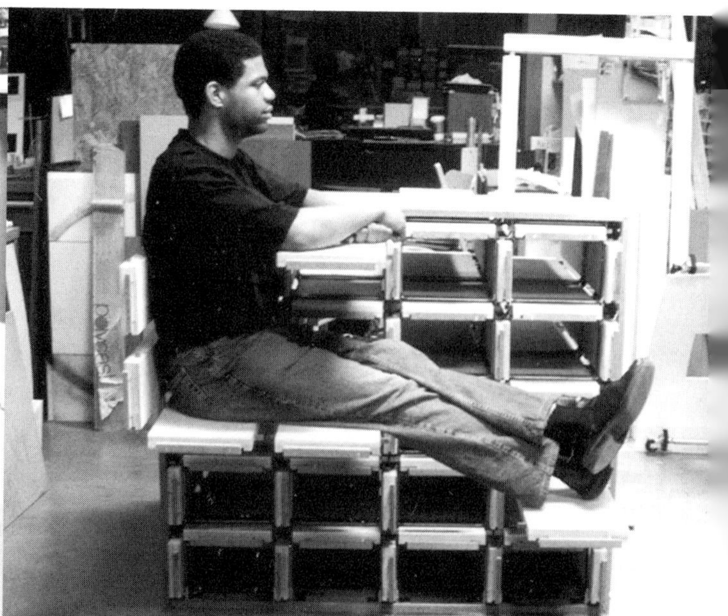

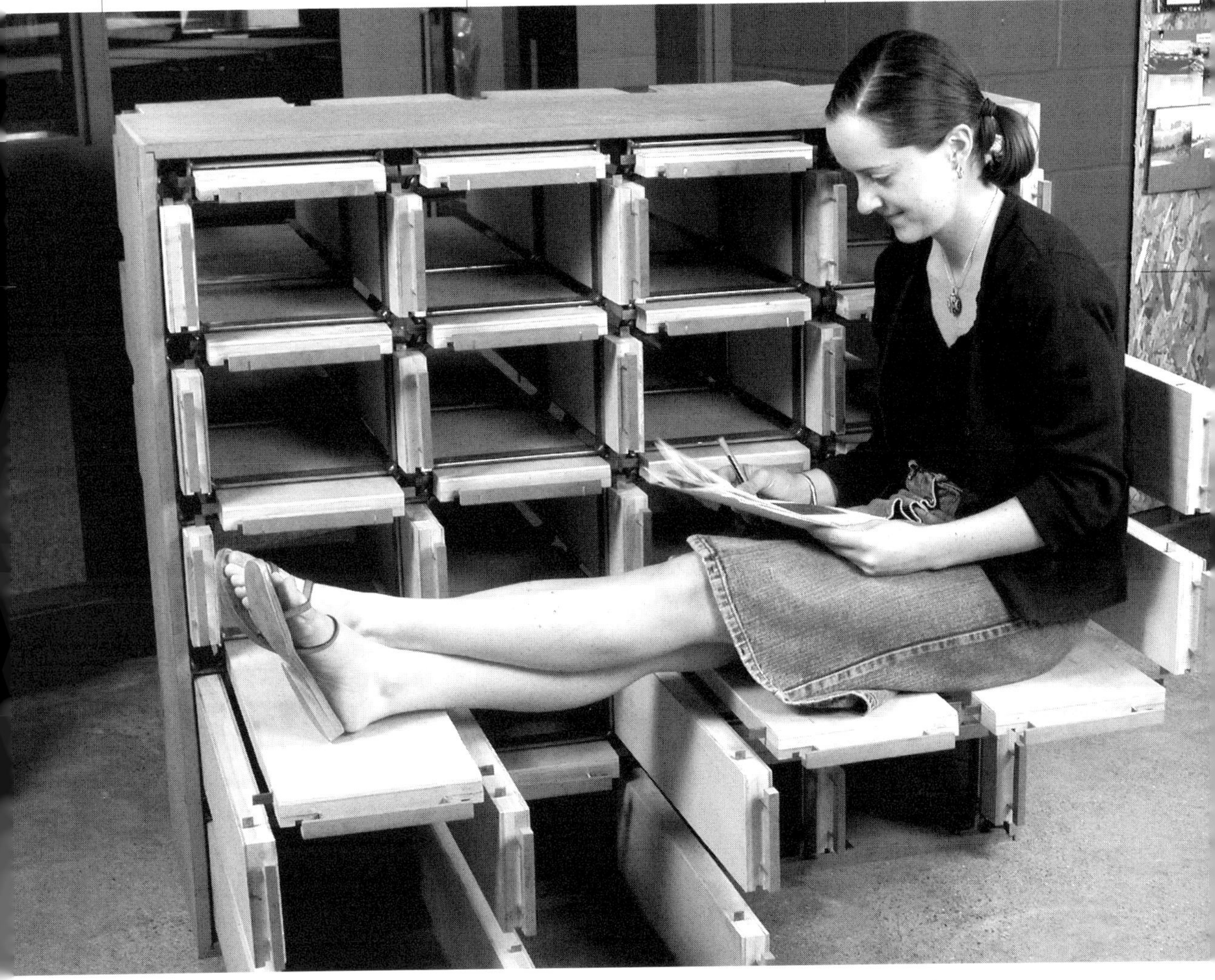

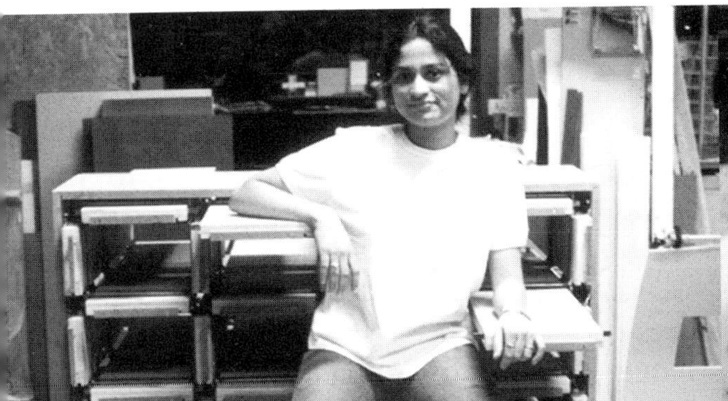

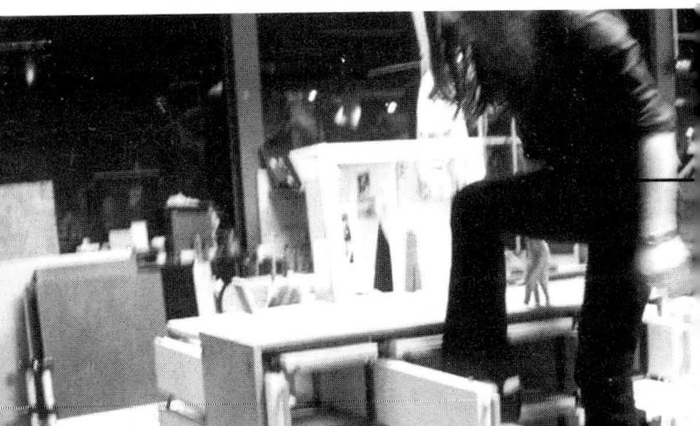

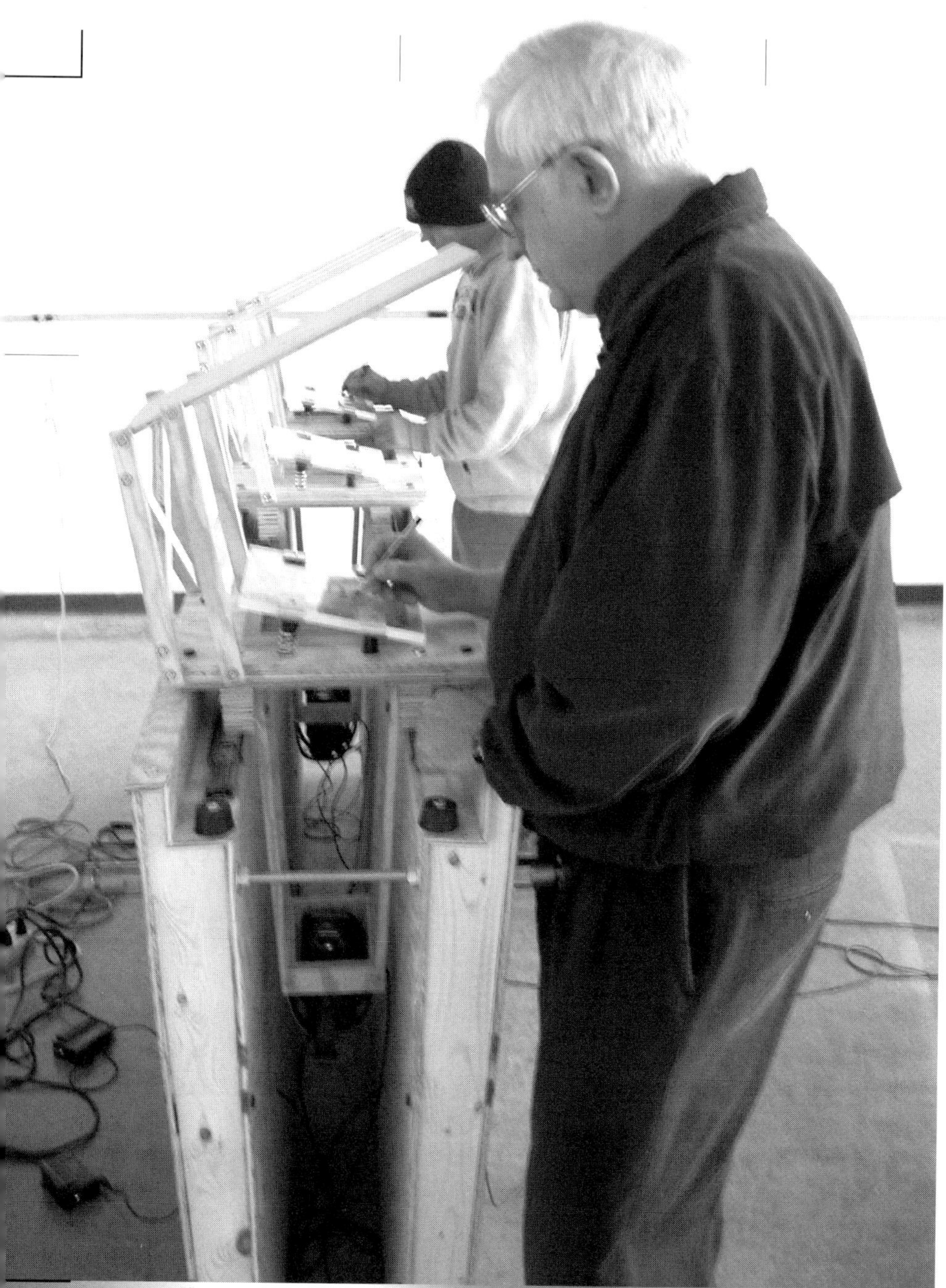

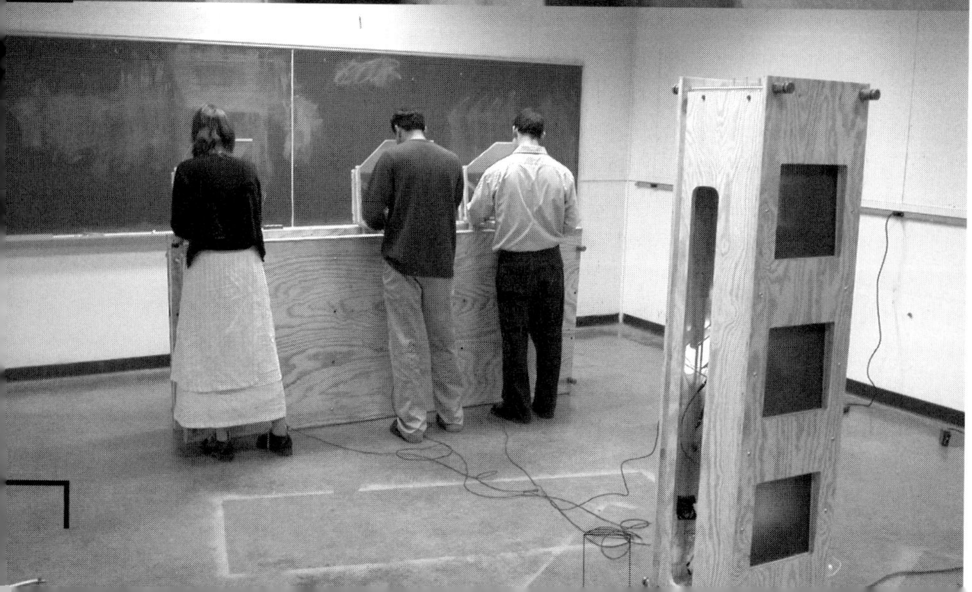

The Group Confessional by Todd Beyerlein

Passing the rock is a traditional event that takes place around a camp-sized fire that is kindled with tobacco and sage at the site of the American Indian Family Health Center. As the community members sit around the fire, one or more may intentionally bring a hand-sized stone into the circle. Once exposed, the member holding the rock is allowed to speak to any member against whom she or he may have a specific complaint. This type of confession is common among many groups within Detroit's Urban Native community. The Health Center also occupies a de-sanctified Catholic Church where they hold their community social events as well as tutorial programs for both the youth and elderly. Todd's project takes advantage of both of these scenarios by flipping the concept of the confidential Catholic confessional and allowing the community to experience a *public confessional* that allows them to document important words of wisdom or confess on individual issues.

1979 classic *Being There*, directed by Hal Ashby and based on a screenplay by Jerzy Kosinski whose main character, CHANCE, an illiterate gardener, is accidentally mistaken for a genius, becomes the country's hottest politician, and is desired as its sexiest male amidst the *videot* culture that thrives on manufactured images and fantasies of power. Both films critique and expose the underpinnings of our social and political environment and question the undercurrents of power and control in relation to such aspects of identity as race, class, gender and sexuality.

"Design as a research proposal and implementation can be called interrogative when it takes a risk . . ."
Krzysztof Wodiczko

Introducing the *risk*: the MACHINE

ma-chine n. 1 apparatus using or applying mechanical power, having several interrelated parts. 3 controlling system of an organization, etc.

The Oxford Pocket Dictionary and Thesaurus, 1997

The idea of a machine emerges as analogous to the stereotypically masculine connotations of the films used in this studio and, at the same time, compels critiques of American masculinity as a social construct. The very word machine relates to masculine stereotypes: It is power-driven and controls its own function and outcome; hence it connotes a *controlling system*. In *Dr. Strangelove* we see masculine power and control exercised over nations and humanity. The actual and imagined machine is an extension of what man is capable of—DESTRUCTION. The bomb brings about the total obliteration of land and society. In *Being There* we see man as machine, a dumb, TV-generated object/human. Chance is designed and manufactured by man's own video environment. *Being There* is a scathing critique of 1970s popular and political culture, which Kosinski envisions as projecting America's millennial destiny.

Students' interrogative design projects take on fictitious, cinematic texts and their authentic historical contexts as springboards for generating arguments about social issues concerning present design and architectural practices. Each student creates a contextualized, spatial machine (the unfamiliar) to communicate her or his development of a constructed language of architecture. The studio uses machine as a metaphor and poses it against an environmental landscape. As a design tool, the machine helps to remove the student from the familiar or previously conceived notions of architectural design (i.e., a house, an institutionalized structure or general form making). It pushes them to interrogate aspects of design, as well as serving as an imperative to work within the language of architecture to actually construct these projects. The majority of the students in this studio have never physically or critically built anything using the architectural materials that they reference daily. These projects give them an opportunity to invent / reinvent elements of design and communicate an idea through research, detail, and material.

This studio does NOT X-ist?

"I am __ invisible ___.
No, I am not a spook like those who haunted Edgar Allan Poe; nor am I one of your Hollywood-movie ectoplasms. I am ____ of substance, of flesh and bone, fiber and liquids—and I might even be said to possess a mind. I am invisible, understand, simply because people refuse to see me. Like the bodiless heads you see sometimes in the circus sideshows, it is as though I have been surrounded by mirrors of hard, distorting glass. When they approach me they see only my surroundings, themselves, or figments of their imagination—indeed, everything and anything except me."

Ralph Ellison, *Invisible Man*[6]

The third project challenged students to bring praxis and theory together while working on site and with a client. The client is the American Indian Family Health Center, whose Director, Lucy Harrison, identifies herself ethnically as an Ojibwa Native. During the 1950s and 60s under the Relocation Act for the People of the First Nation (Native Americans), the U.S. cities promised to relocate the Native Americans from the reservations and into the urban mainstream. Many American cities today are populated with a critical mass of Native Americans but politically their voice and concerns are rarely heard. Within this context, Lucy and I decided that the excerpt from Ralph Ellison's Invisible Man would provide a catalyst to begin questioning popular representations of the Native public. Detroit's Native American (Urban Natives) population is approximately 12,000 and growing. The health center is one of the largest in the country and services Urban Natives from many ethnic backgrounds. The Center was created to assist in obtaining proper health care in an environment that is concerned with cultural preferences for cure, care, and social interactions.

This studio requires, in addition to seeking assistance from other disciplines, students to participate in the events organized by the Native community and involve its members in the design process. Eager for interaction, the studio takes part in weekly community socials and solstice events called Pow Wows. The specific project agendas were to be decided by meetings with the community and studio/student

The Urban Native Threshold by Anjali Hulbanni
Threshold into American Indian Family Health Center

The Urban Native Threshold, interjects the element of threshold as both sign and symbol to identify the Health Center and the Urban Native as well as welcoming the outside surrounding community that encompasses a more diverse community of people. The signage takes advantage of the Native American *color flag*. This flag is a metaphor for a holistic way of life. The colors used are yellow, black, white, and red. These colors have been said to represent the hues of all living humans. The symbol is one of unity and welcome and is critical to the identity of the Urban Native population. When set in the open position, it bridges the sidewalk where the surrounding community of non-natives walks daily. This simple gesture is to make transparent the Urban Native occupation of the Health Center in hope that others will visit with them. This project is being built on the site and will involve the whole community in its construction.

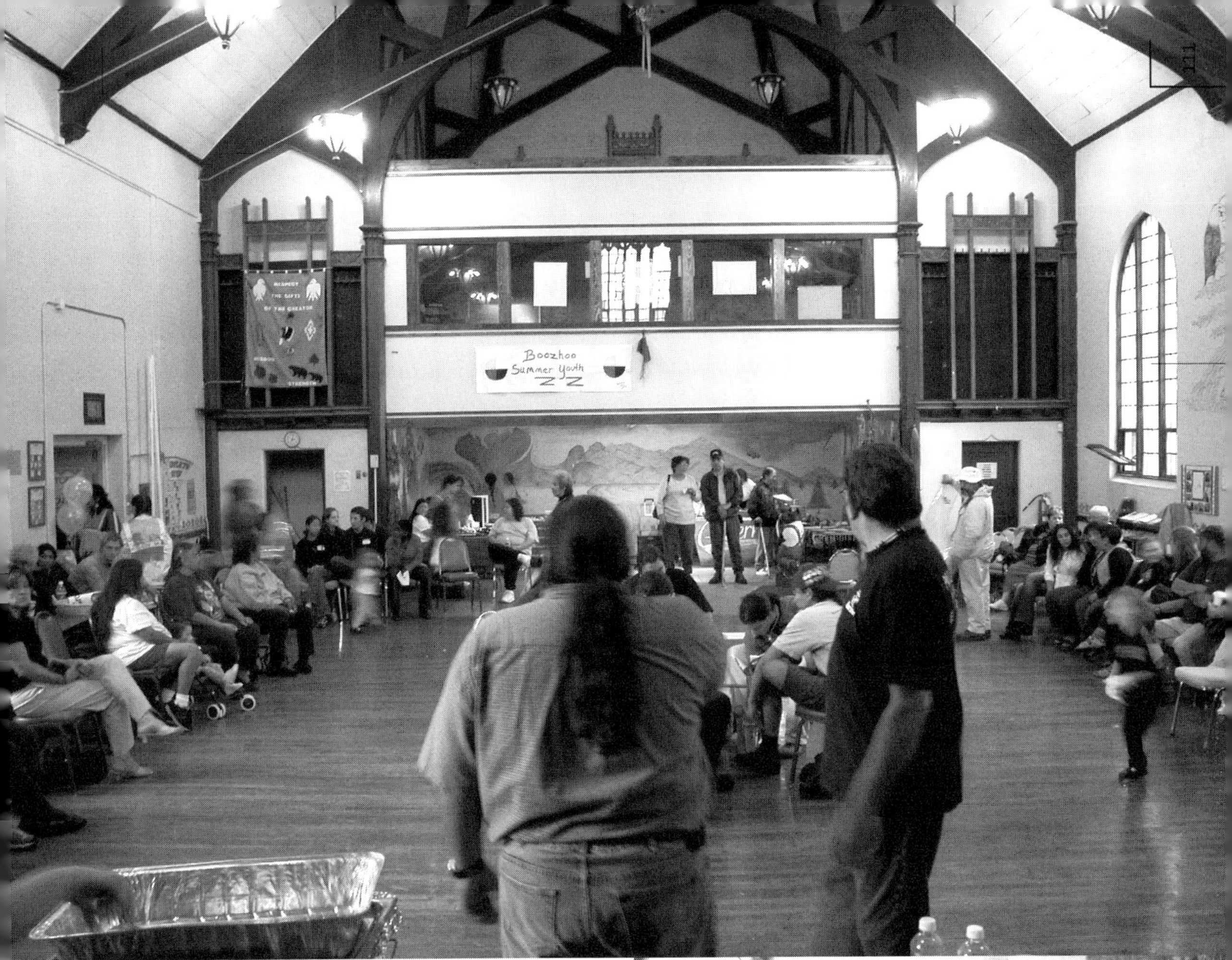
Boozhoo
Summer Youth

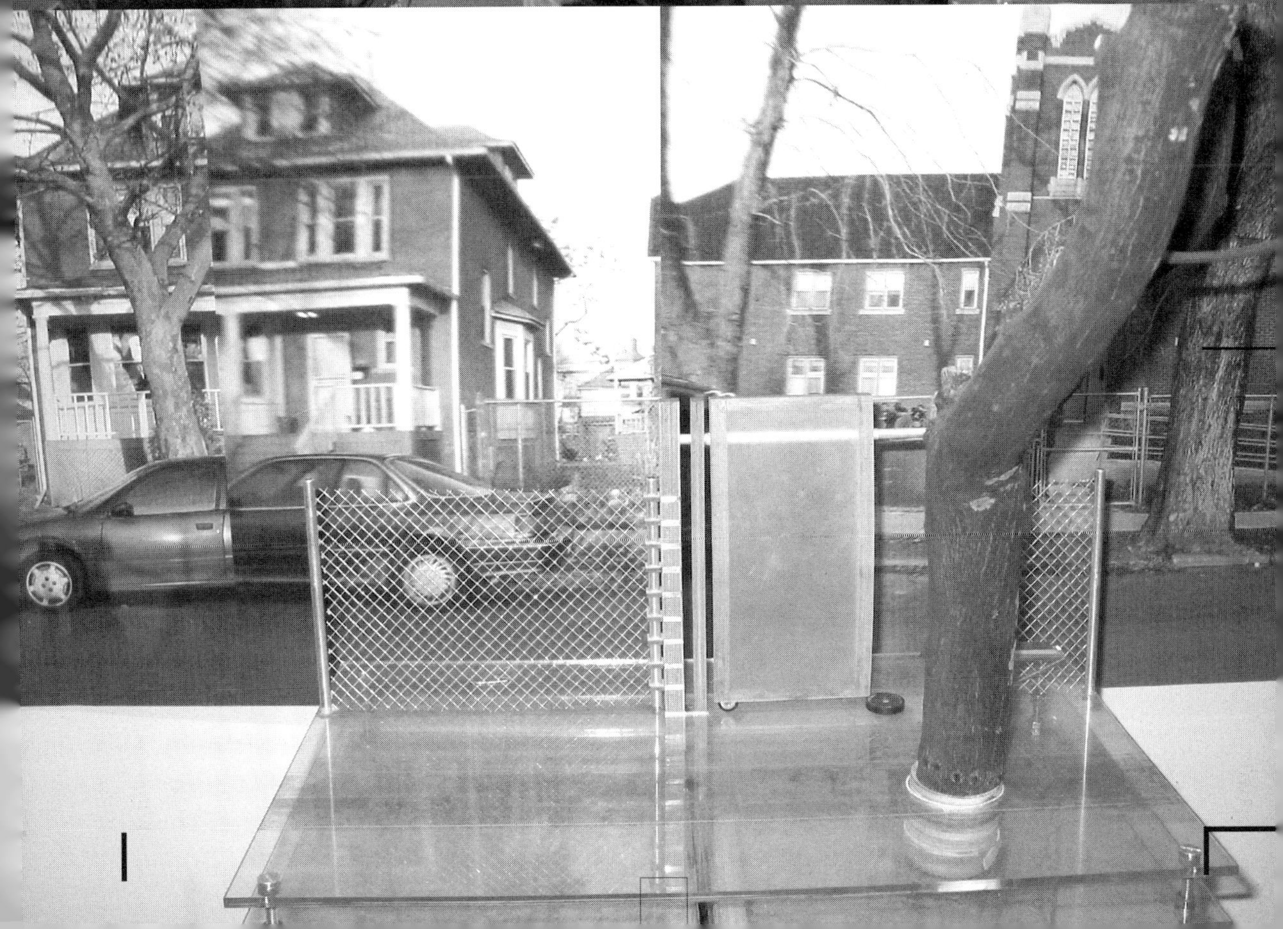

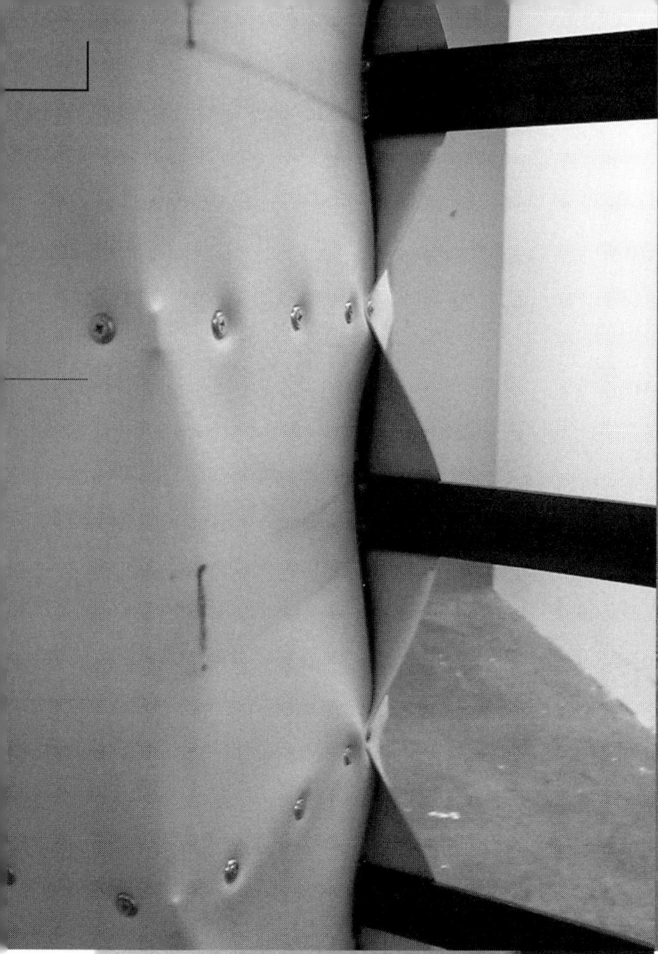
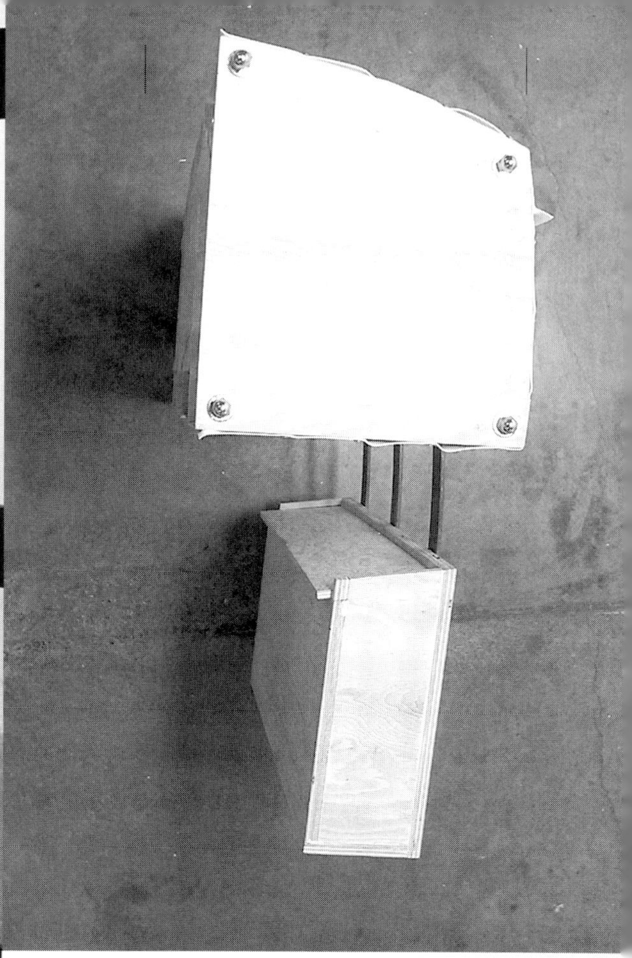
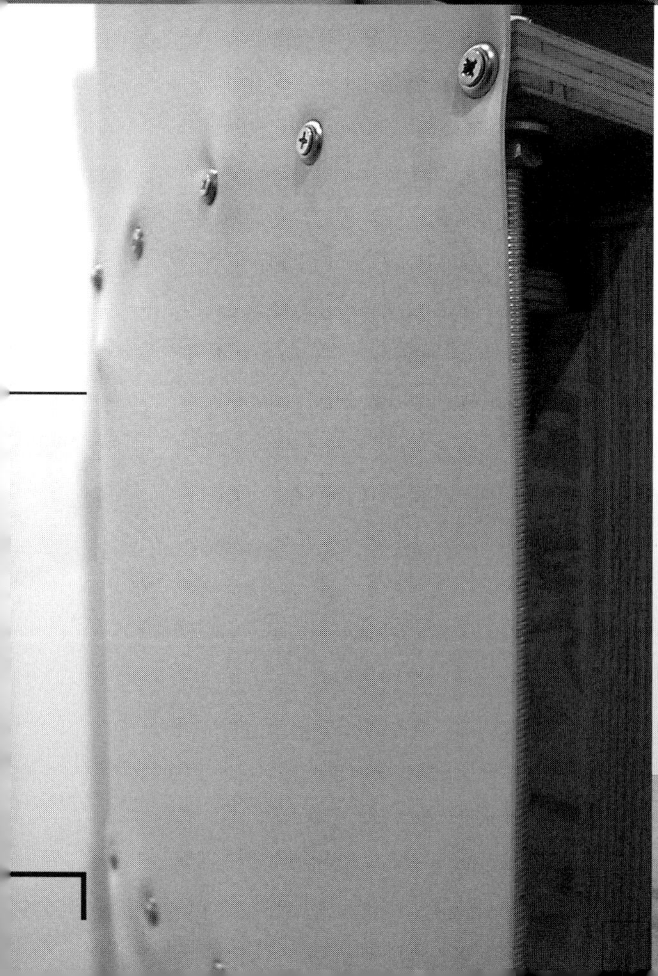
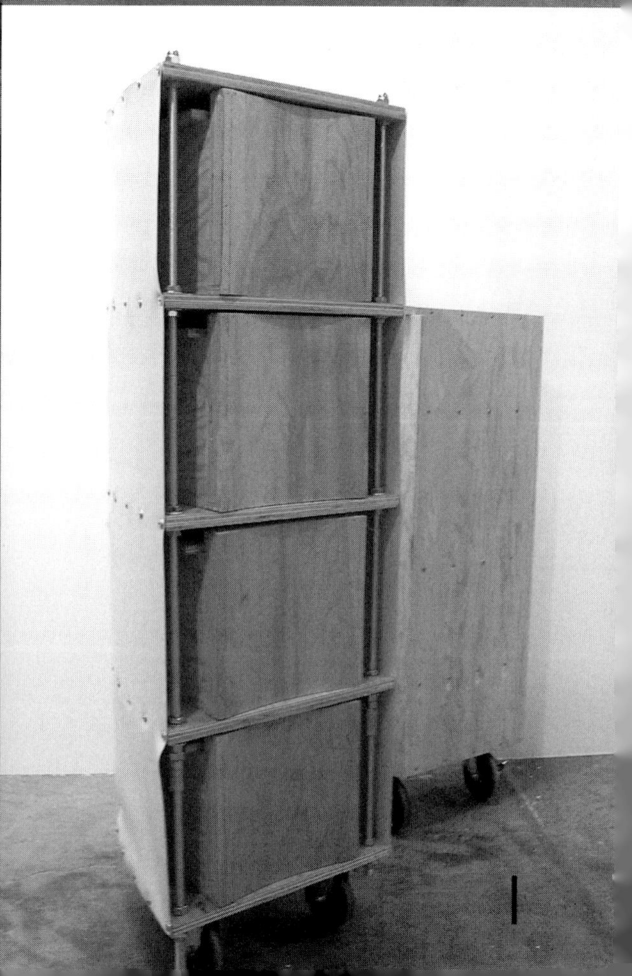

Sweat Lodge Storage Unit by Carrie Dessertine

This project is designed to facilitate the process of a Native American sweat. The initial three-week investigation informed the later project by investigating gender roles that are imbued in a group of people. The intervention is meant to enclose and sanctify space in order to engage in the activities of sweat lodge prayer sessions, a staple of the traditional Native American Culture.

Conception
The angled extension of the object covers and stores the cords of wood used in the sweat and used daily for the fire that burns in the primary yards. The daily function of this insists that it not be fully enclosed but protected from weather. Common construction pallets are altered and replaced as necessary over the life of the unit. The large pallet adjacent to the wood storage is a removable pallet of landscaping rocks, which are the primary material in the sweat process. The chicken wire casing of the rocks would be cut at its farthest right side in order to allow the rocks to flow out of this container onto a slanted plate on the adjacent pallet to the right of the stones. To access these rocks the mobile piece of the project must be separated from the whole. The user is forced to occupy the space created between the two pieces. The choosing of the stones is an important part of the sequence and is done by the person that has called the sweat so that the stones are personalized to the prayer.

Pregnancy
When the heated rocks enter the sweat lodge itself, the metaphorical pregnancy piece of the unit is engaged. The mobile piece that has already been separated from the whole is the container for the four herbal medicines necessary for the activity and prayer that takes place in the sweat lodge. The constricted nature of the space created between the two program pieces and the curved surface of the boxes requires the user to hold the boxes close to their chests as they turn and exit the divide. The curved box creates a feeling of responsibility and emphasizes the fact that the box contains a scared element.

Birth
The sweat is concluded by the smoking of a final pipe and cleansing at the alter mound between the rockpit and the sweat lodge. The third piece of the unit is engaged for this part of the progression. The third piece holds laundered towels that are used by the participants to dry themselves and complete the cleansing. Opening the hinged piece from the piece before accesses the towels. The action of the movement represents birth. The action connects the protective pregnancy piece to the freed/reborn experience of the last piece.

interaction. The students researched the culture and history of both Detroit and the Native American community. The thesis propositions were later explored through small-scale projects that could eventually be built on site.

In conclusion, the pedagogy pursued in these studio projects professes that the *education of the architect* involves interrogative design processes as tools for critiquing social and political spaces that impact our bodies, our space, and our world. The role of the architect must not be passive because the objects *we* desire may have negative implications on *others* if this investigation does not take place. Buildings have lasting impacts on our communities, identities, and the environment.

ENDNOTES

1. Krzysztof Wodiczko, *Critical Vehicles: Writings, Projects, Interviews* (Cambridge, Mass. and London: MIT Press, 1999), p. 16.
2. Education of an Architect: The Irwin S. Chanin School of Architecture of the Cooper Union (New York: Rizzoli, 1988).
3. Leslie Kanes Weisman, *Discrimination by Design: A Feminist Critique of the Man-Made Environment* (Urbana and Chicago: University of Illinois Press, 1994), p. 2.
4. Quetin Tarantino, *Pulp Fiction: a Quentin Tarantino screenplay* (Faber and Faber Limited: Great Britain, 1994), p. 10.
5. Christine Battersby, "Her Body, Her Boundaries: Gender and the Metaphysics of Containment," in Andrew Benjamin, ed., *The Body: Journal of Philosophy and the Visual Arts* (New York: St. Martin's Press, 1993), pp. 31-39.
6. Ralph Ellison, *Invisible Man,* prologue.

SHIFTMENTS

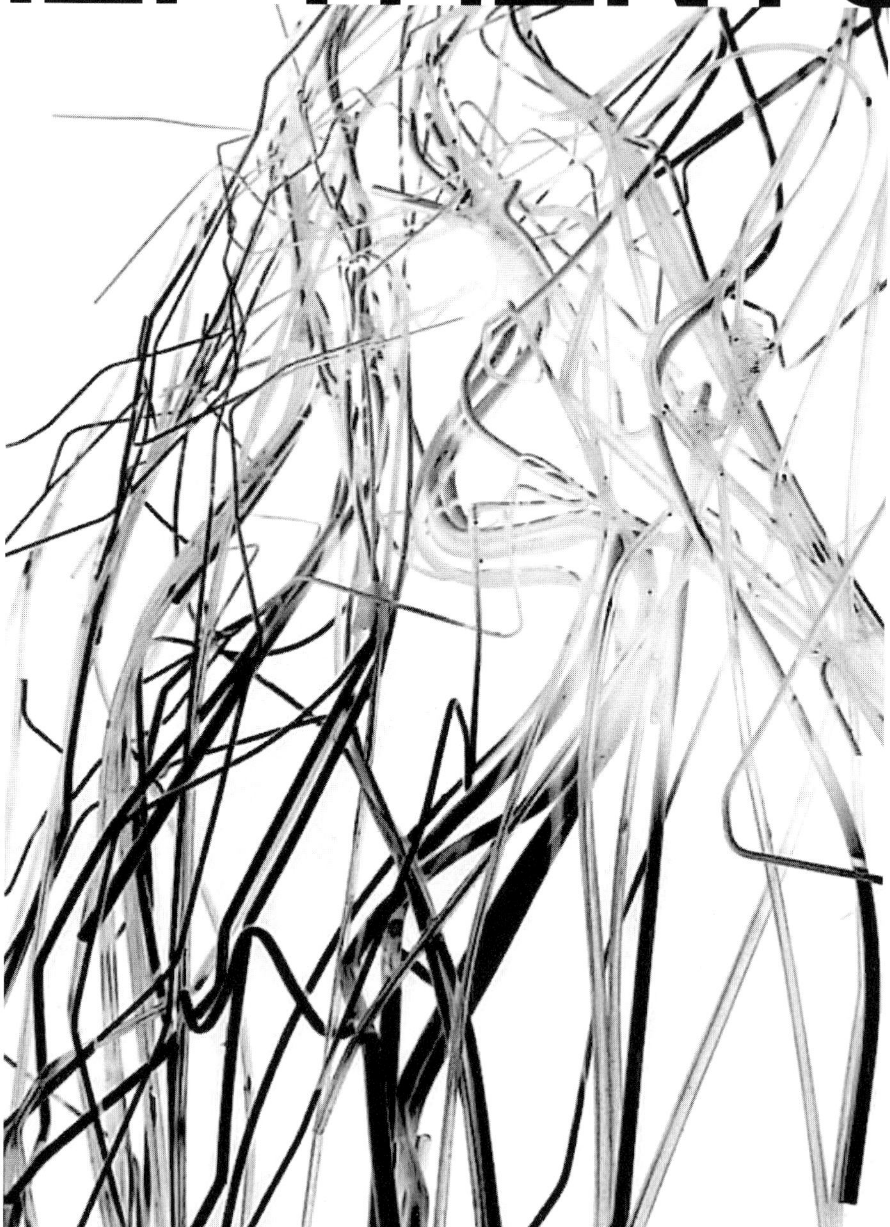

How do we articulate architecture and contemporary theory?

The system relation is no longer matter-form (or substances-attributes); neither is it the continuous development of form nor the continuous variation of matter. It is now a direct relationship between materials and forces. The system intertwines within a varied range of parameters that capture (within non-visible processes) new parameters, generating a re-configured system. Conscious re-configuration is dependent not only on the parameters, but also on the particular conditions setup between them.

Incorporating the computer as a design tool has redefined the way in which we understand architecture. This implementation will be its systematic instrumentalization within the design process, which will allow design to maintain clarity and conceptual precision. In particular the computer reveals alternatives as a shifting field, allowing the scaleless development of the project and opens-up an infinite range of possibilities.

by Jose Salinas

What does it mean to think and re-orient oneself in a system that has lost the conventions of its Euclidian skin?

Seeking a position in a system that is constantly changing and re-shaping itself according to exterior forces, new *shiftment* strategies are developed, generating a simultaneous shifting from an absolute positioning to a relative positioning. Therefore, new systems of representation are developed allowing us to forfeit a deeper understanding of our dynamic positioning within the system. An example of these new systems of representation is the line. The line understood as a diagrammatic technique is a vector—a direction, not a dimension or metric determination. It is a relationship constructed by local operations involving changes of direction. The line is filled by events and is a space of affects, rather than properties. It is a logic of unfinished series, a system of coordinates and dynamic orientations.

As objects turn to codes, colors and intensities, processes of coding and decoding information restructure themselves to develop new systems of information. The system depicts its own territory while movements of deterritorialization and processes of reterritorialization are developed. When these processes take place, the diagram reconfigures itself from the centroid to its periphery and then from the new centroid to the new periphery.

Jose Salinas received a MArch from the Architectural Association. He has worked for Asymptote and is currently principal of KNOBS Design in New York. KNOBS (Knowledge Based System) focuses on architectural design at all scales—furniture, interior, building and urban design—and extends to digital interactive environments and installations. KNOBS is currently exploring inner living spaces, shaped by external machinist systems of information that transform and generate new topological configurations. Jose Salinas is teaching at the Princeton University School of Architecture and has been invited as a guest lecturer at the Harvard University Graduate School of Design.

Jose Salinas completed his project for London in collaboration with Juan I. Aranguen, for Japan in collaboration with Markus Randler and for Greece in collaboration with Noboru Ota.

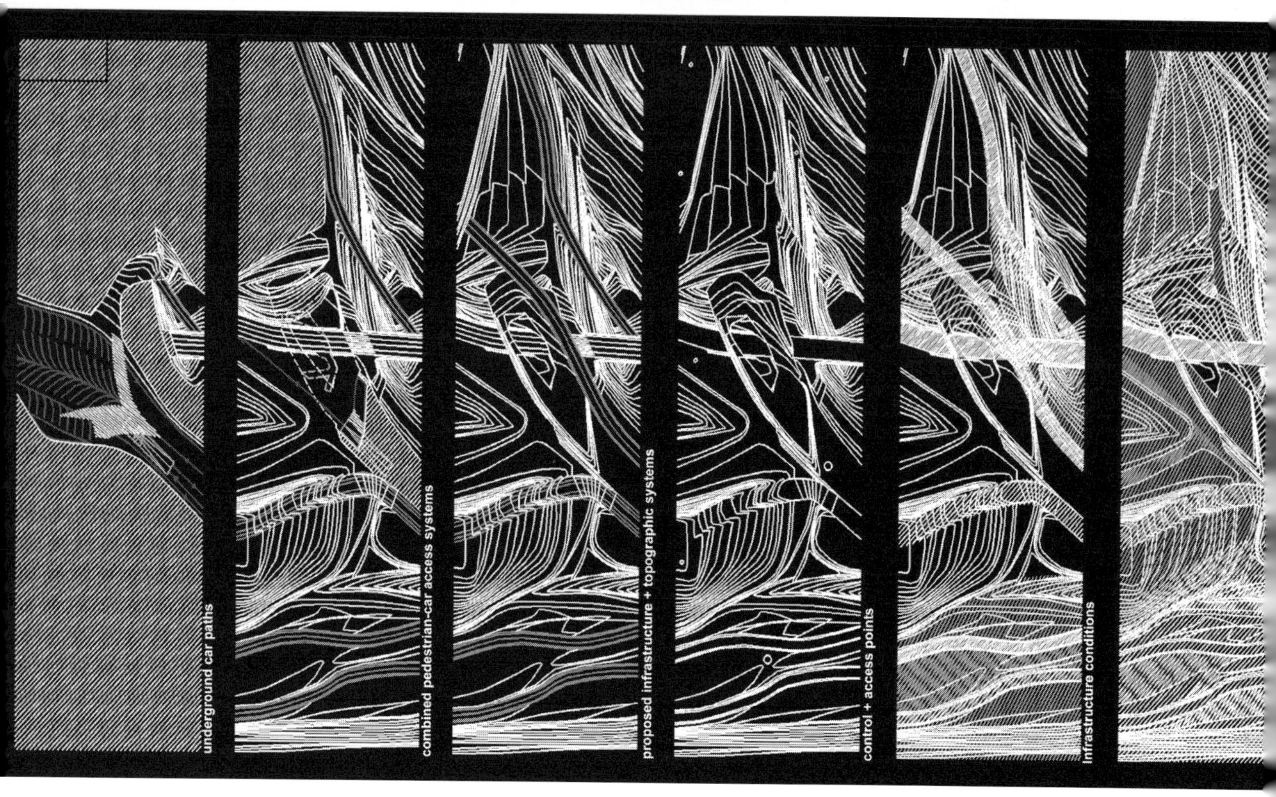

The system is organized by a greater deterritorialization, as the process advances and keeps moving further away from its initial configuration. The system and the associations of one particular set of information with another move through different strata towards alternate spaces, which are the states of the in-between—sometimes stable, other times volatile. Its existence is transitory and ephemeral, behaving as incorporations to one or another. Their relations are not quite localized, as the system is characterized by speeds within the strata.

It is possible to establish horizontal levels if the diagram is read in a vertical way, or vertical levels if the reading is done in a horizontal way, executing an elementary Cartesian reading of the diagram. This reading of the diagram is absolutely literal and fails to represent what the diagram depicts. A diagram's possibilities of development rest in understanding multiple states and directions. This type of diagram has the possibility for multiplicity, allowing spaces of alternatives and nomadic flows. Nomadic flows would generate movements of reterritorialization, as they move independently through different stratas' systems of reference. More important than the information mapped originally in the diagram, are the new configurations rendered in the diagram as it develops as well as its capacity to do so when the diagram is torn in its components. In this type of diagram, the diagonals operate in an unmeasured form in its own centroid moving towards the periphery and colonizing it, reconfiguring a new periphery, opening the possibility for new information to be captured. In this way, movements are generated on an indefinite basis by the information; establishing micro-systems, finding where information crashes, where new paths are. Inside the diagram, as the information stabilizes itself in the strata, it is possible to say that it becomes sedimentary, at least in a short-term span. This information sediment would be called short-term information alternative zones. These nodes of concentration of information belong to a process whose speed is entirely different from the later processes generated. This phenomenon is to be observed as something extremely positive, because when these consequences become non-tolerable the life span of the short-term information alternative zones comes to its end, and becomes the urge for a reorganization of these zones into other alternative zones more suitable to the existing conditions.

The diagram renders alternatives as it behaves as a nomadic monad. Nevertheless, the diagram is not an animation or a simulation that represents literally alternatives of association or exchange of information. The diagram expresses a nomadic monad, because it does not limit itself to a particular set of possibilities within an isolated system. Conversely, it opens an infinite range of possibilities, qualifying as a dynamic system. Its dynamism is not present in the sense that it redundantly has motion, but in the sense that what happens in the system is dependent on speeds. The dynamic diagram has certain qualities within itself that require the constant re-reading and re-definition in order to become the proper tool for understanding the nomadic monads.

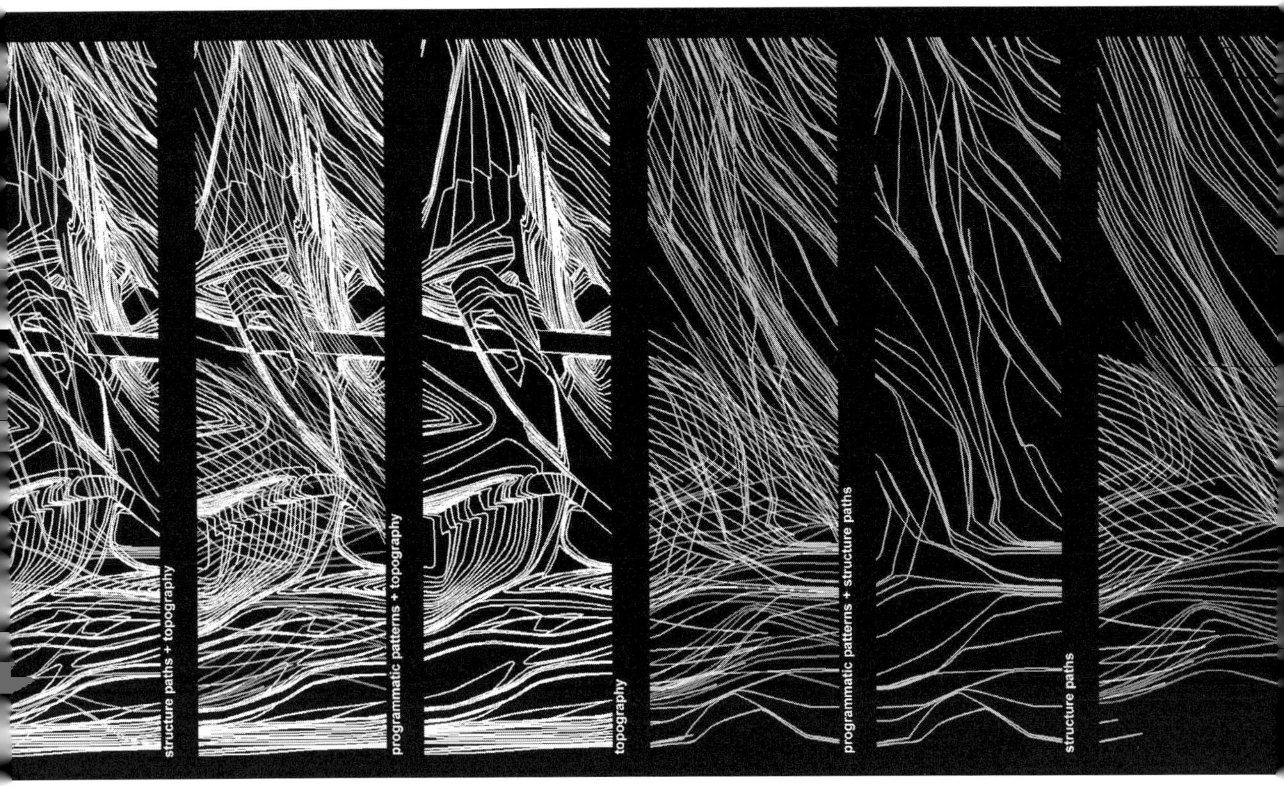

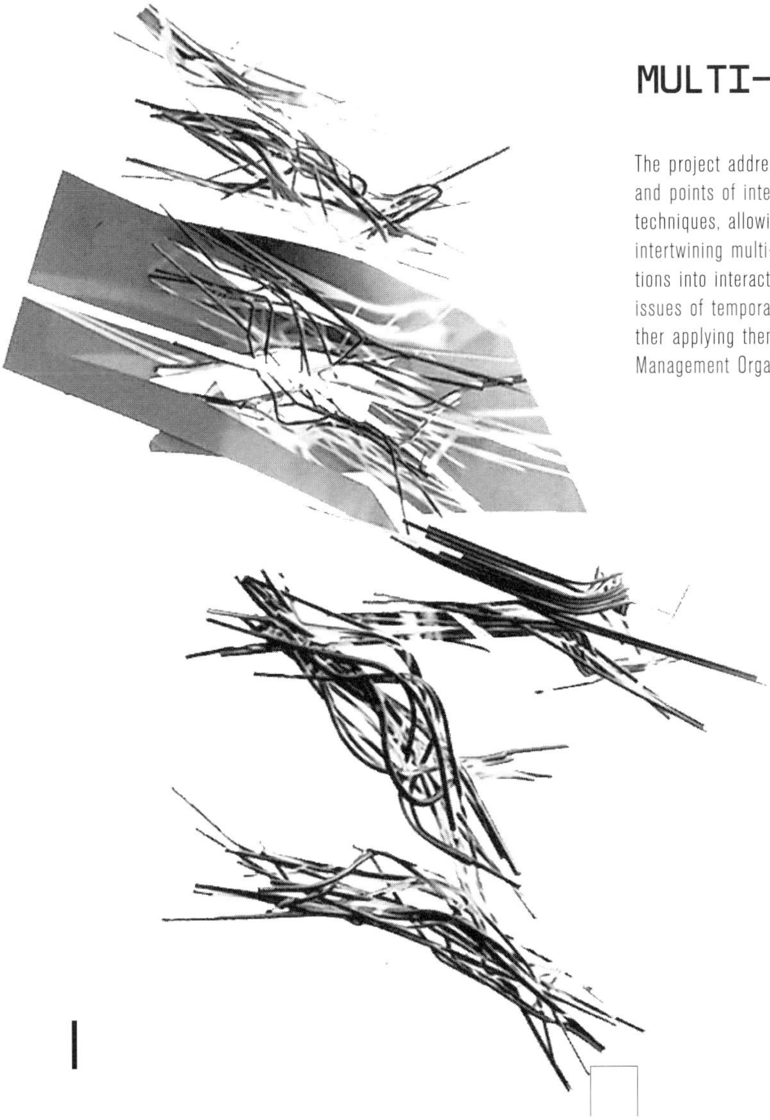

MULTI-LINEAR FIELDS

The project addresses multi-linear conditions such as trajectories and points of intersection, instrumentalized through diagrammatic techniques, allowing the scaleless development of the project by intertwining multi-directional fields. By translating static configurations into interactive ones, the adaptability of the project grasps issues of temporality through various gradients of permanence, further applying them to Management Terminology in order to generate Management Organizations.

GLOWING TOPOLOGIES: TOKI PLASMA RESEARCH PARK

Glowing topologies is an experiment where fluctuating soft lighting patterns interact with each other and with existing natural conditions to generate different programmatic environments. The result is an Artificial Natural Environment (ANE) that fosters the breeding of new ideas and scientific breakthroughs in a scientific community and provides a strong visual identity as part of Japan's new heart in the 21st century.

The urban topological surface is transformed by the interaction of different parameters. Light is understood as a dynamic field of information, where simple expressions generate complex relationships. Transforming and deforming the existing topological surface, light interaction generates and defines the surface appearance, dynamically changing its properties.

Displacement and controlling parameters define the information flows, appearance and materiality. Captured lighting patterns of motion within an endless system of operation are simplified to explore possibilities of transfer phenomena, where the urban system is artificially manipulated and controlled by conscious operators. Skin is said to glow in response to program, existing conditions, and artificial conditions. A glowing volume appears curiously alive because of its dynamic variation by interaction. Artificial light signals the presence of activity, the energy that animates the environment. While fluctuating lighting systems serve to illuminate an object, environment, or task area, others emit low levels of light to foreground the lighting fixture itself. Light emanates from soft, heavy blobs of gel or from bulbs festooned with silicone growths. While most lighting patterns must be shielded from the touch, these objects invite physical contact.

Their dull interior illumination draws attention to the surfaces, infusing their skins with an alien energy, at once comforting and strange. Lighting acts as a field of embedded information. The glow is addition of data within the space. Embedded swamp areas as well as water gardens are included as a variation of the glow. As a result we end up with glowing topologies which are dynamically fluctuating, generating different environmental configurations.

Three specific strategies are depicted as variations through time in different locations: Directional Underwater Lighting, Dynamic Interactive Glowing Landscape, Softly Imprinted Synthetic Light.

Taking in consideration the qualities of the site; its natural presence as well as its natural properties such as the forest and water; and considering water as a generator system, a system that develops dynamically through time, always changing and transforming itself and the different environments that surrounds it; a fluctuating

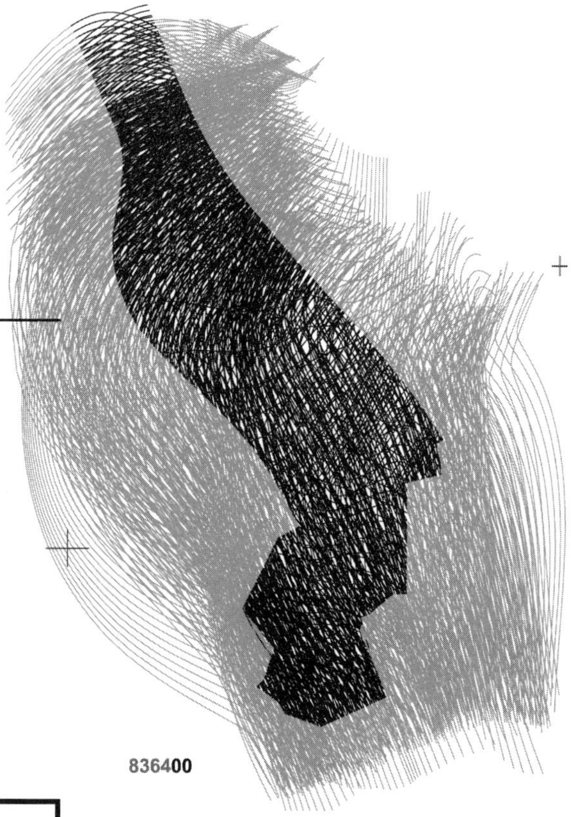

836400

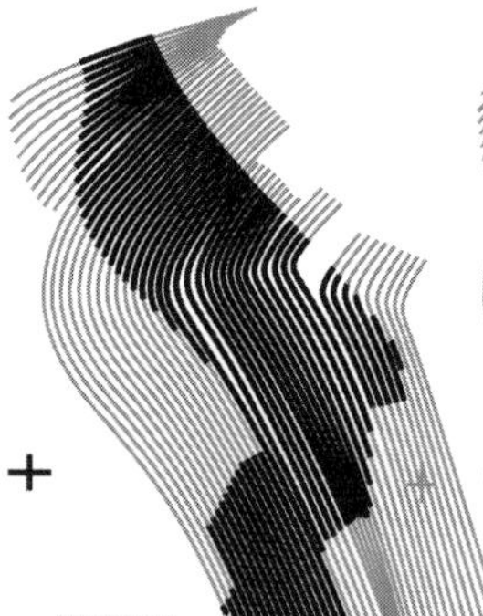

836401

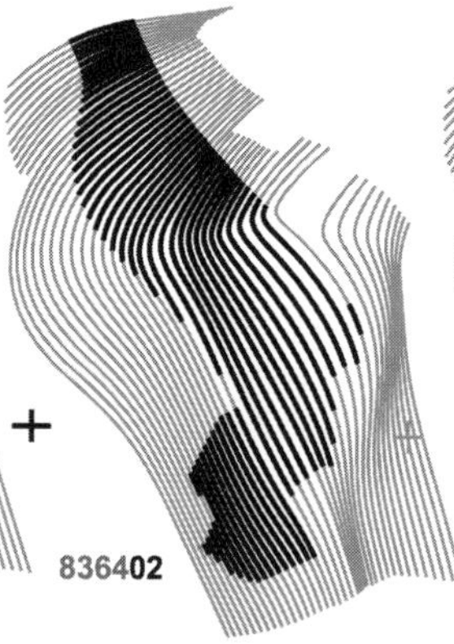

836402

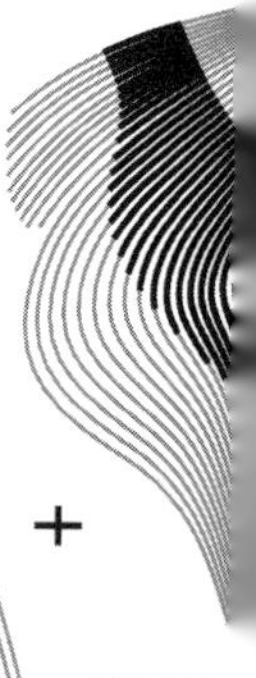

836403

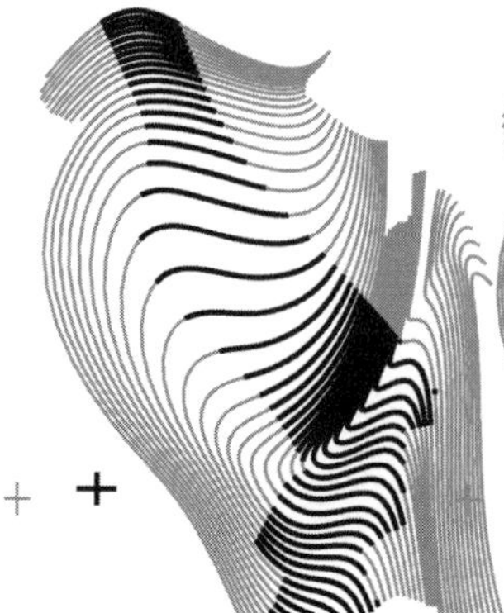

836408

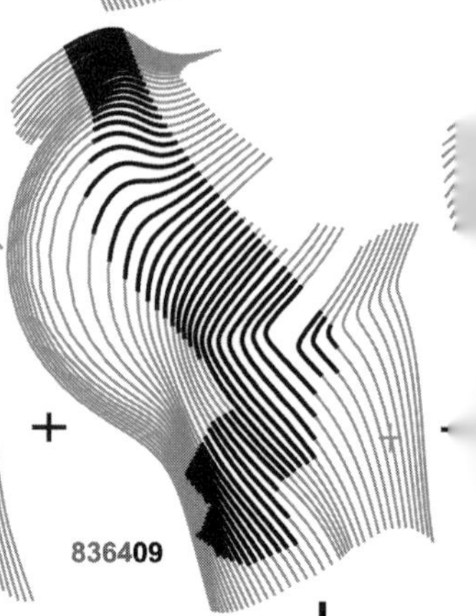

836409

time-interactive lighting system is developed, generating a multiplicity of possible programmatic blended environments.

Sculpturing the landscape by soft pressure allowed a mapping of the site in terms of hardness and a transformation according to the softness of the landscape. Therefore, the landscape morphology became an interactive system where different situations were generated according to programmatic needs.

The two interventions mentioned above create an Artificial Natural Environment that is dynamically embedded between the artificial and the natural layer and allows for programmatic deployment on the area according to the existing conditions as well as proposed artificial conditions. The relationship between the layers defines the possible density. Therefore, the boundaries between the different programs are blurred, as well as the limits between inside and outside, generating the programmatic openness.

The undulating and interweaving layers create a hybrid form of open interior / enclosed exterior, open for the blended programs and undetermined future expansions. Rather than simply arraying buildings as is done traditional urbanism, the urban strategy is to create one dynamic glowing entity, visible from the adjacent motorways as well as from the air. It is intended to provide a strong image of a future science city, which will be flexible enough to assume future additions or variations.

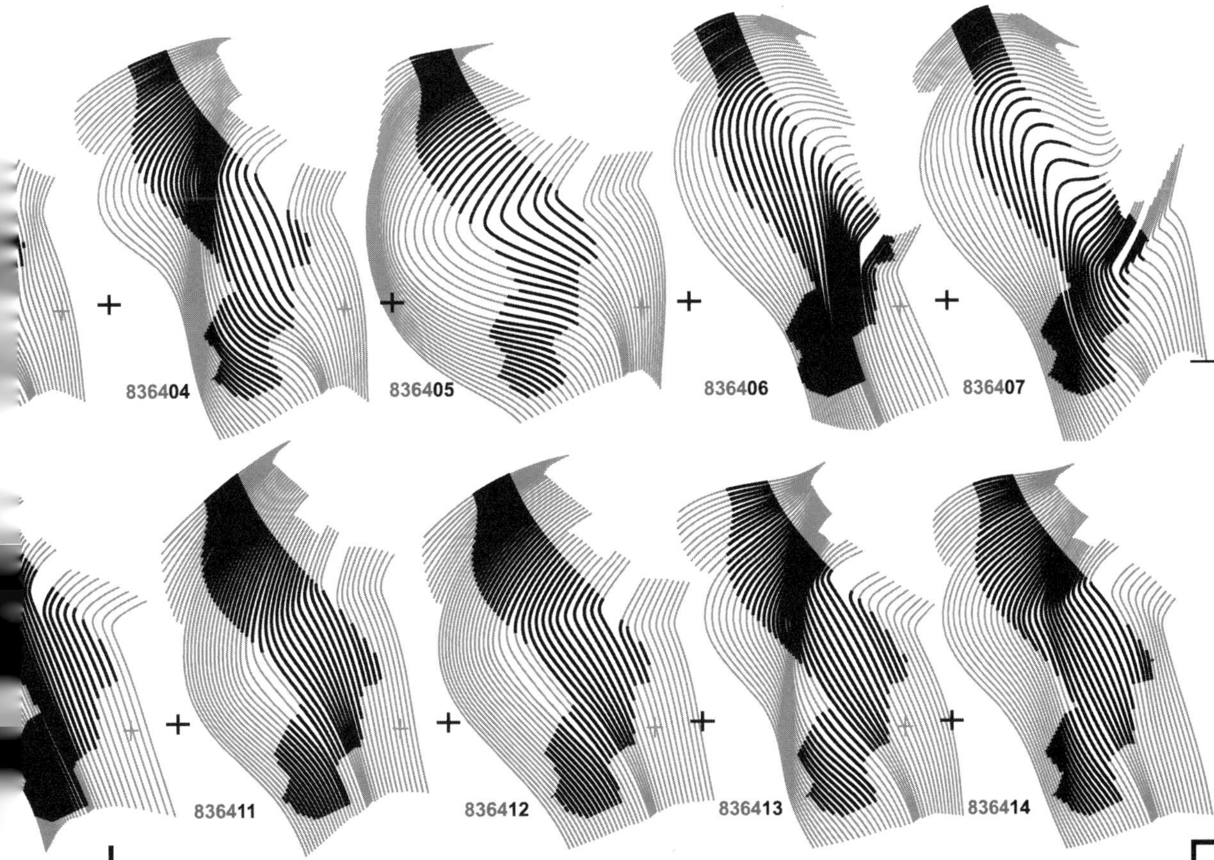

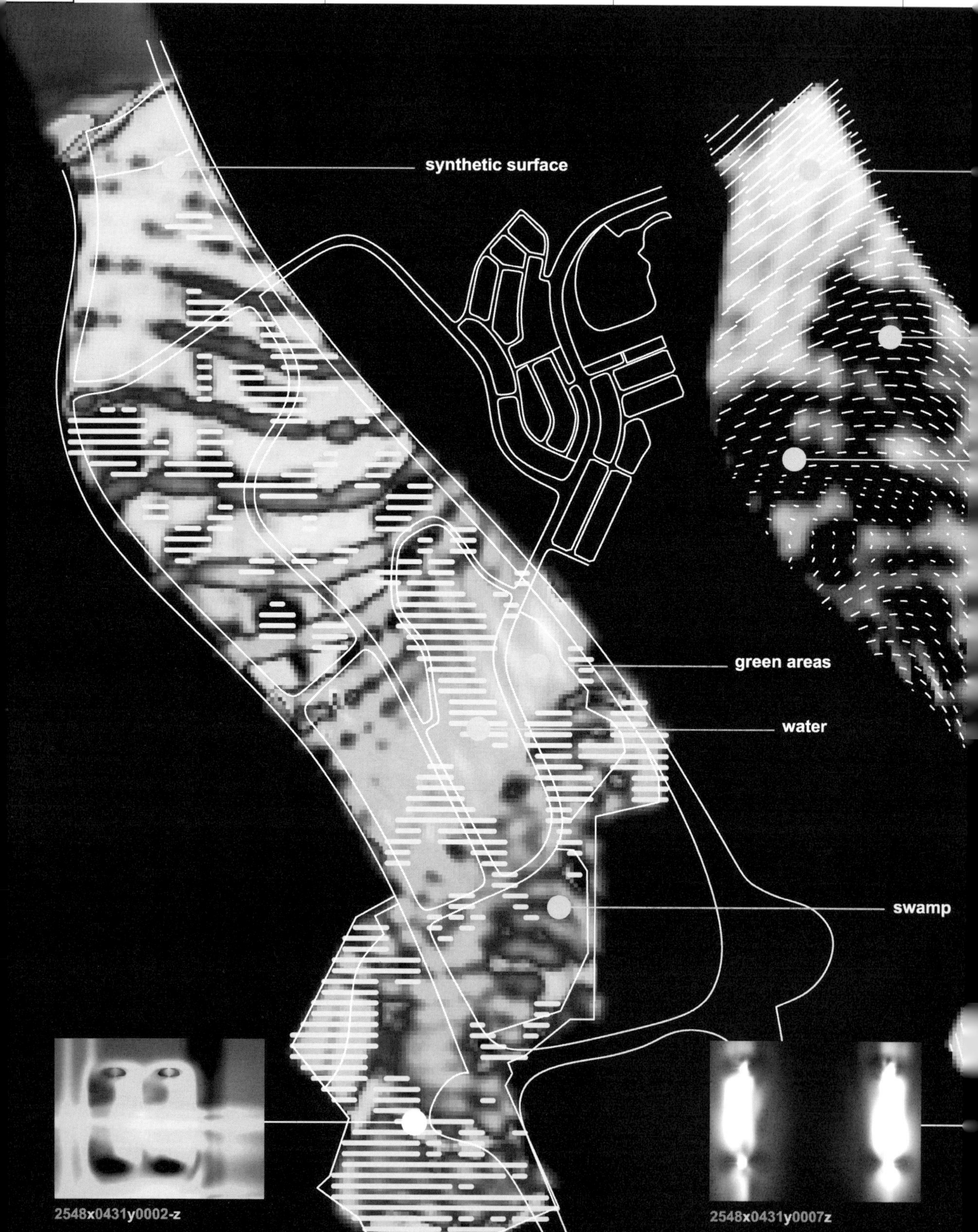
synthetic surface
green areas
water
swamp
2548x0431y0002-z
2548x0431y0007z

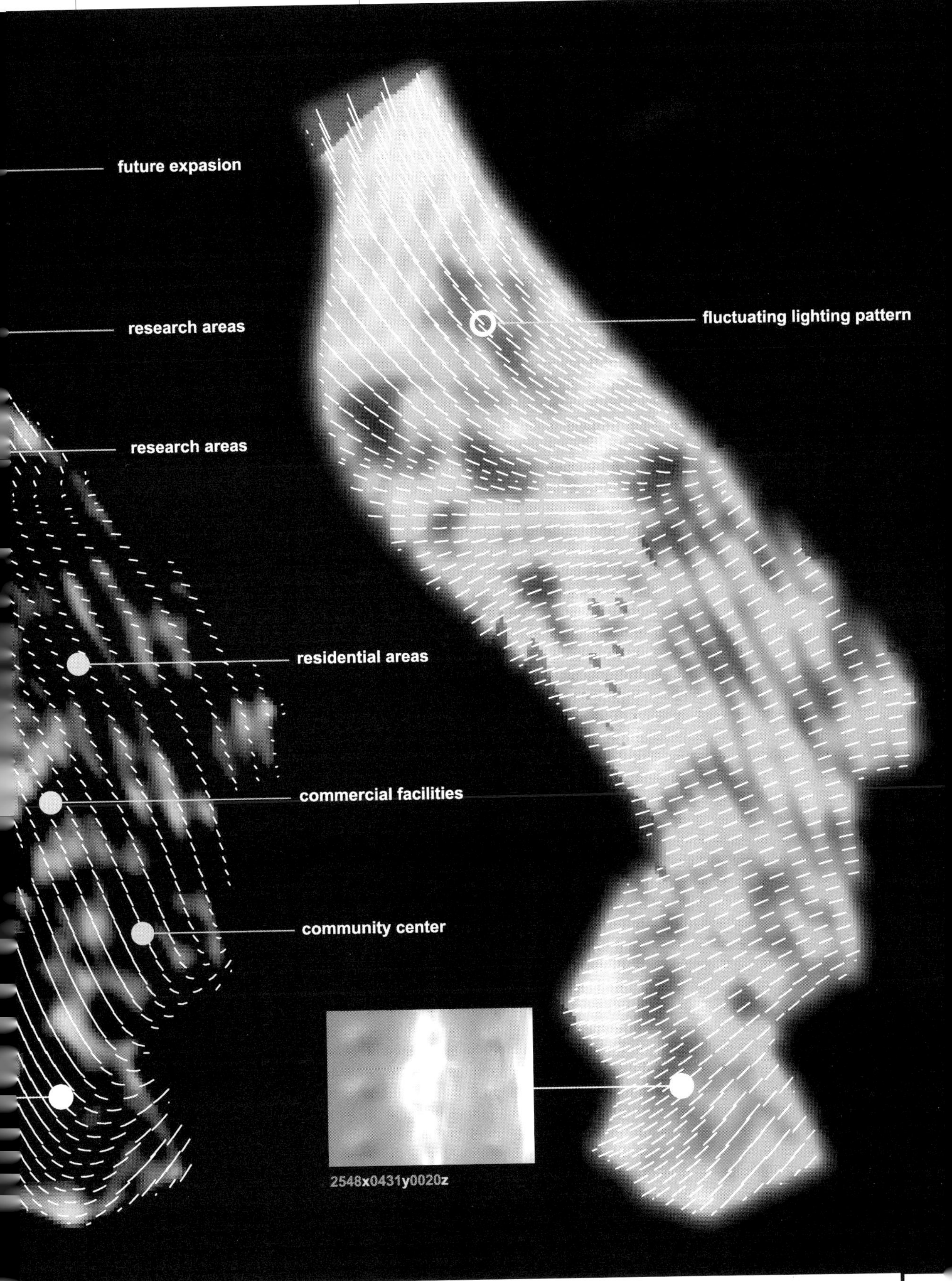
future expasion
research areas
research areas
residential areas
commercial facilities
community center
fluctuating lighting pattern
2548x0431y0020z

INTELLIGENT SURFACE: MEDIA PLATFORM FOR THE 2004 OLYMPIC GAMES

The proposal re-interprets City-Leisure Activities Generators, taking up the Greek notion of Public Space, in particular the Temple surroundings on the Hill as a space of interaction. This proposal also explores the Idea of Journey, both as an interior and as a virtual journey. We are interested in combining these in order to recover the idea of surprise in the event . . .

The proposed topological configuration is then a place where visitors will simultaneously find an environmental space to plug-in and log-on (having access to any information they will request), and a place to rest and start a journey. Therefore, the proposal generates two environments connected by a metaphorical bridge: the exterior one is more a plug-in device display where visitors can feel that they have arrived to a different place and can access information. The interior one is experienced as an open internal exteriority because the visitor will be part of different gradients of filtered visuals. The visitor then participates from the exterior as a voyeur, being part of a differently qualified space, while the interior expresses a different configuration from the exteriority, but in a virtual connection with it. The interior is clustered by a permeable semi-translucent flexible tubular membrane supported by laser-cut stainless steel rings, which host the tubular envelop. The tubular membrane-embedded glowing light patterns generate different environments, alluding to the idea of the interior of an organism.

The structure itself represents the evolution of a primitive topology. The transformation is the genesis of space and opens up a new kind of permeability and connectivity with the exteriority. The project aims to realize mutations and transformations of space through spatial changes and transitions of surface. To mutate and transform the physical space, different glowing techniques are implied to create a more dynamic structural system.

The volume required to store the structure and transportation is around 16.2 m^3. We recommend dividing the volume into three separate conditions (the container dimensions will be 8mx8mx2m): PVC tubular structure (8 m^3), stainless steel rings (12.8 m^3), media station unit and lighting (4 m^3).

The rough cost estimation is around $200,000 USD. For the structure itself the cost is considered $100,000 USD, for the lighting $25,000 USD and $20,000 USD per Media Station Unit.

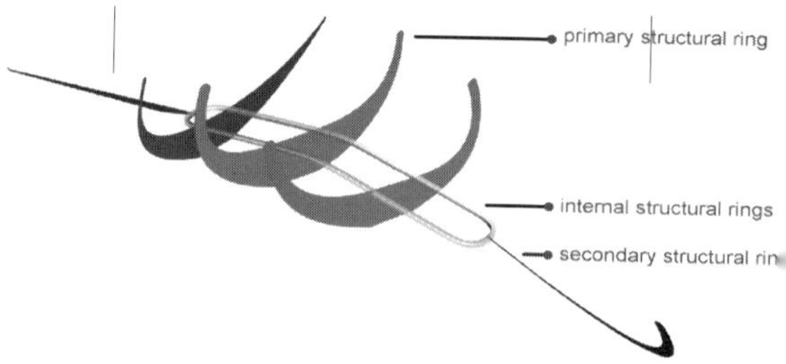

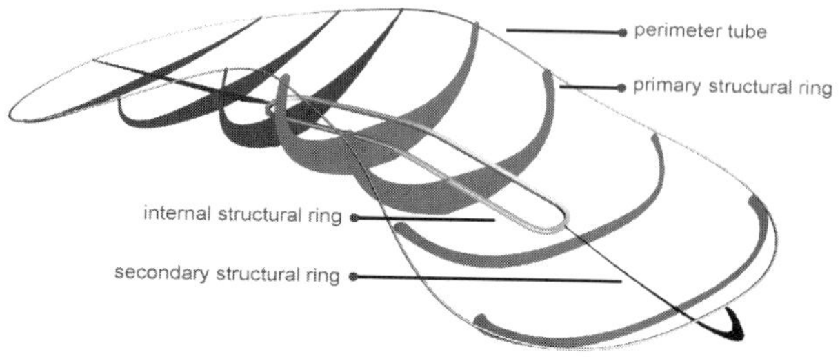

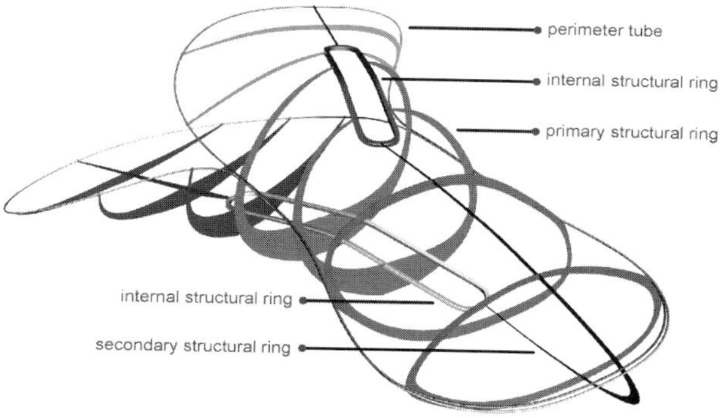

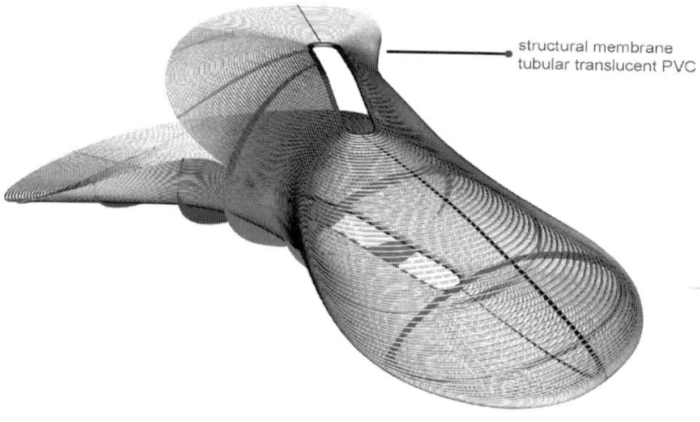

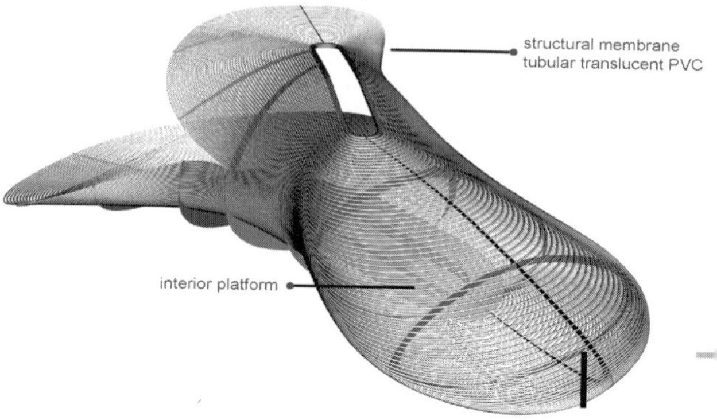

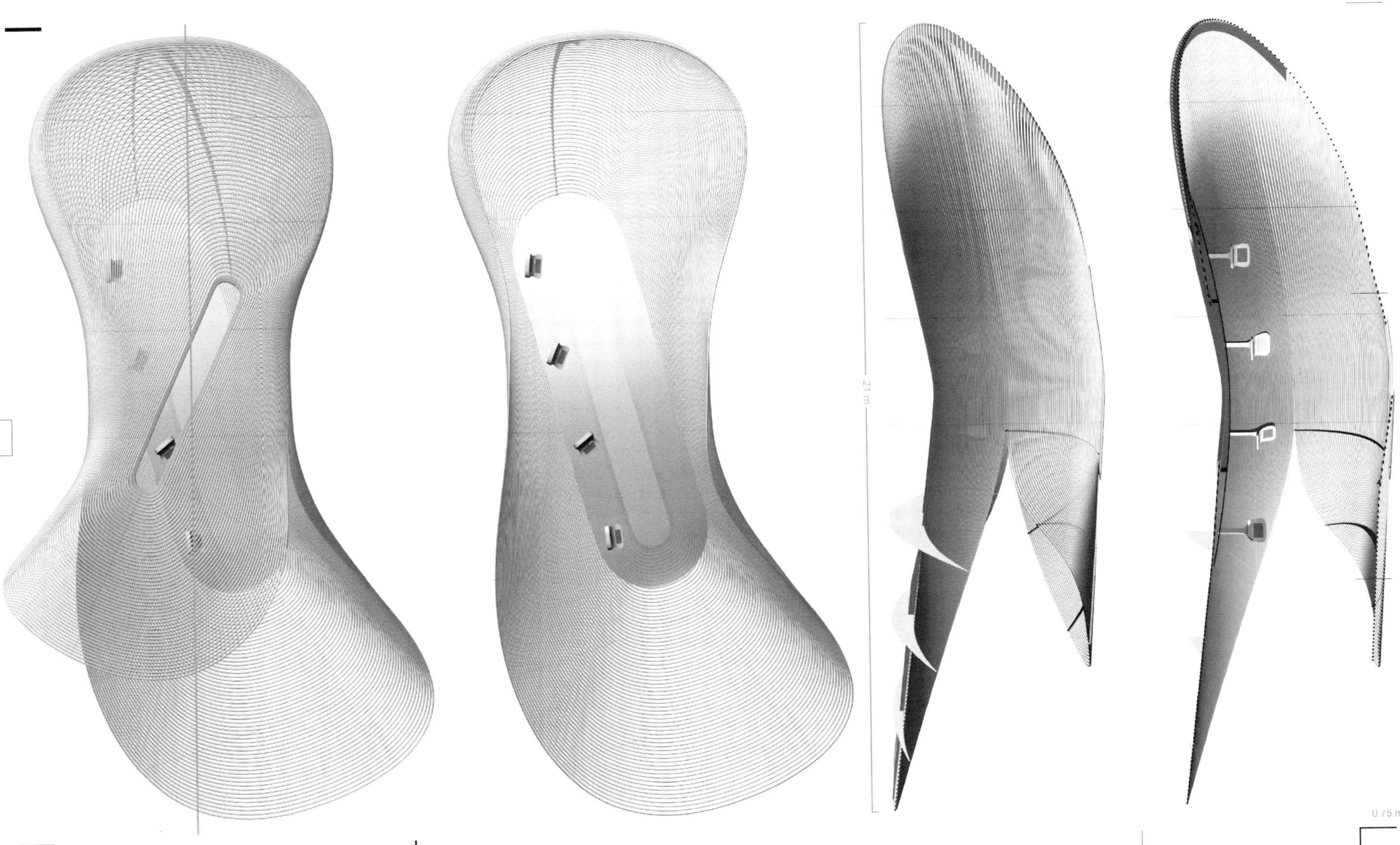
21 m
0 / 5 m

HERMENEUTIC

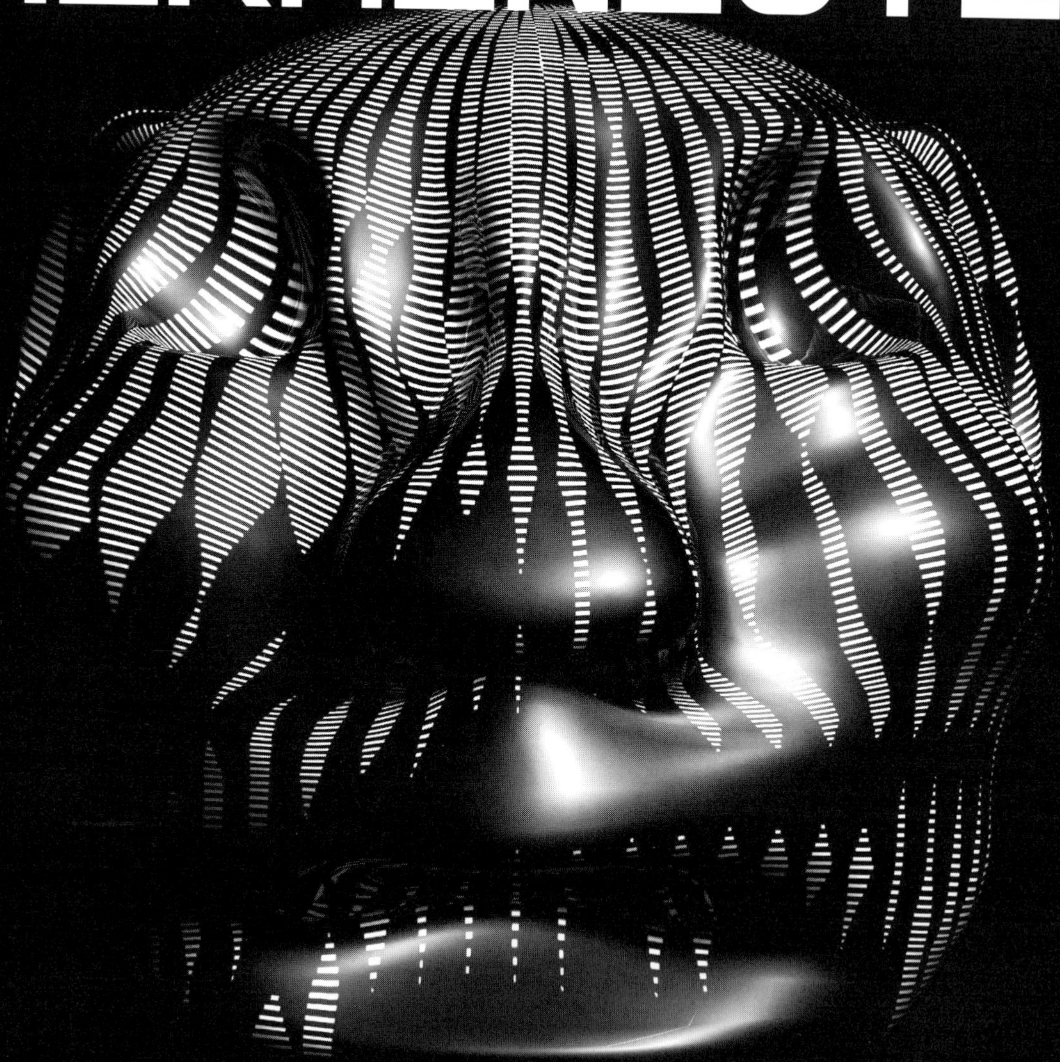

Hermeneutic Topologies, a project by KNOBS Design for *H*

TOPICS

A CONVERSATION WITH JOSE SALINAS

Jose Salinas
I am curious to know, why have you asked me to bring this image of the Hermeneutic Topology?

Jonathan D. Solomon
Well, I'm going to ask you how one applies an education in the manipulation of large scale systems, fields, and change that is registered through difference in repetition, like your projects for London and Japan, and applies it to something very small, like your project for a pavilion in Greece. I thought you would walk me through it, you could explain it to me from the perspective of your practice. The thing about this image from Hermeneutic Topologies is that it throws all that away. It's without scale and without medium. So I thought we better start with that.

JS
The smallest thing I ever designed in school was a piece of furniture. It was an exercise in which we took the example of Reitveld, and studied how he understood space in three dimensions, then produced variations on it. The largest thing I ever designed was the project for a section of London, while at the AA, that was 1km by 2 km.

But at any scale this work focuses on a landscape of information. So the information is defined according to the scale you are working on. In the faces, there is a landscape of information being embedded in the skin, and that defined the topology of the object. At the scale of the pavilion, in Greece, because it is at a small scale, that information is actually structure, and the patterning itself is composed of structural members. A shift in scale or medium is only a shift in what kind of information you have to work with. Of course you need to know what you are after, too. It's like when you start to make some food, first you think, I want to make meat, or I want to make fish, and once you have an idea of what you want you can start to get your pots and add ingredients. These ingredients I understand as information.

JDS
How do you reconcile the changing role of the visual effects, graphic phenomena, across these scales? Doesn't graphic technique, such as a moiré or other repetitive pattern, have different effects when it is at a scale that can be perceived at large then when it is at a scale where it is expressed only in local manifestations?

JS
There is, first, a limit to the complexity of organization that can be addressed in each of these projects. For a student project on the urban scale, for instance, it is very important to define the scope

or limits of your organization. If you had twenty years, perhaps you could solve all those details. But the important thing is that for every space inhabited by people there are systems that allow for that inhabitation: structure, lighting. And how each of those systems are deployed will influence how the space is inhabited. In a building—where do the outlets go? Where is there light? In a city the systems are at a larger scale but they work the same way. In the case of the project in Japan, I avoided so many of those systems that I did not know about or could not control or did not have the resources to go into in any complexity, and primarily focused on designing a lighting system. When you have a large site that you want to bring together somehow, how do you start?

JDS
So this is not a graphic process, so much as an information process? I ask because I am taken by the fearful abstraction of the London diagram, the scale of the pattern in Japan, the one to one ratio of the pavilion, the denatured morphology of the face . . .Is this all the result of processing?

JS
I believe the computer helps me to realize certain complex geometries which are the result of processing this information, in a dynamic way. When you have an object and you cross-section it in three dimensions, suddenly you have much more information than if you made the same drawing as a two-dimensional, orthogonal drawing. In topological theory, if you cut a surface you break the consistency of it, you are adding a boundary condition. Even though when you render it the object seems the same, in terms of the information it embodies it is not the same. This requires you to take a position, constantly, towards how you manipulate form.

JDS
You are a digital media tutor. When you are instructing a student in the use of a processing tool, does your session become a de facto design critique?

JS
When I teach computation as a tool, I encounter students who only want assistance with a technical problem; you can tell they want to know only some function or another so they can move on. What I find more interesting is talking to students who really want to understand something new or different through the tool. It could be just a technical problem, but it could also be a theoretical problem, relating to operations on topology. Sometimes when I go into theories of topology with a student who has called me over for help with a technical problem, I can see in his face he is thinking, "What the hell is this guy telling me!?" So I try to position myself in between. I am not the critic, so I cannot really tell a student to do his or her work a certain way. But, on the other hand, if I show them one technique or another it will condition the way they approach their project all together and have a tremendous effect on it. It could become a constraint for them.

But you asked me an interesting question before about visual effects. There are practices which focus on the visual effect, and these would tend to use the computer for generating the ends of visualization, trying this material and this model until it looks just right. I try to use the computer to make visual patterns that contain embedded information, so that this scheme that you see contains an embedded system of which the visual patterns are an effect only. It is the information itself which I am more concerned about.

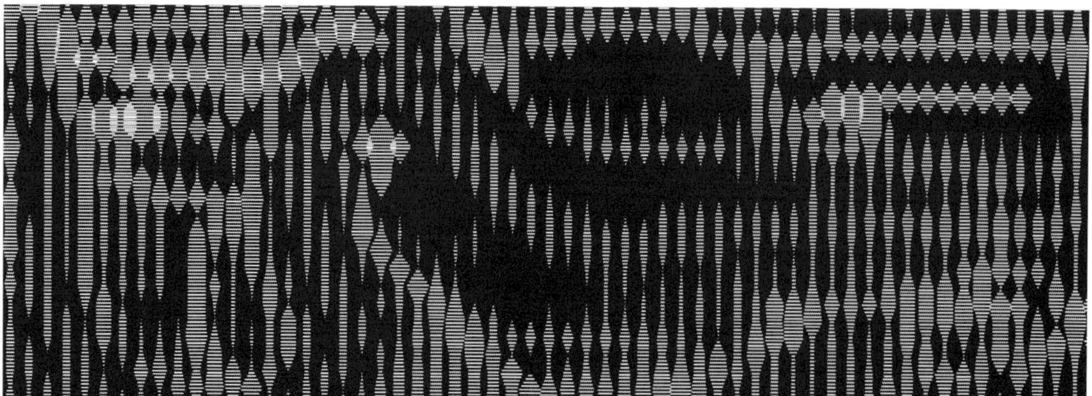

JDS
I confess I read a certain paranoia about information in these faces. These were in a show on surveillance technologies?

JS
"Homeland Insecurity," yes.

JDS
So is information a neutral tool in your work, or does it have positive or negative connotations?

JS
The curator of this show asked me to develop something which would comment on how new security systems and surveillance systems have transformed our lives, even our appearances, in ways that we may not realize. It was a challenge to do something that would be disturbing. The whole idea came from looking at the picture in my passport, on my visa. There is a picture of a face, color-coded, with a pattern overlaid on it. I thought, oh, so when I go somewhere with my passport, my face is reduced to this two-dimensional pattern of overlaid information that a machine can read. I do not think this is negative so much as part of our nature. Nietzsche said, when you remove a person's mask, there is always another mask beneath it. I am imagining these masks as layers of information embedded on the face.

JDS
What are you working on now?

JS
Right now I have four projects going on. I did a World Trade Center memorial, of course, I have an exhibition in Copenhagen, also one in Paris as at the Batofar Multimedia Event, and we did an entry for the Nam June Paik museum, in Korea.

JDS
Unfortunately, you had to have a license to enter that one.

JS
Yes. A friend of mine has a license. I would get one here, but, I don't know how long I will stay. And besides when you get a license here, it's only for New York State! For now I am treating all my work as a research project, I am still learning. I am enjoying myself here, I am doing what I want at last for the time being. It's hard to find clients here, a client who will give you money, because who is going to hire someone who has no experience or resources? But that doesn't have to be limiting. What we do is not necessarily building. We, educated in architecture, can do a lot of things, perform and produce in all sorts of ways. You are an example: it is the students just out of school who are producing the documents on architecture for the public. The lesson is, if you give the students responsibility, they will perform as professionals. They will be the ones to bring in the motivation and energy.

JDS
Maybe years from now we will feel differently.

FOUR FROM

All images courtesy of G Tects, Ominvore, WORK, and Maria Sieira

> G TECTS

> OMNIVORE

> WORKac

> MARIA SIEIRA

A young architect asks: why New York?

NEW YORK

by Jennifer Ferng

The life of a designer is often a haze of late nights, meetings with clients, and repetition. The boundaries between life and work are often indistinguishable. The belief in design as an unassailable force of everyday life is often manifest in the way a designer works and operates. In the course of study for a design professional, an architect, the ideas of architecture and urbanism go hand-in-hand. Young designers are often thrust into the all-encompassing nature of studio culture, which makes no distinction between the practicality of daily living, an urban lifestyle, and the ideals enforced by the dictates of the profession. According to Alice Chung, a partner in the graphic design firm Omnivore, Inc. "Some people have a real division between work and non-work. I feel like it is very integrated and, for me, there are no divisions. I am always thinking about the work, which is part of me." It's no surprise, then, that the life of the designer is also inextricably linked to the pulse of the city in which he or she resides. However, it begs the question: Are cities necessary for the incubation of creativity and design, or is the idea of urbanity—a network of shared ideas across several thresholds—simply just an idea within the collective consciousness?

Four promising groups, ranging from educators to graphic designers to practicing architects, in New York—arguably the great loci of urbanity in the United States, if not the world—were interviewed

Jennifer Ferng is a History, Theory, Criticism PhD candidate at MIT. Her research focuses on theorizing new technologies within the context of architectural precedents, history of science, and modern art. She has been a Visiting Assistant Professor at Pratt Institute and a studio instructor at the Parsons School of Design.

G TECTS LLC is a New York-based award winning design firm. G TECTS LLC pursues both conceptual projects and built work with a particular interest in exploring relationships between electronic information technologies and architecture. G TECTS LLC has developed a strong set of relationships with expert consultants and specialists in various fields of fabrication and construction to enable us to consider a varied range of specialized projects. Since 1999, G TECTS LLC has developed a client list including Lincoln Center, Issey Miyake, The Dermot Company and Equinox Fitness.

Omnivore, Inc. is a small but prolific design studio founded by Alice Chung and Karen Hsu in 2002. Focusing primarily on design for art, architecture and culture-related clients, Omnivore's work spans print, web, motion and environmental design. Omnivore has been involved in numerous projects for museum and academic institutions in New York, Boston and Philadelphia as well as collaborations with OMA. Recent Omnivore projects have been featured in Print *magazine,* WWD Beauty Biz *magazine.*

WORKac consists of Amale Andraos, Jens Holm and Dan Wood. They have recently completed a temporary boutique in Rockefeller Center to launch Target's new line of Isaac Mizrahi-designed clothing annd are working on several residential and commercial projects in New York, the Bahamas and Rhode Island.

Maria Sieira is an architect in New York. She is currently teaching at Pratt Institute and working on a book on architecture and film. She holds a B.A. in Architecture with Theater from Yale University and a MArch from the University of Pennsylvania.

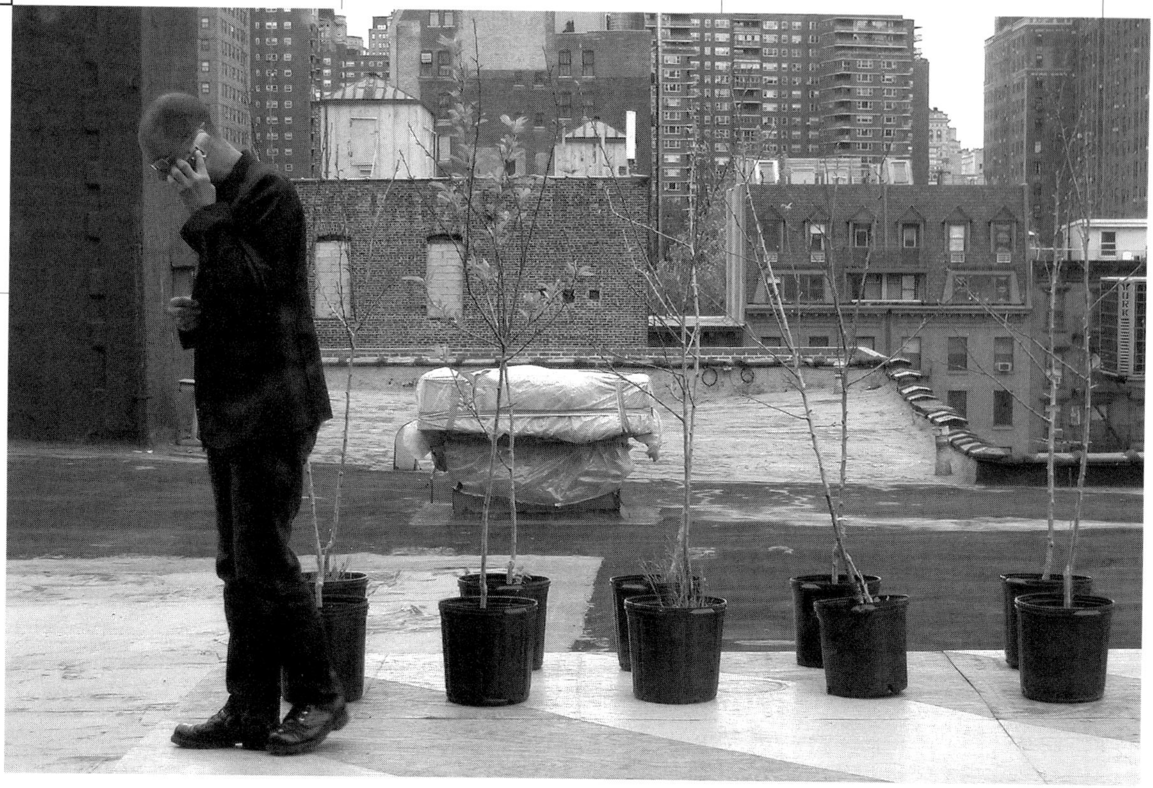

Gordon Kipping of G Tects, on the deck outside his office. >

to see if that question could be answered or at least challenged in an introspective manner. While the interviewed designers are not native New Yorkers, they have gravitated towards the city in both common and uncommon channels; some were schooled here, some have just decided that they wanted to live here. Regardless, all of these designers represent a diverse set of opinions. Gordon Kipping of G Tects is Canadian, while Maria Sieira is American-educated but Spanish in origin. The partners of Work Architecture Company—Amale Andraos, Jens Holm, and Dan Wood—come from three different regions—respectively, the Middle East, Europe, and North America—while Karen Hsu of Omnivore Inc. is originally from Oregon. Many of the questions addressed include, among others: they need to learn and the need to teach; the practicalities of being a young professional in a challenging environment; and the identity of the designer within intersecting disciplines. Further, it will briefly examine, through these diverse design practices, the ability of the city to support and nurture the lives of these young professionals, either through clientele, creativity or practice. Does the city need them, or do they need the city? Or is it all just a perfectly reciprocal relationship?

G Tects, composed of Gordon Kipping, Joseph Lee, and Ayako Mamuro, emphasize that New York's cachet includes innumerable resources such as galleries and other types of creative locations that inspire the development of architecture. For the designers, the city acts as a disseminator of contact and information while at the same time maintaining a highly concentrated amount of media at its core. The city often acts as more of an identity marker than a physical repository of future building sites. In today's climate, the experimental or the non-conventional is not as entrenched as it was a hundred years ago. However, despite its public reputation as an intense and modern city, very few contemporary buildings in New York represent radical innovations in architecture. Presently, it seems that hype is far more interesting than the actual city itself. Recently, other American cities have shown a greater propensity to build innovative buildings. Zaha Hadid's first American building, the Rosenthal Center for Contemporary Arts in Cincinnati, Ohio, springs up in the middle of the country as an example that stimulating commissions may emerge from smaller, less historically progressive cities.

New York has an exciting but brief history compared to its global counterparts. In actuality, its building activity has been rather subdued in recent years. According to Kipping, "If you are here long enough, you seem to think you are at the center, but there are other centers such as Paris, London, Barcelona, or Madrid. Corbusier in the 1920s proposed Ville Radieuse for Paris, to tear down almost twenty-five percent of it, and of course, it didn't happen. Here they take down twenty-five percent of the Lower East Side and build these cruciform towers...it takes up miles and miles. You look at it, and it's not beautiful, but it is pretty radical and incredible that it actually took place. That's some of the greatness of New York."

For Omnivore Inc., a graphic design firm started by Alice Chung and Karen Hsu, whose workload include both local and non-local clients, their ideal is a virtual office allowing both partners to work from anywhere, communicate from each of their respective residences in Manhattan.

The pedestrian quality of the city is extremely attractive for these two designers. New York is a model city that provides projects and also sustains social interests, but even the 24-hour lifestyle of Manhattan has its limitations. Hsu jokes, "We've wanted to order food at 10:30 PM, and the kitchens are usually closed by then. It's the cliché of the city that never sleeps, unless you live in certain neighborhoods or are willing to eat Domino's and deli fare."

While many other metropolitan areas such as Los Angeles contain numerous high profile academic institutions, teaching in New York imparts a different type of urban education on the designer. The work of filmmakers Wim Wenders and Steven Soderbergh provides a framework for the film and architecture explorations dictated by Maria Sieira, who is currently a Visiting Instructor at the Pratt Institute in Brooklyn, New York. Her graduate seminar invites students to view recent films, draw their own individual analyses, and discuss the meaning of the film's central and architectural themes. Sieira understands the practice of architecture as an intellectual experience, as a discipline not bound by the strict parameters of building or form making, but as an academic and practical engagement with ideas and external environments. New York possesses a high concentration of educational institutions such as the Cooper Union, Columbia University, the Pratt Institute, Parsons School of Design, New York University, and the City University of New York, which combine to create a highly enlightening and extensive architectural dialogue between educator, practitioners, and those in between. Thesis projects, which often take as their hypothetical situations popular sites like the Highline corridor that runs from 34th Street to the West Village and Roosevelt Island, provide alternative visions of what New York could possibly become. As an educator, Sieira argues, "I think it is a mistake to try to understand architectural education as years you spend in school. In a way, it is more about acquiring critical

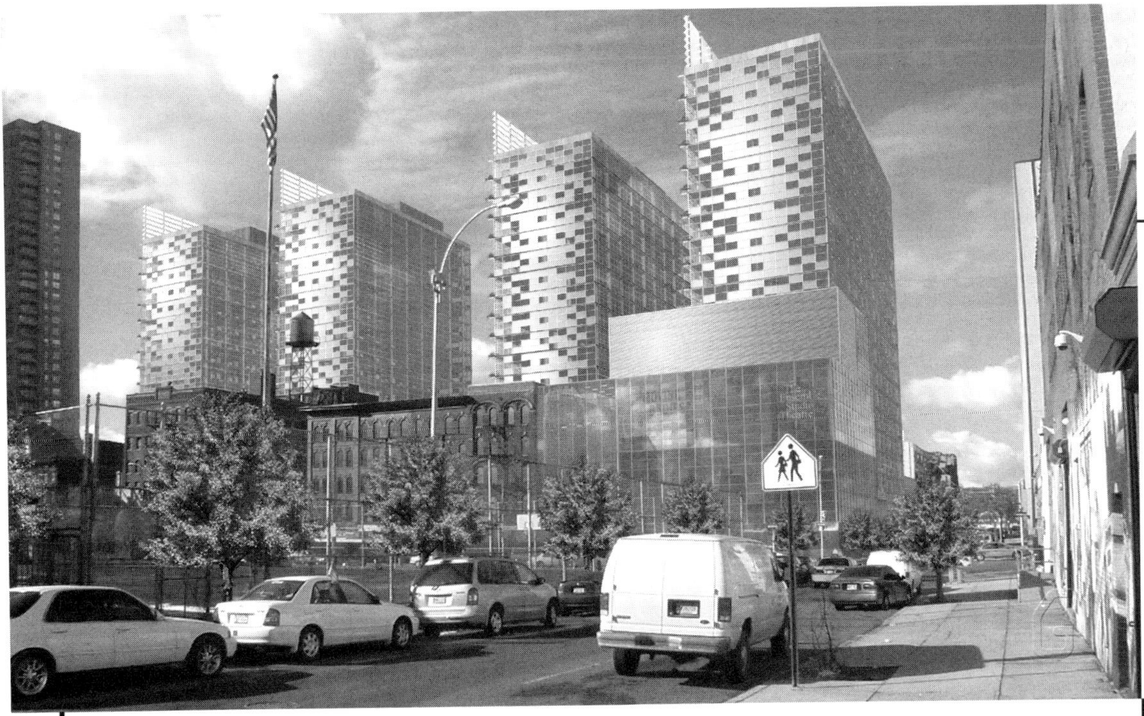

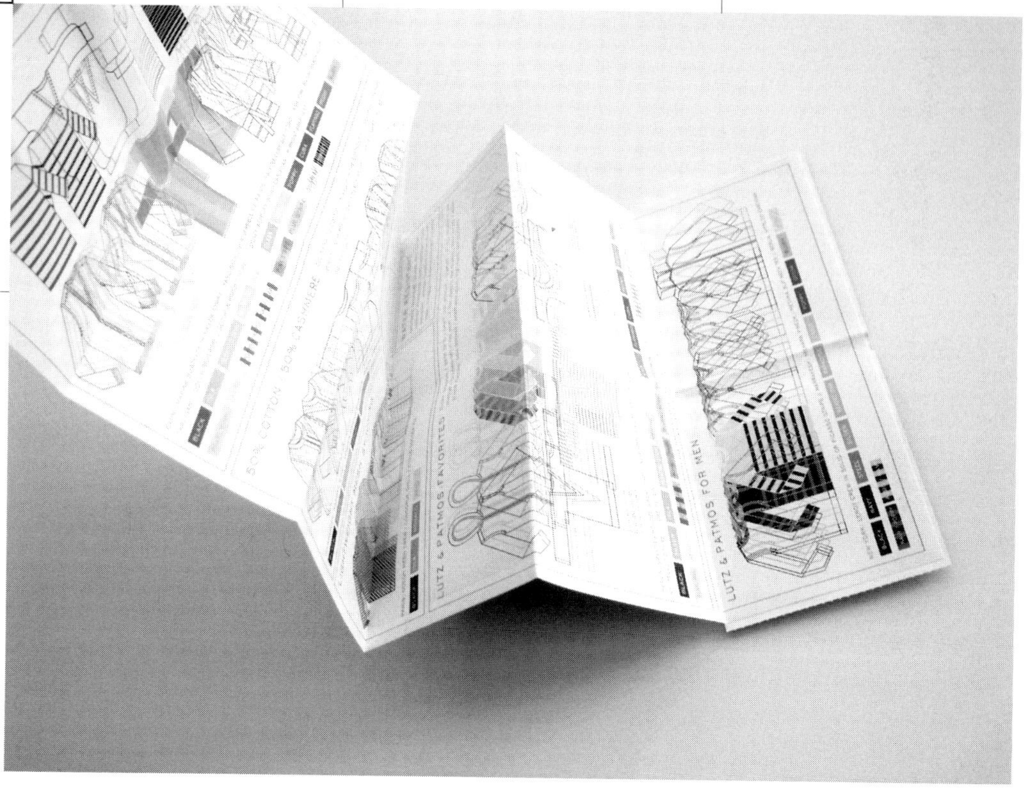

^ Detail of a Lutx & Patmos catalog designed by Omnivore

and analytical skills that you need to continue in education throughout your professional life. It is a mistake to find the perfect education that will give you the perfect architect." Sieira believes that reading and writing are essential elements that link an architect to the intellectual components of design. By picking up a book and reading your way through architecture, you constantly reinterpret how architecture can be framed and developed through different texts and authors.

Building a new reality is certainly not easy; the bridge between theory and practice is a crux that has remained in design discourse since the beginning. Occasionally, the breach is mended when the designer practices and teaches, but even in this case, the balance is often shifted in favor of one over the other. Dan Wood of Work Architecture Company notes, "Theory itself has not had a very good impact on buildings, especially in America. America's contribution to architectural theory has been postmodernism and the blob—neither of which has resulted in very good architecture." Andraos agrees completely, remarking that "It is ironic that the one architect who has built successfully in the blob idiom, Frank Gehry, is also one of the most diametrically opposed to theory."

New York hosts a supportive, active, and accomplished design community. What makes this possible is that the city is able to contain both American and foreign influences. According to Sieira, "The East Coast is certainly not the norm, and the architects who are practicing and teaching in the New York metropolitan area are not necessarily doing what everyone else in the country is doing." While Work Architecture Company similarly perceives New York as an inspirational social environment, they also acknowledge the city's decline as a design center. When asked about the relevance of New York as a design capital, members of Work agreed that New York had lost its influence over the years.

Currently the most exciting cities—and the ones that are in current academic vogue—are those experiencing accelerated transition such as Shanghai, with its rapid growth and skyscrapers, and Beijing, home to the next Olympic games. Even particular European cities seem to overtake New York in their risk-taking and unusual policies; Amale Andraos says, "London is, in many ways, becoming a much more adventuresome urban condition. There are new buildings there by Herzog and deMeuron, Libeskind, and Foster." Dan Wood adds, "Even the Millennium Wheel is interesting. Nothing like that could happen in New York these days, not without a major change in the way the city approaches projects." In a recent competition to redesign the highline—an abandoned elevated track on the West side of Manhattan—over 720 entries indicated that New York invokes a great passion and desire to effect change for the city and for the community. For example, social democracy, decent housing, a black market, and an elongated swimming pool were some of the featured proposals that vowed to inject something back into New York's public space. However, as far as these projects were in the public realm, none seemed be within the realm of public reality. Though such ideas may not find a home in Manhattan they are more than ample fodder for other architectural projects elsewhere.

As Omnivore Inc., Alice Chung and Karen Hsu embody a playful yet serious tact towards the projects they collectively undertake; their graphic design evokes a quirky sensibility that tries to respond specifically to different client needs. Both Chung and Hsu immensely enjoy working with architects as well as others in the art and design community such as artists, museums, galleries, filmmakers, and industrial designers. While these professionals also bring a degree of design experience and visual acuity to the collective process but do admit that architects have the tendency to impose their own experiences onto graphic design. Chung explains, "Working with architects is sometimes difficult; some come back to us with specific graphic design *solutions*, but the skills are not always so easily transferable." Architects often approach graphic design if it were an another exercise in spatial orientation-which it often is not. Often, there is a greater, nuanced quality in graphic design that helps mediate not just the world of two-dimensional, but between all dimensions.

Despite different working methods, the cooperative nature of architecture and graphic design can generate productive and provocative results. For example, Hsu, while working for the graphic-design firm 2x4, worked with the Office for Metropolitan Architecture on the Guggenheim Las Vegas, situated at the Guggenheim Hermitage Hotel. The team, along with firm principals Michael Rock and Georgie Stout, developed a typographic approach, both as surface and volume, to be integrated into the building's architecture. From the Cor-Ten steel facade to the dimensional letters of the museum's main entrance, a graphic approach to building an environment is one that 2x4 has played a leading role in accomplishing.

Another unique aspect of the four designers profiled in this piece is their collective stalwart bravery in starting an independent professional practice, making not only designers out of each of these individuals, but also business owners. Chung and Hsu share an all-or-nothing work ethic towards their projects. Their eventual partnership, independent of 2x4, was perhaps inevitable. When asked about the anxiety or even uncertainty of starting and sustaining a practice, Hsu laughs gently, "Maybe this is all hubris, but I never thought that we would fail. There are different levels of succeeding; there is getting by; there is doing very well...it was always a fear, but there is always the Starbucks down the block."

Amale Andraos, Jens Holm, and Dan Wood, who formed the practice Work Architecture Company, shared a common experience working for Rem Koolhaas at the Office for Metropolitan Architecture. It is often challenging for a newly formed practice to escape the influence of their mother firm as well as forge an entirely separate organization with a new agenda. Wood explains that certain aspects of starting a business are more advantageous than in Europe. "The United States is still miles ahead in its approach to intellectual property, contract documents, fees, etc," he says. "Getting clients to agree is still a challenge, but for us, there is an excitement in trying to build a more traditional work structure."

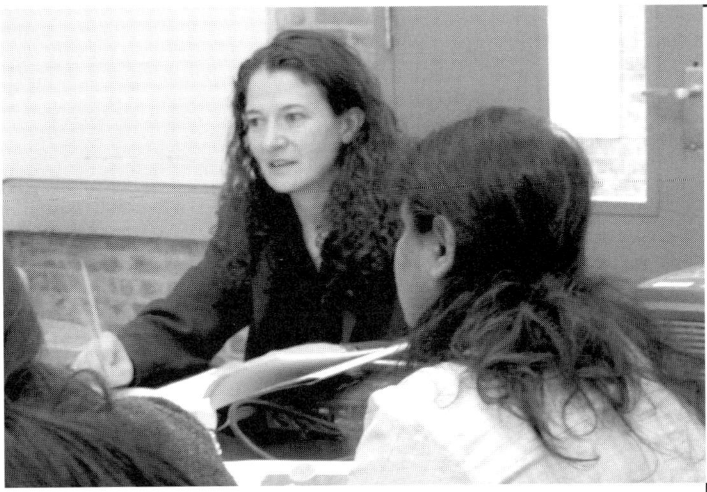

< Maria Sieira hosts a meeting

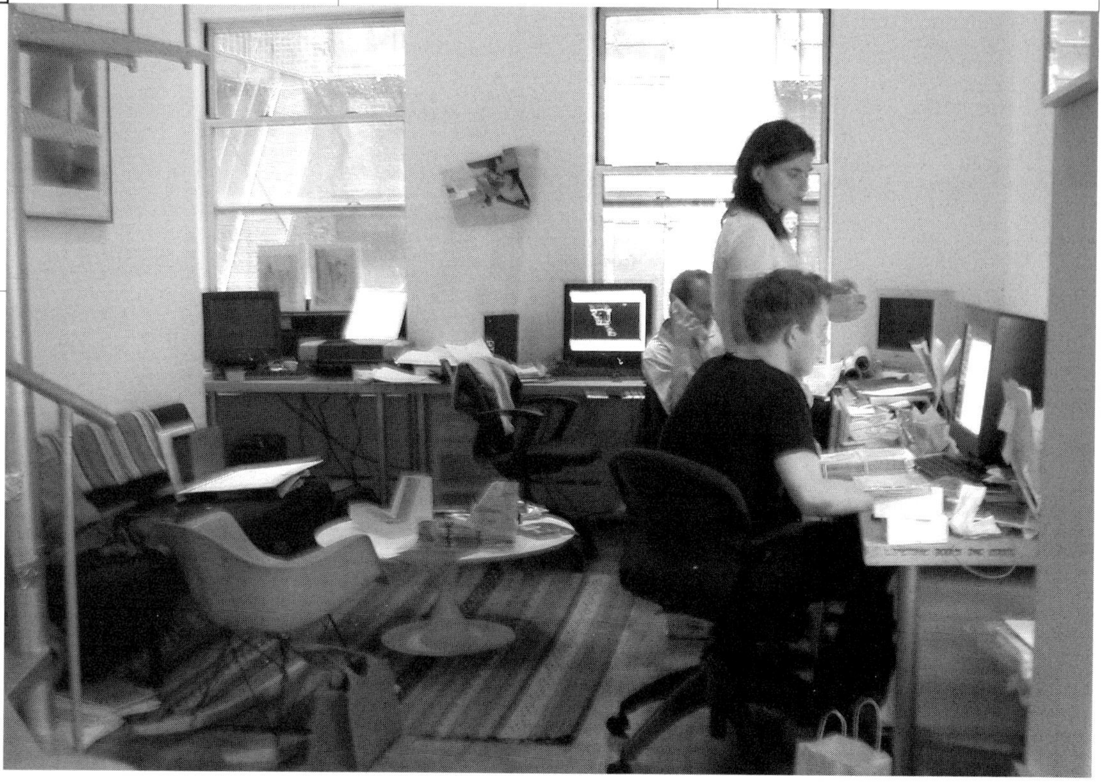

Gordon Kipping explains that one of the reasons for independent practice is that, in some ways, he feels his generation has made it an absolute priority to follow a path that would definitively lead towards the completion of a project. He assertively says, "Younger or new graduates are not always sure of what they don't know, so they think they are being passed over because they are young. I've been practicing at least for ten years, and I'm still learning. I will still learn until I'm 60, 70, until I retire." The inclusion of related fields such as sustainable design, civil engineering, urban planning and policy, and design-build practices also provides for greater synergies; having greater control over what kind of work you do and with whom you do it makes the possibilities even greater.

Additionally, the mode of architectural practice has significantly changed with new tools such as animation software, faster computers, laser cutters, and rapid prototyping machines—but how have institutional and educational processes intangibly affected the ways in which current young designers shape their environment, peers, projects, and their individual trajectories? In Maria Sieira's projects, the architecture of film plays a significant part in her role as a writer and educator; she heavily advocates for architecture as an intellectual obligation. Sieira says, "I always had the suspicion that teaching studio was a way of learning about architecture. It is a way of doing architecture." She began her teaching career at the University of Missouri with computer animation courses and studio classes; the focus of her first studio concentrated on developing a new prototype theater for independent films which would be as good as the outlets for mainstream movies. She soon discovered that the young filmmakers at the Sundance Film Festival and other similar venues were extremely interested in having someone theorize new types of film and provide a unique perspective on their work. Her career, in part, began in Missouri, yet Sieira persists that she eventually was drawn back to New York since the city offers an exciting and intellectual environment for architecture. Places such as the BAM Rose Cinema as well as Pratt Institute and the surrounding Fort Greene area of Brooklyn provided Sieira with abundant resources and provocative ideas for her work. Sieira affirms, "What has happened in the last twenty years in terms of architectural theory is significant. I would like to understand architecture as something other than the making of objects or form. Architecture should be a bigger field of study, more of a discipline rather than a limited practice."

Independent design practices like Sieira's allow for a unique amount of conceptualization and research. The designer, having control over his or her time, is better equipped to manage and allot time for both practical and theoretical pursuits. Holm, of Work, also stresses, "We approach all of our work from the standpoint of concept. It is an intellectual approach, but it is also strongly rooted in reality. In many ways, current discourse and theory do not mix with the reality of practice." Wood summarizes their mutual design goals by stating, "For us, the real stimulation is reconceptualizing the relationships between physical space and virtual space, bridging branding and architecture...and pitting ambition against the building code."

Diverse experiences are necessary for intellectual and technical growth in a field as expansive and competitive as design. An emphasis on the extreme importance of collaboration, creative control, peer support, and an open-minded practice of design is a common perspective that ties these various ambitions together. Presently, there is even more flexibility in how one chooses to become a designer. Simultaneously alternating between educated student and experienced professional, physical-space maker and virtual designer, the young designer attempts to carve an exclusive space both for him/her self and for his or her work—especially the type of work that will allow the greatest amount of freedom and personal satisfaction.

Even after attempting to divulge some enlightened opinions upon the question and importance of the designed environment on designing that environment, there was no real consensus or uniform explanation among these four groups of designers as to why their city is ultimately essential to design. But New York itself is important for many reasons—for trends; for cultural resources; for diversity; for work; for colleagues; and for intellectual expansion. All of these things in themselves comprise what we know as design and ultimately guide us towards a more motivated and informed aesthetic of our world. While New York is a huge metropolis and a universal emblem. It is, at the same time, a city where one can find individual meaning and direction. You do not necessarily have to come to New York to succeed as a designer, but somehow the city becomes that essential urban network, inspiring and challenging any designer, pushing him or her towards the intended or even accidental destination. Compared to other global centers, New York may not be at its pinnacle right now, but it is determined and waiting for its chance to surprise us with distinct innovation. In spite of the chaos of mass transportation, crowded bodies, and disproportionate economies, the city allows for a generous amount of success and failure in design, both of which provide relatively exciting consequences. These four groups of designers will most likely leave an imprint on New York, and most assuredly, the city will leave an imprint on them.

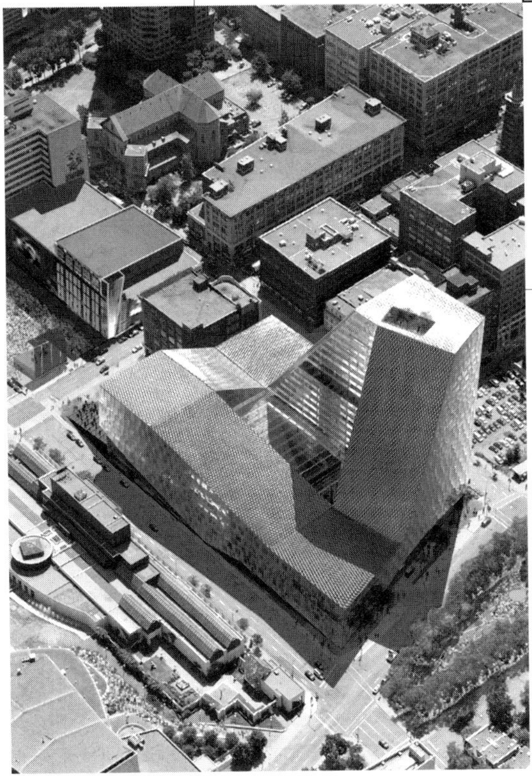

< A project by work for a site in Montreal

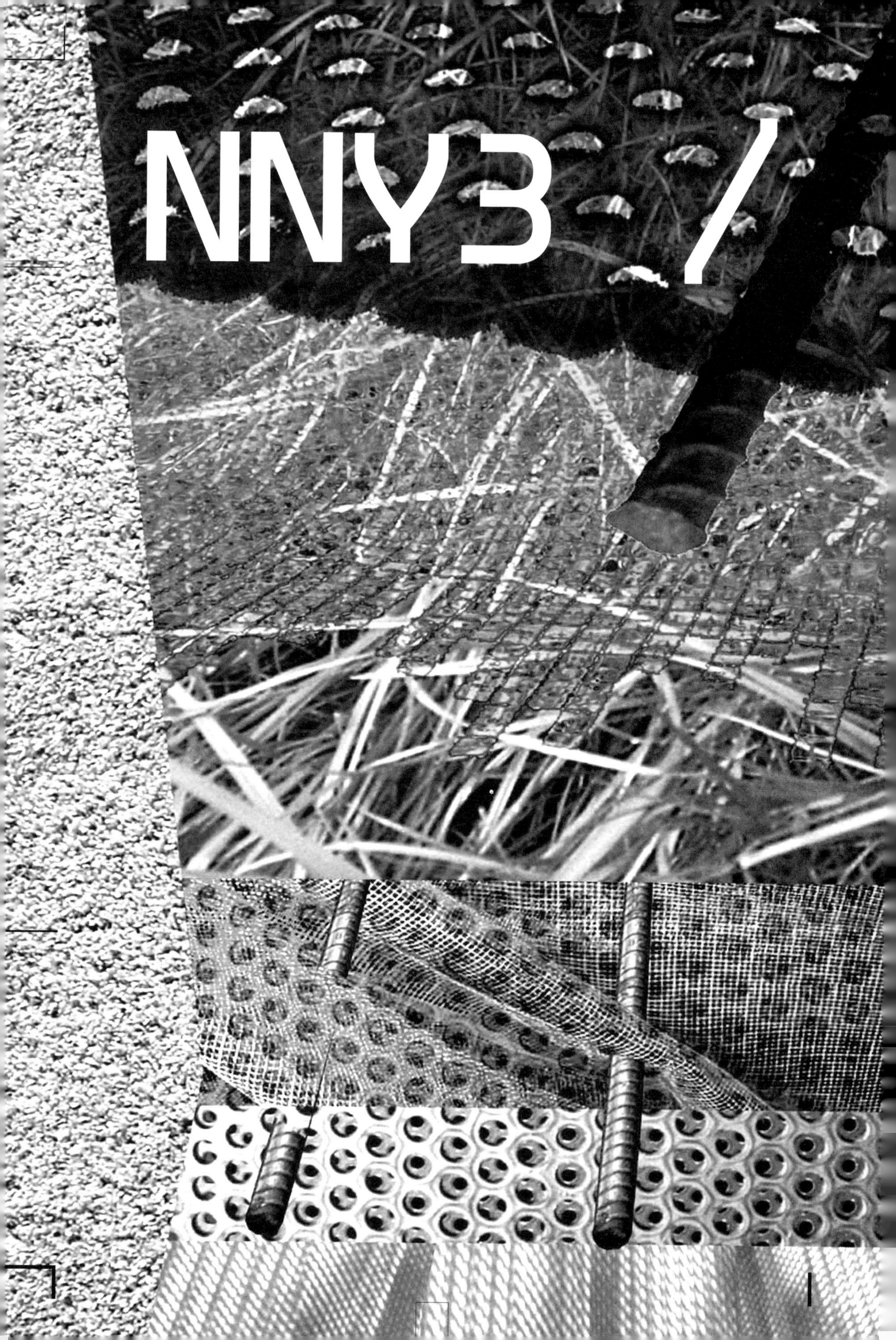
NNY3 /

Two projects from SYSTEMarchitects

WARM-UP

by SYSTEMArchitects

The Devil with Boobs opened on Broadway this April. Pulitzer prize-winning author Dario Fo's play was performed the first time for American audiences. Two weeks before the show opened, Rosalie Genevro, director of the Architectural League, received a letter from the show's producer thanking her for the generous donation of foam to the Material for the Arts program from which the set for the play had been made. This would be the second life for that odd 3000 square feet of foam.

The foam took on a first life when the Architectural League asked *system* to design the exhibition for their newNew York3 (nNY3) show involving over 17 projects and almost as many firms. The nNY3 exhibition is the third in a series promoting architectural projects of high merit from within the five boroughs of New York. Included in nNY3 are ten projects completed under the Robin Hood Library Program, four selected community centers designed and built by the New York City Housing Authority (NYCHA) as well as the proposed East River ferry terminals designed by Kennedy Violich Architects and sponsored by the EDC (Economic Development Corporation). The dual program given *system* was to design an exhibit that ties these myriad projects together; design an installation that does not damage the landmark interior of the Urban Center's left wing gallery. The *system* response engages that complexity with another set of spaces

SYSTEMarchitects is an architecture and research firm based in New York. Recent SYSTEM projects include the seCCA HOME House Competition, a series of three green/off-the-grid houses in Australia, a house in Wellfleet Massachusetts and the Fall 2002 nNY3 Installation for the Architectural League. The office is also featured in the Architectural Record's 2001 Design Vanguard and.

Jeremy Edmiston [New York State License #025793–Partner] holds a Master in Architecture from Columbia University and a Bachelor in Architecture from the University of Technology, Sydney. Jeremy has lectured and served as visiting Professor in the schools of Architecture at Columbia University, Roger Williams University, and The City College of CUNY.

Douglas Gauthier [New York State License #024334–Partner] holds a Master in Architecture from Columbia University and a Bachelor in Architecture and Art History from the University of Notre Dame. Douglas has lectured at a various institutions while serving as a studio professor in several universities including Columbia GSAP, CCAC, RWU, Yale, City College, Barnard and Princeton.

nNY3 project team:
Josef Jelinek, team leader; Sarkis Arakelyan; Marlon Cruz; Jorge Fontan; Salomon Frausto; Henry Grosman; Se Hyuk Jung; Ioanna Karagiannakou; Yarek Karawczyk; Maciej Kusmierski; Megumi Mieno; Anna Misanvu; Marco Montalto; Stanley Pikul; Christian Soberanis; Chiyomi Ueoka.

P.S.1 Exhibition project team:
Sarkis Arakelyan; Amber Lynn Bard; Jeremy Carvalho; Tam Duong; Rose Evans; Jorge Fontan; Salomon Frausto; Kobi Pinto; Henry Grosman; Josef Jelinek; Jane Kim; Maciej Kusmierski; Yarek Krawczyk; Christian Soberanis.

Structural Engineers
Buro Happold, Craig Schwitter and Cristobal Correa

All images courtesy of SYSTEMarchitects

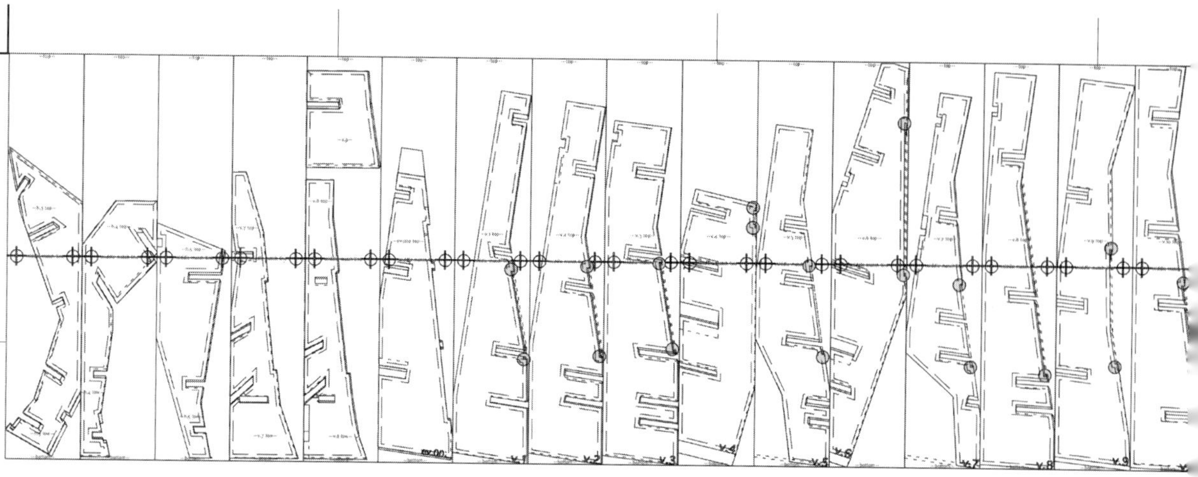
v.1
v.2
v.3
v.4
v.5
v.6
v.7
v.8
v.9

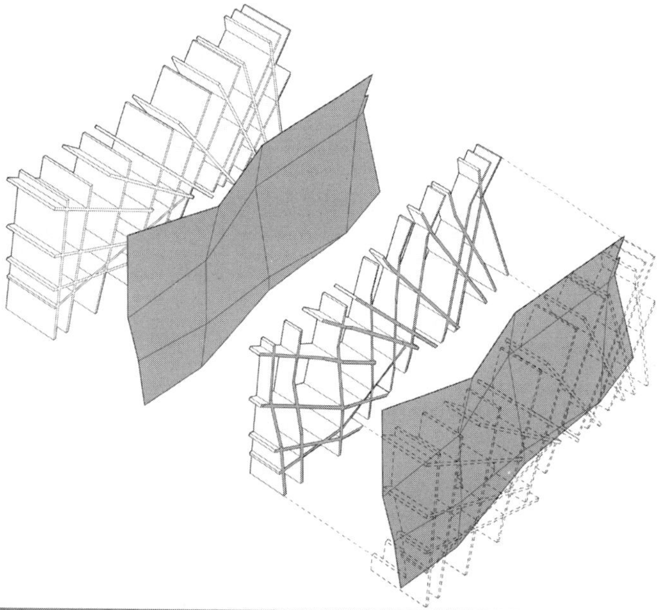

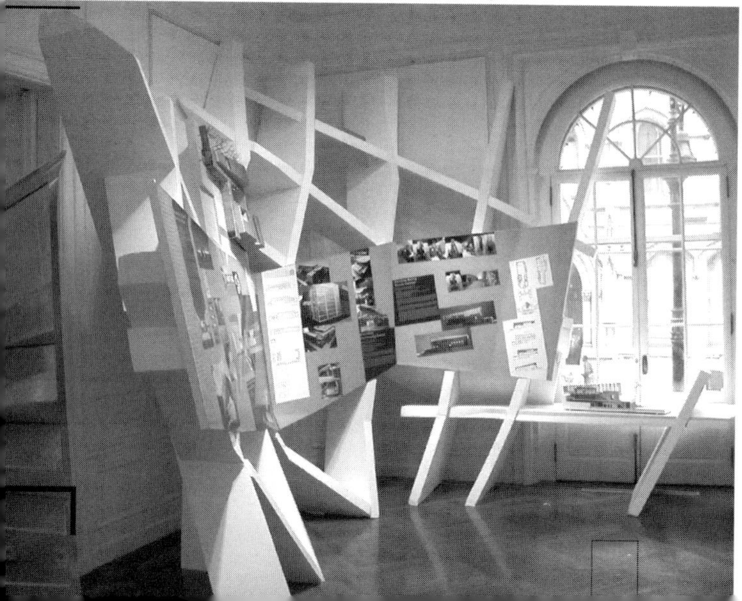

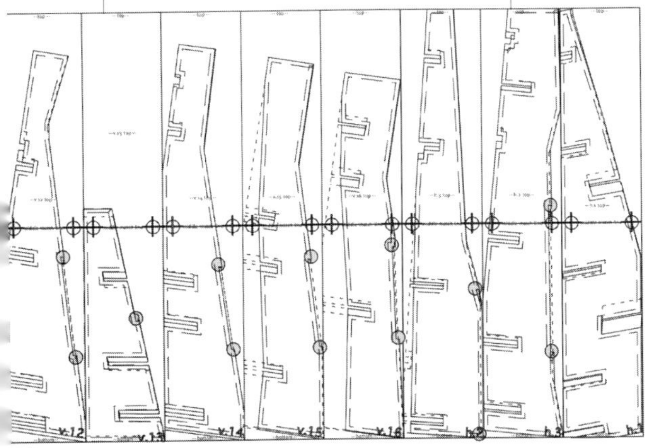

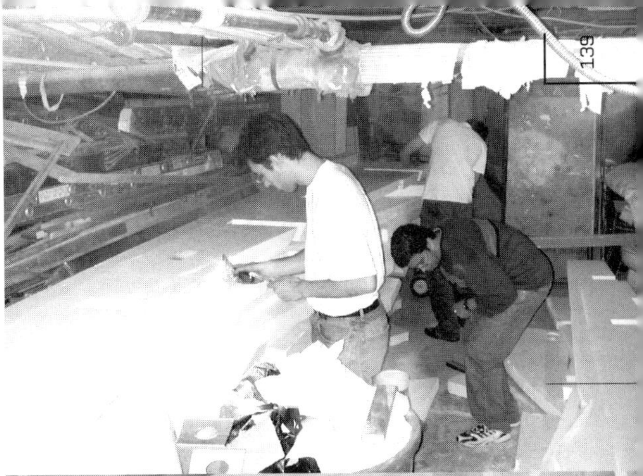

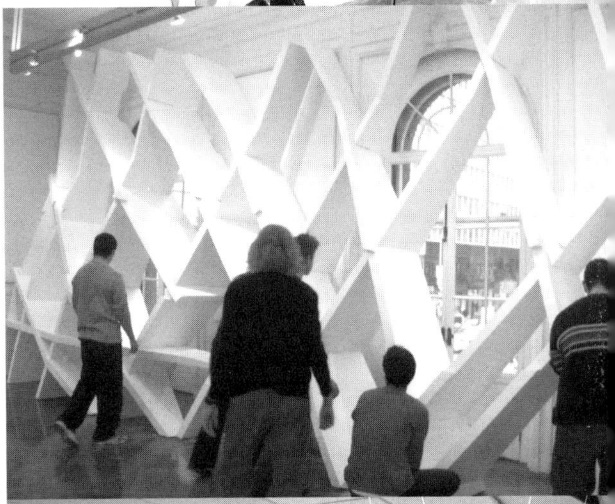

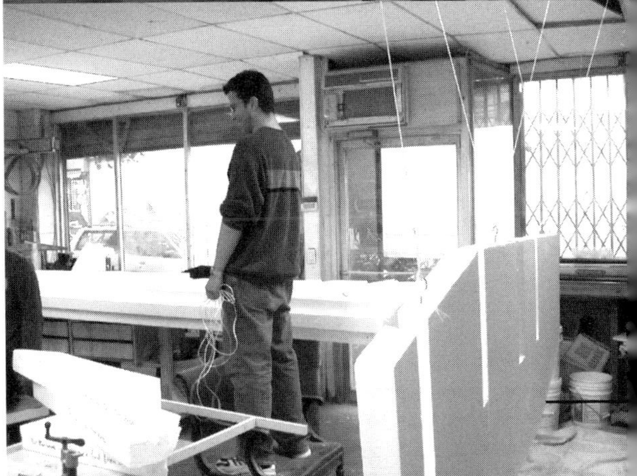

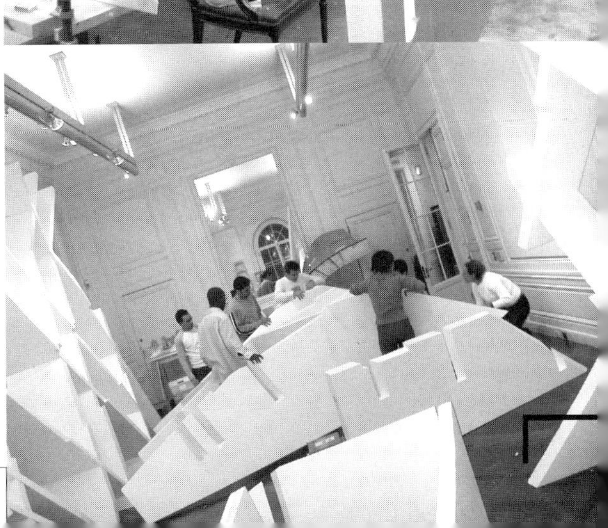

within the existing gallery. In order to bring these disparate elements together *system* chose a spatially driven strategy over an object—or furniture-driven strategy. The images, drawings and models of the projects presented in the exhibition are nested in and on the ribs and overall surface texture pulling out from the gallery walls.

Such an extensive design on a small budget employs either the digital labor of milling machines or the analog labor of architecture students. It is an irony or an opportunistic collusion that the lectures, exhibitions and symposium provided by the Architectural League are the first forum where many New York City students engage architectural culture outside of the university. An institution that provides another network within the city, and *system,* where both partners teach, would now combine to enlist—for 30% of the installation budget—students to construct and install the exhibition.

The strategy for nNY3 is to re-skin the gallery walls using another idealized surface that shapes and affects the flow of the viewer and then to embed the exhibition material in this spatially changing system. These new walls/surfaces employ a series of folded planes supported by ribs that are more responsive to the geometry of the folded surface lines than to any orthogonal support system. The planes of the walls are stripped away, exposing the ribs, removing the surface until the amount of folded wall left intact is just enough to display the work. This project is interested in the spatial remaking of the gallery space that the surface strategy provides, as well as in the filigree and depth left by exposing the rib structure. The filigree of the ribs allows daytime sunlight and the night's action, noise and street-light into the installation through the large gallery windows that the ribs. The ribs are also glimpsed from the adjoining gallery and entrance area to tease and provoke curiosity.

The foam surfboard construction is both delicate and strong, leaning against the walls and windows of the gallery, touching only the floor and the top

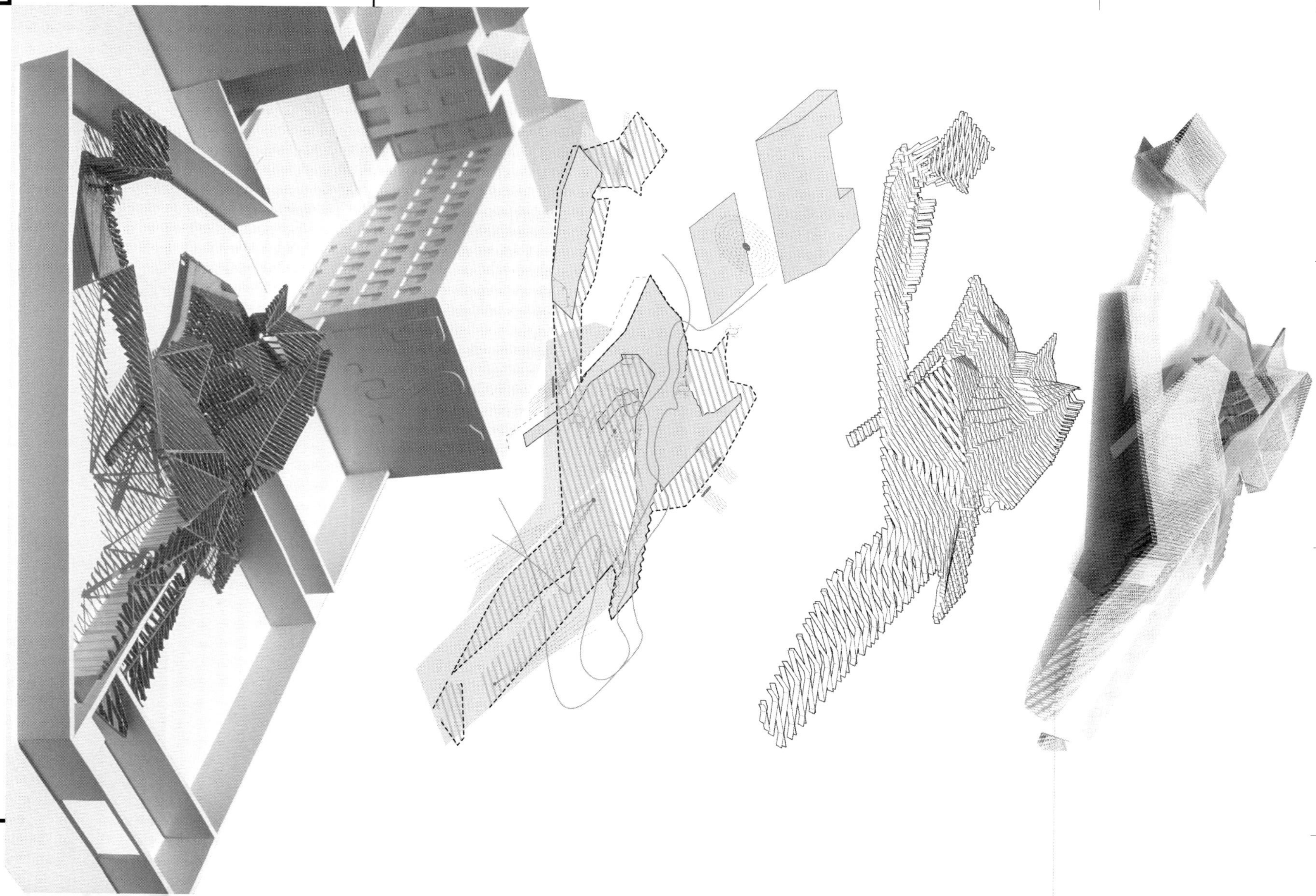

of the walls, did not damage either surface. Foam has many advantages including cost, workability and weight but its tendency towards the landfill isn't easily reconciled and might have proven to be a deal-breaker within the green sympathies and constraints adhered to by the Architectural League. That is, if not for Materials for the Arts. Recycling as a program of re-use is where the Materials for the Arts program was the key to taking the advantages given by foam and as it turns out allowing the project to become part of another system of production within the city—or for the *Devil with Boobs*.

The budget and schedule didn't quite provide for milling the 150 pieces of foam needed. Option two was concocting a human milling machine—which proved to be a group of 9 architecture students from City College's and Columbia University's architecture schools. Precise, full-scale pattern or template drawings for each piece of foam were printed in the office. This pattern made from the 3D computer model with the depth of each piece was projected onto the flat surface of the drawing. This depth and the uniquely angled cuts were color-coded, reducing the complexities of shape, angles and location of the foam knife to a set of clear processes. The foam pieces and the plotter paper were limited by a 36" wide dimension but the length of 16' and the 3" thickness were accommodated by the coded line work. The production team first pasted the numbered patterns onto the foam, cut the foam to the patterns using a table saw or hot wire and finally painted the pieces the exact color of the gallery wall. This work was done in a Yonkers workshop, which quickly filled with cut foam. Running out of workspace the team rented a large truck and did much of the painting and finish work in the truck or on the street.

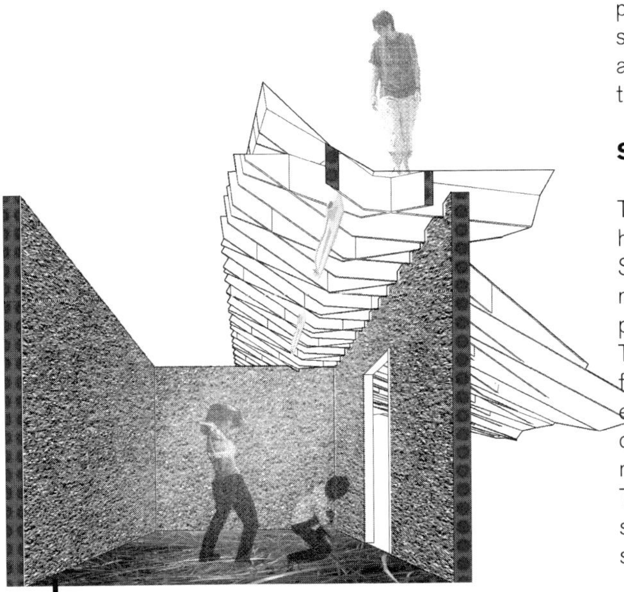

That same truck delivered the finished foam pieces to the League where the assembly team sorted the pieces and began stitching the wall together. Joining the panels required a small team delicately lifting and sliding the panels on the floor. The joints were not glued so raising the wall off the floor required a pair of hands at each joint for support while the section was lifted against the wall. Every able-bodied person at the Urban Center who lent a hand or two raising each of the four sections in only a few minutes augmented the installation team. The computer model had transformed rectangular pieces of foam into abstract ribs that formed the new gallery surface. These walls were rigid and brittle. Each rib dovetailed together with four or five adjacent ribs. The geometry sustained a twisting surface that turned the corner of the gallery. In the computer these pieces were easily connected and disengaged from one another without any rule of mass. The foam however, while perfectly aligned in the final position, in certain locations, could not be fitted to four pieces simultaneously. The angle of the joints produced twisting in some of the panels only as they were sliding into their joints. This created an intentional break and facilitated the invention of the on-site dowel joint.

Digital three-dimensional modeling does not always follow specific rules of gravity and the ribs alone do not have a lateral support system. Locking ribs into their final place depended on the display panels or the sections of the folded wall notched into the ribs. Before these were put in, the ribs on their own elongated the sections up to ten feet longer than designed. The physicality of the pieces, as well as their weight and geometry, obstructed any seamless installation. However, once the colluding systems of rib and surface were locked—the accuracy of the computer model transposed into a full-sized foam construction was continuously shocking. The process of cutting the foam from the pattern never seemed completely accurate, yet on-site, the pieces always slotted together making a strong mesh of the ribs.

SYSTEMsystems

Two projects using similar methods are presented here—the nNY3 installation and the 2003 P.S.1 Summer Warm-Up competition proposal. The relationship between the students and these two projects is an operative or even opportunistic one. The projects do not rely on stable, recognized form and program such as the house—but instead engage the students through the ingenuity and difference of making program and form with a responsive non-intuitive construction method. The interesting play here is that the institutions sponsoring P.S.1 and nNY3 assume that the students are willing to work on these projects.

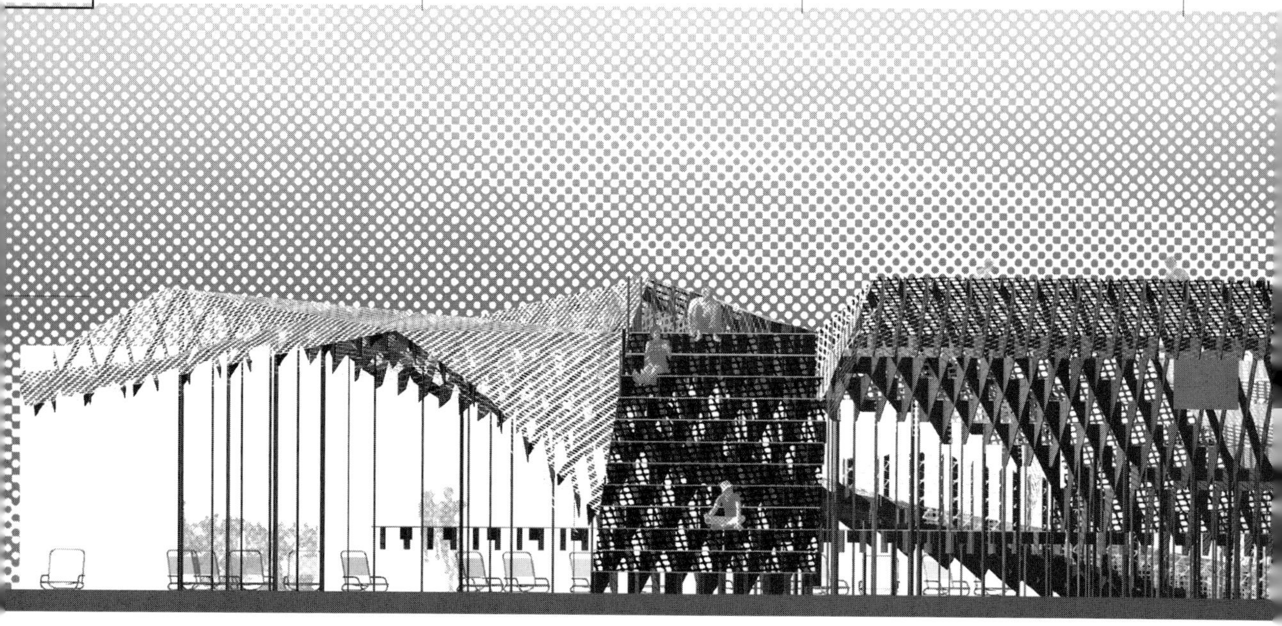

To that end *system* set up the budgets for each project where 30% of the nNY3 and 20% of the lager P.S.1 budget were reserved for the student work. Both projects make special efforts to engage the students involved in the project production and installation and P.S.1 hosts a summer of activities that include international guest DJs, events and parties. On the weekend, young residents of the neighborhood and surrounding boroughs can go to the museum to get relief from the oppressive urban heat. Families with children play in the forecourt during the day and as the shadows lengthen the dancing starts. The Warm-Up program expects the creation of an outdoor fantasy space.

Both projects share a construction methodology that is taken from computer-generated form. In nNY3 the structure is made of notched, angled pieces and cut from large-scale pieces of painted foam. Warm-Up uses a plywood structure cut out by computer-driven water-jet system. The P.S.1 proposal, the second generation of the process, uses steel X-clips, plastic grating, plastic netting, Astroturf, sod, hard foam, sprinklers and water equipment. Warm-Up goes beyond transforming the spatial condition of an existing exhibition space. The spaces are driven by programmatic requirements based on viewing but in the P.S.1 proposal, rather than inhabiting a transformed gallery space the construction is itself habitable. Using a surface method for design, Warm-Up Bridge propositions the walls of the gallery's forecourt. They functionally and visually succumb when confronted by the bridge's diaphanous weave.

With the bridge as its design model, the Warm-Up project takes on the spatial criteria of up, down, over and under, all the while connecting P.S.1's small and large courtyard galleries. Occupy-able in its undercroft, it's also transverse-able, dance-uponable and sit-uponable in its up-and-over filigree structure. Roughly half the bridge is made up of bleachers and ramps, while the rest of the surface provides a moiré of shade that traces the sun's

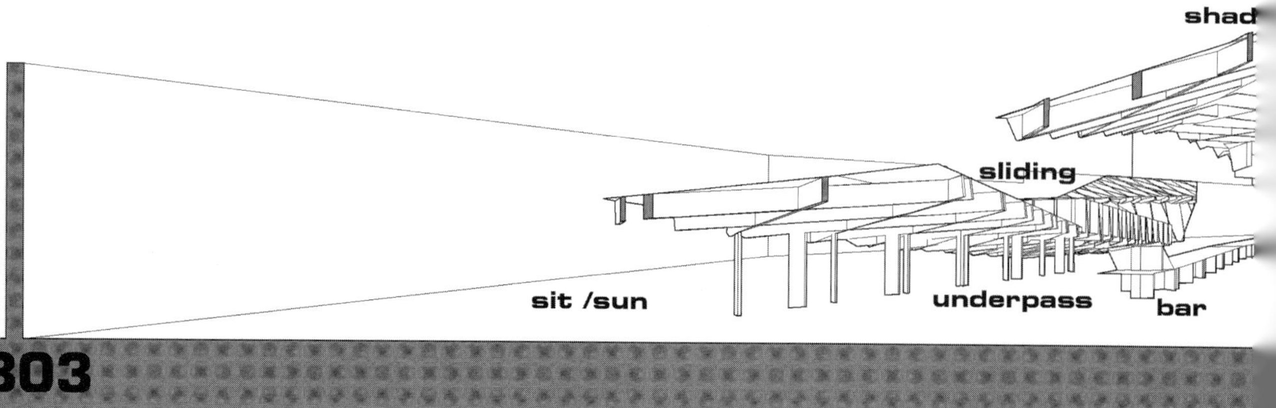

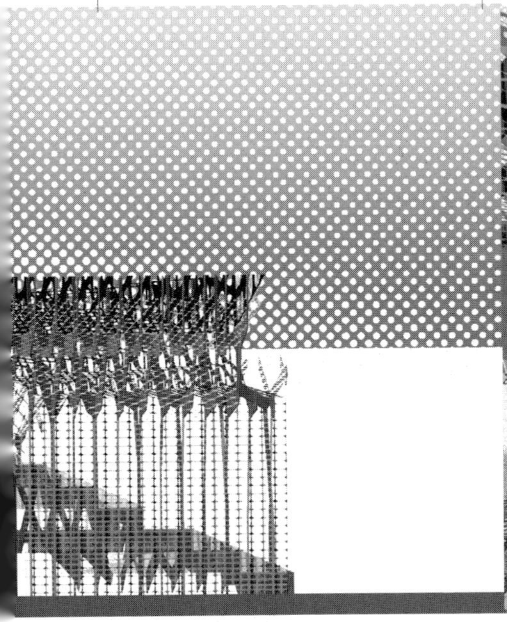

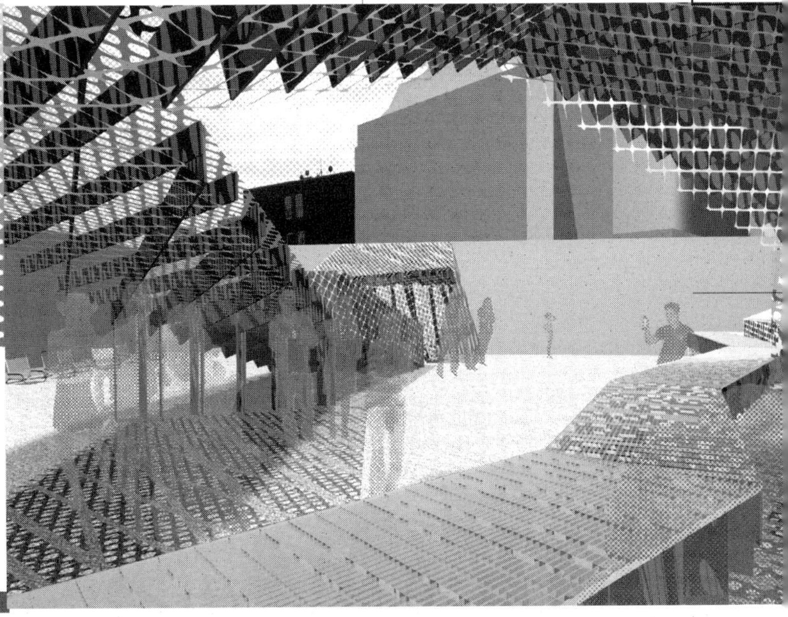

movement across the grounds and walls. That moiré is comprised of grating, the woven-rib structure and plastic netting holding the structure in tension. The ramp/bleachers flow up and over the existing 15-foot walls, and fold into a 70 foot long bar. The shading starts at the entrance of the courtyard and forks back to the bleachers and into an Astroturf-covered wet slippy-slide that empties into a shallow pool.

Both projects were done while the partners at *system* were teaching design studios. Students from City College, Princeton and Columbia University, work in the office. The process of designing these projects shared a great deal with the design concepts, methods and techniques in our teaching approach. In some ways these projects parallel process within the realms of practice and the academy. In many ways this structure is paramount in the work of *system*. In the 2ndNATURE—a manifesto proposal—architecture is used to define Nature. In defining a practice of architecture *system* uses a mixed assemblage of procedures, positions and consequences, to render a condition. This condition is fed by what this assemblage can do. Practice includes research, competitions, writing, work, teaching, consulting, and of course, building. Research topics frame and inform built or intended to be built work, without serving as a direct manifestation of the research. Each project presented proposes some sort of invention associated with the design. *system* believes there is an emerging school of architecture that is blatantly interested in working on the questions of more operative processes of design. Armed with invention rather than prescription, we are curious about how to use technology as a means of reconceiving the economies and aesthetics of building. This parallel processing makes hierarchies seem tangential to the real work that might be done, and privileges the way things work over the way things look.

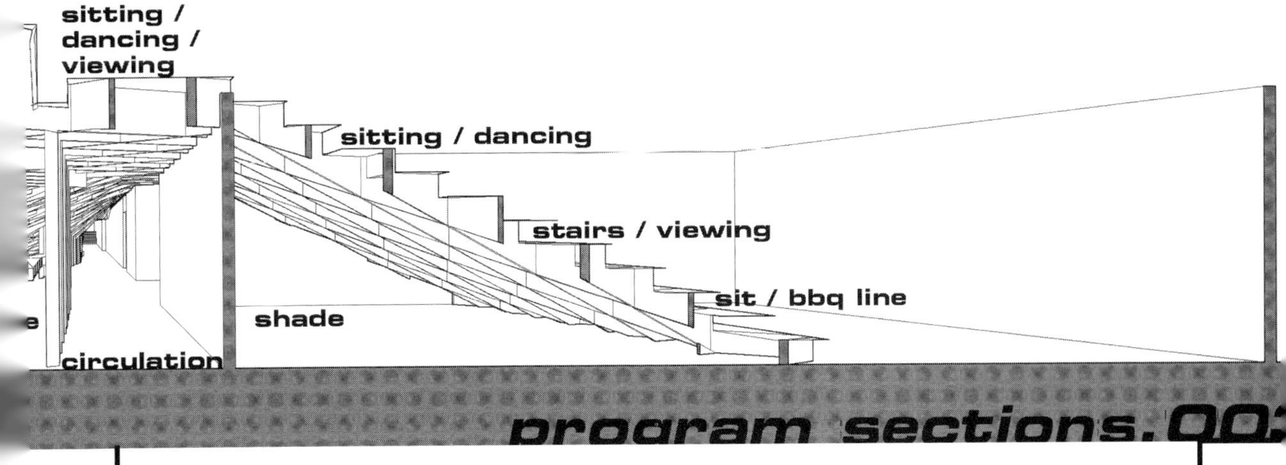

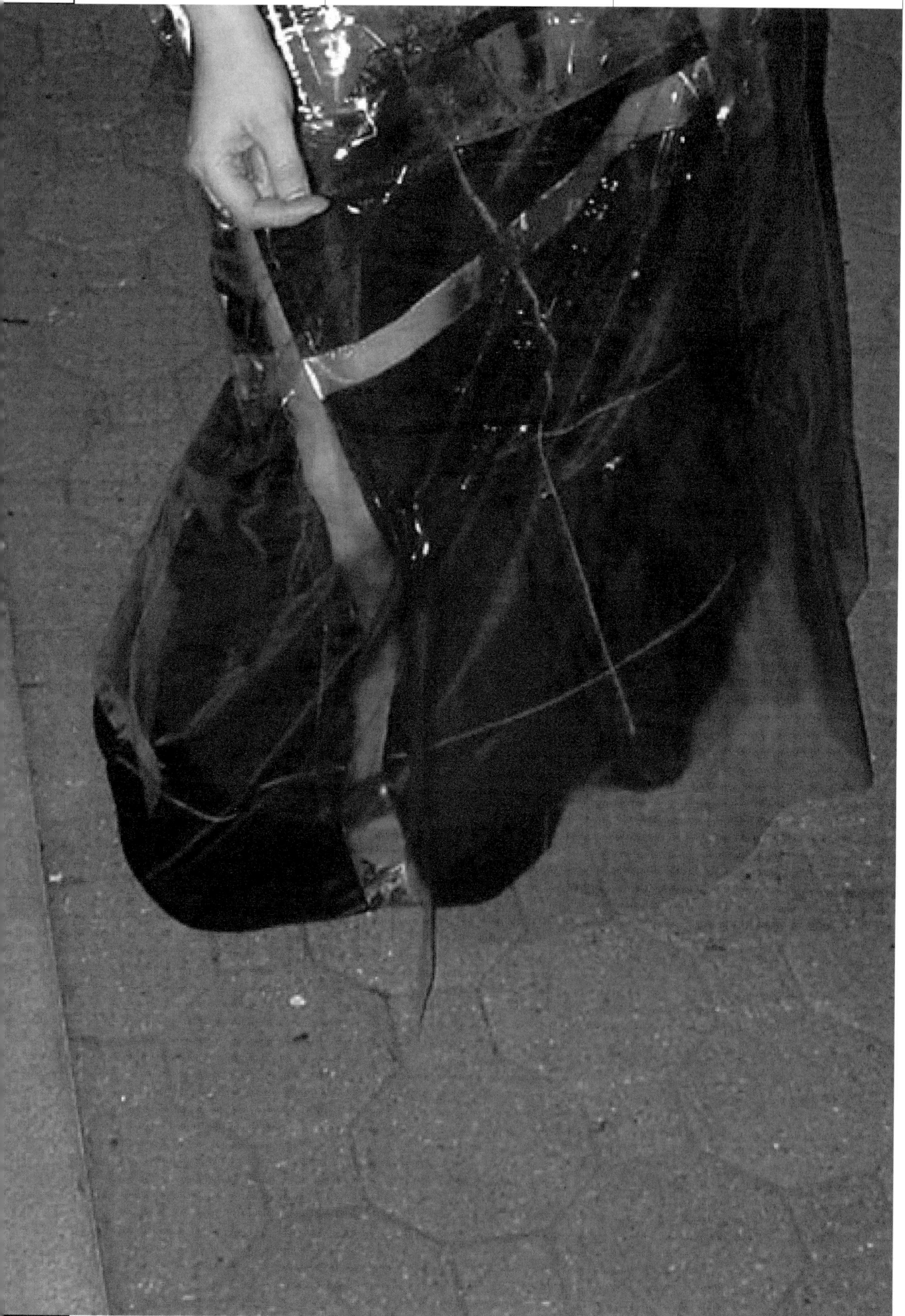

A studio at the Ohio State University

SURVEY SAYS

by Janette Kim

The Assignment:

Make a device that measures the site.
RULE 1. The site is any area that touches High Street in downtown Columbus.
RULE 2. Measurements must be quantitative.

What is worth measuring? A vertical studio of undergraduate and graduate students at the Knowlton School of Architecture at the Ohio State University enacted creative research techniques in the city to identify points of contact between the public and networks of information (systems that include communication, navigation, exchange, ecology, surveillance, and urban infrastructure).

The city cannot be separated from these systems of exchange and infrastructure—and as a result, our access to the city often depends upon our ability to register such networks. By adopting surveying techniques for their own purposes, architects and architecture students alike can play an active role in creating portraits of the city, the public, and civic identity.

With this in mind, students created devices that generate their own systems of information and affect the environment in the process. They reconfigured methods of collection and sampling, tracking technologies, and techniques of information

Janette Kim runs an ongoing project called All of the Above that locates and redesigns sources of information in the physical environment. She currently lives and works in New York City, and is on the faculty at the Rensselaer Polytechnic Institute School of Architecture. The work shown here resulted from the Howard LeFevre fellowship at the Ohio State University from 2002-3. Kim holds an MArch from Princeton University and a BA from Columbia University.

(START)

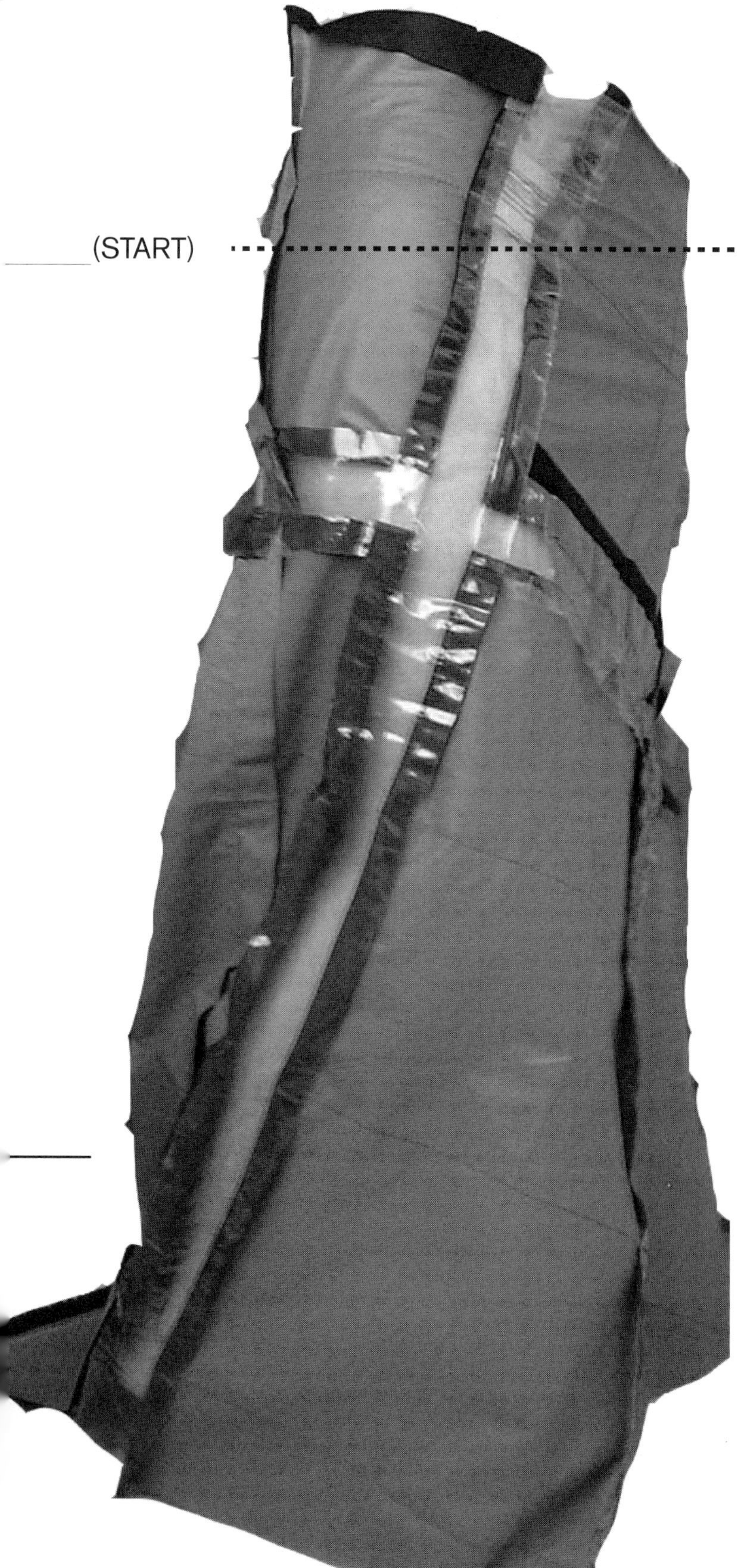

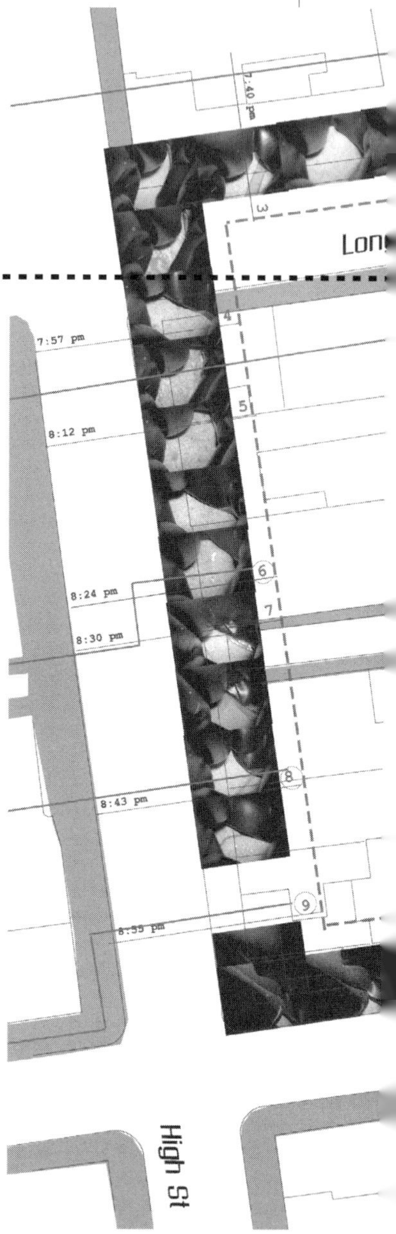

THE PICK-UP SKIRT by Teresa Ball

The Pick Up Skirt collects site information as one leisurely walks around downtown Columbus. Double-sided sticky film on the bottom of the skirt accumulates *data* (i.e. dirt and cigarette butts) from the sidewalk, and then is periodically placed inside the clear display window—the outer layer of the skirt. In this way actual pieces of the site are juxtaposed with the standard map of the site visible in the stitching of the lining. These site samples also give the user privacy. The Pick Up Skirt contains a pneumatic tube that triggers a camera to take photographs of the ground with each step.

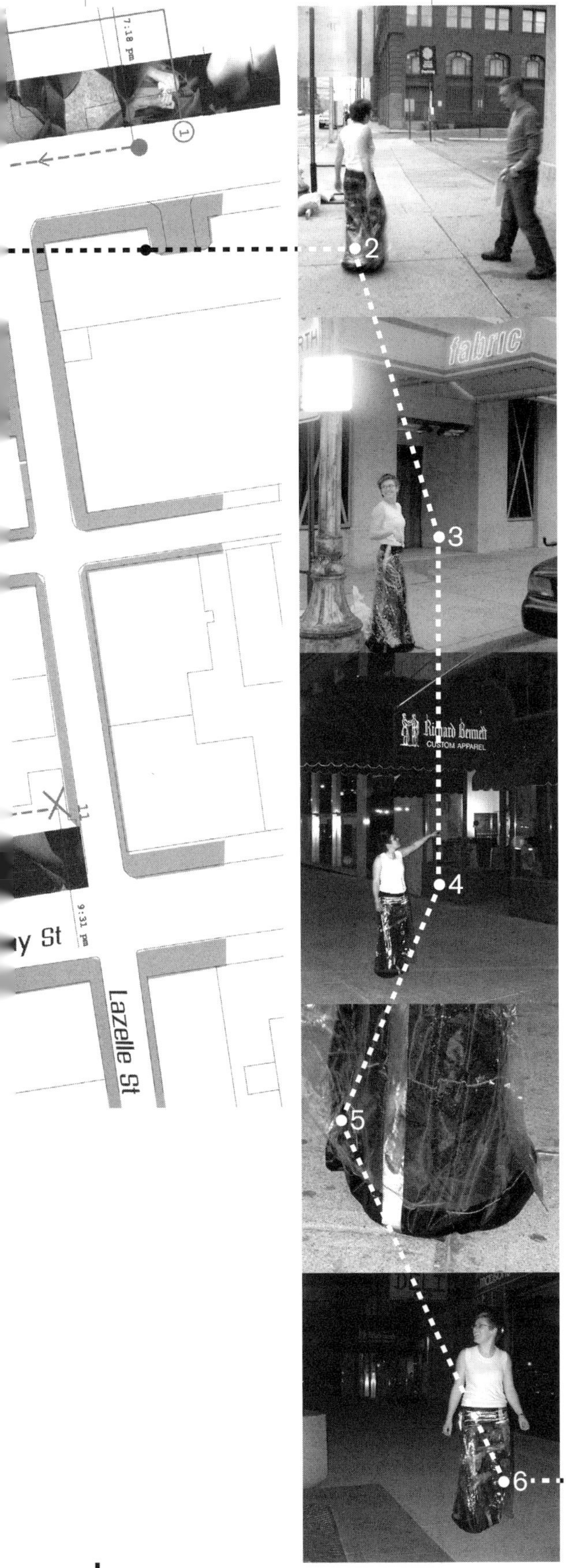

visualization to provide glimpses of urban activity and systems of value often overlooked. The studio was encouraged to explore both the possibilities and limitations of measurements—these devices not only make urban activity visible, but often generate inconclusive or contradictory readings. In this way, the act of measuring, or the attempt to measure, became the subject itself. More important than any set of data produced by the device is the affect of the device directly within the site, affecting the public's use of space and calling attention to the thresholds between spaces of universal and restricted access.

Site is not something that precedes architecture—it is made through architecture, and through an analysis of our environment. Thus, by making a device that measures the site, students of architecture create the context in which architecture operates.

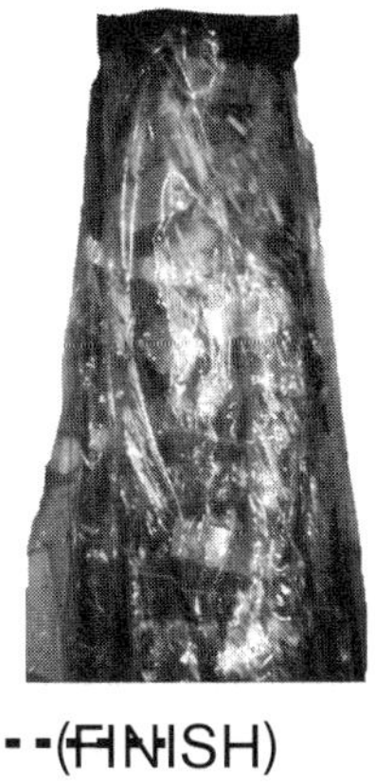

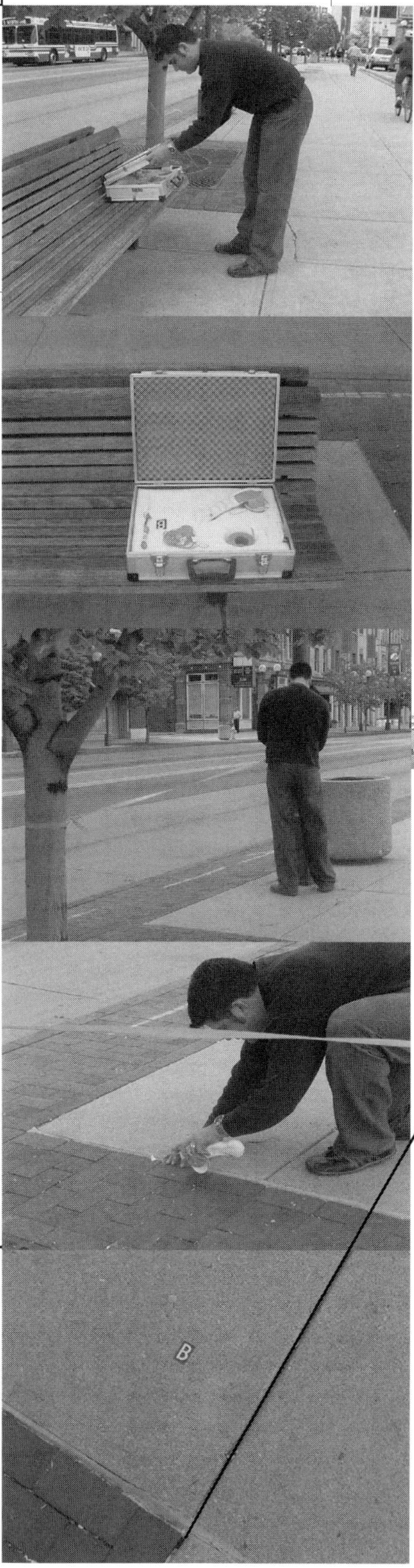

VALUE SYSTEM by Vasy McCoy

The device creates a new VALUE SYSTEM for the city by using the methods of the biologist, the forensic scientist, and the witch doctor. The scientist adds points for any nearby street furniture that adds value to the site (fountains, benches, planters, etc.), and subtracts points for any inconsistencies of material (i.e. cracks). He or she uses a handheld device to measure cracks in each section, producing a new map of string that denotes the length of crack in each section. After appraising each lot, a grade is given and the site is thus reorganized according to the values imposed on it by the scientist.

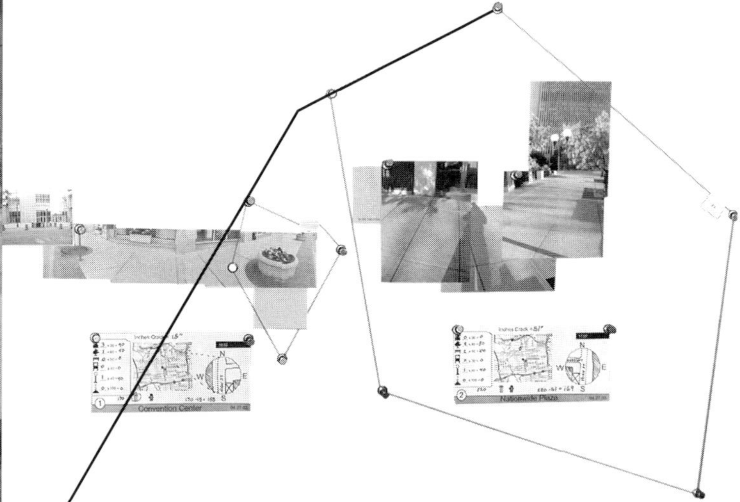

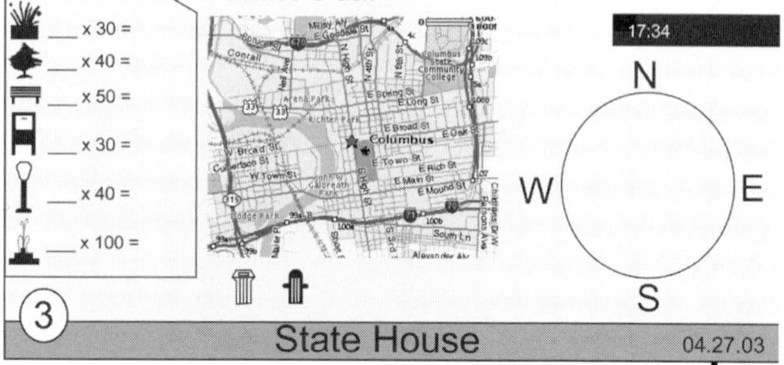

The GROWBOT uses electronically controlled motors, Global Positioning Systems and VOX technology to redefine the urban landscape as a reaction to noise pollution. The GROWBOT is a patch of grass on wheels that moves when it hears sound and stops when the sound source fades. The device carries a GPS receiver that creates a map of the area that it traverses.

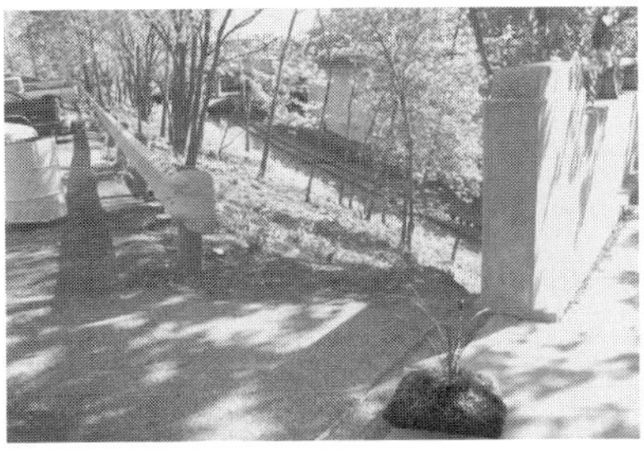

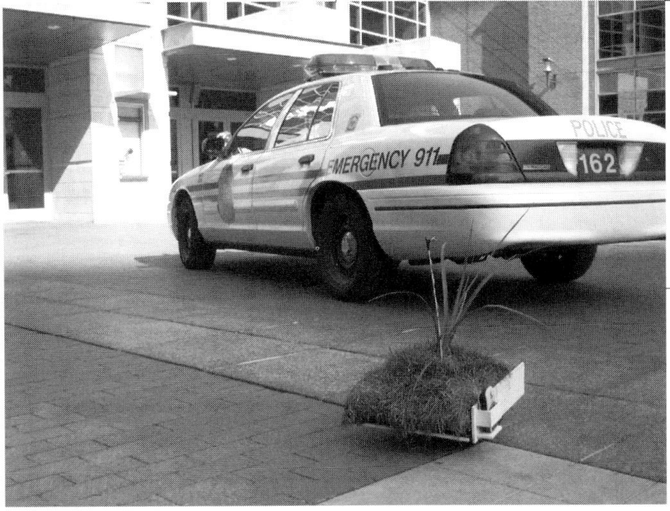

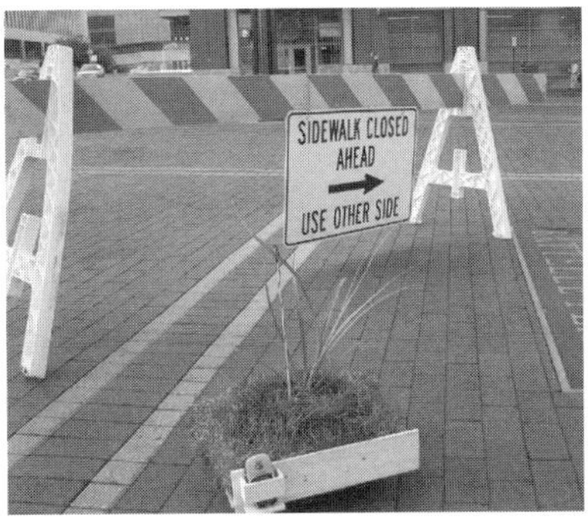

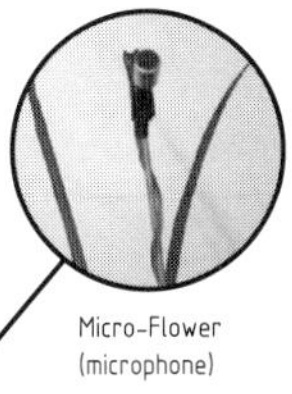
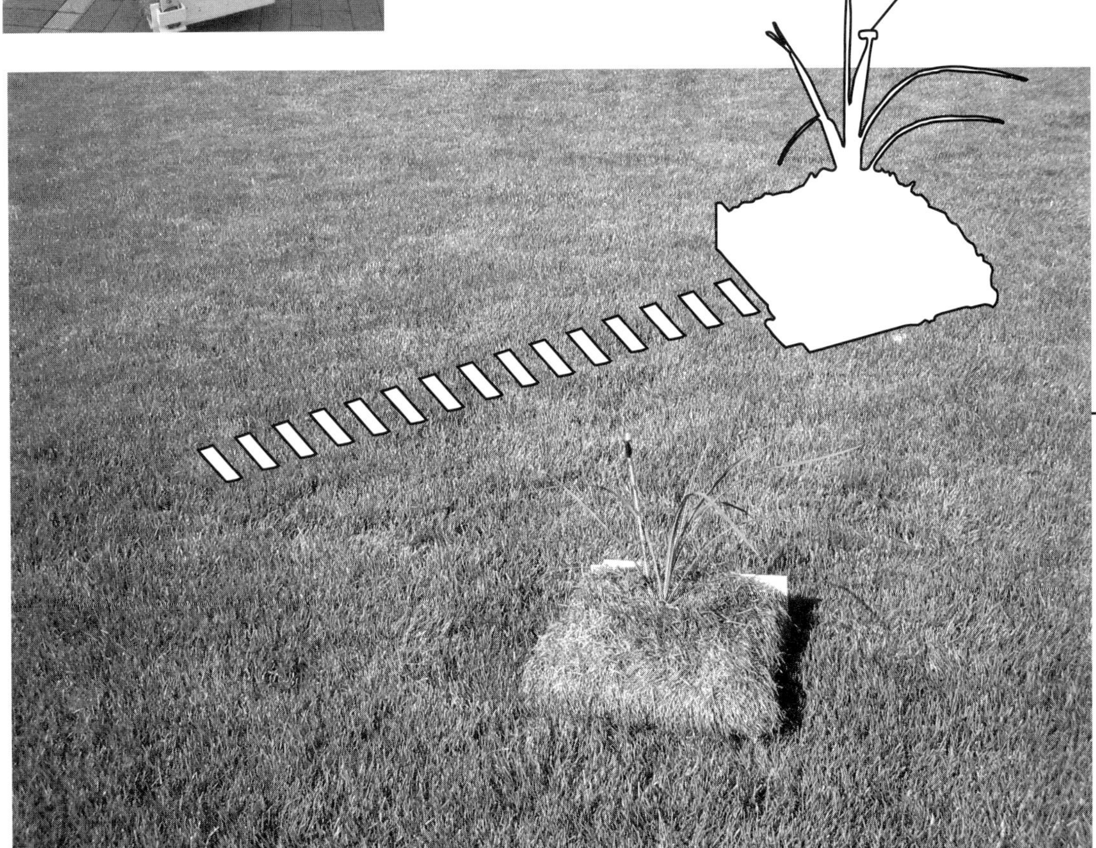

PEDMEASURE by Sofia Castricone

The device is a bicycle that measures pedestrian traffic. The bicycle is locked to an existing post, tree, or parking meter across the sidewalk from a motion sensor transmitter. When pedestrians pass between the bicycle and the transmitter, a motor is activated to momentarily cover the lens of a camera. The result is a measure of frequency, density, and quantity of pedestrians.

Because the device only works at distances of 6 feet or less the project not only produces quantitative data but also questions what is in fact measurable. Like the early explorers of the world, the measurable parts of the city can be mapped but the immeasurable is the unknown, or the land of the sea monsters

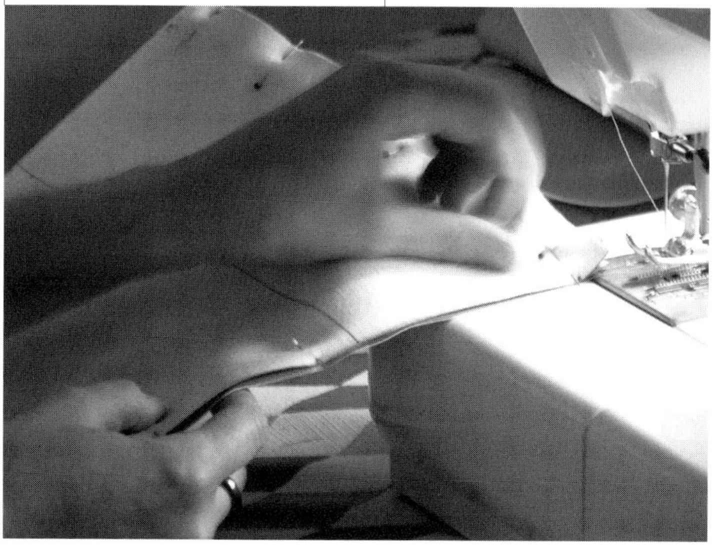

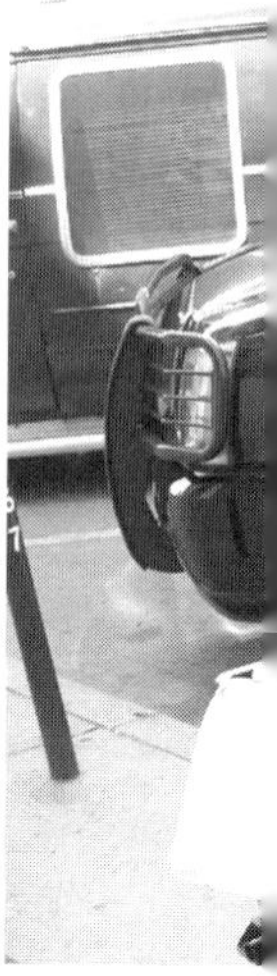

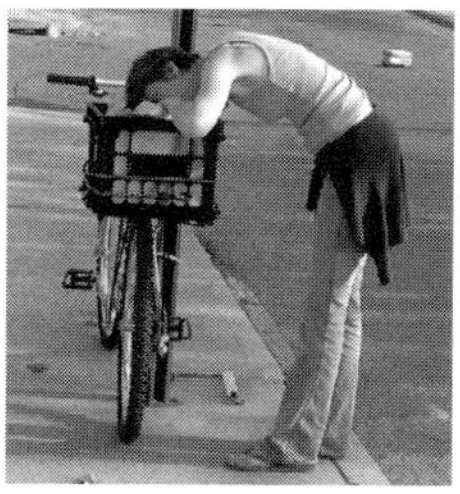

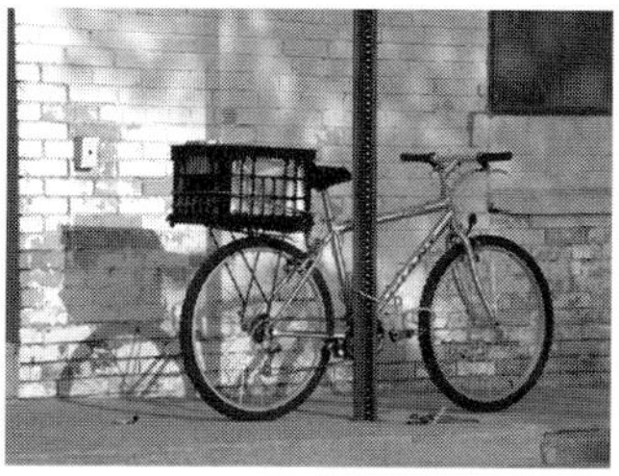

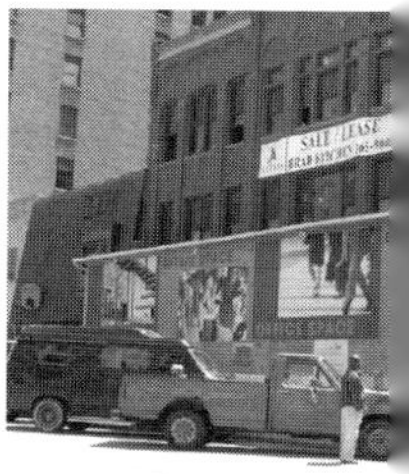

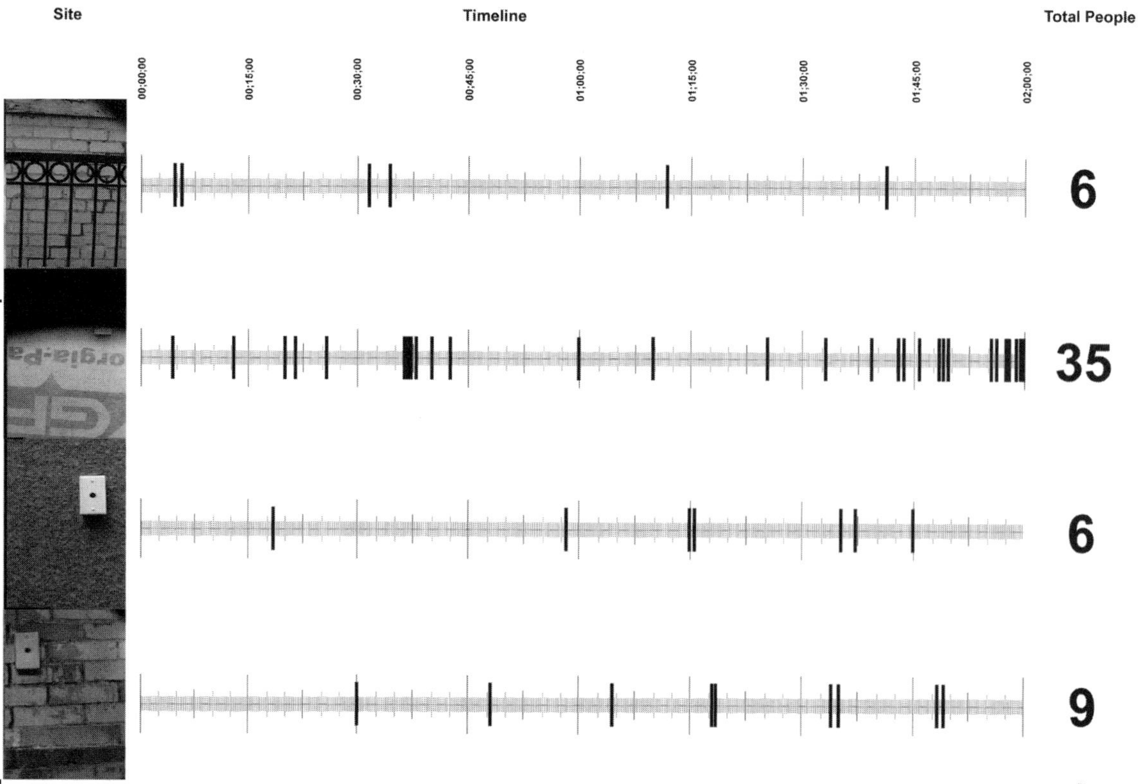

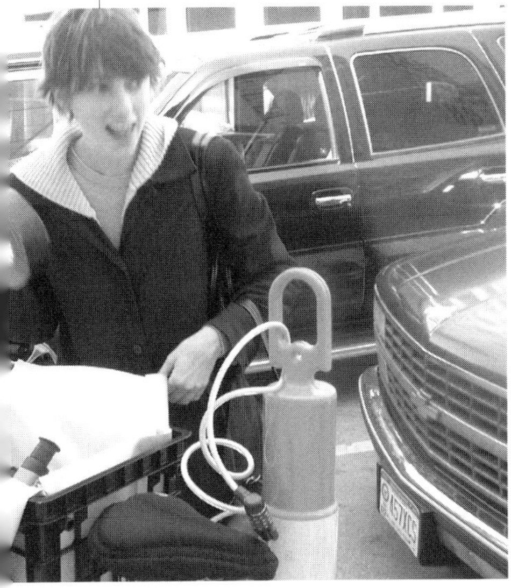

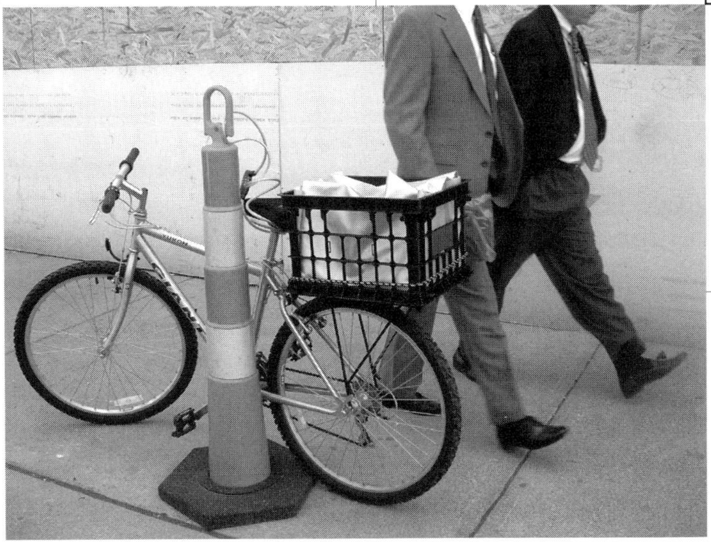

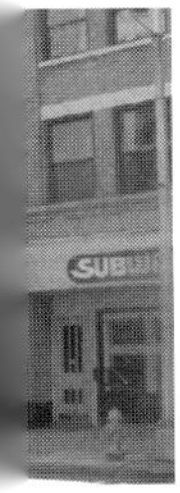

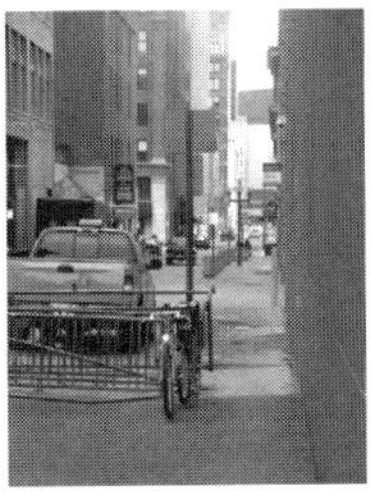

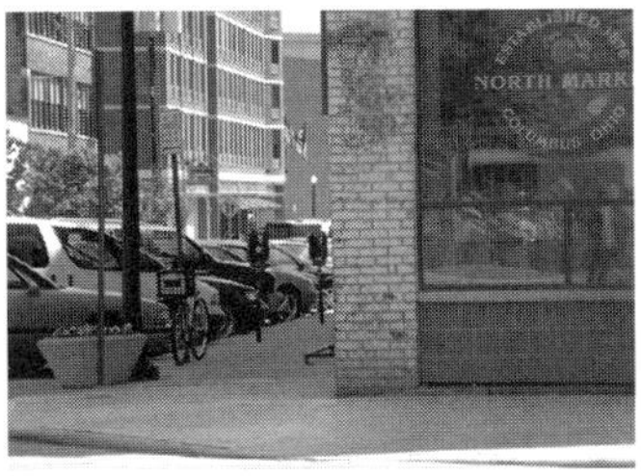

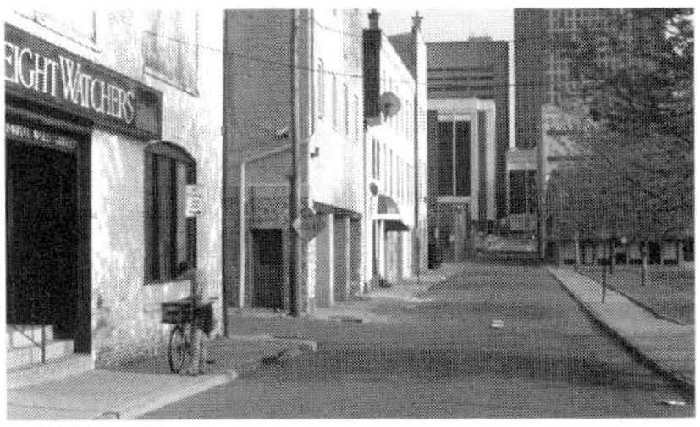

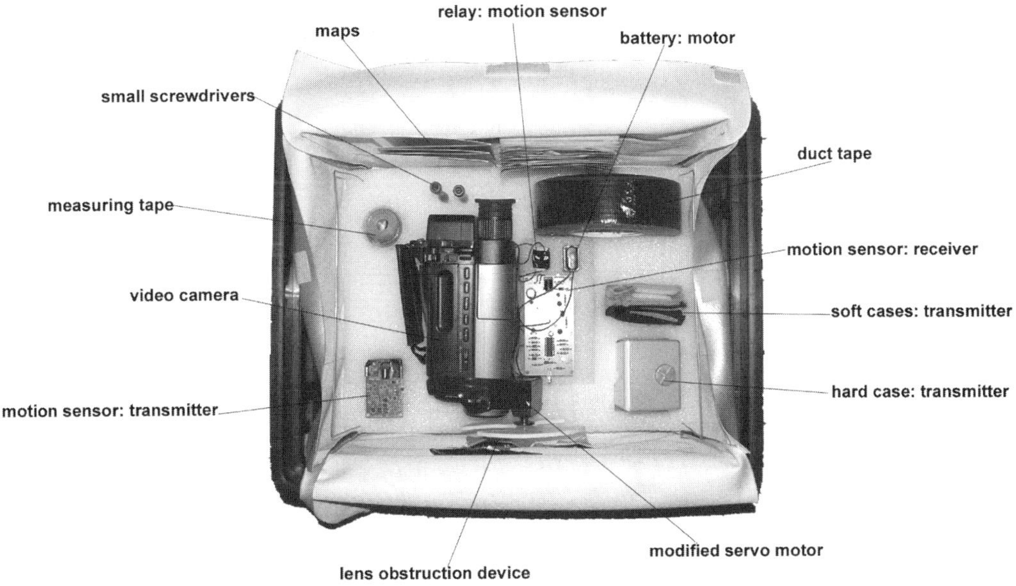
relay: motion sensor
maps
battery: motor
small screwdrivers
duct tape
measuring tape
motion sensor: receiver
video camera
soft cases: transmitter
hard case: transmitter
motion sensor: transmitter
modified servo motor
lens obstruction device

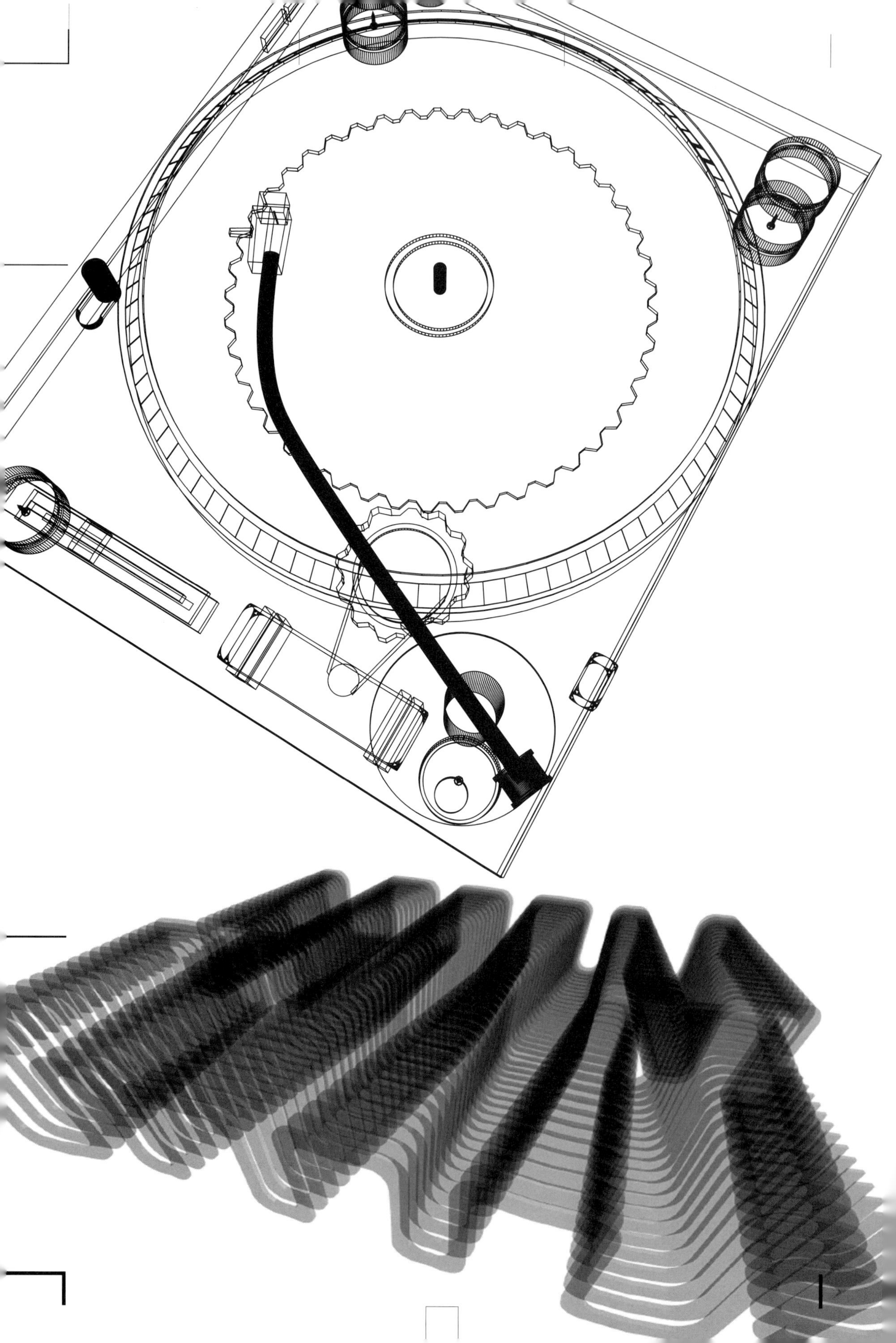

Building for beats

TRANSMAT

by M1

Sleeper Studio

Sited within a room which has informally served electronic artists for well over a decade, the renovation occurs in a 300 sq. foot space through the introduction of a series of new elements and surfaces designed to support, display and equip the production of electronic music.

The studio responds primarily to the client's unique way of working—sitting on the floor, surrounded by instruments and other rack-mounted equipment. The studio, however, is intended to accommodate other DJs, many who come from outside the country, and not only produce music in the space, but also live in the studio for short periods of time. The space must therefore be capable of switching between modes of activity and inactivity at any time of day or night.

Two zones programmatically differentiate the studio: the principal working platform and the sleeping area. Both are distinguished from the existing entry floor plane through the introduction of a raised platform and a natural woven fiber floor covering which resists electrostatic build-up. The platform is also slightly separated from the existing walls, allowing for indirect lighting to illuminate the studio while creating a flexible cavity for the many power and signal cables.

M1 is a multi-disciplinary practice engaged in the material production of objects, artifacts, identities and spaces. Recent projects include a number of built projects in Detroit including 6 salon, offices for the Stategic Group and a pair of recording studios. Their work has recently been exhibited in Detroit, Los Angeles and Austin.

Chris Benfield holds a BFA from the University of Michigan and a MFA from the Cranbrook Academy of Art. He has taught and lectured at a number of schools including the College for Creative Studies in Detroit, University of Maryland, Beaver College and Cranbrook. His work has been exhibited in museums and galleries across the United States and in Japan.

Christopher Puzaio graduated from the Architecture Department at the Cranbrook Academy of Art in 2002. His work has been exhibited in a number of cities through the United States and is in the collection of DaimlerChyrsler in Berlin. He currently lives and works in San Diego.

Christian Unverzagt holds BS in Architecture from the University of Michigan and an MArch from the Southern California Institute of Architecture (SCI-Arc). Founding designer of the Michigan Architecture Papers, *he has received several awards for his design work. He is also a Lecturer in Architecture at the University of Michigan's Taubman College.*

Sleeper Studio Project Team:
Chris Benfield, Chris Puzio, Christian Unverzagt with Ryan Kelley, Peter Warren & Andre Sandifer. Models by Martha Merzig and Neil Meredith Jr.

M1@M1DTW.com

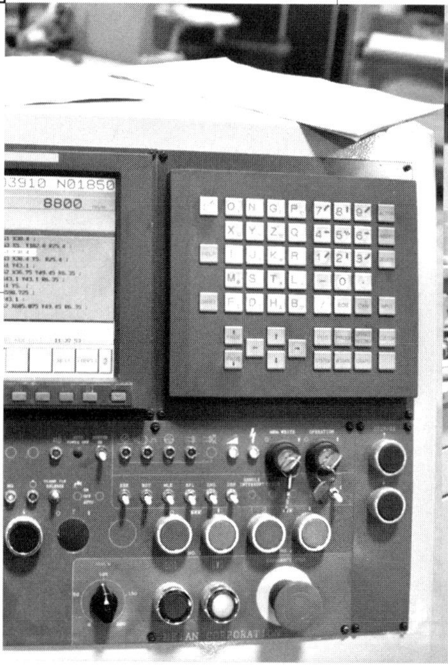
03910 N01850
8800

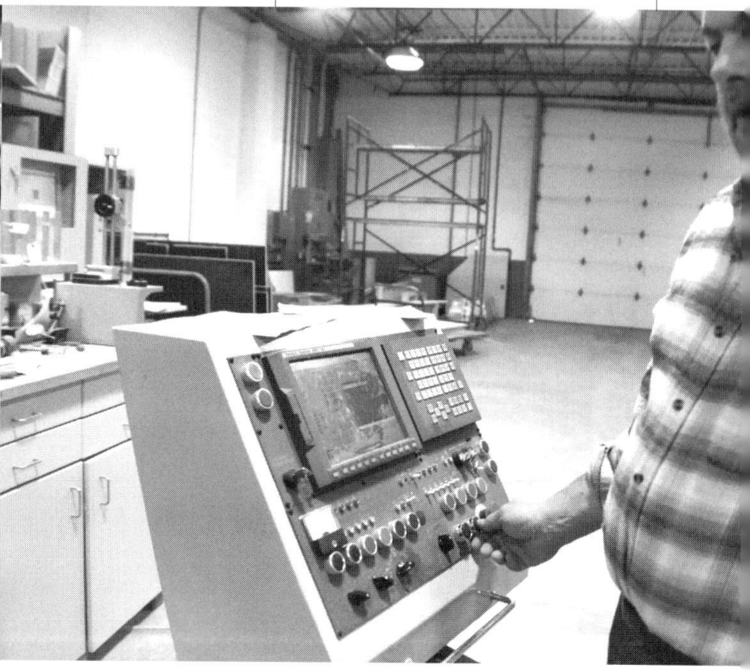

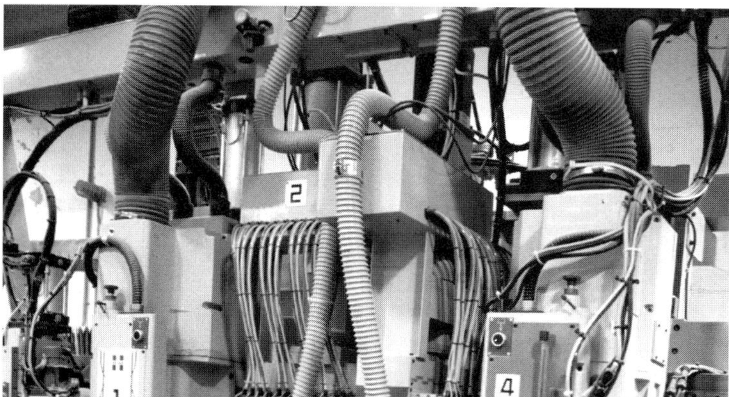
2
1
3
4

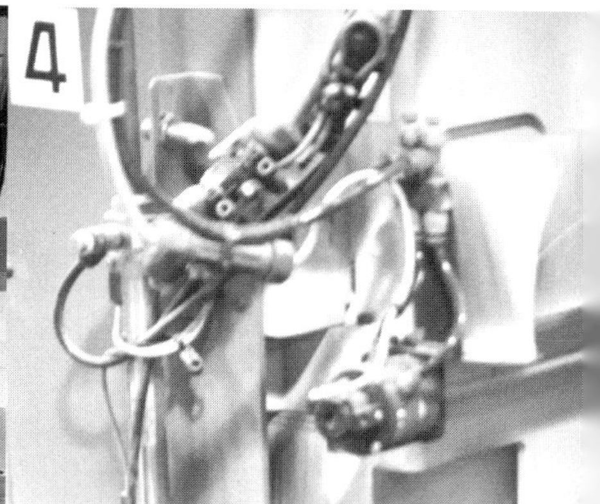
4

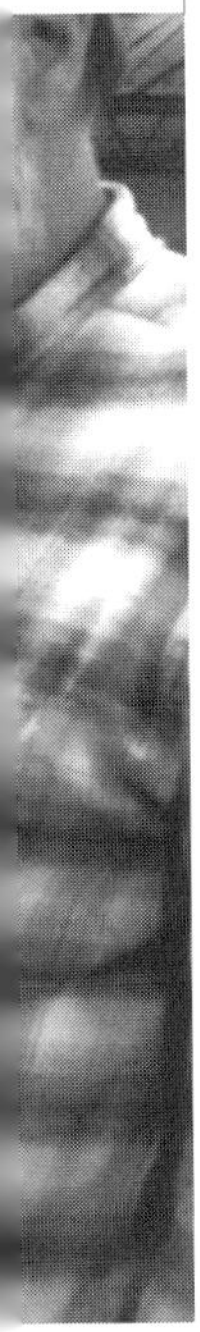

A pair of L-shaped *super frames* both line and divide the space while hosting a field of tiles made from materials with various acoustical and visual properties. This allows the studio to be acoustically *tuned* and to help regulate light from the clerestory windows. The frame profiles—cut from a finely laminated plywood sealed with a phenolic resin coating—transform as they wrap over the windows from the ceiling to the wall serving as a working surface, small seating area and studio storage. Both the frame and tiles are cut directly from digital profiles using CNC milling equipment.

In contrast to the lightweight framework and tiles, 17-gauge laser-cut steel is used to construct a series of independent objects, including an equipment storage unit, light reflectors and a loft ladder. In other areas, the steel is a surface which covers the egg crate-like frames to provide a seat or desktop. The white powder-coated steel also identifies key surfaces of activity (or inactivity) especially in low-light conditions.

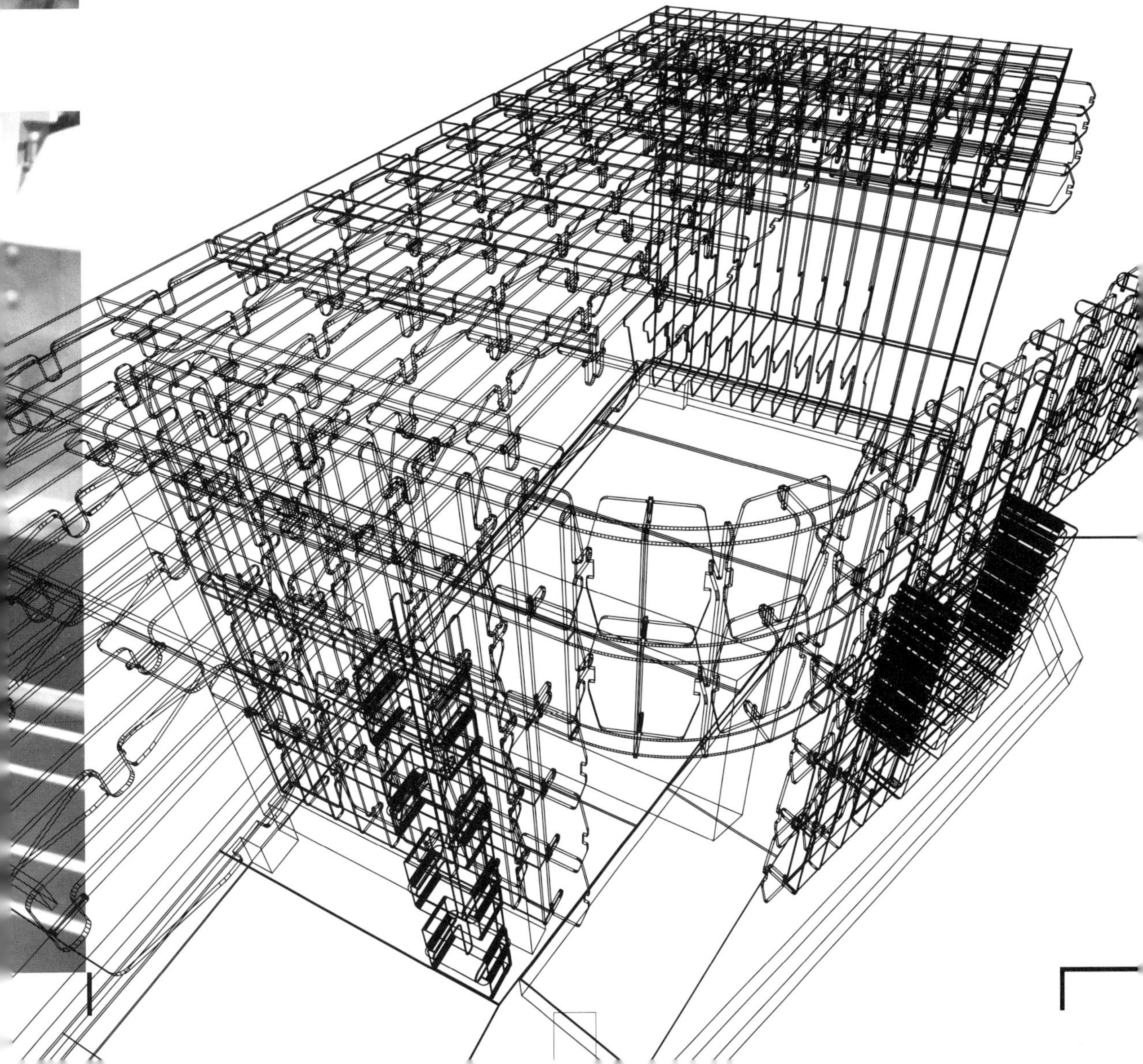

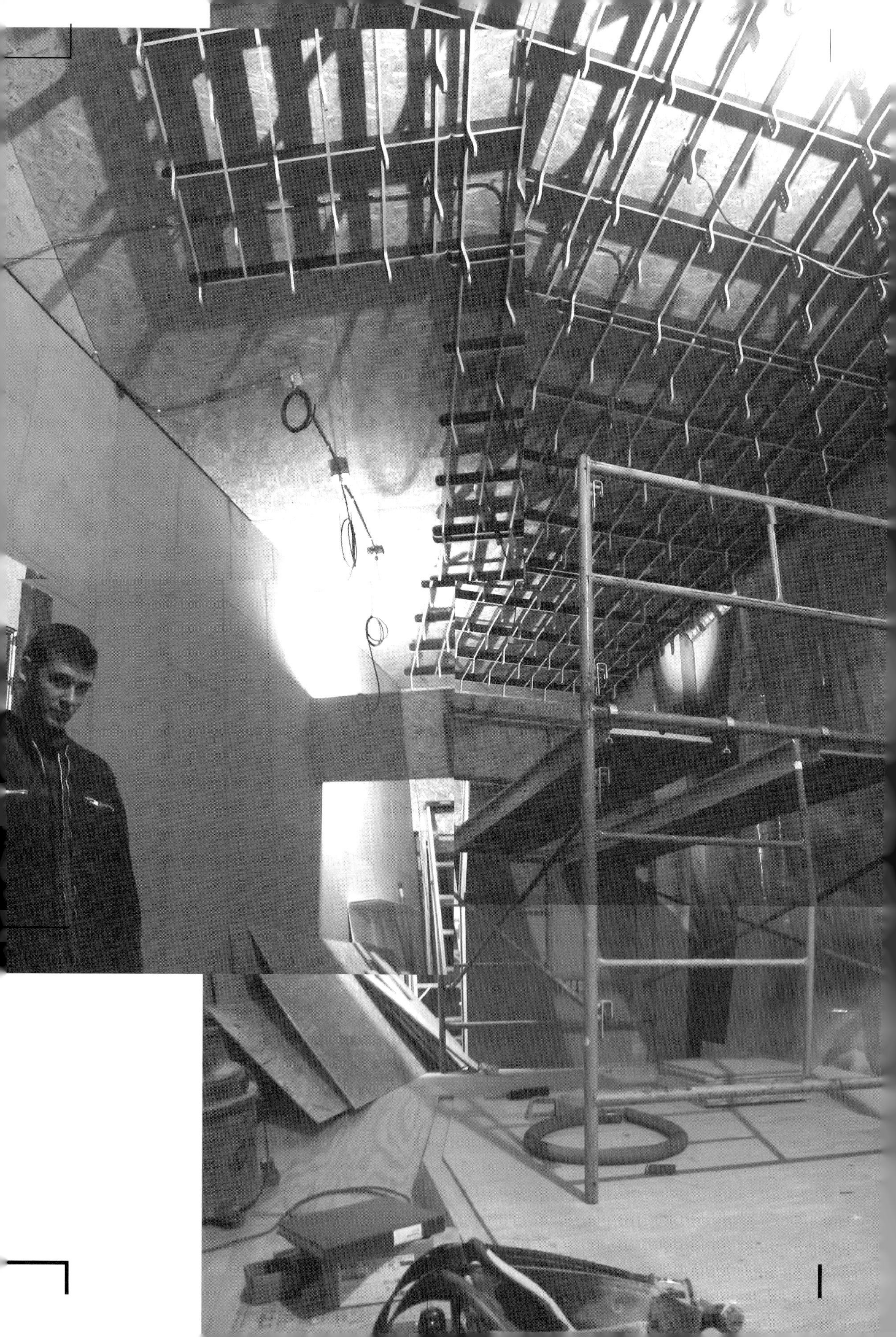

SONICBOOM

As the flight speed of an aircraft approaches the speed of sound, a compression of sound waves occurs. When the flight speed becomes greater than the speed of sound, or supersonic—the resulting shock waves produce a sonic boom. This is not unlike the condition the pioneers of electronic music put forth to the city of Detroit and the world. The level of music production in the city surpassed the masses to such a degree that it has taken well over a decade to catch up.

The sleeper studio is not intended to be simply a functional recording studio, but rather a space which will support the continuing redefinition of Detroit and a progression of the sound arts—in other words, a site for the production of further sonic booms.

Detroit's reputation in the world of electronic music permeates the globe. The city acts as both a center and a hub for the production and distribution of the artist DJs and their product recordings. And while both conventional and emerging systems of music distribution allow their work to be heard across the globe simultaneously, the artist can only exist in one place at any given moment. While physical distance and time itself have created a market for the DJ as performer, these same demands counteract the conditions which initially permitted the production of music which led to their demand. The sleeper studio attempts to allow both of these conditions to co-exist and therefore is not intended as a reclusive retreat, but rather a space for the production of music which is consciously aware of its position relative to these two often contradictory systems.

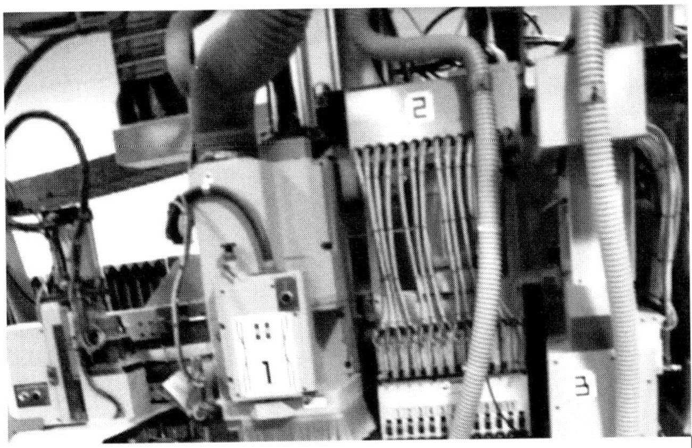

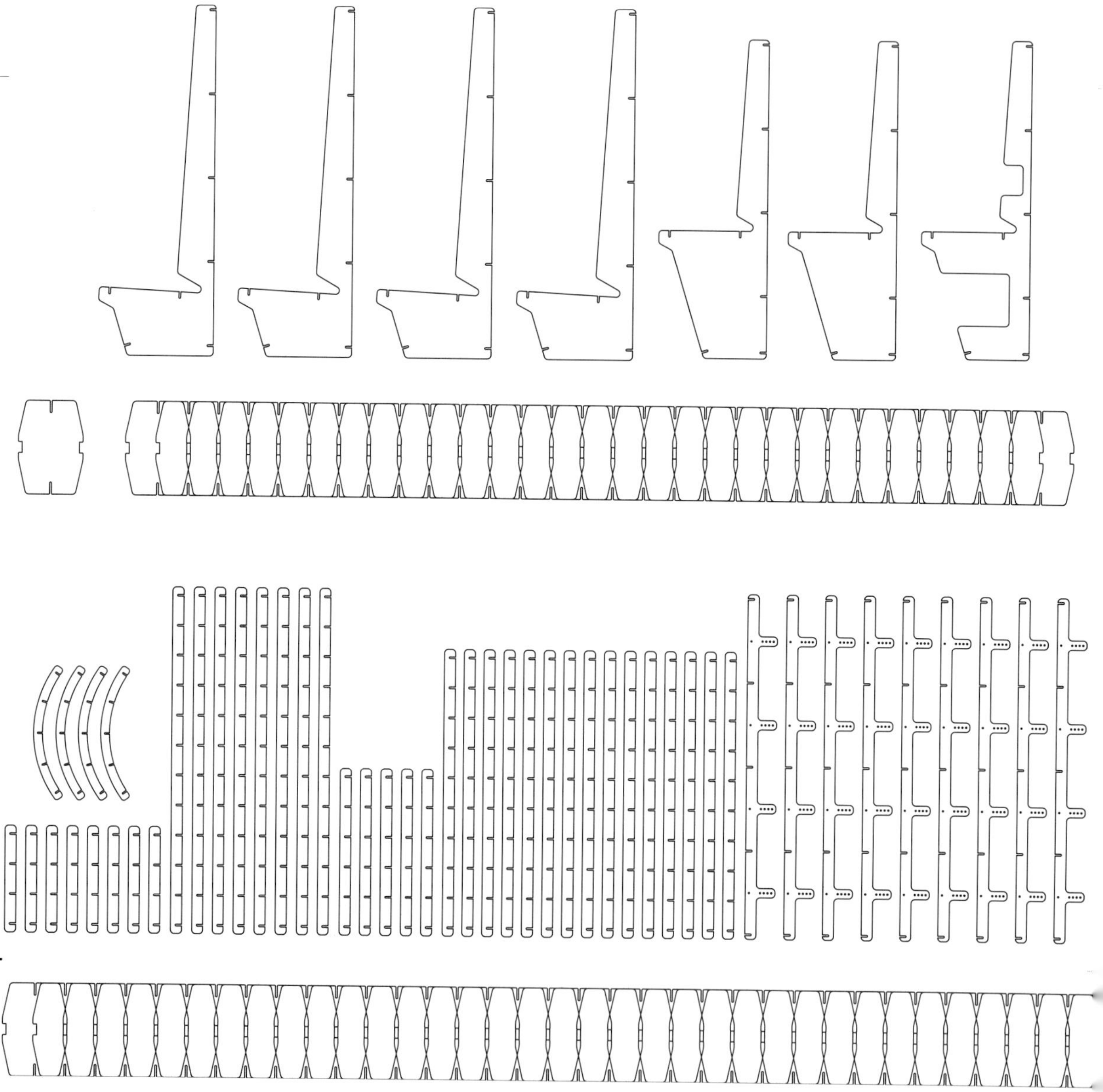

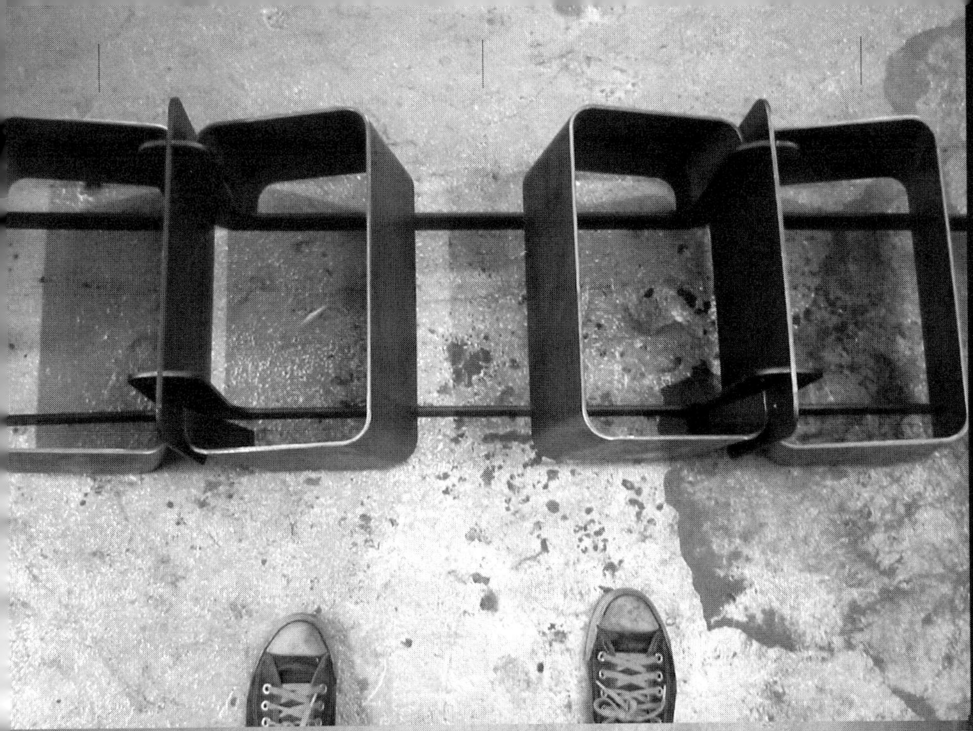
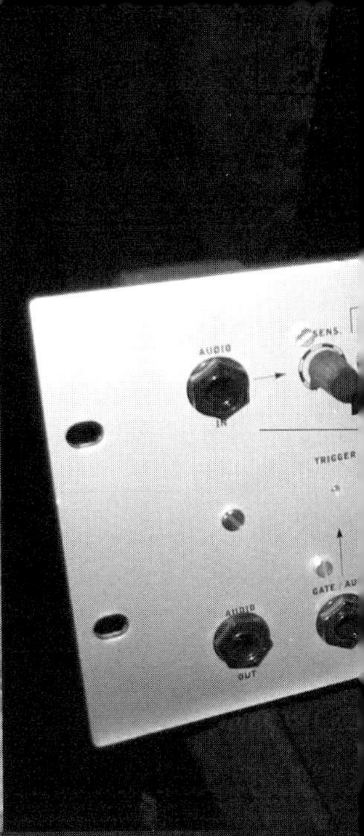
AUDIO
IN
SENS.
TRIGGER
GATE / AU
AUDIO
OUT
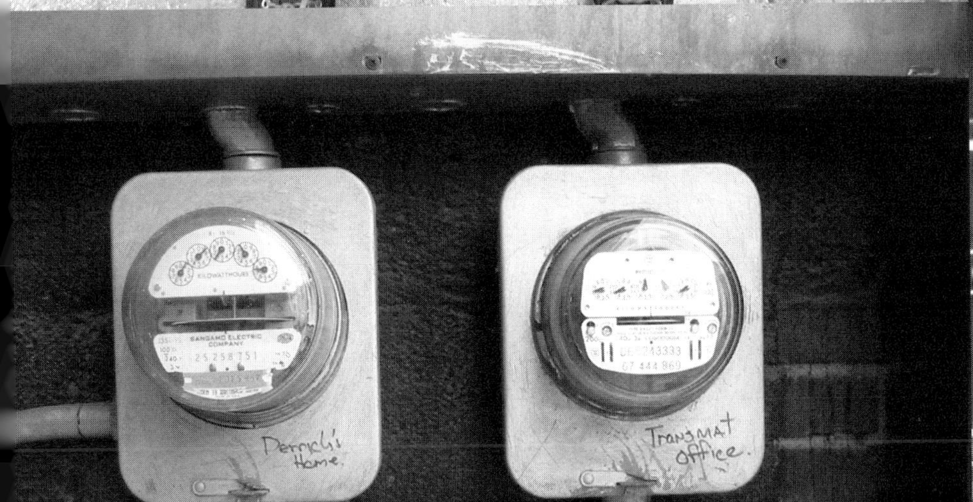
KILOWATTHOURS
SANGAMO ELECTRIC COMPANY
Derrick's Home
Transmat Office
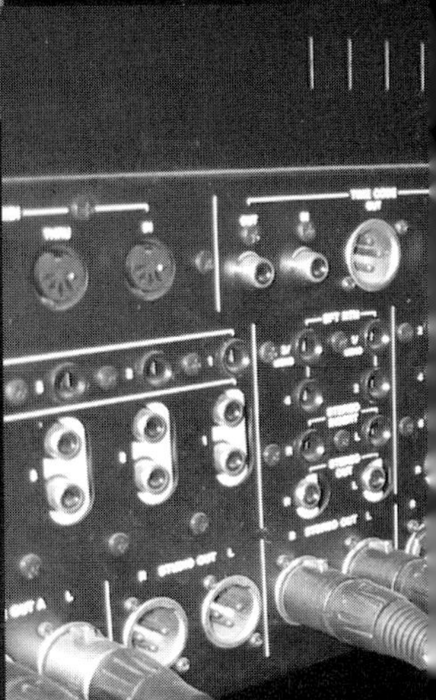
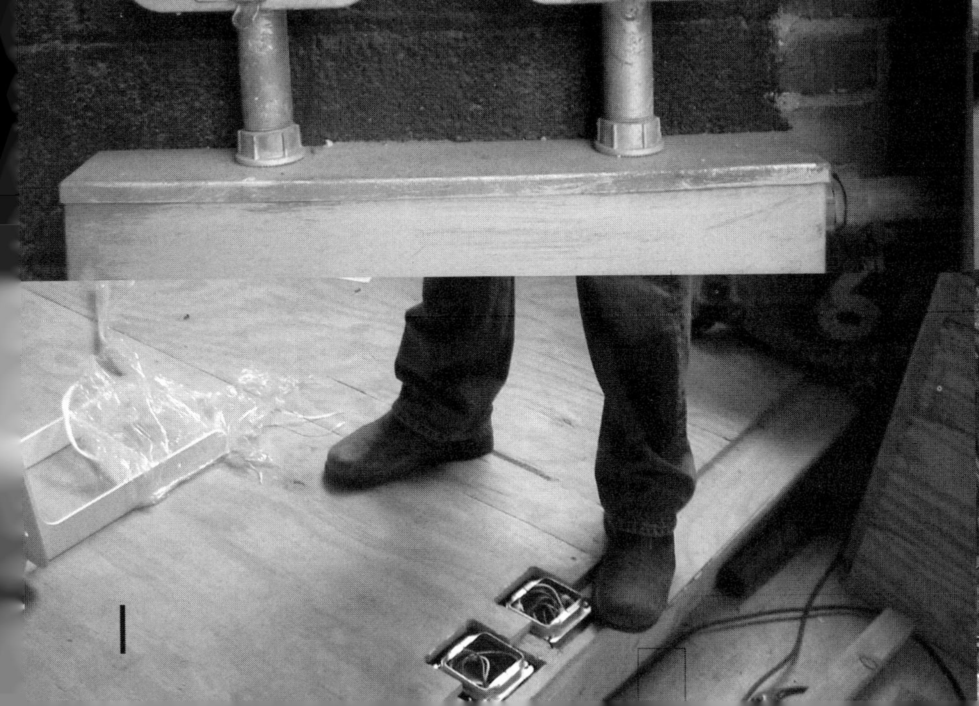
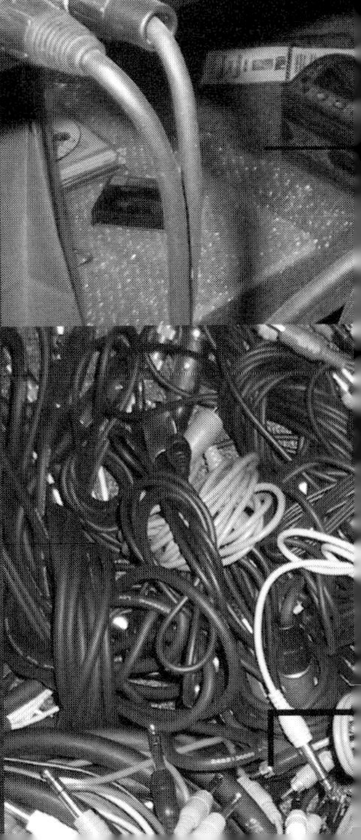

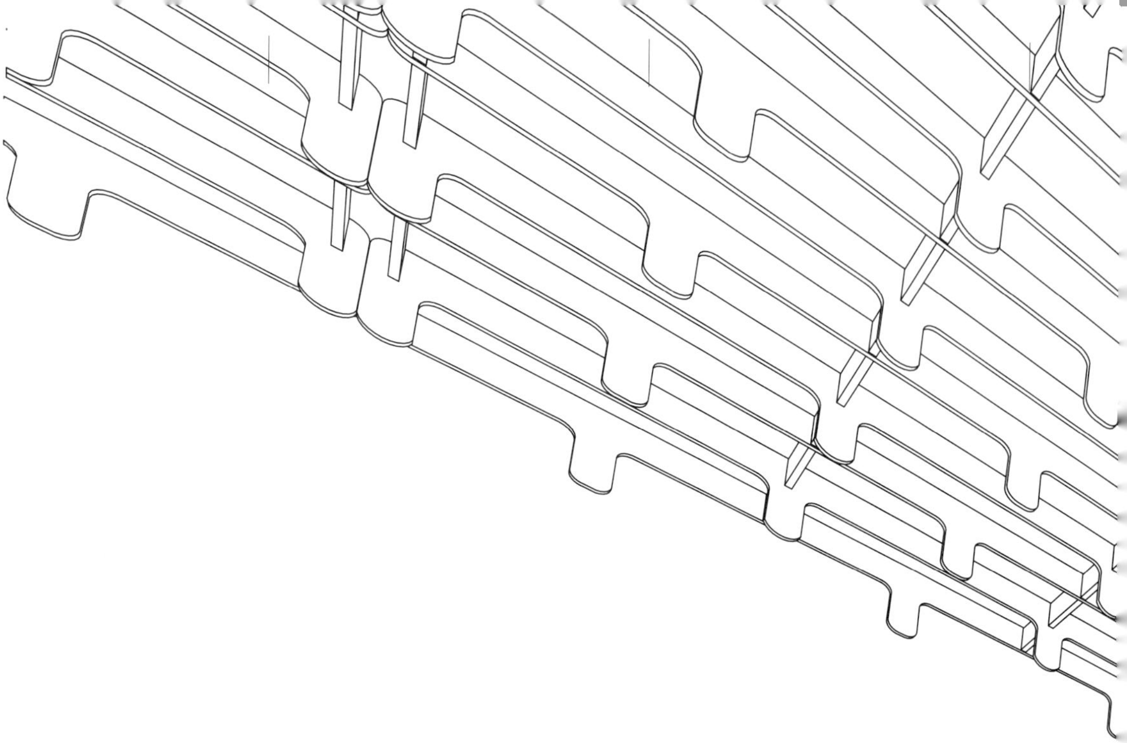

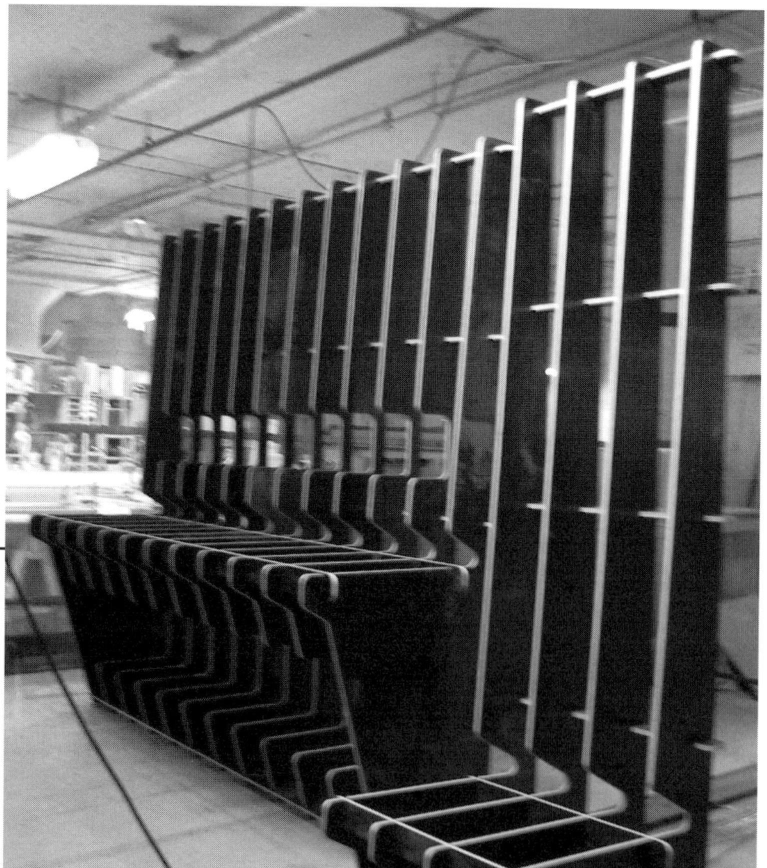

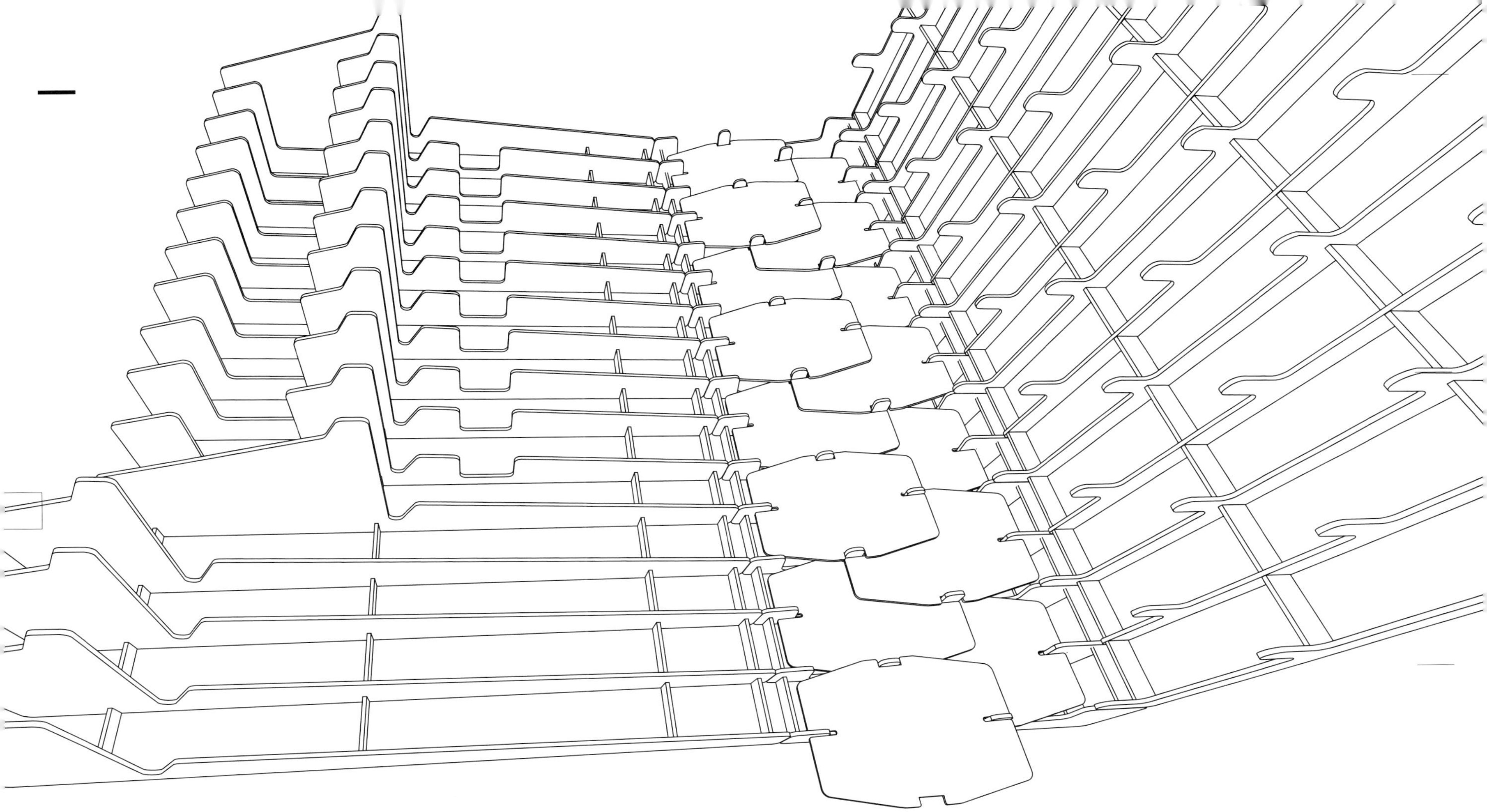

YOU ARE THE

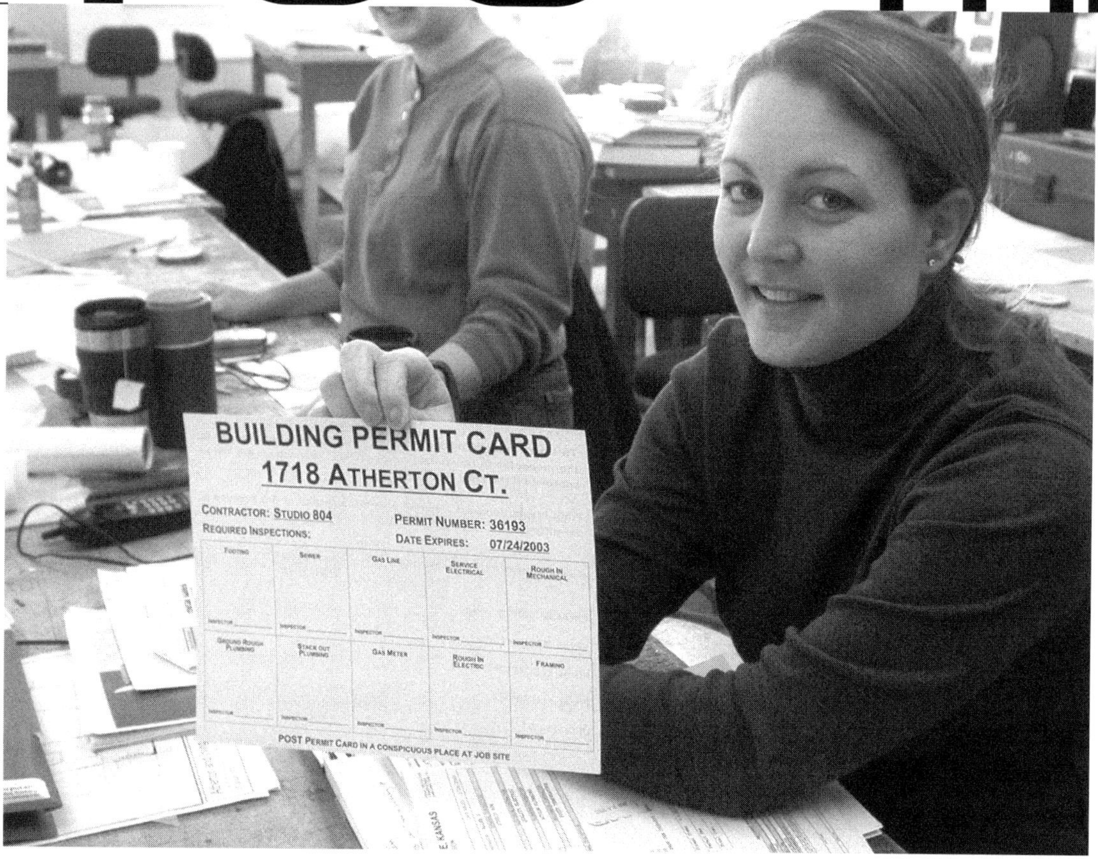

> Erin Shea, third year graduate student, holds the permit for 1718 Atherton Ct.

Studio 804 has built its 5th house

ARCHITECT

All images courtesy of Dan Rockhill

by Lindsey Mahoney

"You are the architect." With these four words 19 students leave the fantasy world of traditional design studios to design and build their first real project. In this unique design-build program, where students are faced with the challenges of architectural practice on the way to making their design solutions a reality.

Studio 804, Inc. operates as a not-for-profit outgrowth of the University of Kansas School of Architecture and Urban Design Masters' program. Under the leadership of Professors Dan Rockhill and Kent Spreckelmeyer, third-year graduate students and fifth-year undergraduate students collaborate to design and build an affordable residence for a family in Lawrence, Kansas. Students are given the opportunity to explore first-hand the inner workings of the architectural profession in an intensive four-month process that culminates with the completion of an affordable residence incorporating sustainable design and ADA accessibility.

Billy Williams, a former 804 student: "You begin this project and think, 'Last semester I was building little wooden models and this semester I'm building a house,'" says Billy, "It's a pretty daunting task." Students begin the semester in January with a two-week design charette in which all 19 students submit design solutions for the site and program.

Lindsey Mahoney participated in the design and construction of Studio 804's fifth house at 1718 Atherton Court in Lawrence, Kansas. She graduated in May 2003 with a BArch degree from the University of Kansas School of Architecture and Urban Design. She is currently working as a staff architect for International Architects Atelier in Kansas City, Missouri.

Students enrolled in Design Studio 804 are majoring in architecture either as graduate students or as fifth-year undergraduates. Kansas University's Bachelor of Architecture degree is a five-year professional program.

Studio 804:
Jean Dodd, graduate student
Erin Shea, graduate student
Brian Spainhour, graduate student
Kyle Unruh, fifth-year senior
Lindsey Mahoney, fifth-year senior
Kevin Gillian, fifth-year senior
Jessica Fishback, fifth-year senior
Diane Mansfield, graduate student
Carl Drafall, fifth-year senior
Christina Boehne, fifth-year senior
Dirk Henke, fifth-year senior
Lindsey Piant, a fifth-year senior
Brian Garvey, fifth-year senior
Michael J. Schaefer, graduate student
Evan Fox, fifth-year senior
Frank Louis, graduate student
Izumi Kitajima, graduate student
Christina Assmann, graduate student
Christine Prescott, graduate student

Professors:
Dan Rockhill
Kent Spreckelmeyer

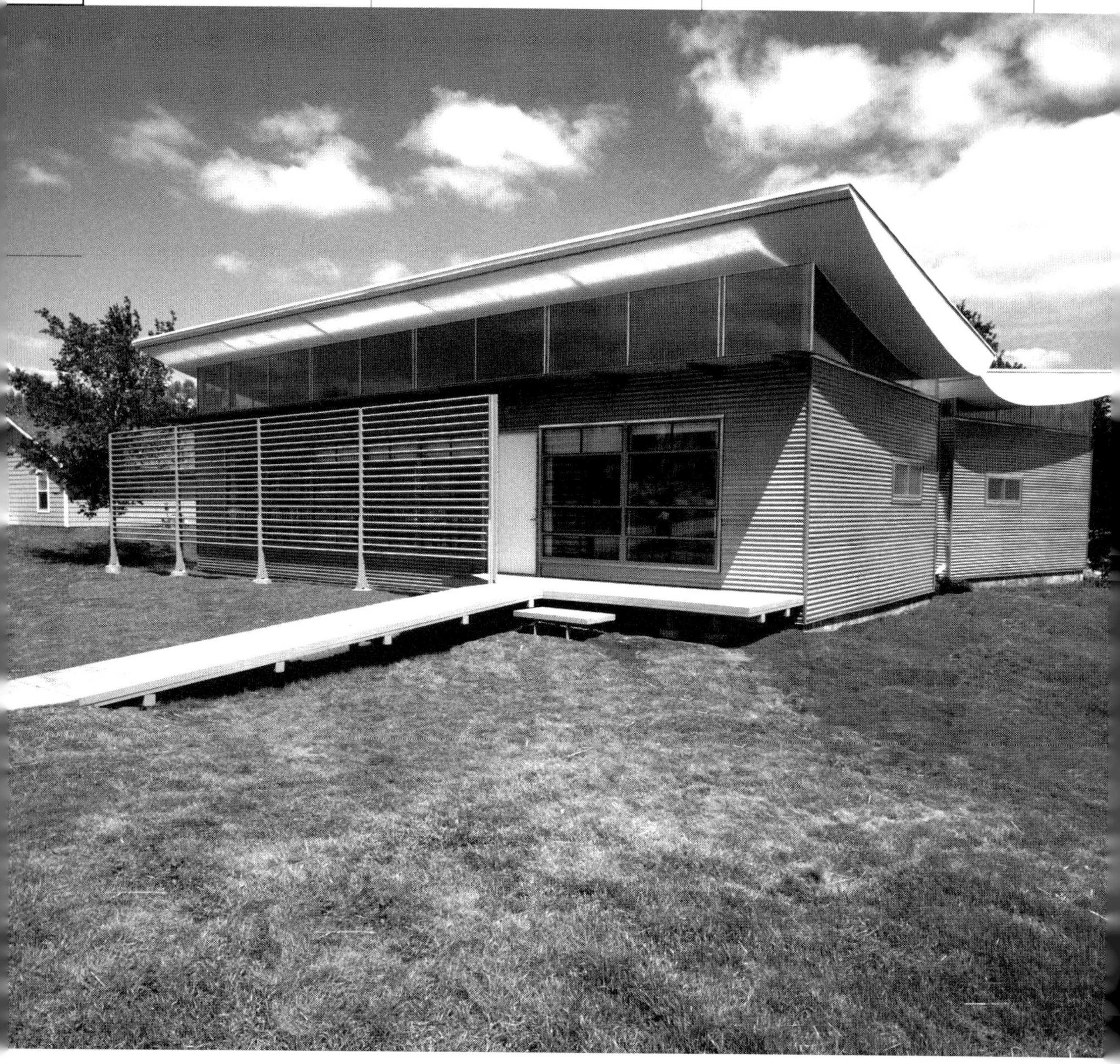

In contrast to traditional studio sequences in which students focus solely on their own work, Studio 804 students are encouraged to share ideas and build upon one another's work. There is no ownership of ideas. Students cluster similar ideas and collaborate to arrive at two schemes by the end of the first week. Students are then asked to select one scheme to pursue as a group. One former Studio 804 student recalls that, "[The house was] only possible through constant debate and discussion, design and redesign, and a lot of advice from our instructor. The communication and teamwork between everyone involved was key to our success."

In addition to design, students are responsible for post-occupancy evaluations of past Studio 804 houses, looking for ways to improve and build upon

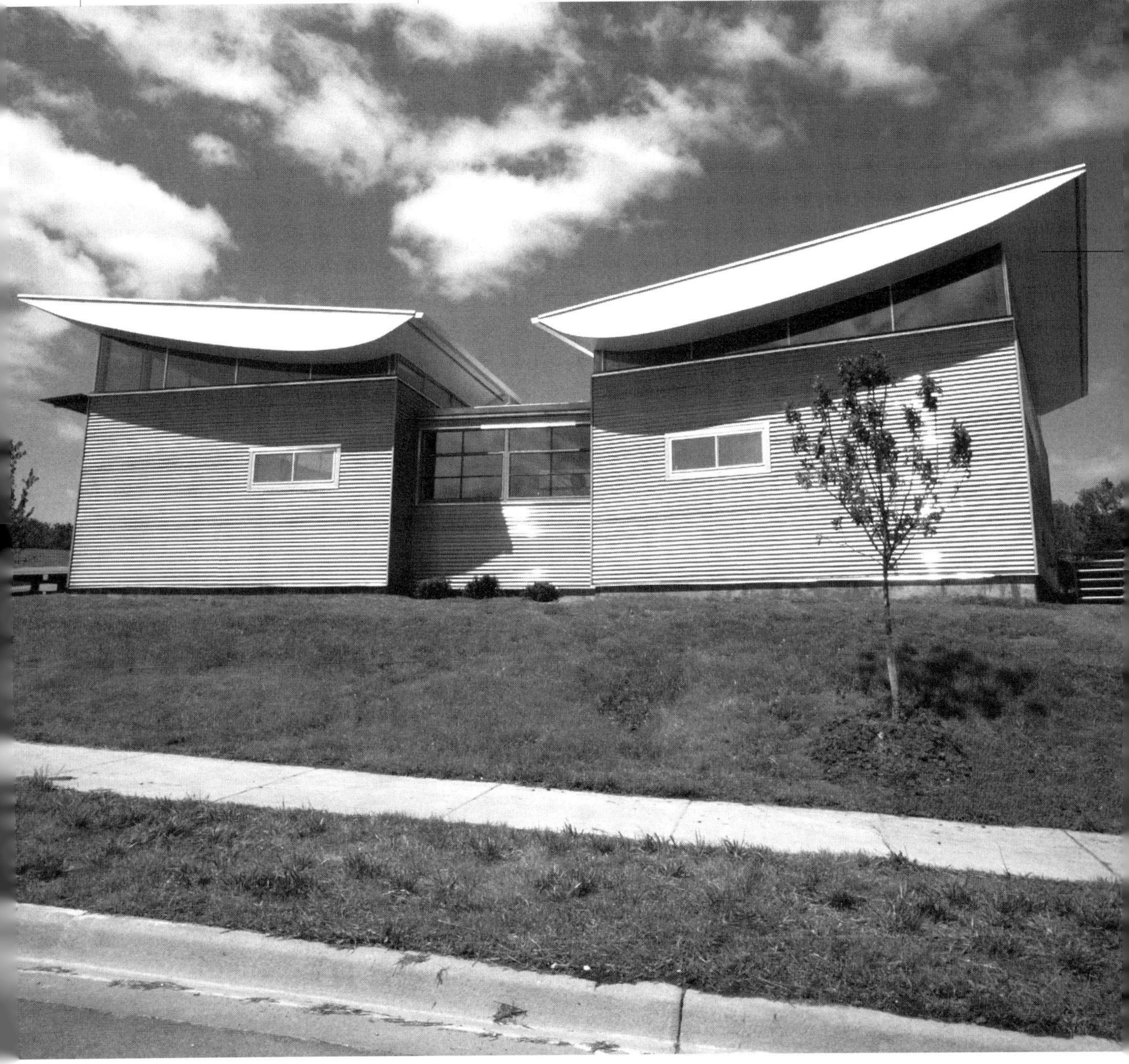

the successes of past projects. Students investigate energy consumption, material durability, and the livability of the houses. Students conduct materials investigation, sustainable design and accessibility research. Working with neighborhood, city, and ADA organizations, students are immersed in the many dimensions of practice.

At the end of two weeks students present their design solution to the client, Tenants-to-Homeowners, (a Lawrence-based not-for-profit organization) for approval. Students break ground and begin construction in late January. All aspects of construction are completed by the students, except those required by law to be carried out by licensed professionals (plumbing, electric, and HVAC).

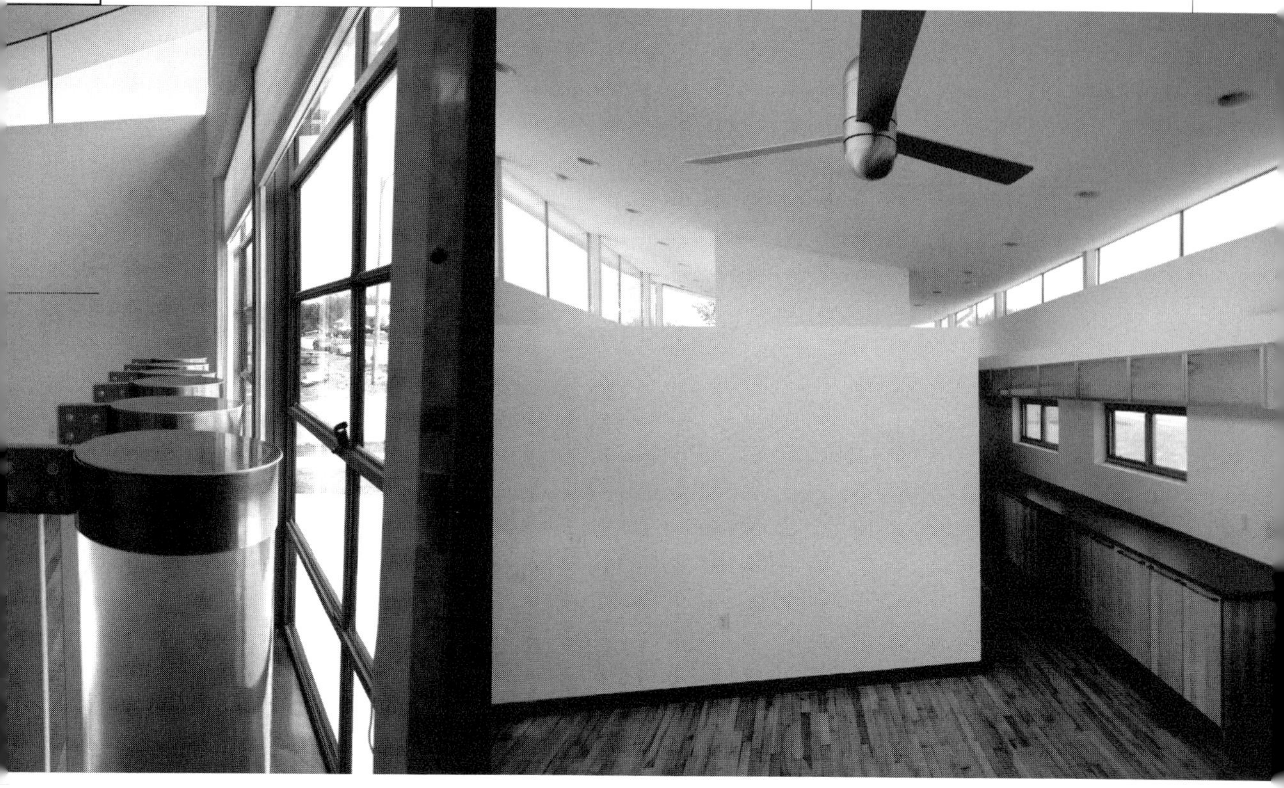

In a design-build studio, students learn things that textbooks can not teach. There is no better time to ask questions than in the field, and no better resource than a plumber or electrician on the job site. Through this experience, students begin to view architecture not as a set of plans, but as a union of materials, surfaces, connections, and ideas. Students are faced with questions rarely visited in traditional design studios—How do we keep water out? How is it insulated? How do two materials meet? How do we actually build it? Is it possible in our budget? Students, as future designers, learn to appreciate the fact that someone actually has to build every detail they imagine.

Perhaps most of the learning achieved in this intense process is the realization that architecture is much more than drawing a few lines on paper. Studio 804 teaches its students to consider the impact of each line they draw. Students are quick to realize that design never stops. Many details are worked out on the back of a 2x4 at the construction site. Students discover the value of such a hands-on approach. There is no better place to teach flashing details than on the site with a full-scale mock-up. Through this approach, materials and details can be tested and revised, and students are able to explore possible solutions.

Ideally, Students who participate in Studio 804 enter the architectural profession with an increased confidence and sensitivity. While many students graduate and look for a firm to teach them how a building goes together, students of Studio 804 leave with the advantage of experience in design, construction, marketing, client relations, and communications experience. The experience is intended to instill in future designers an increased attention to detail and respect for construction. Students leave the experience with an invaluable lesson in teamwork, design, and construction that shapes them into wiser and more sensible future architects.

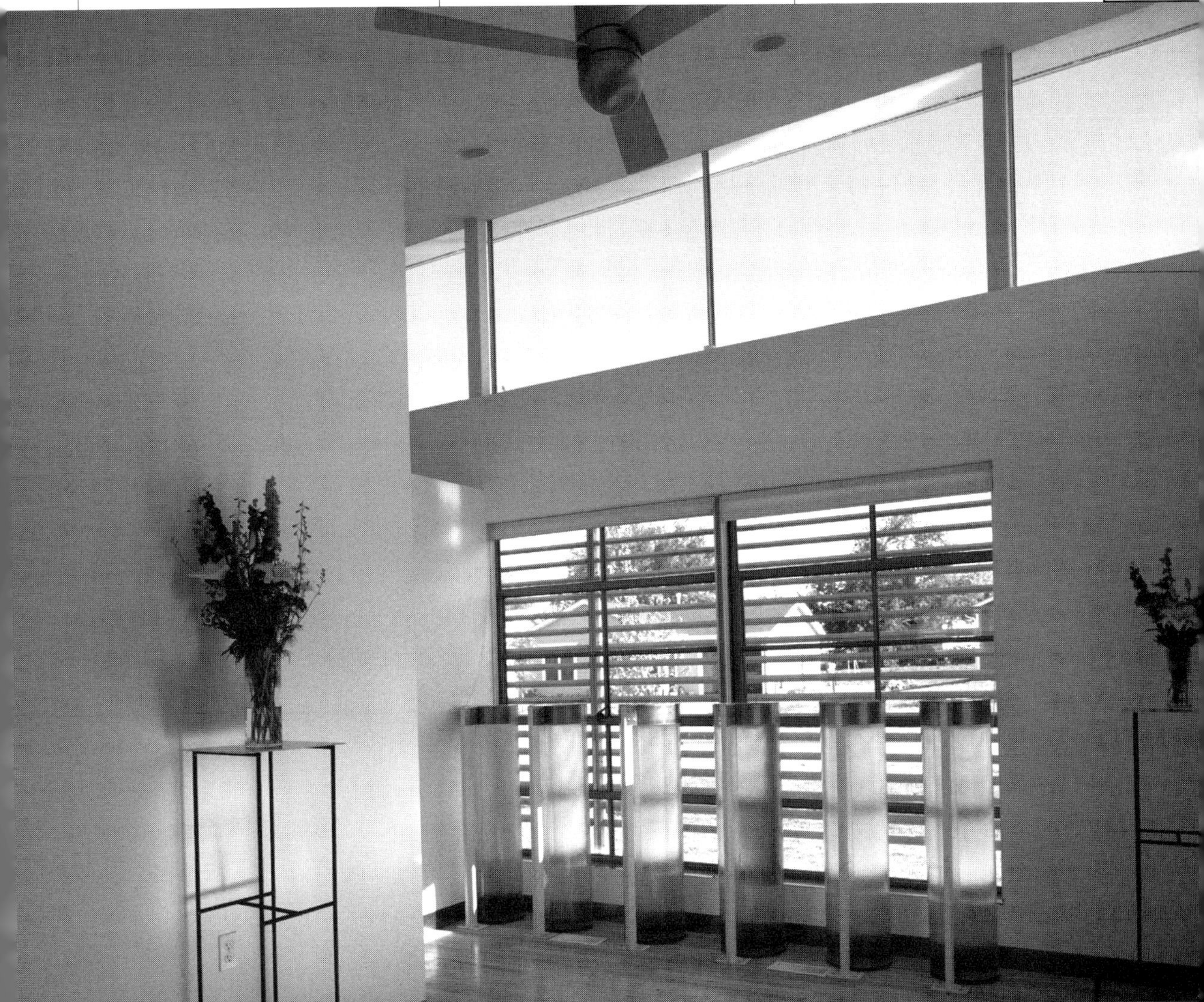

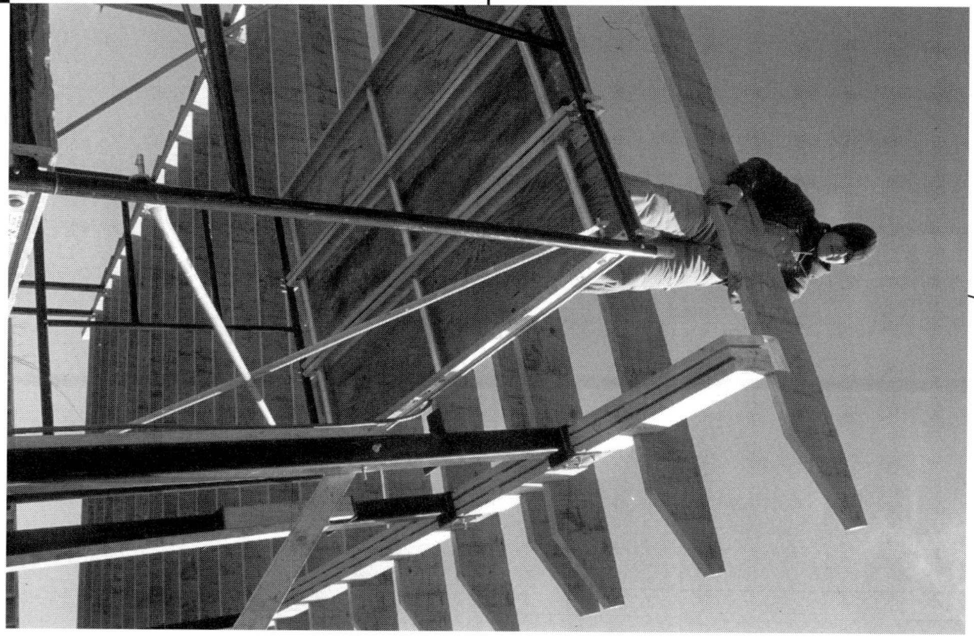

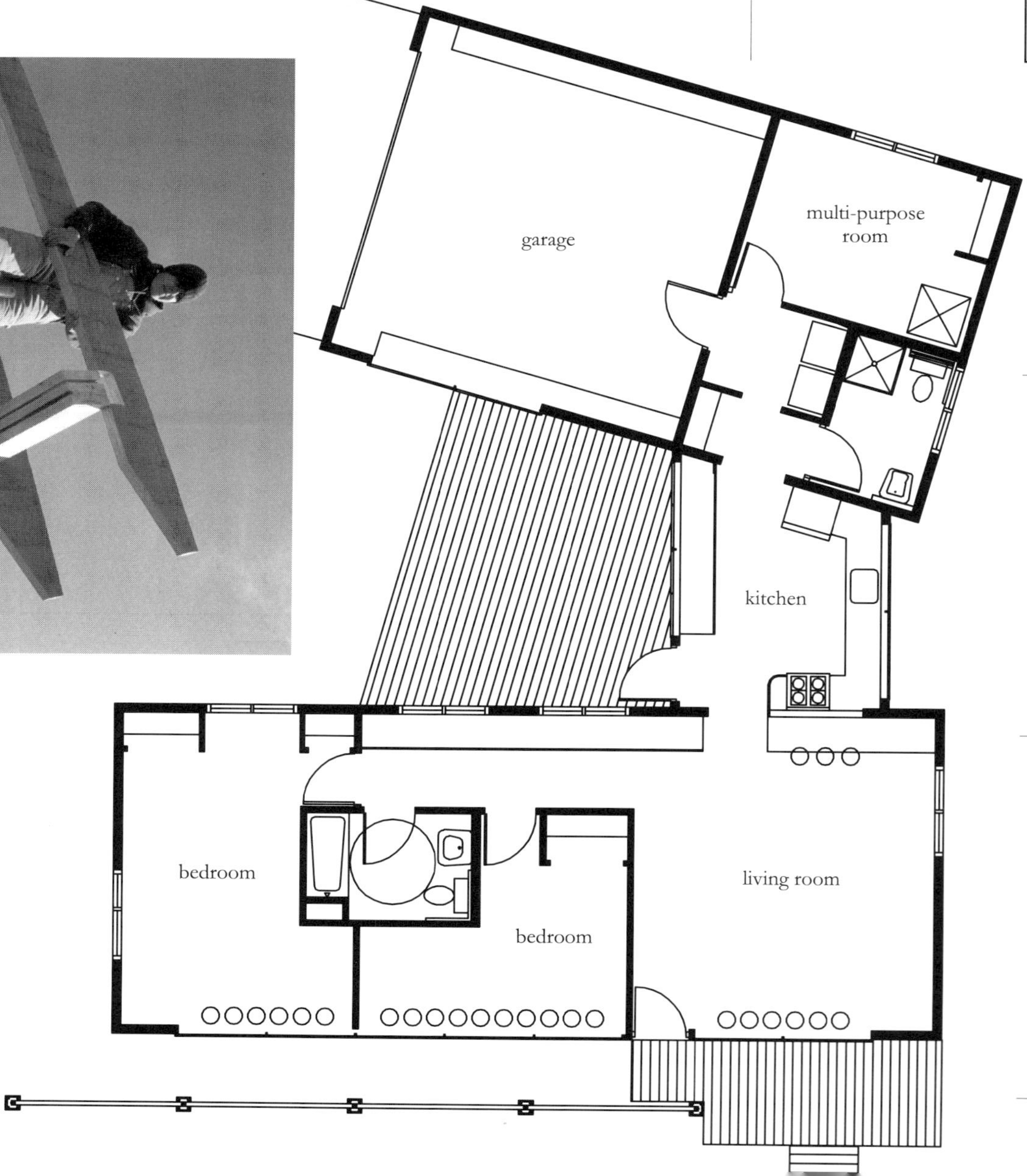
garage
multi-purpose
room
kitchen
bedroom
bedroom
living room

BUILD YOUR OWN: AFFORDABLE HOUSING

Each spring, Studio 804 undertakes the task of providing alternatives to the local affordable housing initiative. Construction of the fifth house designed and built by the studio was completed in May 2003. The studio works within the constraints of a limited budget and break-neck schedule to create a unique design that reflects evolving family needs. The design seeks to maximize energy efficiency, natural light, and accessibility, while maintaining a high level of design excellence.

Energy Efficiency

Broad south orientation maximizes solar exposure for winter heat gain
Livable spaces are oriented to the south, optimizing solar gain and daylight.
Roof overhangs and shading screen block high summer sun, yet allow in lower winter sun
White single-ply membrane roof reflects sunlight, reducing cooling costs
Thermal mass absorbs heat throughout the day, slowly releasing heat at night
Operable windows allow cross-ventilation
Insulated window shades prevent nighttime heat loss
Deciduous trees provide summer shading, yet allow direct sunlight in the winter
Coniferous trees provide north wind buffer
Insulation is maximized in roof, walls, floor, and crawlspace
Super-insulated windows reduce thermal loss above light shelf
Highly reflective interior materials enhance daylighting, reducing electricity costs
Garage is passively heated through large windows on the south
Higher efficiency mechanical, electrical, and plumbing systems are used

Sustainability

Site resources, including native trees, are preserved
Corrugated steel functions as a low-maintenance, recyclable exterior material
Laminated veneer lumber, used for roof framing, lessens need for large timbers
High fly ash content concrete and gravel recycled from crushed concrete are used
Waste recycling occurs throughout construction
North swale blocks winter winds and absorbs water run-off

Innovative Design

Design is compliant with ADA regulations for handicapped accessibility
Multi-purpose area provides a flexible space for changing family needs
Kitchen serves as a naturally-lighted activity center
Open floor plan eases circulation
An accessible courtyard, protected from the street, provides for dining and socializing
Storage is integrated into circulation space
Garage is accessed from the rear, leaving the front of the house open to the neighborhood
Crawl space facilitates utility changes over time
Common materials are used in creative ways

Cost Effectiveness

Construction generates minimal waste
Concrete formwork is reused for sub-flooring and framing
Low-maintenance materials reduce time and money devoted to upkeep
Materials are salvaged from area buildings slated for demolition
Use of regional materials reduces transportation costs

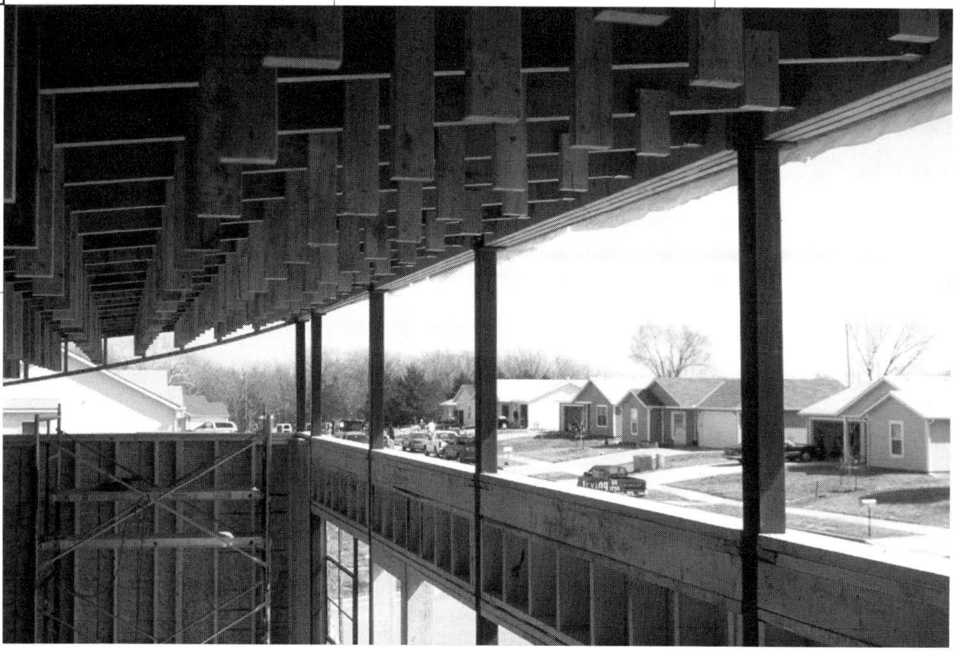

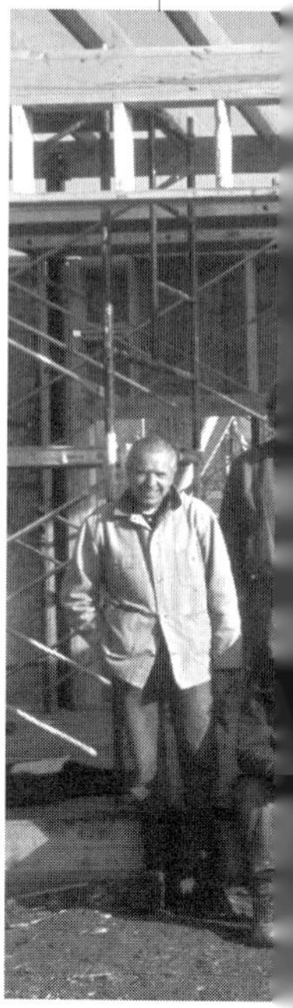

STUDIO 804: SPECIFICATIONS

Lindsey Mahoney and Lindsey Piant

Studio 804 is a not-for-profit organization that is operated 5 months of the year by 19 architecture students under the leadership of two professors. Students participate in an intensive design-build process each spring that culminates in the construction of an affordable house that is sold to a family in the Lawrence, Kansas, community. Students work in collaboration with Tenants to Homeowners, a local not-for-profit organization, that acts as the client for the construction of the house. The design-build program offers students the opportunity to work with real clients, neighborhood associations, limited budgets and local building codes, while establishing a community-university partnership. The studio incorporates innovative design, ADA accessibility, and sustainability in a house that is sold to a qualified buyer. This is the fifth house to be designed and built by the studio. The students began construction on January 28th, 2003.

Energy Efficiency

Studio 804 operates with the understanding that affordable design is not limited to initial construction costs. The house responds to these issues by using passive solar design as a means of decreasing energy consumption to reduce energy bills. Maximum insulation in the ceiling, walls, crawlspace, and clerestory helps to keep energy costs down while super-insulated glass is used in the clerestory windows to reduce thermal loss through the glazing. A white single-ply membrane roof reflects sunlight to minimize summer heat gain. Natural daylighting is maximized throughout the house through the use of highly reflective interior materials, reducing electricity costs.

Sustainability

The design-build studio strives to achieve an environmentally responsible design by incorporating regional, recycled, recyclable, and salvaged materials whenever possible. High fly ash content concrete and gravel recycled from crushed concrete are used as a means of reducing landfill waste. Industrial steel windows were salvaged from an area building slated for demolition. Corrugated steel siding is used on the exterior of the house as a low-maintenance, recyclable material. To avoid destruction of large timbers, laminated veneer lumber is used for roof framing. Recycling and efforts to minimize waste occur in the construction process as well. Concrete formwork is dismantled and reused as sub-flooring and framing material. Site waste, such as wood scraps, nails and metal, are all recycled at the end of their use.

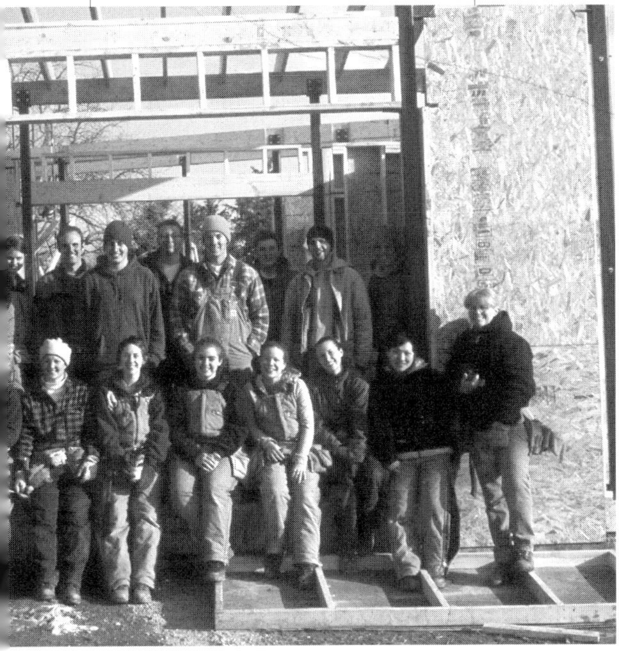

Accessibility

The design-build studio works to make environments that are accessible to everyone, not only financially but also physically. Care is taken to ensure that ramps, turnarounds, fixtures, and door widths fully comply with ADA regulations for handicapped accessibility. Designing with accessibility in mind, the design-build studio ensures that the home will continue to meet the needs of its occupants over time. The house's multi-purpose room in the north wing accommodates live-in nursing or caretaking staff. It is separated from the main bedrooms to ensure privacy for both the occupants and staff.

Design Features

1. The length of the south façade is maximized to improve passive solar benefits for winter heat gain and daylighting. Carefully calculated roof overhangs and a louvered shading screen block the high summer sun, yet allow lower winter sun to enter the house. Operable windows, on the north and south sides, provide cross ventilation. Super-insulated glass above the light shelf minimizes heat loss. Water tubes, used as a thermal mass behind the south glazing, absorb heat through the day and release it at night. Cellular insulated window shades prevent nighttime heat loss.

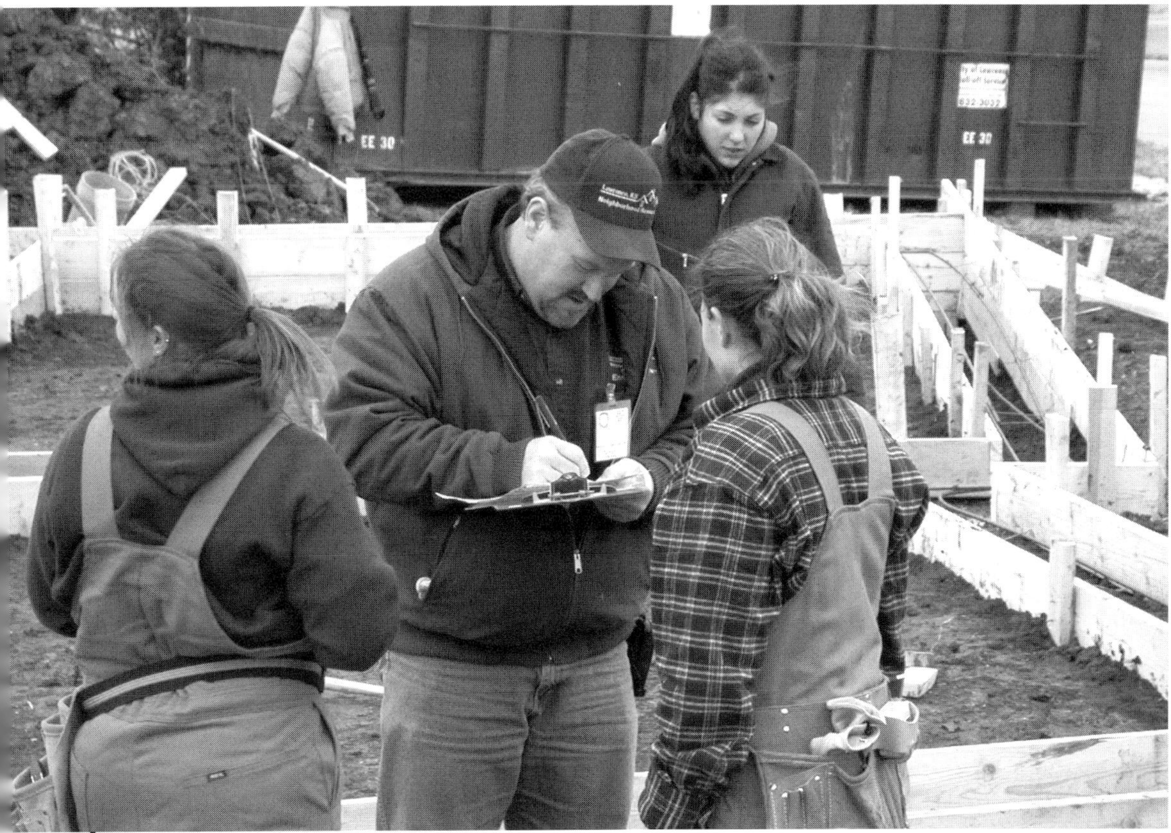

2. Site consideration influences the house's orientation, landscape, and passive solar opportunities. Orienting the house to maximize southern exposure achieves optimum passive solar benefits. Preservation of site resources, such as native trees, is considered in the location of the house. Additional plantings include deciduous trees on the south to provide summer shade and coniferous trees on the north to provide a wind buffer. A north swale blocks winter winds and absorbs run-off.

3. Green materials and sustainable practices are used to achieve environmentally responsible design. High fly ash content concrete, gravel recycled from crushed concrete, and recycled content insulation and gypsum are used throughout. Materials salvaged from area buildings slated for demolition, such as industrial steel windows, are re-used as high-end materials for little or no cost. Maple flooring is re-used from an area gymnasium, in lieu of basic-grade carpet, which is poorer for indoor air quality and recyclability.

4. Garage emphasis is minimized with access from the rear, leaving the front of the house open to the neighborhood. Focus is aimed at neighborhood socialization. The front yard is more approachable at a pedestrian scale. In this design, the placement of the garage to the north allows the livable spaces to take advantage of the south exposure for winter heat gain and daylighting.

5. A truly cost-effective house continues to be affordable after the occupant moves in. Energy efficiency and low-maintenance materials contribute to the reduction of the house's life cycle costs. Care with construction waste contributes to the house's cost-effectiveness. Concrete formwork is reused for sub-flooring and framing materials. Regional materials are used to reduce transportation costs and pollution created in traveling great distances.

6. Storage is maximized throughout the house as an integral part of the architectural aesthetic. Integrating storage systems into what is typically circulation creates more useable space. The north storage wall acts as an insulated buffer to the livable spaces, reducing heat loss along the north exposure. A multi-purpose space, separated from the main bedrooms, provides a flexible space for changing family needs and storage space near the garage. The house is constructed on a generous 5' crawl space, adding long-term storage.

7. The kitchen is designed as an activity center with light entering from east and west. It functions as a *hinge* to create a separation of living zones between the north and south wings. The north wing serves the more service-oriented functions of the house such as the garage and laundry room, while the south wing contains the living spaces. The kitchen is thoughtfully located with access to the garage, outdoor patio space, and living room.

8. A courtyard with privacy from the street, offers an area for outdoor dining, children's recreation and socialization with neighbors. This space incorporates convenient access from the kitchen and garage for ease of movement between indoor and outdoor activities. The defined edges of the space create an outdoor room that is ideal for barbeques, birthday parties, and other social gatherings. In addition to the west courtyard, a low sitting wall is located along the front of the house to encourage neighborhood socialization.

Floor Plan Analysis

The plan is hinged around the kitchen, creating two wings, north and south. This narrows the depth of the bays to allow more natural daylight to enter the building. The north wing, containing the garage, serves as a buffer to the cold north winds, protecting the living spaces in the south wing. The south facade of the north wing is glazed to passively heat the garage slab for energy efficiency.

The multi-purpose space in the north wing addresses changing family needs. Possible functions include: teenager's bedroom, grandparent's room, nurse / caretaker's room, office and/or shop. This space is separated from the main living area to offer hierarchy of public and private living zones in the house.

The kitchen is designed as an activity center with light from the east and west. It offers ease of access to the garage, patio, and living room.

The garage is minimized with access from the rear, leaving the front of the house to respond to the neighborhood, in lieu of the car. Less emphasis is placed on the garage for *curb appeal*, and instead, focus is aimed at neighborhood socialization.

The design is complaint with ADA regulations for handicapped accessibility. Careful attention is given to bathroom turnarounds, ramps, and door openings. The garage is designed to enable a handicapped vehicle to meet loading and unloading needs.

The outdoor courtyard space is designed with privacy from the street and easy access from the kitchen to provide an enjoyable area for engaging the homes' exterior.

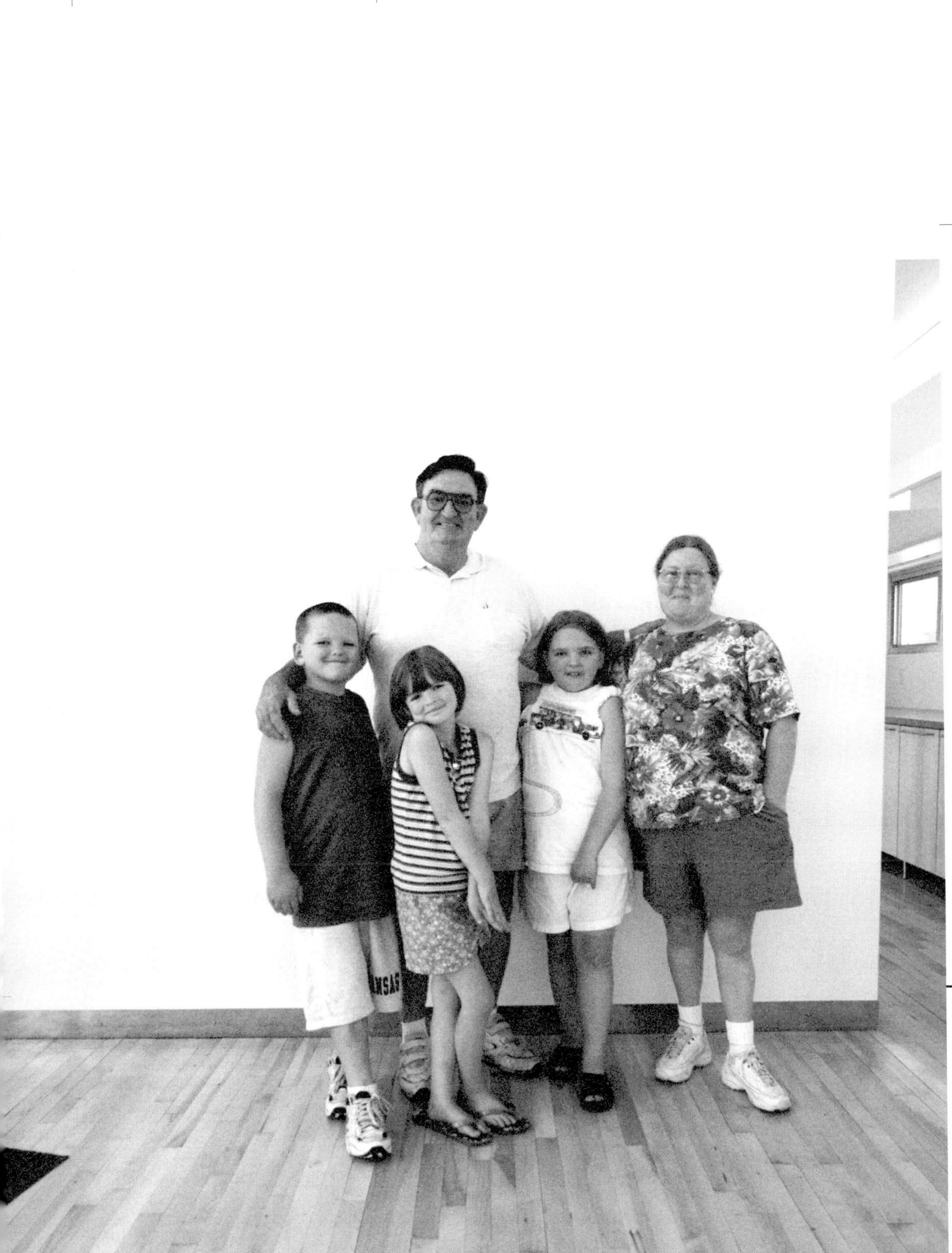

The Owners of a New Home: Roy and Constance Frazier with their children, Donald, Ava and Katie

FROM DES MOINES

Jonathan D. Solomon
We wanted to talk to you about your Des Moines Vision Plan from its beginnings in a Yale studio to its current realization—with an eye—given our constituency—towards your experiences working on the same projects as an educator and as a professional.

Emily Abruzzo
I'm not quite clear on how the work first started; I know you had a studio at Yale that began work on it . . . But, what I think might be interesting to talk about is how the students projects affected the way that you saw it; or, how you approached it, beginning as an elucidator and then becoming the architect for the project. How did those two conditions—which are very different in terms of who you might look at things—how maybe how they affected what you eventually did for the city?

Mario Gandelsonas
Its an old story, but the suggestion of working on DM came from Bruce Graham. He asked me what kind of city I would like to work with, I gave him a grocery list of conditions which would make a city ideal for me. I said I want a small city—so I was already thinking about that second tier. I was thinking about that because I was also thinking implementation, which was a question that was raised by Bruce Graham, him being president of the largest office in the world and being essentially pragmatic. He saw the interest in what I was doing, but he asked me the question, how can we use it? From his point of view that was the crucial question.

I said that I can't really look at my work as something that will be used. I look at this as basic research; In the same way, there is a possibility for an impact on the real world.

So we discussed the city. I said a small city; immediately I said a city with a river, because I thought that geography was important; I though that location was symbolically important. He I said I'd like the city not to be on the coast—I thought about that because, for me, symbolically. . . I wanted that middle ground that hasn't received the impact from the Atlantic or Pacific and doesn't have to deal with the weight of hundreds of years of history like the old east. And its not like mid century like Los Angeles. So I said I want something that is in a way indefinable but can serve as a platform for thinking the future without that weight of history. So it was a very schematic and diagrammatic way of looking at things.

I said I'd like to work with a city with a wealthy community that will have the ability to implement things and who would be willing to do things; to change. A forward looking city. And a city where

Mario Gandelsonas speaks with 306090 about education and practice

TO SHANGHAI

I can find a group of sophisticated people who understand about art. He said, well, I have your city, it's Des Moines.

It's the heartland, so, symbolically, its exactly what you want. It has a very strong economy, which is a well-kept secret. That's because of their role in the insurance business—they're the third international insurance center. And he said that they have an art center; a museum—that's a real jewel. For a city to have that, you need people who understand about art.

So they helped me and I started my long tradition of itinerant studios. This was one of the option studios. When I said I was going to do a studio in Des Moines, I thought that the students would be like, 'what is he talking about?' But they thought that it was the coolest thing. This was like '88. They thought it was so strange as an idea.

So we went to Des Moines, and immediately got the support of the city planning department, which provided us with all the plans, all the drawings, all the photographs. Actually, the first project, to go back to the pedagogical question, for me was structure around the question of representation. Let's call it representation and tourism. Because this is bunch of people who don't have the faintest idea what this is—it's not like you go to Paris and you can buy a guide—they are supposed to, in a way, draw an architectural and urban guide to Des Moines.

I asked them to bring their camera and dozens of rolls of film. That was one of the exercises—to spend a lot of time photographing the place. I used the same technique I have used ever since, which was not to go immediately but to look at the drawing, and to try to develop and idea of about what that city was about on the basis of the drawing—without even knowing what the buildings are. In the end, we all discovered the same few things.

The studio was basically about discovering Des Moines, and I decided that it was so successful that we needed to repeat it, and I did it again in the next year. They brought us back and we refined the analysis and discovered more things. At that point, I felt I had in my hands the tools to come and propose a new way of starting a master plan and a new way of developing the idea of planning without the notion of master—and the substitution of the word Master with Vision. That's where we came up with the term.

EA
How do you think your work for the Vision Plan would have been different had you just been hired by the city of Des Moines to look at the city

and work on it, as opposed to doing it in a studio environment?

MG
I never thought about that, but I think what the studio work brought was a richness of approaches that I tried not to unify and compress into a globalizing approach. That definitely affected the very idea of the Vision Plan, which was a multiplicity of approaches and the idea that everything should be more than one. That is, that there couldn't be just one solution but that planning process should generate alternatives. So I never thought about that think that directly related to the studio situation where you're given a project and, in the end, you don't end up with a project, but a number of alternative to the project. So I would say that the influence was really deep, because it destabilized the very notion of master planning because the master plan presupposes a single picture. The master plan is linked to time, there are a number of phases—thought of in the short term, the medium term, the long term—and you know that you're supposed to revise it every so many years. But here the very short-term plan was not really finished. The idea was related, from my perspective, to a fact that I learned in reading early 20th century master plans (like the 1929 New York plan where you get a discussion between the American way of planning and the European way of planning; related to very different political systems). I've always had that in mind, except that I felt that concept was just a philosophical concept and it needed to be brought in to the present through the discussion of the economic questions together with the political question, and the basic question—the relationship between planning, the market, the business sector, and the government. That, in a way, is articulated though the idea of alternatives, because one of the of the things the business sector hates is the fact that you come and. . .but I thought of it idealistically as a process of negotiation.

EA
Well, its certainly an amazing success in getting an entire city to rethink the way it exists; I'm wondering how that success has influenced how you teach your other studios now-for example, the Shanghai studio, which seems to have a similar idea to it, but maybe not?

MG
Maybe not. There are two questions here. The success of the plan is one thing; the success of studio is a different story. I think if we are going to talk pedagogical issues and their relationship to reality, it is a very difficult question, we might need to address first—I'm rephrasing the question. I do believe the benefits of trying to articulate and not use. Articulation is a term I really like, because its not just a simple relationship. Every element in the relationship has its own logic, and by putting them together, they are both going to be modified. It destabilizes both education and reality. I could never separate theory from reality—I think that theory needs to feed from reality and reality can be informed by theory. When theories going on a limb, detaching themselves from reality I find very negative; as well as I find reality without grounding on theory also problematic.

I see my work as a multiplicity of practices: research is one, teaching is another, design practice is another one; the dissemination of architectural ideas is another. . .In a way the success of Des Moines pushed me to look into something else—because, why should I do it again? And was it pertinent? Because that was something I started in the 70s and 80s. And in the meantime, the world had changed. So I wanted to move on.

The news was flooded with what was happening in China—its been asleep for 5000 years and suddenly things are happening. I also stumbled across a booklet that the Chinese consulate had put out in New York. I read something that really hit me: the Chinese said, 'America was the leading cultural nation of the 20th century; China will be the equivalent in the 21st century.' I thought, 'My god, this is pretentious;' but, then, 'I like that!' Because I like ambitious ideas. Its like the Burnham plan for Chicago. So I thought, I need to look into that.

EA
Maybe an interesting thing to segue into would be . . . you seem to be a big proponent of publishing student work, as we've seen with Shanghai Reflections. That's something, of course, that we're interested in because it's what we aim to do in a way. . .I'm curious who you think the audience is for that kind of thing and how does it make students think about their work differently?

MG
Well, I have a very particular way of doing it. It may not really coincide with the way you see it, because I'm on the other side of the table. There are three different ways, among many others, of teaching design. One is the old Beaux Arts systems, which is being perpetuated even today. When you look at teacher like John Hedjuk, etcetera. there are a set of very strict rules on the basis of which the design studio is organized. There are also a very limited number of formal options that are suggested or imposed on the students—this is one extreme. There is another one which is like a free-for-all and where there is a lot of freedom. There's something in between where I like to locate myself where the rules are quite strict; the formal repertoire is actually quite open, but what, for me, is important is the

enactment of the rules or the a given repertoire. And the understanding of the notion of developing a project. That presupposes a relationship between the teacher and the student where they trust each other. The key for me in this type of relationship is that the teacher listens to the student, which, in general, doesn't happen.

Listening is a rhetorical figure for the teacher detecting in the students work—in the visual manifestations and in the concepts—the more powerful ideas that have a potential for developing in a project. It's more a late 19th/early 20th century Freudian concept, which for me is absolutely valid in the 21st century—to understand that architecture doesn't really take place strictly or solely at the conscious level, but constantly weaves the conscious with unconscious.

The extremely difficult position of the teacher of a studio is to be able to connect to both levels. Obviously, to be able to connect to the unconscious is something that we can't control, which puts you in a difficult situation—its not like teaching math. So you need maximum receptivity while at the same time, you deal with the boundary that separates student and teacher. So I don't know if that's clear.

What's important is that, at the same time, you need to build up the confidence of the student and her or his own capability. The problem is that, with the first method, its perhaps more efficient in terms of teaching because you are giving rules and feeding things. So this is really more difficult because the student feels on the edge of some precipice where the teacher is not entirely there protecting him or her. You need to show the student that he or she is doing the right move—because there is also failure and dead ends . . . It a little bit more complicated. What's good in a school is when you can have both experiences.

Mario Gandelsonas, currently a professor of architecture at Princeton University, has taught at Yale, Harvard, the University of Illinois, and the University of Southern California. He was a founder and editor of the journal Oppositions *His book* The Urban Text *was one of the first to use the computer to analyze urban forms. His most recent book is* X-Urbanism: Architecture and the American City

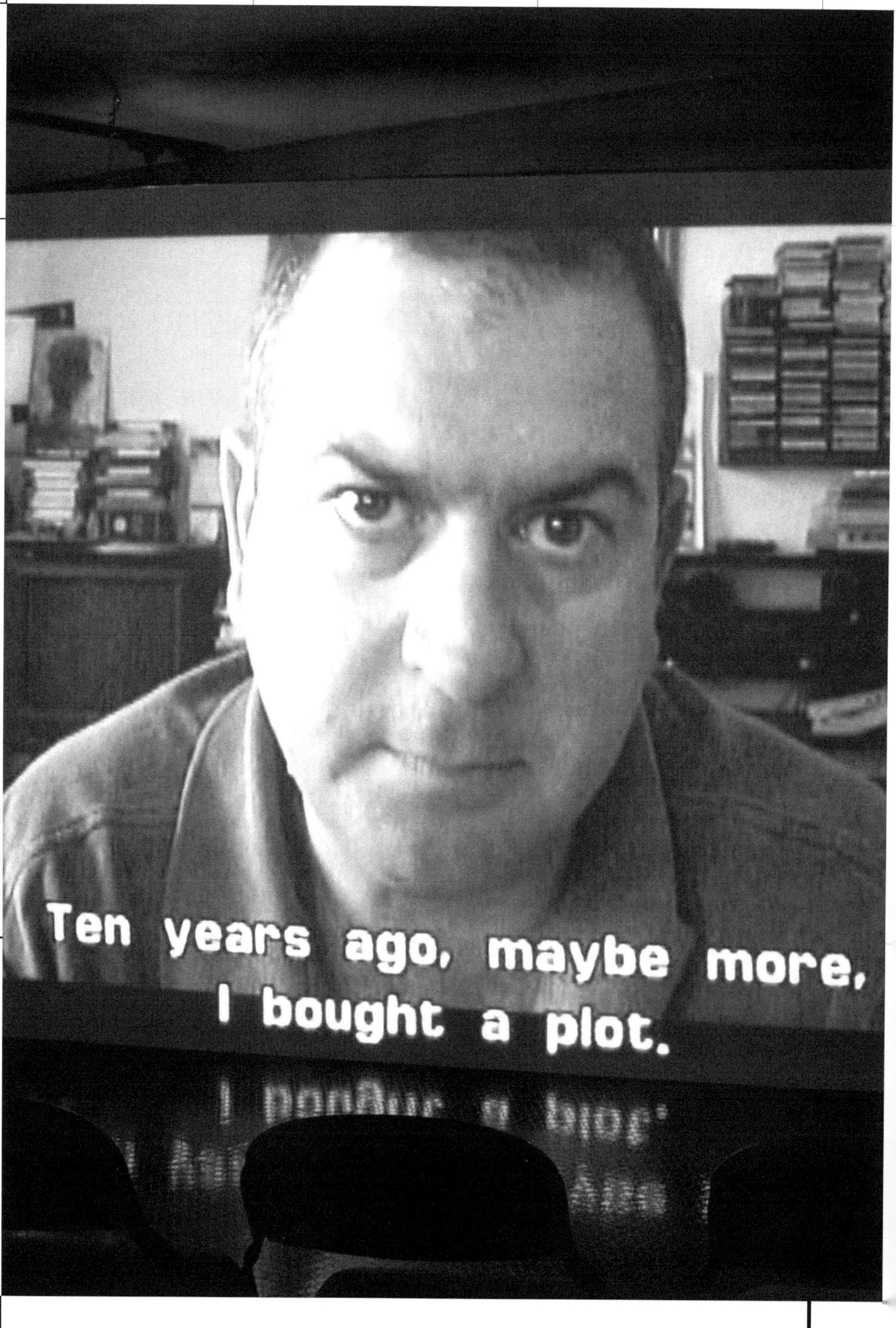

Film Still from Avi Mograbi's *Happy Birthday, Mr. Mograbi*

All images courtesy of Mohammed Sharif / UCR/California Museum of Photography, University of California Riverside

10.60 Design Collaborative build an exhibition for 4 Palestinian and 4 Israeli film makers

ONE GROUND

by Mohamed Sharif

Pedagogy *in Vivo*

The design and construction process was entirely collaborative in spirit. Regular design and client team meetings, held at the museum from November 2002 to February 2003, were central to the formulation of a design strategy and its realization. Artists participating in the exhibit also contributed to the process by means of a vital and often challenging E-mail exchange. Dialogue enabled the design team to distill the needs and desires of each exhibited artist and to identify the nature, or character, of the presentation of each specific work. Indeed, the most significant pedagogic imperatives of the design effort draw from this engagement.

Practitioners, teacher and students quickly shed their preconceived design solutions for this environment and endeavored to look, listen, converse and repeat the discursive cycle with all involved. The use of a large-scale model combined with frequent walkthroughs and the use of full-scale cardboard mock-ups enabled the team to verify the design approach. Consequently, issues related to scale, disposition, and image to surface proportions were fine-tuned for each gallery space.

For all involved the installation provided the luxury of working, at full scale, on classic architectural binaries and devices (anticipation and delay, path

Artists and works:
Measures of Distance, *Mona Hatoum*
Border, *Michal Rovner*
Waiting, *Rashid Masharawi*
Promises, *Justine Shapiro & B.Z. Goldberg*
Dew, Encounters, Neither Black Nor White, *Ori Gersht*
From Texas with Love, *Emily Jacir*
Chronicle of a Disappearance, *Elia Suleiman*
Happy Birthday Mr. Mograbi, *Avi Mograbi*

Client:
UCR/California Museum of Photography, University of California Riverside (Museum Director: Jonathan Green; Assistant Curator: Mitra Abbaspour).

Installation design team:
10.60 Design Collaborative: Joel Blank, Jennifer Myers, Mohamed Sharif and Susie Tashiro; with Felix Monasakanian and Nebi Nazar, Students in the Department of Architecture, College of Environmental Design, California Polytechnic State University, Pomona

Volunteer installation construction team:
Museum staff and volunteers and 10.60 Design Collaborative with Rodolfo Gonzalez and Hugo Ventura, 4th and 5th year students in the Department of Architecture at California Polytechnic State University, Pomona. Construction was directed and coordinated by Brett Perkins of UCR/California Museum of Photography, University of California, Riverside.

10.60 Design Collaborative is:

Joel Blank *BArch/TP, AIA; a Los Angeles based architect, trained in Israel and Spain.*

Jennifer Myers *BFA, BS Env Des; a Los Angeles based designer, trained at Art Center College of Design and Marshall University.*

Mohamed Sharif *BSc Arch, MSc Arch; Assistant Professor in the Department of Architecture, College of Environmental Design, California Polytechnic State University, Pomona; trained at the Scott Sutherland School of Architecture, Aberdeen, Scotland and Illinois Institute of Technology.*

Susie Tashiro *BA Arch, MArch; a Los Angeles based architect, trained at UC Berkeley.*

Photographic credits:
UCR/California Museum of Photography, University of California Riverside.

http://www.cmp.ucr.edu/oneground

and meander, parts and wholes, and frame and content). Setting out to engender substantial visceral engagement in a setting that is normally associated with short attention spans, the team focused on situating an economy of surfaces and spaces that worked with measures of over or under-scaling.

Room, walls, and an entry station were designed as mute objects: undemonstrative and either just-too-big or just-too-small. Especially in the main gallery these objects sit like strange pieces of furniture, each somewhat related to the other, each somewhat related to one of the four gallery walls and each establishing its own subtle and slightly disjointed private zone. For example, the very large tilted screens at either side of the mezzanine level bridge activate the volume of the main gallery and provoke a spatial and corporeal tension. Serving as a continuum between the two floors their taut and looming presence is felt by viewers below and on the bridge.

Animated by projections, the strange and slightly awkward objects engage the viewer in a manner that provokes pause or that momentarily arrests visual drift. Surfaces flicker and substantial bodies define spaces. Within this conceptual framework, and with modest means, a tangible sense of unease s transmitted; without melodrama it provokes an atmosphere resonating with the existential subject matter of the films themselves.

Overall, the team of designers, architects, teacher and students was horizontal and flexible in its design approach and each participant presented an equal share in the conception of the installation. This spirit extended to the realization of the installation itself, wherein the work incorporated the intelligence and improvisational skills of all those involved. This process was an opportunity for all to explore a creative and nimble praxis where design imperatives thrive at the intersection between the built and the imagined. That is in the realms of critical, vital and palpable ideas.

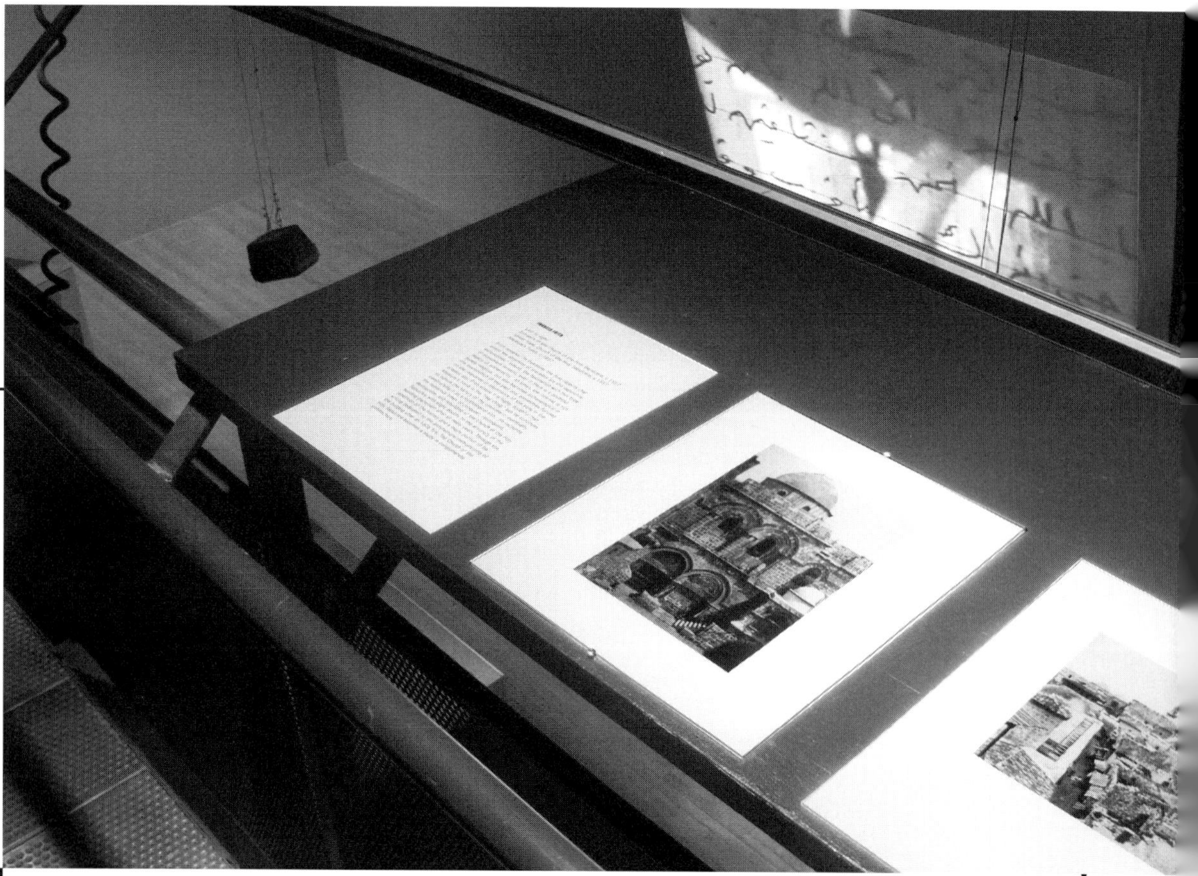

Installation Composition

The museum (renovated by Stanley Saitowitz in 1990) is located in an historic three-storey building on Main Street, off the pedestrian mall in Riverside. The main gallery, on the 1st floor, is almost square in disposition, 2500 sq. feet in area and almost 19 feet in height. A narrow bridge, at the mezzanine level, connects east and west galleries on the 2nd floor and hovers at about 9 feet or so above the main gallery. Located in the center of the main gallery is a column that travels upwards through the bridge. Attached to the column are two high-powered projectors. On the 2nd floor, galleries are more intimate in size and character than the open space of the main gallery below.

The exhibit content is situated in four spaces (one in the main gallery on the 1st floor, another on the mezzanine level bridge above the main gallery, and two at either end of the bridge on the 2nd floor). Four artists' works are shown in the main gallery. These pieces are considerably shorter than the other four works on the 2nd floor. The 2nd floor spaces each seat about twenty or so visitors. Depending on visitor number and degree of conviviality museum visitors are free to select which film to view. The bridge between the two spaces is a kind of open room where photographs and historic information related to 19th century Palestine are displayed.

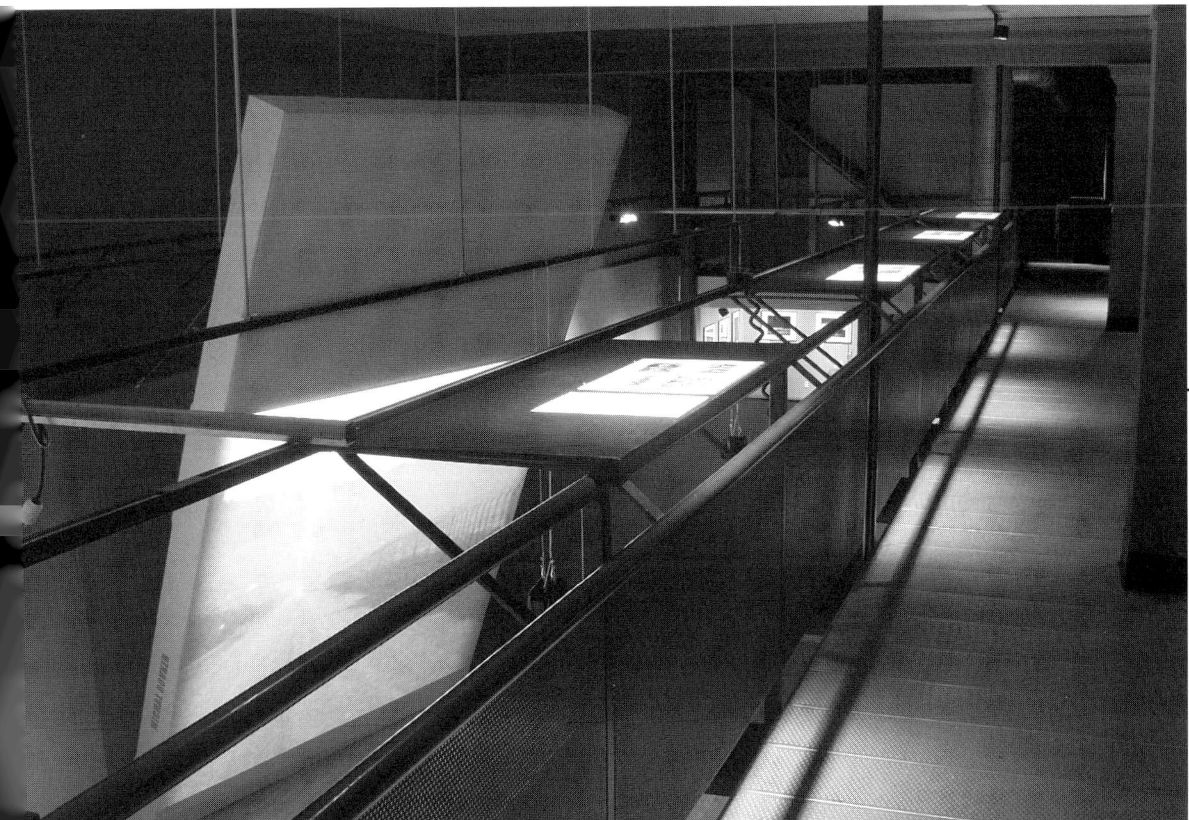

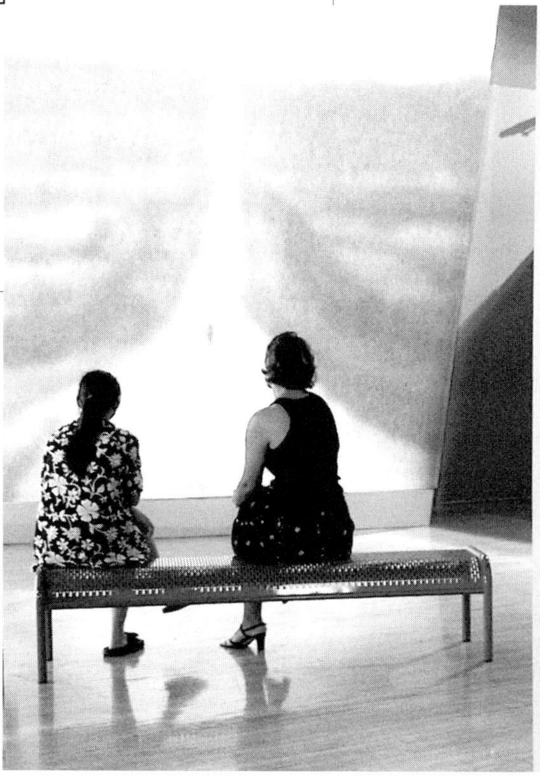
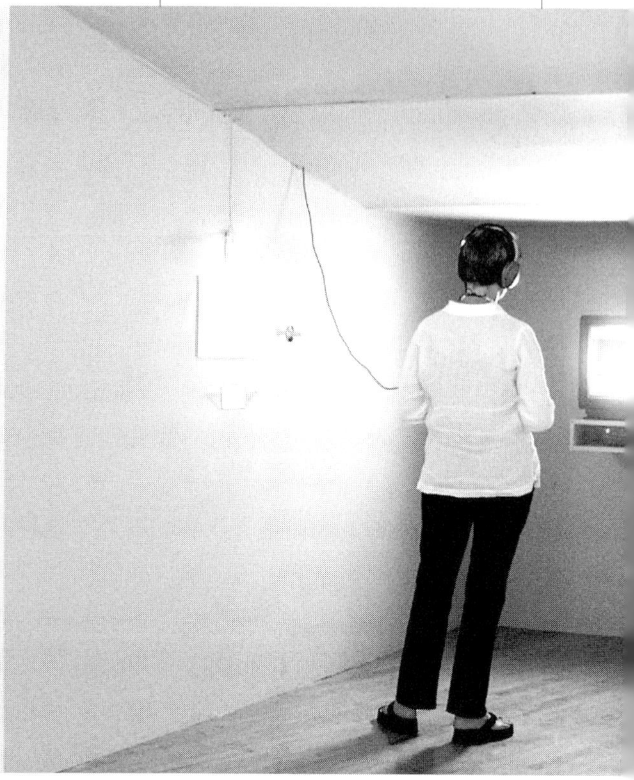
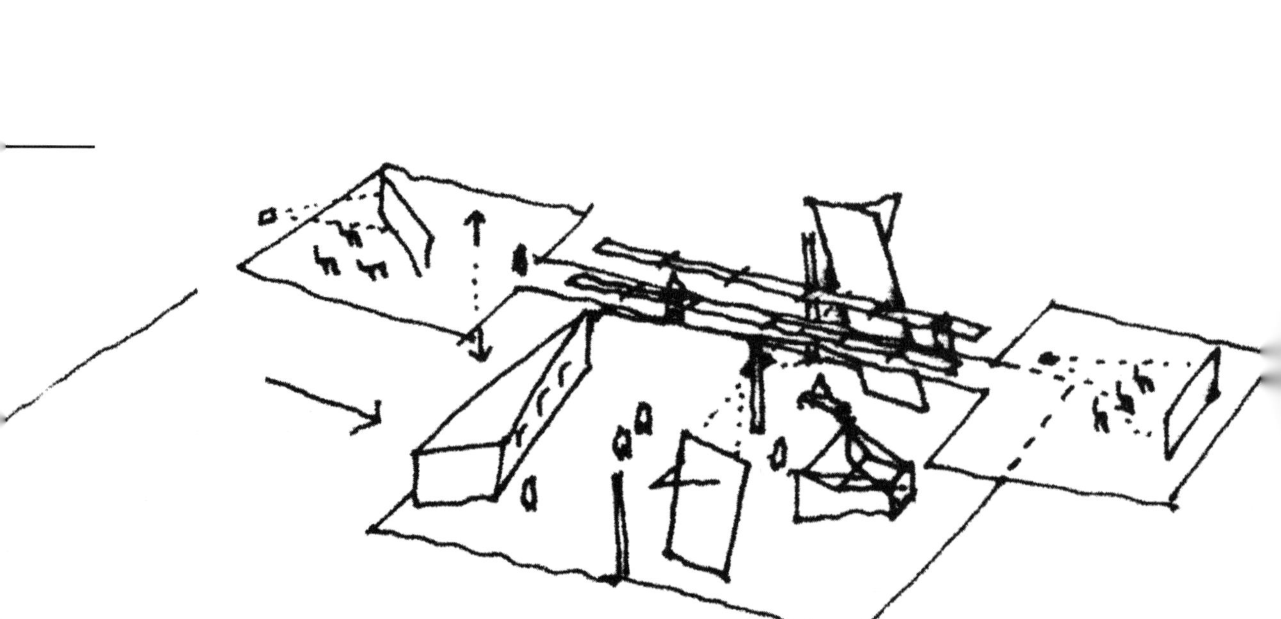

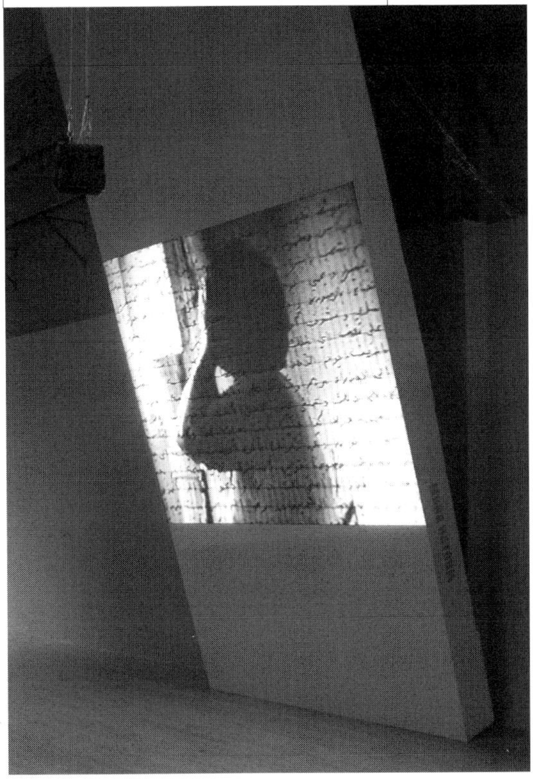

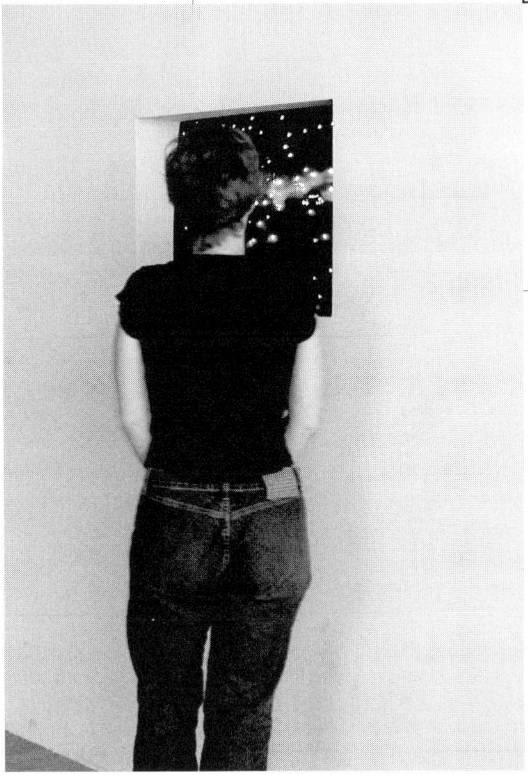

Installation Components and Surfaces:

Mounted on the wall immediately adjacent to the exhibit entrance are excerpts from an e-mail exchange that had developed between the artists, designers and curators during the design process.

A large wedge shaped object, an acute triangle in plan, whose longest wall acts as an information screen and establishes the threshold between museum and exhibit, marks the entrance. It is about one foot shorter than the bridge overhead. On the other side of the wall, in the main gallery, the object contains three television screens that display three silent painterly works by Ori Gersht.

In the main gallery are situated two large tilting screens. Constructed of 1"x12" wood frames and sheathed in cardboard and muslin, these screens hang off the existing walls at an angle of about ten degrees by means of cable attachments at the top. The screen to the left (12' wide x 18' high) is where Michal Rovner's film is projected and the screen to the right (8' wide x 18' high) is where Mona Hatoum's is shown. Audio speakers hover directly above the viewing space in front of each tilting screen so as to concentrate sound for each film.

At the far end of the gallery, directly opposite to the large wedge like object, is a small trapezoidal room (flaring to a width of 8 feet at the entrance from about a width of 4 feet at the far end). At the far end a small television set and DVD player are perched on a one-legged table. Hanging off the sidewalls are two sets of headphones and remote controls for operating the CD player accompanying Emily Jacir's film. The ceiling in the room is raked from a short 7 feet at the entrance to a very short 4½' at the far end so as to amplify the perspectival qualities of the image on the screen

An 8' high x 12' wide screen (constructed like the large ones in the main gallery) is situated in each of the viewing spaces on the second floor. Films by Justine Shapiro and B. Z. Goldberg, Rashid Masharawi, Avi Mograbi and Elia Suleiman are shown in the west space. The east space features the same works by Goldberg, Mograbi and Suleiman.

The guardrails on the bridge between the two spaces serve as continuous horizontal frames for ten large black plywood panels (five on each side) displaying photographs and historic information related to 19th century Palestine.

From the exhibit curators' statement:

Artists have frequently been able to cut through the immediate politics of a conflict to seek out the essential truths that acknowledge the importance of each human being and define the human condition. *One Ground* presents a multi-part program with the intention of creating a dynamic and rich neutral ground for dialogue. *One Ground* centers around a two-part exhibition that addresses some of the metaphorical issues that come out of the politically charged region of Israel and Palestine.

Featured in the museum's main gallery is the work of four Israeli and four Palestinian contemporary film and video artists. *One Ground* differentiates itself from other exhibitions concerning the Middle East because of its shift in focus from social documentary footage that depicts the literal events of political conflict to the presentation of works that address the more conceptual and universal issues of exile, loss, belonging, identity and home. The emphasis on these issues highlights the complexity and specificity of the conflict in this region from the diverse viewpoints of each side as well as the layered cultural and political history of the region without reducing the conflict to a death tally or extremist battleground. These featured works focus on the heightened emotional and psychological experience of living in this region on a daily basis as a means of suggesting in the most powerful and visceral terms tangible human solutions that seem to be unavailable in the political sphere.

The second section of the exhibition draws on the vast photographic resource of the museum's Keystone-Mast stereograph collection, the largest stereo photographic collection in the world, to look at historical representations of the region. In addition to a selection of stereo prints showing the cultural richness of this region this section of the exhibition will also feature an online interactive presentation of the photographic albums of Francis Frith from the 1850s and 60s, which include images of Egypt, Sinai, Jerusalem, and Palestine. Since many of these images were taken from the specific outsider viewpoint of Christian European travelers these photographs provide both a historical context and a counter-viewpoint to the contemporary films. Together the historical images and the contemporary films compliment each other showing how the current situation rests on complex and layered histories, sentiments, and experiences. *One Ground* has taken shape simultaneously

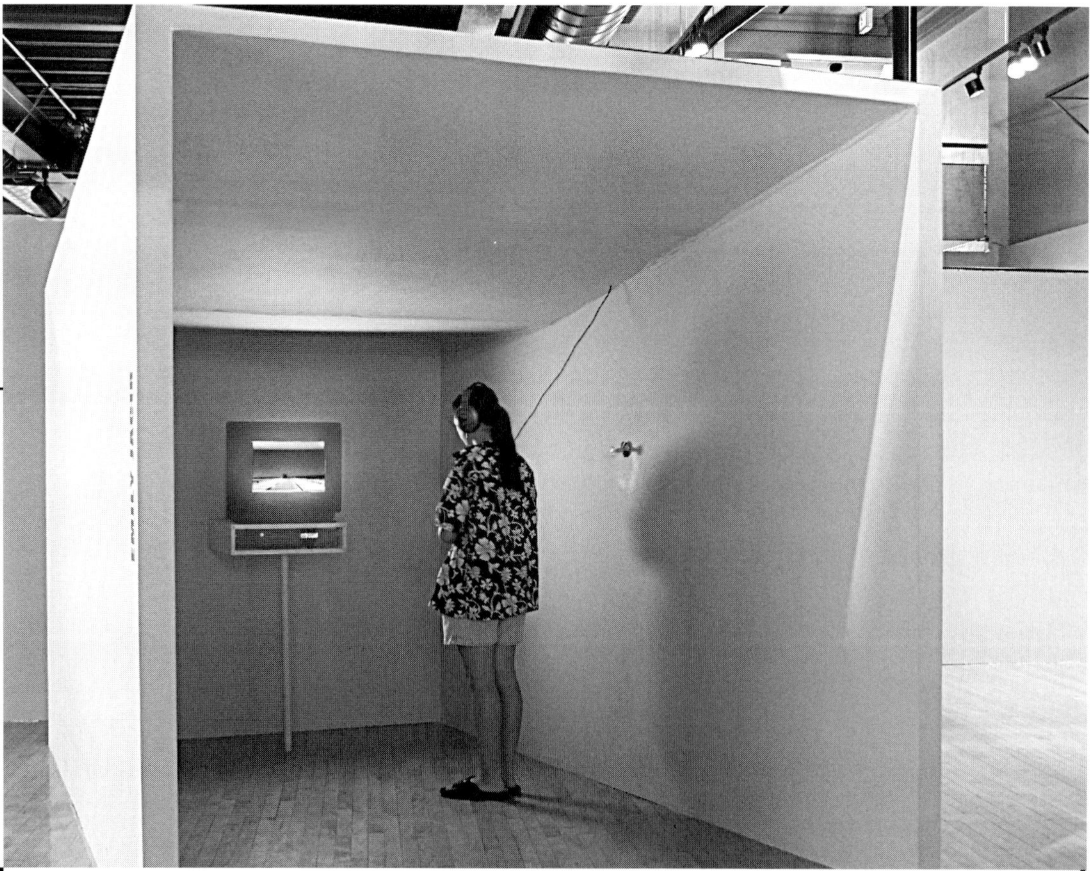

as the result of a dialogue and as a platform for dialogue. Given the realities of the Middle East it is clear that it would be dishonest and unjust to suggest the illusion that a working dialogue exists between Palestinians and Israelis; however, UCR/CMP sees the exhibition and the dialogue that it generates as equally important. Both have the great possibility of enlarging the audiences'—especially American audiences'—understanding and sensitivity to both the current causes and the roots of enormous suffering and seemingly endless state of crisis between Palestinians and Israelis. The show and the dialogue offer the possibility of a neutral ground; but also go beyond the endless dialogue- and -reconciliation meetings and conversations and allow the strength of each artist's film to evoke experiences, relationships and desires central to the human character and in this way make the conflict an issue of vital interest to all citizens of the world.

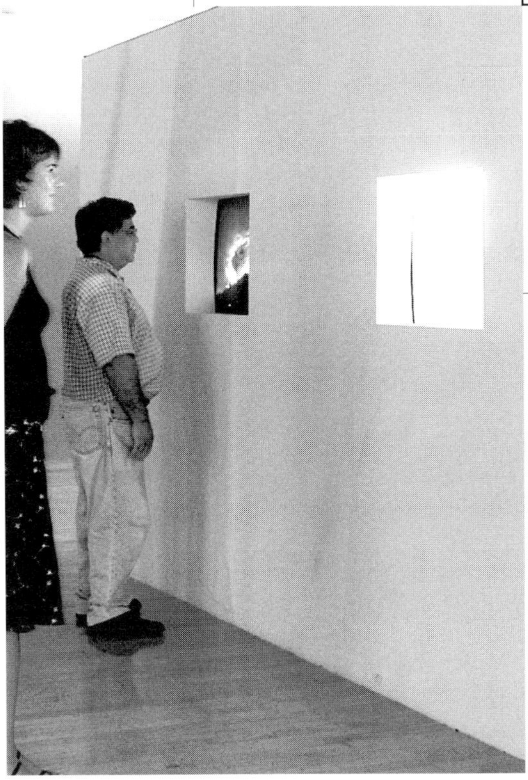

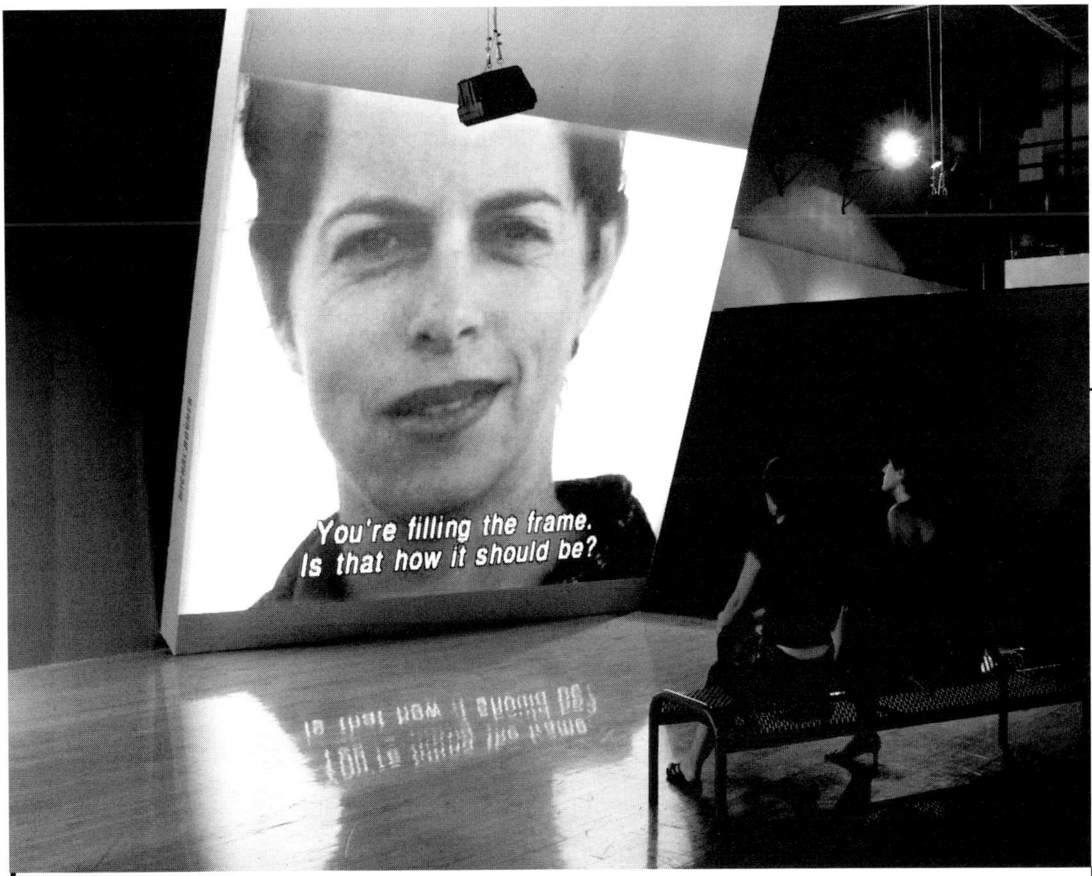

< Film Still from Michal Rovner's *Border*

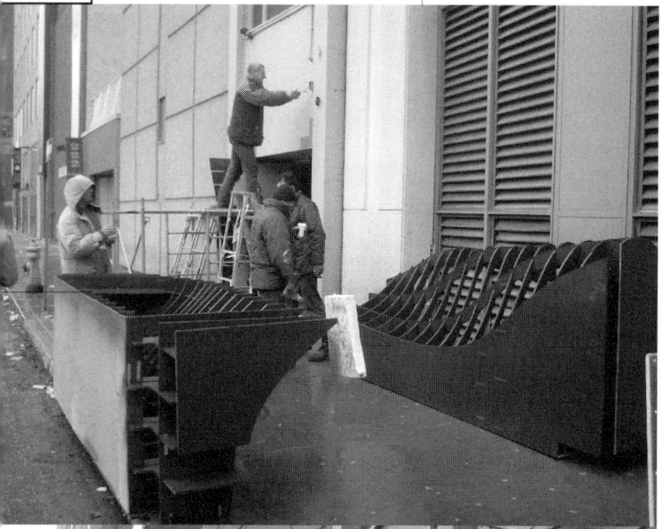
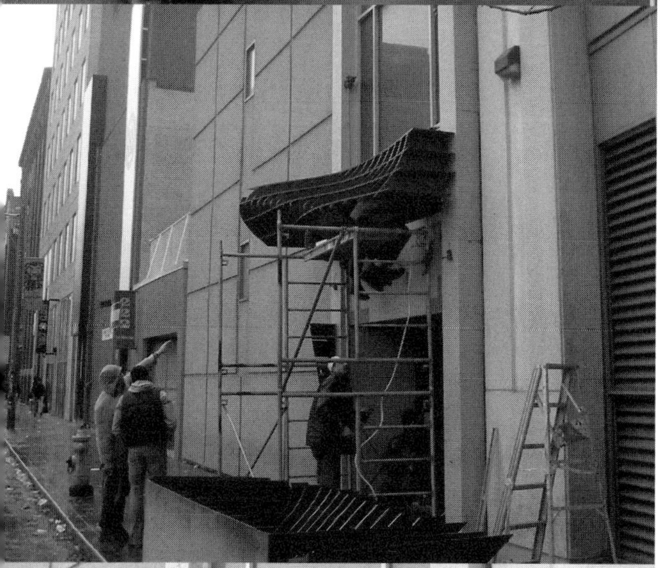
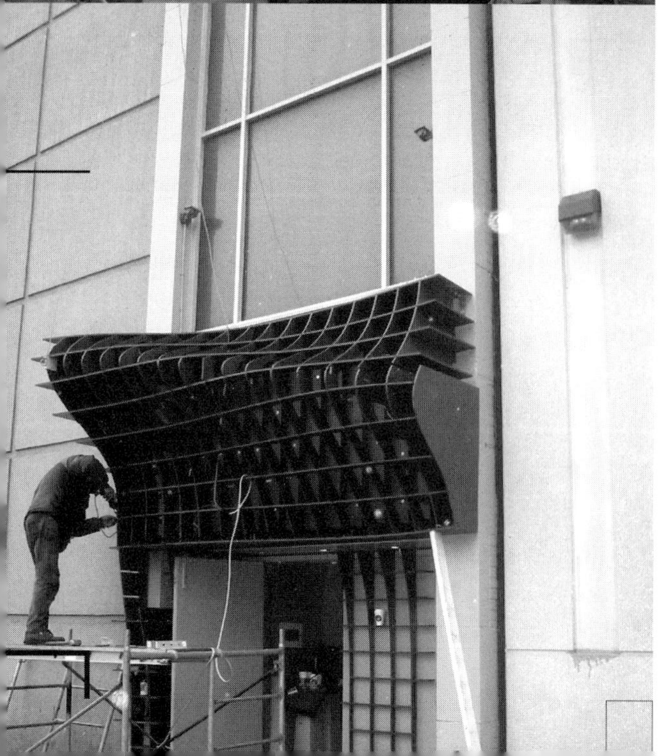
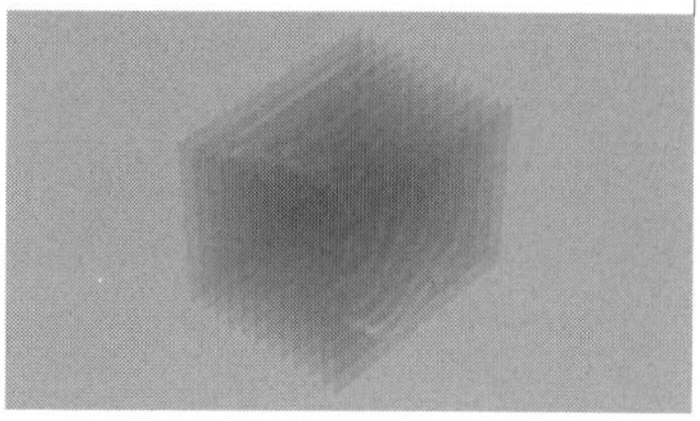
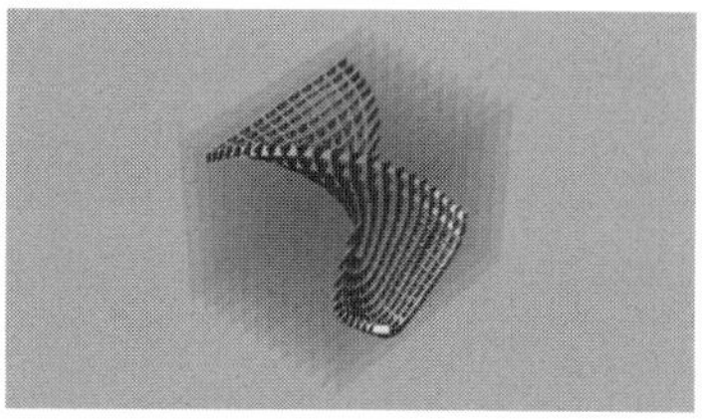
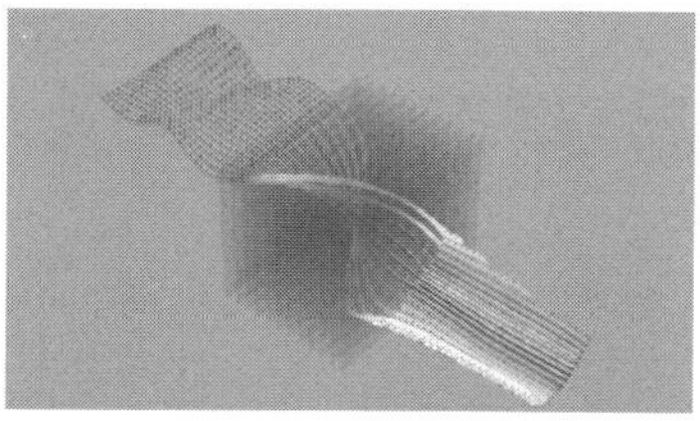
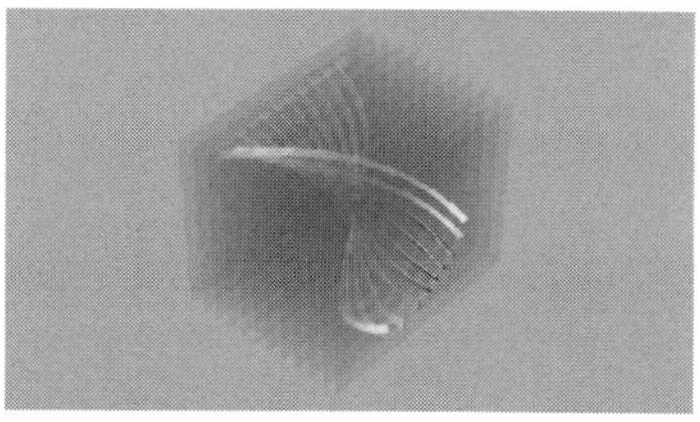
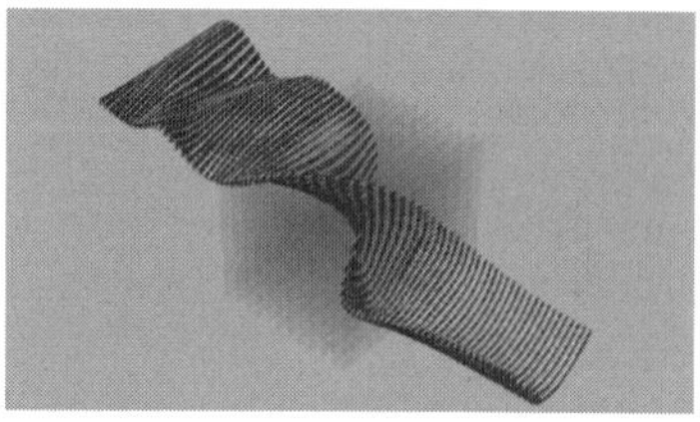
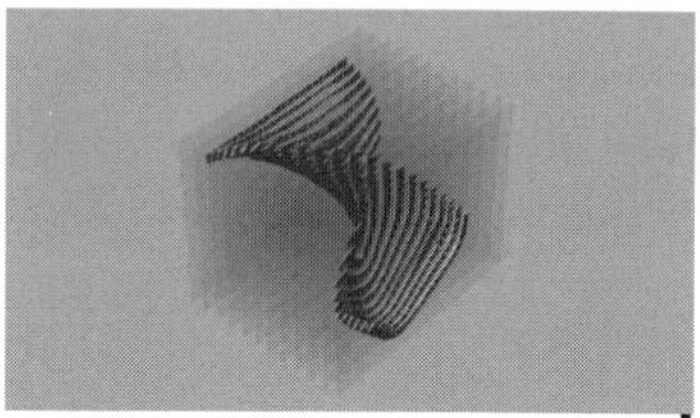

CAD, CNC and chocolate in Toronto

FAÇADE

by Richard Tseng and Saeed Tadrissi

Exploring the possibilities of creating architecture using CAD/CAM (computer assisted design and computer assisted manufacturing) technologies was the goal of the University of Toronto's global architecture program, which teamed with the University of Catalunya in Barcelona in the summer of 2002. During a two month studio, twelve students, selected for the traveling studio for their advanced computer skills, were encouraged to learn and utilize the production software Topsolid (developed by Bernard Cache) and were introduced to the usage of Control Numerical Coordinates (known as CNC) for the fabrication of 1:1 prototypes.

Unlike traditional academic settings where projects rarely leave their digital environments save for in the form of scaled prototypes or study models, it was important that the studio see the projects develop from the digital to the real. The designs would then have to take into account the machinery and software available to students in order to make that transition.

Without the help of contractors or builders, the translation from digital model to actualized form required the architecture students to take into account all construction and tectonic details needed to construct the form. This required more precise 3D modeling techniques, as the digital

Richard Tseng received a BS in Urban Design from Concordia University and a MArch from the University of Toronto. He completed a design studio in CAD/CAM production and its implementation in architecture at the Universidad de Catalunya in Barcelona.

Saeed Tadrissi received a BS in Molecular Biology and a Certificate in Advanced Computer Animation and Modeling from the Information Technology Design Center, both at the University of Toronto. He also completed an advanced digital studio in CAD/CAM productions at the Universidad de Catalunya in Barcelona (under the supervision of Bernard Cache of Objectile).

Tseng and Tadrissi founded the digital design studio, Tsquared2. Since its conception, Tsquared2 has successfully utilized the digital environment as its central mechanism in architectural design and manufacturing.

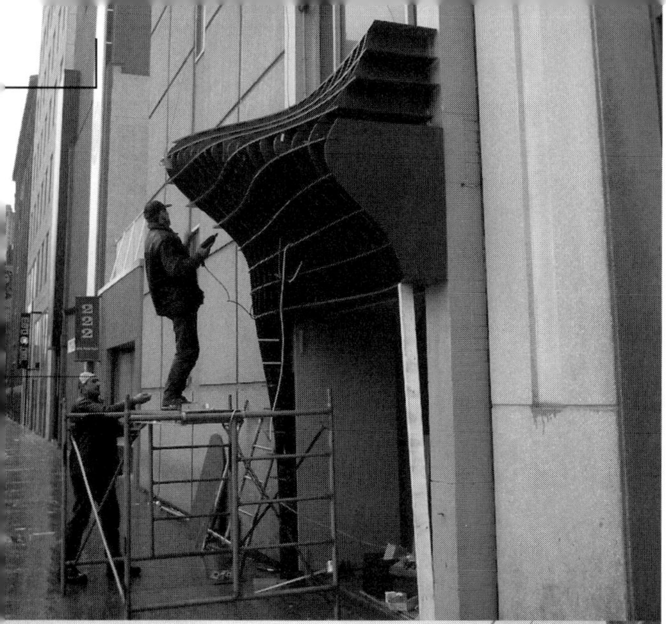

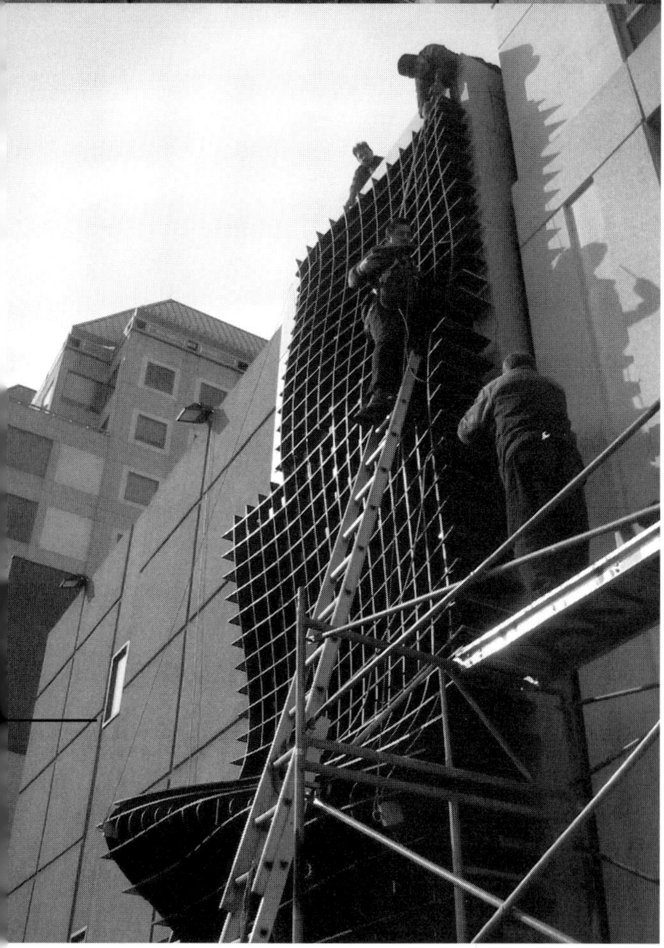

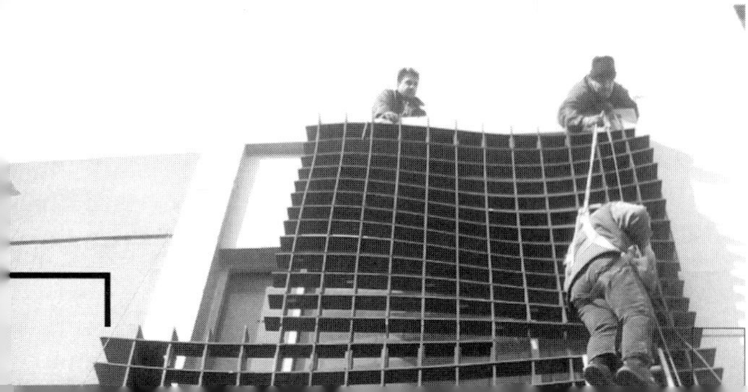

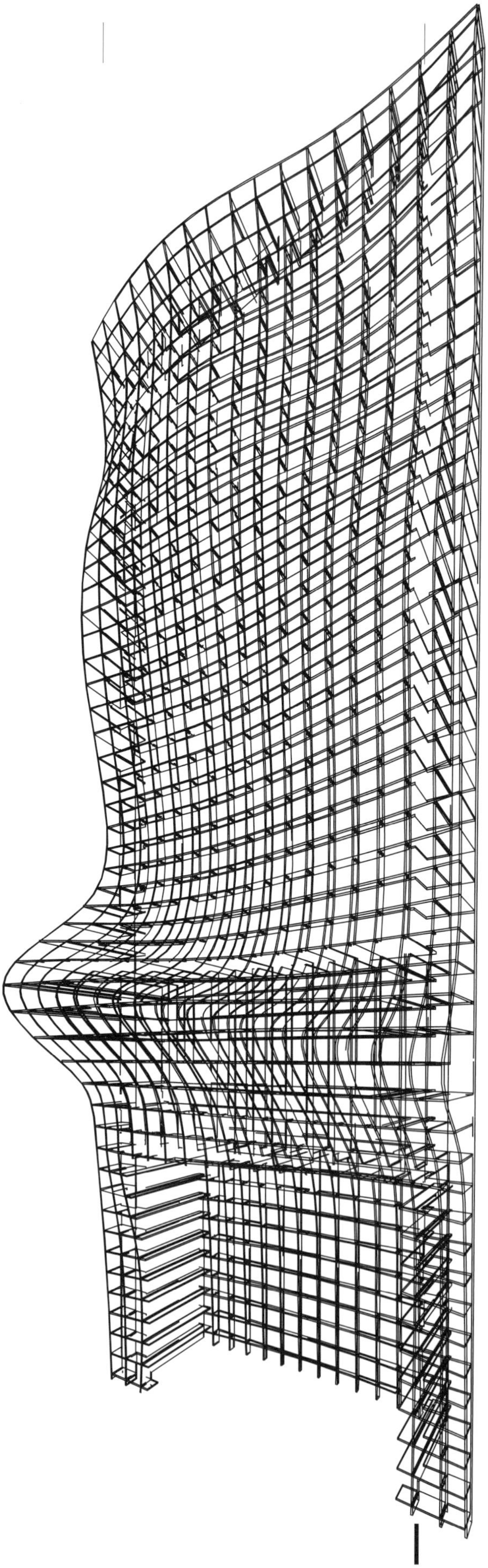

models would now be used for more than a mere visualization, or image, of the project. A result of this method of working is an increased amount of control for the architect; that is, he or she has the additional benefit of dictating the very construction or assemblage of the final product.

The student groups began by creating scale study models from 3D NURBS surfaces using a laser cutter. The use of the laser cutter forced students to back-think the 3-dimensional forms that they designed into 2-dimensional planes. This same process would then help the students extract 2 dimensional coordinates which were transferable to either given production machine (laser cutter or the CNC machine).

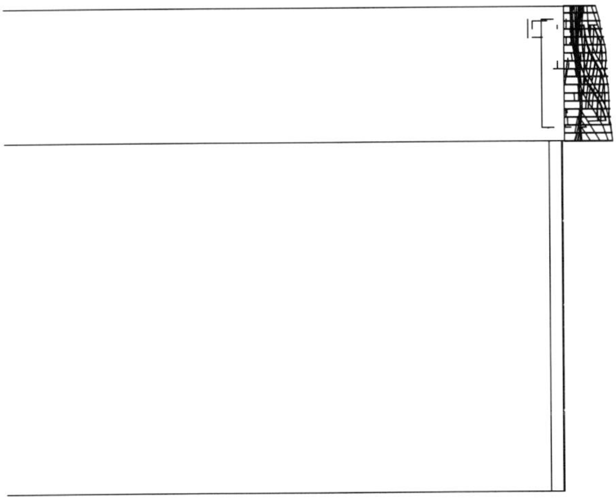

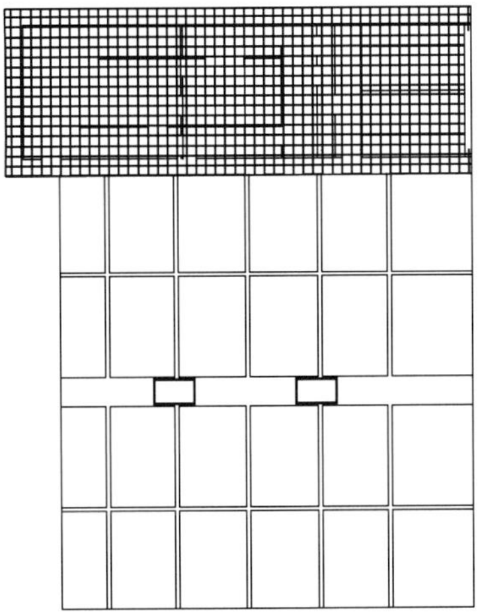

FAÇADE

The methods we explored at the University of Catalunya in Barcelona were the bases for a new design approach in our own work, as shown here with a project to design and build a new façade for a nightclub in Toronto. Functional requirements of the façade were to attract the attention of the public as well as to provide weather protection for the club's patrons. The design had to allow for the installation of two signs for the nightclub. An undulating surface was designed and adjusted in order to accommodate all of the above as well as the existing doorway and double-swing doors. A simple tongue-and-groove system was utilized for the assembly of the pieces. The dimensions of the plywood and the CNC machine dictated the size of each section to be used in construction.

This process allowed the group to utilize the techniques learned in an academic setting to translate the digital model into a physical project. The simple, direct processes allowed the near-exact shape and form of the 3D digital model to be created in a cost-effective and timely manner using the CAD/CAM technology.

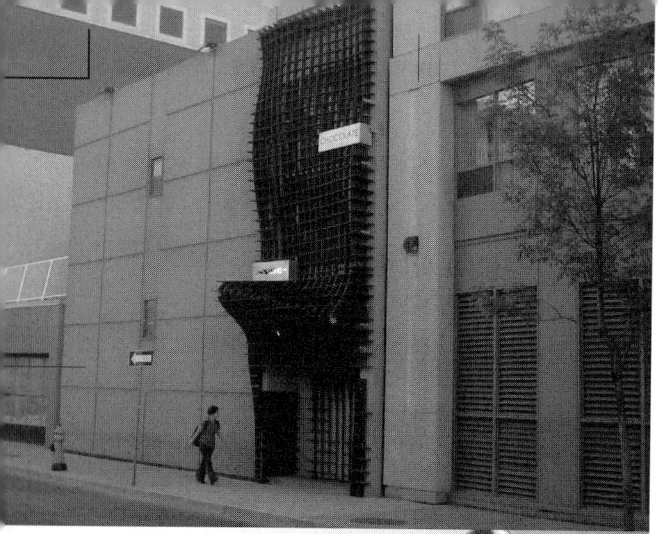

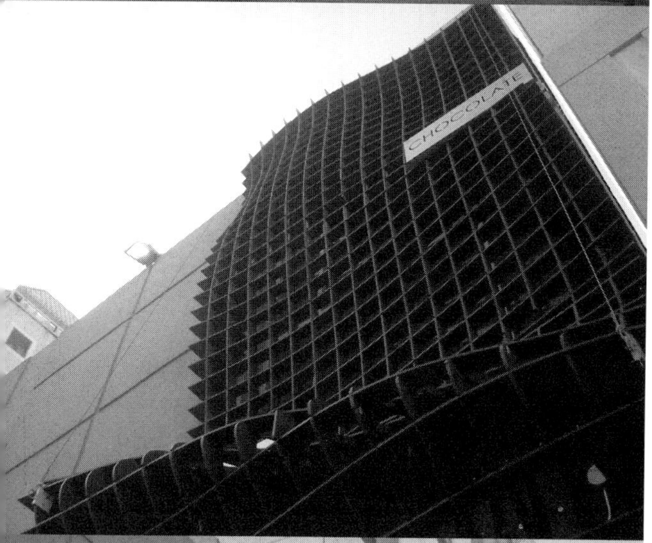

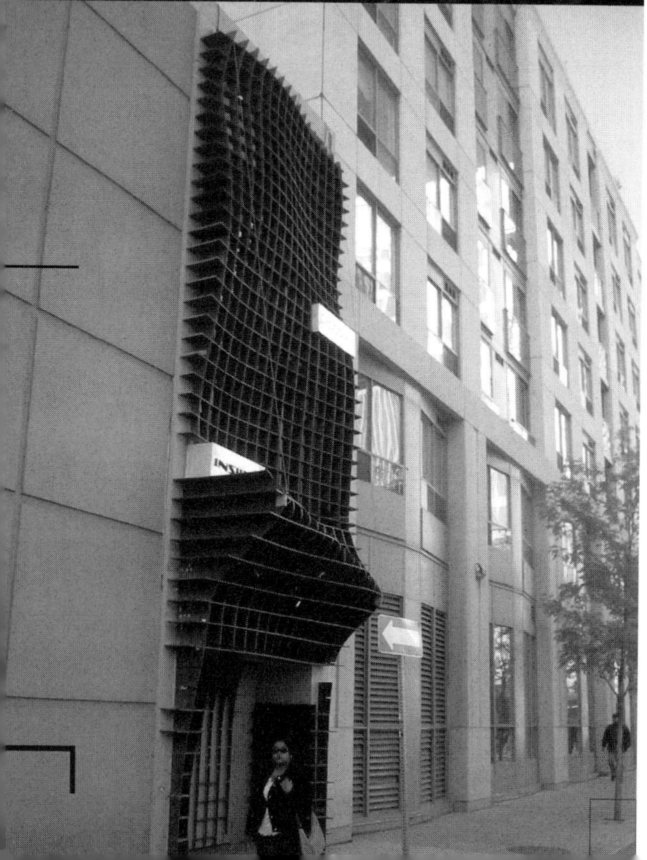

HOW TO: BUILD YOUR OWN FAÇADE

Digital Prep and Fabrication:

1. Using a NURBS modeling program (such as Rhinoceros), create a digital surface that approximates the desired size and shape of the building you intend to cover.
2. Extrude the middle section to create a canopy that will not extend further than the city limits for signage.
3. Pull the undulating model inward on the bottom portion to accommodate the existing doorway.
4. Incorporate as many needed cavities for the installation of the signage.
5. Utilize a tongue-and-groove system for the assembly of all the pieces by dissecting the 3D digital model into six different pieces for ease of construction and installation. When determining the section sizes, be sure to take into account the limitations of the size for material used (standard 4'x8' sheets of plywood) and the machine used for fabrication (here, the CNC machine).
6. Section the 3D model two-directionally, so as to create an interlocking grid pattern that will act to stabilize and form the final shape of the façade.
7. Extract and convert the 2D profiles of the digital model into CAD files. Be sure to score a number onto each piece for easy locating during the assembly process.
8. Translate the coordinates into G-codes for the CNC machine (using the milling software Master Cam).
9. Cut the profiles and paint.

Assembly:

1. Assemble and fasten the six major pieces. Secure these pieces with weather-proof L-shape brackets for extra support.
2. Spray the six major pieces with a transparent weatherproof coating and ship to the site.
3. Install the façade from the bottom piece up to the top.
4. Secure to the building with stainless steel U channels. Attach these both to the pieces and anchored to the concrete façade.
5. Use two cables for extra support of the canopy area. Run these to the top of the building.

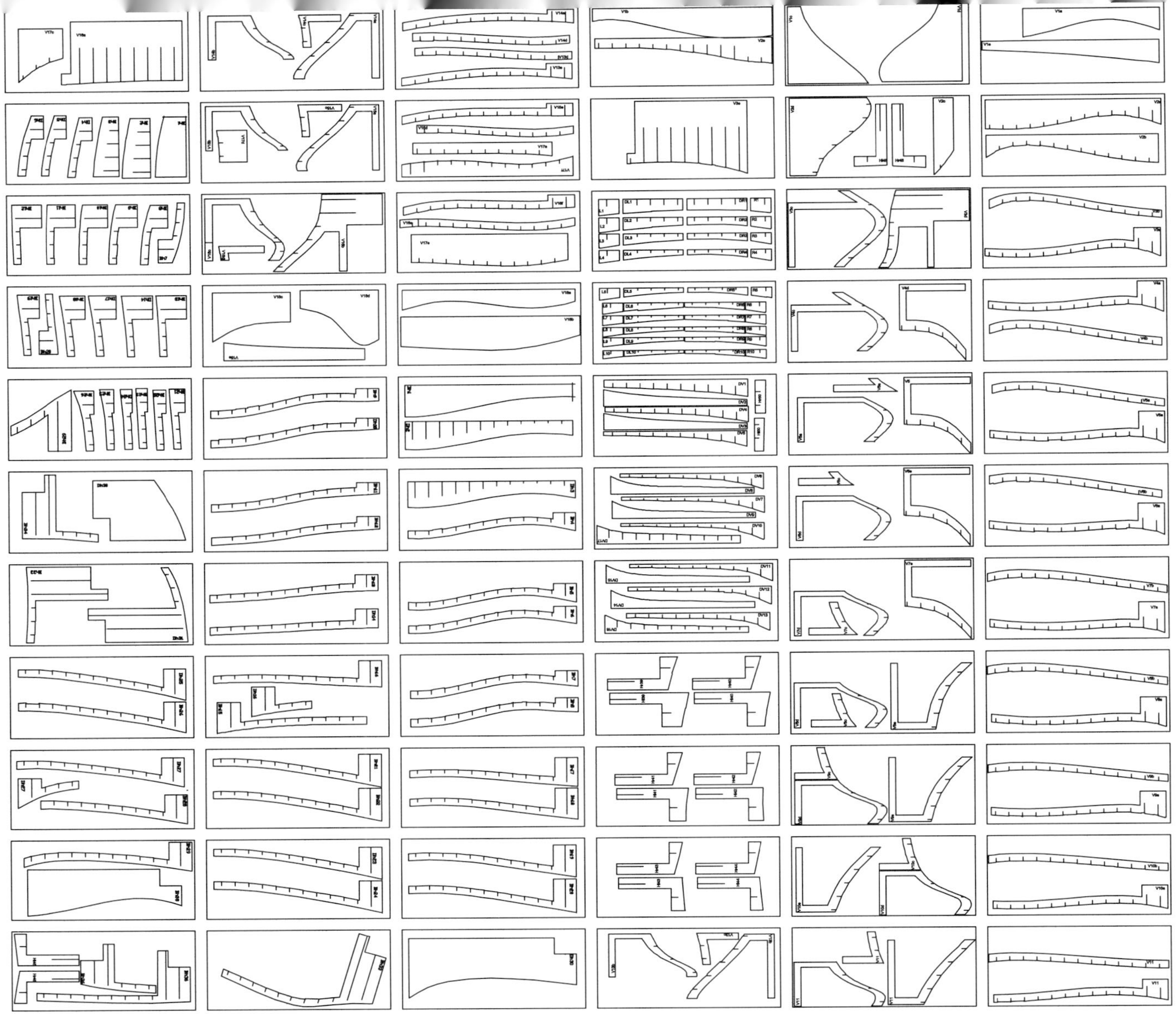

306090 05 was made possible by a grant from the Richard H. Driehaus Foundation

For their generous contributions,
306090 wishes to thank:

Richard H. Driehaus Foundation
The Graham Foundation for Advanced Studies in the Fine Arts
Robbin Dripps and Lucia Phiney

and

The School of Architecture, Princeton University
The Rensselaer Polytechnic Institute
The Hillier Group
The Michael Sorkin Studio

M. Christine Boyer
Beatriz Colomina
Claire Flom
Leslie and Peter Flom
Jason and Wendy Flom
David L. Hays
Allen and Ruth Kramer
Anne R. Kreeger
Nancy Laing
Kevin Lippert
Sadashiv Mallya
Lora and Tom Sandberg
Richard Solomon

Emily Abruzzo holds a BA from Columbia University and a MArch from Princeton University. Her thesis research examined the shifting role of the museum in the modern urban environment.

Brigid Boyle holds a BA in architecture from Princeton University. She lives and works in New York.

Alexander Briseno holds both a BArch and a MArch from the University of Michigan. He is a designer living and working in Brooklyn and is on the visiting faculty at Pratt Institute. He recently completed research travels as a Booth Fellow on the palimpsestic nature of Italian cities.

Lynne DeSilva Johnson holds a double BA in Sociology and Studio Arts from Swarthmore College. A writer, artist and teacher living in Brooklyn, she is also working towards an MArch from SAUDLA at the City University of New York. Her work focuses on architectural pedagogy, psychogeography and socio-spatial practice in the 21st century city.

Eva Hagberg improbably holds a BA in Architecture from Princeton University. She advocates architectural literacy and writes for the Architectural League in New York.

Cara Soh holds a MS in Historic Preservation from Columbia University and a BArch and MArch from the University of Michigan. She is a designer living and working in Brooklyn.

Jonathan D. Solomon holds a BA from Columbia University and a MArch from Princeton University. He teaches at the City College of New York. and is the author of Pamphlet Architecture No. 26: *13 Projects for the Sheridan Expressway.*

Andrew Yang holds a BA from the University of Chicago. He is an editor at *PRINT* magazine and contributes to *Surface, ARTnews*, and *Frame.*

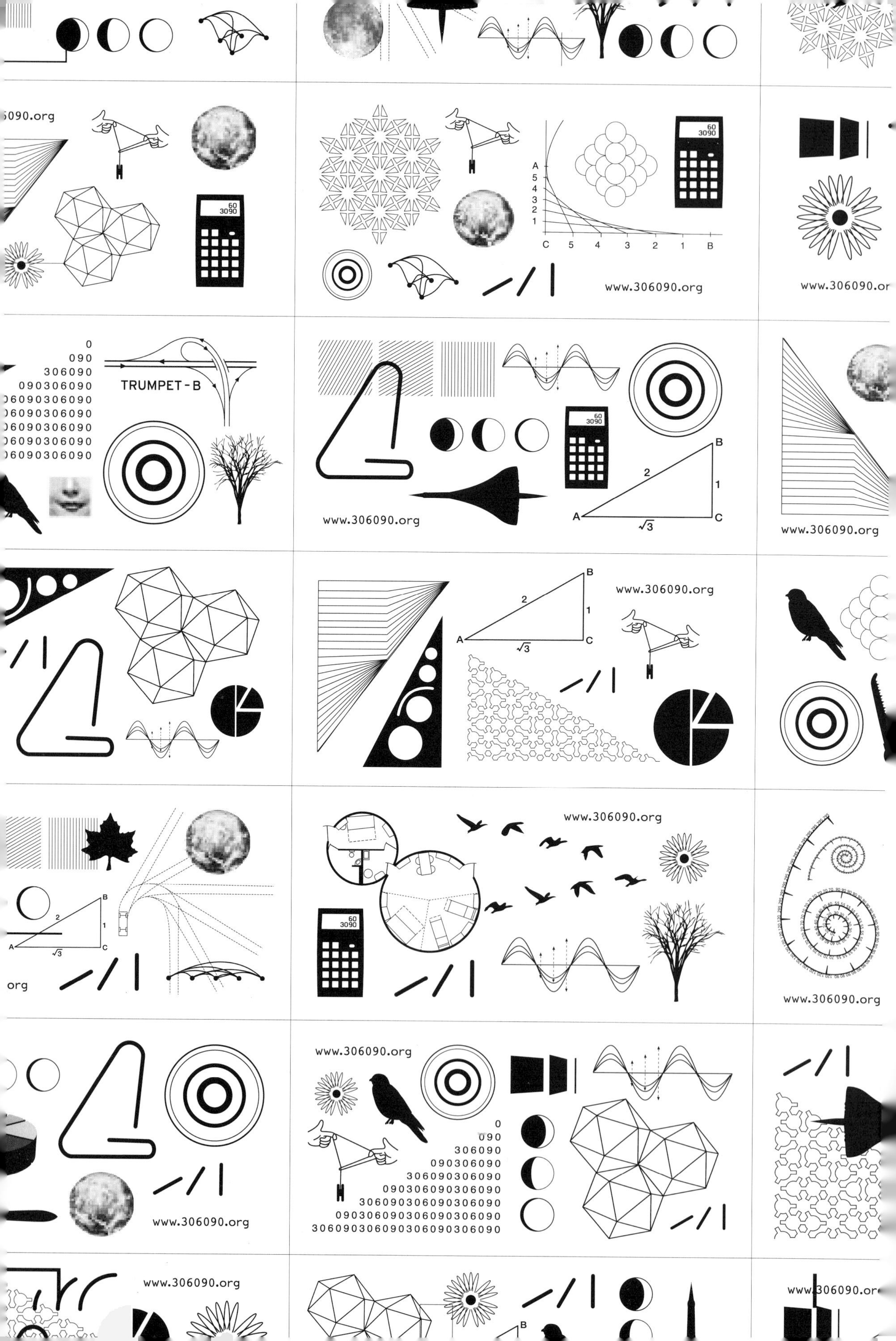

www.306090.org
60
3090
A
5
4
3
2
1
C
B
TRUMPET-B
0
090
306090
090306090
306090306090
090306090306090
306090306090306090
090306090306090306090
306090306090306090306090
2
1
√3